The Golden Fleece

The Golden Fleece

*Manipulation and Independence
in Humanitarian Action*

EDITED BY

Antonio Donini

FOREWORD BY

Lt. Gen (Ret) the Honorable Roméo Dallaire

Kumarian Press
An Imprint of Stylus Publishing

Published by Stylus Publishing, LLC
22883 Quicksilver Drive
Sterling, Virginia 20166–2102

Bulk Purchases
Quantity discounts are available
for use in workshops and for staff
development.
Call 1–800–232–0223

Library of Congress Cataloging-in-Publication Data

The golden fleece : manipulation and independence in humanitarian action / edited by
Antonio Donini. — 1st ed.
        p. cm.
   Includes bibliographical references and index.
   ISBN 978–1–56549–487–9 (cloth : alk. paper) — ISBN 978–1–56549–488–6 (pbk.
: alk. paper) — ISBN 978–1–56549–489–3 (library networkable e-edition) — ISBN
978–1–56549–490–9 (consumer e-edition) 1. International relief—Political aspects. 2.
Humanitarian assistance—Political aspects. 3. Humanitarian intervention—Political as-
pects. 4. Nongovernmental organizations. 5. International agencies. I. Donini, Antonio.
   HV553.G65 2013
   361.2'6—dc23

2012016566

Printed in the United States of America

∞All first editions printed on acid free paper that meets the American National Standards
   Institute Z39-48 Standard. .

First Edition, 2012

1 0   9   8   7   6   5   4   3   2

Contents

PART THREE
THEMATIC CHAPTERS

PART FOUR
CONCLUSIONS

Tables and Figures

Abbreviations

ACF	Action Contre la Faim (Action against Hunger)
AMISOM	African Union Mission to Somalia
ARS	Alliance for the Re-liberation of Somalia
AU	African Union
AUPD	African Union Panel for Darfur
BBC	British Broadcasting Corporation
CAP	Consolidated Appeals Process (United Nations)
CERF	Central Emergency Response Fund
CGDK	Coalition Government of Democratic Kampuchea
CIA	Central Intelligence Agency
CNN	Cable News Network
COIN	Counter insurgency
COMECON	Council for Mutual Economic Assistance
CPA	Comprehensive Peace Agreement
CRS	Catholic Relief Services
CSO	Civil Society Organization
DK	Democratic Kampuchea
DCPSF	Darfur Community Peace and Stability Fund
DOD	(US) Department of Defense
DRC	Democratic Republic of the Congo
EAD	Economic Affairs Division (Pakistan)
ECHO	European Commission Humanitarian Office
FAO	Food and Agriculture Organization of the United Nations
FAR	Forces Armées Rwandaises

FATA	Federally Administered Tribal Areas
FDMA	FATA Disaster Management Authority
FIRUP	Food Insecurity Response to Urban Populations
FRC	Federal Relief Commission
FSNAU	(Somalia) Food Security and Nutrition Analysis Unit
FUNCINPEC	United Front Party
GoP	Government of Pakistan
GWOT	Global War on Terrorism
HC	Humanitarian Coordinator
HCR	High Commissioner for Refugees
HCT	Humanitarian Country Team
HRF	Humanitarian Response Fund (UN)
IASC	Inter-Agency Standing Committee
ICC	International Criminal Court
ICG	International Crisis Group
ICRC	International Committee of the Red Cross
ICU	Islamic Courts Union
IDB	Inter-American Development Bank
IDP	Internally Displaced Person
IFI	International Financial Institutions
IFRC	International Federation of Red Cross and Red Crescent Societies
IGAD	Intergovernmental Authority on Development
IRC	International Rescue Committee
IHRC	Interim Haiti Reconstruction Commission
IHL	International Humanitarian Law
IMF	International Monetary Fund
INGO	International Nongovernmental Organization
IOM	International Organization for Migration
IRIN	Integrated Regional Information Network

ISAF	International Security Assistance Force (in Afghanistan)
ISI	(Pakistan) Inter-Services Intelligence
IVS	International Voluntary Services
JCA	Joint Church Aid
JEM	Justice and Equality Movement
JMST	Joint Mediation Support Team
KR	Khmer Rouge
KPK	Khyber Pakhtunkhwa (formerly North-West Frontier Province)
LTTE	Liberation Tigers of Tamil Eelam
MCC	Mennonite Central Committee
MINUSTAH	UN Mission for the Stabilization of Haiti
MSF	Médecins Sans Frontières
NATO	North Atlantic Treaty Organization
NDMA	National Disaster Management Authority
NGO	Nongovernmental Organization
NOC	No Objection Certificate
NWFP	North-West Frontier Province
OAS	Organization of American States
OCHA	(UN) Office for the Coordination of Humanitarian Affairs
ODA	Official Development Assistance
ODI	Overseas Development Institute
OECD/DAC	Organization for Economic Cooperation and Development/Development Assistance Committee
OEEC	Organisation for European Economic Co-operation
OFAC	Office of Foreign Assets Control
OFDA	Office for Disaster Assistance (USAID)
OHCHR	(UN) Office of the High Commissioner for Human Rights

PA	Palestinian Authority
PDMA	Provincial Disaster Management Authority
PIH	Partners in Health
PLO	Palestine Liberation Organization
PRT	Provincial Reconstruction Team
RC	Resident Coordinator
RPF	Rwandan Patriotic Front
R2P	Responsibility to Protect (initiative)
SACB	Somalia Aid Coordination Body
SEATO	Southeast Asia Treaty Organization
SLM	Sudan Liberation Movement
SLM/AW	Sudan Liberation Army/Abdul Wahid Nour faction
SLM/MM	Sudan Liberation Army/Mini Minnawi Faction
SPLA	Sudan People's Liberation Army
SRSG	Special Representative of the (UN) Secretary-General
SSG	Special Support Group for Pakistani IDPs
TFG	Transitional Federal Government
TNG	Transitional National Government
TTP	Tehrik-e-Talibaan Pakistan
UN	United Nations
UNAMA	United Nations Assistance Mission in Afghanistan
UNAMID	African Union/United Nations Mission in Darfur
UNAMIR	United Nations Assistance Mission for Rwanda
UNBRO	United Nations Border Relief Operation
UNCTAD	UN Conference on Trade and Development
UNDG	UN Development Group
UNDP	United Nations Development Programme
UNDPA	UN Department of Political Affairs

UNDSS	United Nations Department of Safety and Security
UNHAS	United Nations Humanitarian Air Services
UNHCR	United Nations High Commissioner for Refugees
UNICEF	United Nations Children's Fund
UNITAF	United Nations Task Force
UNMIS	United Nations Mission in Sudan
UNOSOM	United Nations Operation in Somalia
UNRWA	United Nations Relief and Works Agency for Palestine Refugees
UNSC	United Nations Security Council
USAID	United States Agency for International Development
VNCS	Vietnam Christian Service
WASH	Water, Sanitation, and Hygiene
WFP	(United Nations) World Food Programme
WHO	World Health Organization

Foreword

LT. GEN (RET) THE HONORABLE ROMÉO DALLAIRE

In the first days of the offensive in Afghanistan, former US secretary of state Colin Powell commended humanitarian nongovernmental organizations (NGOs) as a "force multiplier"[1] of the American military. His speech provoked outrage among civil society leaders, who denounced NGOs that engage in civil-military cooperation as "pawns in the war on terror"[2] that imperil the humanitarian imperatives of neutrality, impartiality, and independence. But this NGO rhetoric is not in line with reality. Neutrality as envisioned by humanitarian NGOs is rarely, if ever, manifested in the field. The principle of neutrality calls for external actors to abstain from any activities that would afford a political or military advantage to one side over another. Yet in many settings, neutrality is but an "aspiration,"[3] a "myth,"[4] and an "impossibility."

Adhering to the principle of neutrality is an extreme position that can only be held by the International Committee of the Red Cross (ICRC) and, to some extent, by Médecins Sans Frontières (MSF), and very few others. Even then, these organizations have struggled to uphold their neutral positions. Neutrality is, and has always been, subjective and context specific.

The environment in which humanitarians and peacekeepers work is the same—when we intervene, we are all outside entities that have no ambitions to overtly occupy or change a society or failing state. However, we can be dragged rapidly, through casualties, into a confrontational and even belligerent set of circumstances. So just as the humanitarian neutrality argument is used as a shield to be able to function as freely as possible within a conflict zone, the nation builders, security forces, and development people also have to build the mantra of being altruistic with their influence and resources to assist in attenuating the humanitarian crisis. The fact that we approach the situation from two different angles should compel us to bring about a more progressive philosophy of intervention—assistance that goes beyond conflict resolution into the realm of conflict prevention.

There is no post-modern instrument that has been created to generate complementary efforts of humanitarians and others, a void that creates a reticence on the part of the political entities to get engaged in far more proactive ways. There is not enough dialogue or innovative debate on either side to propel humanitarian efforts into a more proactive stance and effectively influence the political dimension to get engaged early and significantly.

As amply demonstrated in this book, the sacrosanct principles of neutrality and humanitarian space have been used and abused by many in ways that ultimately benefit killers rather than victims of armed conflict. The delivery of humanitarian assistance in complex and ambiguous crisis situations is dependent on having access to airports, securing strategic transport corridors, and protecting humanitarian workers, vital tasks that can be carried out only by military forces operating without a partisan agenda. In an environment where it is growing increasingly difficult for humanitarian relief organizations to keep staff on the ground, the international community must move to embrace effective civil-military interaction.

Both the soldier and the relief worker, the general and the doctor, have roles to play in a complex crisis. While these roles are separate and distinct, cooperation on the ground can save the lives of the populations we are attempting to protect and enhance the safety of those who are providing relief. NGOs loudly called for troops to intervene in Somalia, Rwanda, and Darfur, but once military forces were deployed, cooperation did not always ensue.

Humanitarian organizations also cannot—and should not—be expected to be the fig leaf for states' failure to intervene politically to prevent or solve crises. Humanitarians alone cannot be expected to solve the root causes of conflict. In fact, if donors and politicians did their job, there would be less need for the gigantic humanitarian enterprise of the twenty-first century, also well described in this volume. A more serviceable humanitarian enterprise could be smaller and more focused, concentrating on what it can do best, which is to save the lives of people in extreme situations.

We must learn from the past and avoid repeating our mistakes, mistakes that cost the lives of the very people we are trying to protect. The authors of this book are seasoned humanitarians who have come together to better understand the manipulation of humanitarian action by all players in this industry. Their findings are sobering. They highlight the obstacles but also detail the opportunities for improvement. Change requires a better understanding of how the temptation to manipulate humanitarian action works and strategies to overcome the built-in disincentives of the humanitarian business to reform itself.

Change is possible, and we are not condemned to repeat the past if we are willing to learn from our mistakes and move on. *Peux ce que veux. Allons-y*—If there is a will, there is a way. Let's go for it.

Chapter 1

Introduction

Antonio Donini

The Golden Fleece

According to ancient Greek myth, Jason and his band of Argonauts set out on a quest to find the fleece of a golden-haired, winged ram. Success would result in Jason achieving the throne of Iolcus in Thessaly. Some versions of the legend emphasize the fleece, others the quest. There have been many interpretations of what the fleece might mean: power, forgiveness, the riches of the East, sun reflecting on the sea, alchemy. In modern usage *to fleece* means to shear the fleece from an animal, such as a sheep, but it also means to con or to trick someone out of money.

The political economy of humanitarian action embodies all of these concepts and more—if not in fact, then certainly in perception and popular observation. The quest for independence, and, by extension, respect for the humanitarian imperative, has long been subject to manipulation by governments, warlords, public opinion, disembodied *realpolitik,* and the calculations of humanitarians themselves. The results have often been less than golden.

This book delves into questions that are rarely asked and seldom answered. To what extent—if any—have the manipulators of humanitarian action, including humanitarian agencies themselves, achieved the objectives of their manipulation? Would humanitarian action, shorn of manipulation, be more effective in saving and protecting lives? Is political manipulation greater today than at other times in history, or are we experiencing fluctuations within a standard historically consistent bandwidth? Does the dramatic growth of the aid enterprise in the last two decades open up humanitarian action to greater manipulation? Our book examines a variety of geographic and thematic contexts to shed light on these questions and offers some observations about whether and where possibilities for change exist, change that could point toward Thessaly.

1

In this book we use *instrumentalization* as shorthand for the use of humanitarian action or rhetoric as a tool to pursue political, security, military, development, economic, and other non-humanitarian goals. *Instrumentalization* is not quite the same as *politicization* or *manipulation*, though it contains elements of both. The following chapters unpack these terms by illustrating the many ways in which humanitarian action is misused. Examples include the blatant abuse and distortion of relief operations to achieve political objectives that are often antithetical to humanitarianism and lead to increased rather than reduced mortality. They also include more subtle manipulations arising from the convergence of interests between aid workers and their organizations around agendas related to globalization, peace consolidation, nation-building, human rights, and justice. We also examine how humanitarians themselves have manipulated governments, international organizations, the donating public, and even intended beneficiaries in support of lofty partisan or institutional objectives.

We take a long view, starting with the origins of organized humanitarianism in the mid-nineteenth century. Three distinct periods in humanitarian action are identified: pre-1945, 1945 to the end of the Cold War, and from 1990 onward. The immediate post–World War II years saw a rush of norm making with important changes to international humanitarian law, human rights law, and refugee law that set the parameters for future relief operations. After 1990, the end of East-West confrontation saw a reduction in proxy wars, but myriad unresolved quarrels within states burst into flame, generating major displacement of, and harm to, civilians. Rather than a period of peace dividends and consensual problem solving, the 1990s were scarred by an increase in global turmoil and suffering—along with a growth in the humanitarian apparatus and questions about its core purpose.

In the twenty-plus years since the end of the Cold War, organized humanitarian action has blossomed from a relatively marginal activity in the shadow of interstate wars to a central tenet of the West's approach to crisis and conflict. Humanitarians are no longer confined to providing succor outside the theater of conflict. Intervening beyond borders has now become the norm. In 2012, humanitarian agencies are expected to disburse close to US$20 billion in support of those affected by disasters, manmade or not, and for the maintenance and development of the humanitarian system.[1] Humanitarianism, once an endeavor that was mainly voluntary and driven by a sense of mission, is now a business and a profession that, according to one estimate, employs a quarter of a million workers.[2] And this is only the dominant "official" humanitarian enterprise. The contributions of emerging humanitarianisms—both of Islamic and other hues—and those at the national and community levels who, almost invariably, are the first responders when disaster strikes do not make it to the international statistics of compassion. With growth has come power, the power to raise and move resources and personnel, to decide where and where not to intervene, to influence government and the media. Humanitarianism has become part of global governance, if not of government. It has also become a global fig leaf that covers up for global misgovernance. The world's collective unwillingness or inability to prevent conflict, to address the plight of millions in drought- or flood-prone lands, and the growing incidence of climate-related disasters, creates the need for a humanitarian enterprise out of all proportion to what would be required if we had more responsible and just governance in the world. This enterprise continues to evolve in the twenty-first century—with emerging powers including China, India, Brazil, Turkey, and Middle Eastern countries likely to play an increasing role—as does our understanding of vulnerability and of the action needed to help those who find themselves *in extremis* in the face of catastrophic events.

Our starting hypothesis was that although humanitarian thinking and practice have evolved significantly over the past 150 years, there never was a "golden age" when core humanitarian values took precedence over political or other considerations. Several chapters in the book confirm this. Many of the problems and pathologies faced by the humanitarian enterprise today, most notably challenges to the values of humanity, impartiality, neutrality, and independence, are not new. They may seem more pronounced because they are more studied, but today's humanitarian angst may not, in fact, be caused by new threats to its core principles. It may simply result from an increase in the number and severity of concurrent crises; the vast growth of the humanitarian apparatus; the increased ability of governments to dictate the shape of agency programming; more intense real-time scrutiny made possible by improved communication technologies; and the conditions, restrictions, and expectations that this increased scrutiny has generated in the funding environment. Threats to humanitarian principles are very much present throughout history. Today's may be qualitatively and quantitatively different from those of the past, but they are not new. What is clear, however, is that the stakes are higher: more money, more people, higher expectations from a better informed general public, and a growing demand for accountability from those on the receiving end all conspire to place humanitarian action—a relatively low key and minor endeavor for many decades—at the center of the international system. And with centrality comes unprecedented responsibility.

Because humanitarians and donors tend to have short memories, it is important to revisit the past. If instrumentalization has been a constant in the history of humanitarianism, a fundamental question arises about the apparently unbridgeable disconnect between aspirations and reality. Must we accept that saving and protecting lives in crisis situations is an urgent and necessary but always deeply flawed endeavor? Or can humanitarianism be transformed, made immune or less vulnerable to manipulation? Can the gold standard—the mythical *fleece*—ever be attained, or will it remain little more than a dream? There are different ways to answer this question, few of them definitive because of the evolving context in which the humanitarian endeavor exists. Our hope is that the chapters in this book will provide some useful markers for analysts and policymakers as well as for humanitarians themselves. Learning from the past may well help us to navigate the choppy seas of the perpetual present. The quest continues—not for a mythical golden ideal, but for real solutions to real problems that affect the lives of millions. If humanitarians decline to question unethical policy and practice, they risk being complicit with avoidable death and suffering. Being immune to wanton or deliberate loss of life is a stark negation of what it is to be human.

Dramatis Personae

In order to capture the complexity of a "typical" crisis setting, we have, based on the data compiled for this book, developed the following diagram that shows the actors and agendas involved. The "bubbles" indicate the actors that are generally present in a crisis situation, and the arrows show the direction of the pressures they apply in pursuit of their agendas and those that they are subjected to.

Not all actors are present in all crises, and not all arrows represent vectors of instrumentalization. Donors, for example, can have a positive or negative impact on humanitarian action; they can support efforts to enhance protection and provide relief supplies liberally or place conditions that undermine the impartial provision of aid. Similarly, host governments or de facto authorities can block access to particular groups or locations or facilitate the work of humanitarian agencies. Figure 1–1 describes a complex emergency in which there is an outside military intervention and where non-state actors are involved. In a flood or earthquake situation the makeup of the bubbles would be different (and the third-party military might not be present at all). The size of the bubbles would vary with the nature of each crisis and over time.

The bubbles are useful for depicting the different types of interactions and pressures that humanitarian and other actors are subjected to as well as relations, on the one hand, with civil society and affected populations, and on the other hand, with donors, political forces, and the media. Many of the arrows are two way and show the complexity of the potential instru-

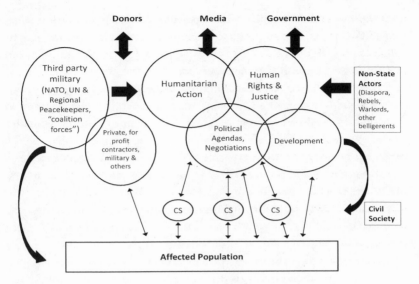

Figure 1–1. Instrumentalization: Actors and Agendas

mentalization flows. For example, donors may subordinate the provision of funds for humanitarian activities to their own political agendas, while at the same time being influenced—or even manipulated—by the perspectives and leverage of aid agencies on the ground. Similarly, it is not unusual for affected populations and/or the civil society organizations purporting to represent them to be caught in a two-way relationship in which they need and receive life-saving help but also use it to advance interests that go beyond a humanitarian remit. Several of the chapters use variations of the bubbles, or what they represent, to illustrate the pressures to which humanitarian action is subjected in a particular context.

Types of Instrumentalization

The use of suffering to achieve political objectives predates organized humanitarianism. Lord Byron, agitating for Greek independence in the 1820s, used the same moral and political levers as did his epigones in the service of Biafra or the boat people fleeing Vietnam.[3] Despite the rhetoric and lip service to principles and accountability—as General Dallaire notes in the Foreword—instrumentalization comes with the territory, and humanitarian actors, however much they dislike it, will always be confronted with partisan agendas. Humanitarians almost always operate in highly politicized and contentious environments where humanitarian values are not a central priority of belligerents or power holders. This conditions what humanitarians can and cannot do. Moreover, their mere presence may be seen by some as a political act, an affront to sovereignty, and an expression of Northern/Western hegemonic agendas.

But can humanitarians be truly nonpartisan in their own actions? For the purposes of our analysis, it is useful to distinguish between partisan politics and a "politics of humanity," that is, the politics of moral resistance against intolerable suffering,[4] because this is where humanitarian theory comes up against reality of power in crisis settings. The former is a politics of transformation and power—whether fueled by greed, grievance, or lofty ideals; the latter derives its legitimacy from universal values, codified in international treaties and instruments (international humanitarian law, the Geneva Conventions). And while humanitarians may resort to political tools, such as lobbying governments or negotiating access, they do not do so for partisan gain but to secure the survival of affected populations. Even though this apolitical balancing act is, as Michael Barnett puts it, "part confidence trick and part self-delusion,"[5] one that often results in humanitarian actors overplaying their claim to a moral high ground, reference to the law and to humanitarian values remains a useful barometer in studying the pitfalls of instrumentalization.

In our chapters we discuss a wide variety of instances of manipulation and politicization. Historically, some were relatively benign—for example, the "disaster inflation" that drives the media and agencies to overestimate needs.[6] Others, like the use of "humanitarian" aid to support the resuscitation of the genocidal Khmer Rouge regime, was deadly and disastrous for Cambodians in need of life-saving assistance and protection (Chapter 11). Similarly, generous assistance to mujahideen factions in the anti-Soviet period of the Afghanistan crisis has had dramatic and long-term consequences that continue to reverberate today (Chapter 4). In some cases instrumentalization may have worked for the instrumentalizers, although it is hard to identify an example of this where human suffering did not increase. In others—as in Afghanistan or Somalia (Chapter 5)—it has backfired spectacularly. Crises of high strategic import have clearly generated great amounts of blow-back from instrumentalization, while in those of lesser political import the independence of humanitarian action can be better protected.

Table 1–1 (pages 8–10) provides a typology of actors and examples of instrumentalization. Our chapters on Darfur, Somalia, Pakistan, and Afghanistan highlight the perils of subordinating humanitarian concerns to political or military agendas. But the same chapters, as well as the historical analysis in Chapters 2 and 3, show that there were moments when the humanitarian imperative did trump political considerations and/or where humanitarian actors were able to resist the pressure to become the hand-maidens of a political enterprise. Chapters 4 and 11 also provide examples of aid agency collaboration to challenge *refoulement* policies and, more recently, to document systematically patterns of harm to civilians associated with the intensification of conflict. In Afghanistan, both coalition forces and the insurgents could not ignore the nonpartisan data collected by the United Nations and other agencies and the resulting media attention and condemnation. To an extent, this obliged warring parties to amend the conduct of hostilities and contributed to the reduction of civilian casualties.

Typologies are of course arbitrary and do not capture nuance. While the agents of instrumentalization are relatively easy to identify, the nature of their objectives and the outcomes of their actions, especially in the longer term, are often murky. For example, our Haiti chapter (Chapter 9) argues that the privatization of aid promoted by the United States and other donors resulted in the "NGO-ization" of the country to the detriment of the Haitian state and civil society. This severely undermined government capacity, including its ability to head off or respond to disasters. This is a pretty straightforward case of manipulation. However, the role played by international NGOs (INGOs) in this process is more difficult to categorize: were they willing agents of instrumentalization in a manner similar to US NGOs in Vietnam (see Chapter 3)? Or were they motivated more by a desire to preserve or expand programs? Or was it a case of poor analysis and programming? And is it possible to draw a link, the chapter on Haiti asks, between this decades-long use and abuse of aid by NGOs and conditions that contributed to the post-earthquake cholera epidemic in 2010?

It is also important to distinguish among active, passive, and default forms of instrumentalization. The active is often blatant, as when a belligerent or a donor denies humanitarian help to a particular vulnerable group. The criminalization of the provision of life-saving assistance to areas controlled by groups proscribed as "terrorist" by the United States or international organizations, such as the Al-Shabab in Somalia or Hamas in Palestine (Chapters 6 and 7), falls into this category, as does the abuse of food aid described in Chapter 10. The Cold War provides many glaring examples perhaps best epitomized by Secretary of State Henry Kissinger in 1976: "Disaster relief is becoming increasingly a major instrument of our foreign policy."[7]

Passive instrumentalization can take more subtle forms ranging from seductive cooption—for example, INGOs gladly accepting donor largesse for assistance projects in Afghanistan and Iraq that were effectively part and parcel of a counter-insurgency agenda—and asking questions later, if at all, about principles. Institutional growth and development at the expense of

Table 1–1. Typology of Instrumentalization

Key Actors	Objective	Examples of Instrumentalization of Aid
A. States		
Donors and other external state actors - political	Geo-strategic advantage	Resuscitation of the Khmer Rouge and denial of asylum to Cambodians in need of life-saving action. Supporting mujahideen to counter Soviet intervention and "pulling" refugees to Pakistan/Iran 1980s. Criminalization of NGO aid to Hamas/Somalia post-9/11.
- military	Security/military/COIN agenda	Hearts and minds, PRTs in Afghanistan/Horn of Africa Misuse of "humanitarian" moniker Militarization of aid, denial of access and "humanitarian war" in Sri Lanka
- economic	Competition for markets/oil/resources	Denial (or manipulation) of food aid (Somalia)
Host state	Political/military advantage Targeting particular groups/ethnic agenda	Denial of access (Sri Lanka, Darfur) to attack particular groups unimpeded Control/harass NGOs (Sri Lanka, Darfur, etc.) Diversion of assistance
Third-party state	Geo-strategic advantage Advance political/military agendas	Afghan refugees in Pakistan/Iran used to support fighters, as buffers, or to counter opponents (DRC) Control of access; diversion of aid

B. Non-State		
Non-state armed actors	Seeking legitimacy Political advantage Greed/economic advantage	Diversion Denial of access Control/abuse of humanitarian assistance Attacks against aid workers
Local community	Optimize self-interest Greed Coping mechanism	Magnification of needs Diversion of aid Denial of aid to others
C. Agencies		
Intl. Organizations - political - humanitarian - development	Political agenda Institutional preservation Attracting (more) funds	Calling for "humanitarian" intervention; subordination of HA to political, "integrated," or "coherent" agendas Low-key approaches/downplaying of protection concerns Safeguarding institutional relations with governments.
INGO/NNGOs	Attracting funds Seeking profile Justifying presence Force multiplier role	Exaggerating/minimizing need/risks; accepting lower standards/keeping quiet Goma, Iraq Afghanistan, Iraq
Advocacy/human rights groups	Profile Naming and shaming Pressure from public opinion	Save Darfur coalition "Feel-good" statements condemning the Taliban Using info from humanitarian groups to advance HR agendas (DRC, Somalia, etc.)

(continues)

Table 1–1 (continued)

D. Other		
Individuals	Self-aggrandizement Sense of mission Political ambition	From Lord Byron manipulating the nascent British media to Bernard Kouchner, enterprising individuals have often "used" the humanitarian pulpit to pursue personal/political agendas.
Media	Sell copy/Prominence Influence agendas	Biased reporting in Darfur Demonization of Taliban in Afghanistan
Religious groups	Influence agendas Anti-west/Jihad	Anti-aid Buddhist clergy in Sri Lanka Attacks against aid workers in Afghanistan, Pakistan, and Somalia
Private-sector actors	Greed/economic gain	For-profit humanitarians Landowners diverting floodwaters into smallholders' land (Pakistan)
Political parties	Electoral gain Influence agendas	"NGOs are worse than warlords" (Afghan politicians) Anti-NGO/anti-western rhetoric (Sri Lanka, Haiti, Somalia)

independence and principle has too often been the default position of NGOs and even international organizations operating in politicized contexts. The pressure to raise and spend funds and to ensure the continuation of projects can constitute instrumentalization by default. The top-down and supply-driven nature of the humanitarian system can lead to other, not necessarily visible, forms of instrumentalization. As the saying goes, when your only tool is a hammer, every problem looks like a nail. Food agencies may well be driven by the supplies at their disposal in determining priorities on the ground. A refugee agency will naturally target groups on the move rather than those that remain behind.

Finally, there is "instrumentalization by story telling." The initial way of telling the story tends to shape the response. The Vietnam War generated massive human suffering, but it was not "told" as a humanitarian crisis. The narrative on one side was about defending the "Free World" and about aggression by the forces of imperialism on the other. Civilian deaths and body counts were reduced to sub-themes. Biafra was a political and military crisis cast almost entirely in humanitarian terms, and it was dealt with almost entirely in that light. More recently, representation by the media and advocacy groups of the conflict in Darfur as one between nomadic "Arabs" and sedentary "blacks" served to simplify and polarize a much more complex reality and to obscure the nature of the displacement and suffering of groups who would not necessarily identify themselves with those labels (Chapter 5). The demonization of the Taliban by Western media and feminist groups had similar effects prior to 2001. The black-and-white discourse focusing on burqas, beards, and buddhas undermined UN and NGO fundraising and the prospects of addressing urgent needs of vulnerable Afghans suffering from the combined effects of war, displacement, and the worst drought in recent history (Chapter 4).

Our Approach

This book is the product of a research community built around the Feinstein International Center at Tufts University. All the authors are either researchers at the center or have been actively associated with the center's research projects. The book builds upon the earlier work of the Humanitarianism and War Project and more recent evidence-based country studies of local perceptions of the work of humanitarian agencies conducted under the Humanitarian Agenda 2015: Principles, Power and Perceptions project.[8] The process started with a paper prepared by Ian Smillie on the "emperor's old clothes" (now in revised form as Chapter 2). The overall approach was then discussed at a meeting of the authors and a few external experts in November

2010 in London and at a second consultation in April 2011 at which the conceptual framework was agreed and chapter drafts were reviewed.

The authors are all committed humanitarians. All have years—in many cases, decades—of experience in crisis countries as aid workers, researchers, or both. All would like to see positive change in how the system functions, and most have been actively engaged in analysis and policy development vis-à-vis donors, UN agencies, and NGOs. In other words, the bedrock of solid experience in crisis and conflict is the inductive base on which our work is built. We are fully aware of two pitfalls in this type of exercise: first, the naiveté in believing that if principles were more universally respected, all would be well with the humanitarian system. And second, the paralyzing cynicism of those who claim that change is impossible and that cosmetic surgery is pointless. We, of course, subscribe to some of the critiques of humanitarian action and add a few of our own. But unlike some critics,[9] we respect the essential humanitarian values of those who devote their energy to reducing the suffering of others. We are wary of losing healthy babies as we deal with the bathwater of instrumentalization.

For us, saving and protecting the lives of people in imminent danger is a fundamentally necessary and worthwhile activity. Humanitarian action is a safety net for the most vulnerable in times of disaster, whatever the source of the calamity. As such, it deserves to be protected and nurtured despite its obvious limitations and imperfections. And while instrumentalization is a constant, so are the efforts to improve the effectiveness of this essential enterprise. Our chapters document this tension—and what happens when the humanitarian guard is lowered. The arrow of history does not travel in a straight line; learning from the past is the best way to ensure that its arc tends toward more progress and justice for the millions whose lives and protection are at risk.

Acknowledgments

This book would not have been possible without the generous grants from Norway, the Netherlands, and Australia that allowed us to conduct the field research on which it is largely based. We owe a huge debt of gratitude to the colleagues and friends who gave of their time and insights, hosted, fed, watered, and sometimes provided logistics and security during the authors' time in the field. They are too numerous to be recorded here. Nonetheless, many of the ideas discussed in the following pages were born of face-to-face conversations, reflections, and verbal jousting with protagonists in the front lines of disaster response. Our interlocutors—government officials,

UN humanitarian and political staff, NGO workers in some of the remotest outposts ranging from Bamiyan to El Geneina—who have wittingly or unwittingly contributed to this book, of course, bear no responsibility for its contents, for which the authors alone are responsible. Throughout the gestation process participants in formal and informal consultations helped us to sharpen our ideas: special thanks to Michael Barnett, Fiona Terry, Mary Anderson, Randolph Kent, Bertrand Taithe, Stephen Hopgood, Raga Alphonsus, Aunohita Mojumdar, Jeevan Sharma, Krystel Carrier-Sabourin, and Tanya Zayed. We are most grateful to the Rockefeller Foundation and the staff at Bellagio (in particular Robert Garris, Nadia Gilardoni, and Linda Marston-Reid) for hosting our final authors' meeting. The congenial atmosphere and surroundings allowed us to refine much of what follows. Thanks are also due to Anita Robbins and her colleagues at the Feinstein International Center for dealing with travel and administrative headaches. Finally, the authors and the editor are greatly indebted to Jim Lance, Alexandra Hartnett, and Joan Laflamme at Kumarian Press for believing in this project and helping it through its many hoops and moving parts.

Part One

SOME LESSONS FROM HISTORY

Chapter 2

The Emperor's Old Clothes

The Self-Created Siege of Humanitarian Action

IAN SMILLIE

Some of them want to use you
Some of them want to get used by you
——"SWEET DREAMS ARE MADE OF THIS,"
—EURYTHMICS*

The Sky Is Falling

Humanitarianism is under threat, under siege, in peril. Humanitarianism as we knew it is dying. Cynical politicians and the military now direct everything; *instrumentalization* is the order of the day. A decade ago Hugo Slim wrote darkly about the challenges of the "new humanitarianism"; five years ago Ian Smillie and Larry Minear wrote about "humanitarian action in a calculating world"; Michael Barnett and Tom Weiss wrote *Humanitarianism in Question*. Today there is talk of "post-modern humanitarianism" and "neo-humanitarianism," in which the old ideas, principles, and norms are dead, moribund, or "ripe targets for manipulation."

This chapter examines instrumentalization and humanitarian action in manmade emergencies over the past century and a half, with a view to explaining how it has changed since the putative "golden age" of humanitarian independence, impartiality, and neutrality. Today, instrumentalization is taken to mean manipulation by donor governments, combatants, and others, although this chapter will examine variations on the theme.

---

*Lyrics from the song "Sweet Dreams Are Made of This" by Eurythmics are used by permission of DVA Limited and Universal Music.

Because the chapter follows a thematic rather than a chronological logic, a discussion of the Boer War is near the end, while Somalia is at the beginning. The cases are clustered under two broad headings: "Humanitarians Using Governments" and "Governments Using Humanitarians." There are subsequent sections on perceptions of neutrality, and a section dealing with double standards, missed opportunities, and "forgotten" emergencies.

Three distinct periods in humanitarian action are commonly identified: pre-1945, 1945 to the end of the Cold War, and from 1990 onward.[1] In the post–World War II period there were distinct and important changes to international humanitarian law and its application, and after 1990, a myriad of unresolved quarrels burst into flame, leading to a period of increased human suffering, along with a growth in the humanitarian apparatus and questions about its ultimate purpose. But after visits to the Balkans in the 1870s, the Boer War, Armenia, Abyssinia, Manchukuo, and Biafra, among others, it may be concluded that although humanitarian thinking and practice have evolved significantly over the past 150 years, there never was a humanitarian golden age.

In all manmade crises, as this chapter will demonstrate, humanitarian action has been constrained and shaped by the agendas of governments, combatants, and donors; by the media; by third-party military and political interests; by considerations of human rights and justice; by the needs and demands of affected populations and their own organizations; and by those seeking commercial gain.

Many of the problems and pathologies faced by the humanitarian enterprise today—most notably challenges to the core values of impartiality, neutrality, and independence—may seem more pronounced because they are more studied. But today's humanitarian angst may not, in fact, be caused by any new threat to its core principles. It may simply result from an increase in the number of concurrent humanitarian crises; the vast growth of the humanitarian apparatus; more intense real-time scrutiny made possible by improved communication technologies; and by the concomitant conditions, restrictions, and expectations that this increased scrutiny has generated in the funding environment. While threats to humanitarian neutrality, impartiality, and independence are not new phenomena, the factors that make them more apparent than in the past make the need to deal with them more urgent and compelling.

Un Souvenir de Solferino[2]

A great deal has been written about how much the world, war, and humanitarianism have changed since the bucolic, uncomplicated days of

Henri Dunant, surveying the field after the 1859 Battle of Solferino. Dunant and his experience in Northern Italy are frequently cited at the beginning of books and articles about today's humanitarian complexity, not as if they are quaintly irrelevant, but as if the remembered classical humanitarianism that emerged after Solferino actually existed.

Thus, Kurt Mills writes about what Dunant created as having been "embraced by European statesmen to ensure the gentlemanly conduct of war," when "humanitarian action, including assisting wounded soldiers and others affected by the war, was seen as an act of compassion rather than an act of politics. This is the classical model of humanitarianism—neutral, impartial, and independent."[3] In an essay on what he calls "neo-humanitarianism," Mills admits that there was always "an element of myth" to this, although by and large, it is this classical and perhaps mythical model that has been cast into so much peril and paradox—either since the end of the Cold War, or since the beginning of the global war on terror, depending on one's age and perspective.

The so-called classical model of humanitarianism was never much more than a model, if not a full-blown myth, and it has never been more than partially embraced by most of the humanitarian agencies that have undertaken humanitarian action since 1859. Few have struggled as hard and as consistently as the International Committee of the Red Cross (ICRC), however, to give the concept meaning. The ICRC has been the gold standard where humanitarian principles are concerned, but it has had consistent competition since the 1860s for space and funding from other humanitarians for whom independence, neutrality, and impartiality were more like guidelines than principles. For them, manipulation—always in a good cause, of course—has been the default position, some using, and some eager to be used. And as this chapter will show, even the ICRC stumbled on its way to the twenty-first century.

This is not to suggest that the 160 years since Solferino have not seen incredible humanitarian valor. Many humanitarian workers have died in the cause, and tens of thousands have given the best years of their lives in valiant and effective humanitarian action. Millions of people lived and continue to live as a result of their work. But neutrality, impartiality, and independence have been observed by most humanitarian organizations with great selectivity ever since the very first Geneva Convention was signed in 1864.

Humanitarians have been used from that day to this as fig leaves to veil government action and inaction in the face of war crimes and genocide. Humanitarians have been paid, manipulated, and "embedded" with singular disregard for humanitarian principles. They have been routinely ignored, even in cases of obvious humanitarian need and enormous public outcry.

They have been silent when they should have spoken out, and they have spoken out—taking sides—when they should have remained silent. Then as now, they have called for military intervention to end the worst atrocities, and on the few occasions when they got their wish, they mostly lived to regret it. None of this began with the wars in Iraq and Afghanistan. It did not begin with the post–Cold War return of Western armies to distant lands. The struggle to give meaning to the basic tenets of "classical humanitarianism" was as real on the day they were first enunciated as it is today.

Humanitarians Using Governments

Somalia: Play With Puppy, Puppy Lick Your Face[4]

> History is never the fairy tale of innocent victims, oppressive gunmen, and caring outsiders that the humanitarian narrative so often presents.
>
> —DAVID RIEFF[5]

In December 1992, the first of twenty-eight thousand American troops poured ashore at Mogadishu in full combat gear. The event was covered by dozens of already-present international reporters and cameramen on the beach wearing jeans and t-shirts. The difference in attire was a clear indication of very different realities and a metaphor for much of what had transpired up to that moment.

Somalia was a failed state, a Cold War pawn left to the devices of clan factions, warlords, and gangsters. Fighting had displaced tens of thousands of people, and famine stalked the land. The major relief organizations were there, but Somalia was dangerous for them. Aid workers were threatened and killed, and relief supplies were regularly stolen. Agencies hired armed guards to protect their staff and their convoys, and this soon turned into an expensive and dangerous protection racket.

The international media was slow to notice Somalia, but that began to change as humanitarian agencies ramped up their appeals for funding and protection. In 1991, reporters on their way to or from the Gulf War stopped in Somalia and began what would become a growing refrain: the United States was willing to expend great amounts of human, military, and financial capital in the Balkans and the oil-rich Gulf, but not in Africa. As the 1992 US presidential race gathered steam, UN Secretary General Boutros Boutros-Ghali criticized the Security Council for ignoring Africa and for its single-minded focus on what he called a "white man's war" in the Balkans.

Large American NGOs, notably CARE, harassed by Somali military factions and alarmed by fighting around Bardera, upped the ante, calling for US military support as well as more relief supplies. Estimates of the number of deaths from starvation escalated.

Michael Maren, an alumnus of the Peace Corps, Catholic Relief Services, and the United States Agency for International Development (USAID), but no longer a friend of NGOs, wrote that humanitarian agencies, led by CARE, had asked for military assistance assuming that the military would serve their interests in facilitating humanitarian assistance. But of course it didn't work out quite that way. "No sooner had the soldiers landed than the aid organizations began to complain about them: they did too much, they did too little; they failed to disarm the factions; they were violating human rights in their attempts to disarm the factions. Aid agencies were dismayed to find that the soldiers were acting like soldiers."[6]

Soon there were Cobra attack helicopters strafing the streets of Mogadishu, and when a Black Hawk helicopter went down in the midst of an attempt to capture warlord Mohamed Farrah Aidid, things moved from bad to worse. The new man in the White House extracted the Marines as quickly as he could, and Somalia soon disappeared from American and European television screens.

Somalia made the Clinton administration wary of further African adventures, and when the United States might have contributed to halting genocide in Rwanda (only months after the last US troops had left Somalia), it did not, going so far as to block consensus in the Security Council on UN action.

Perhaps the jury is still out on the role that humanitarian agencies played in Somalia. Certainly there was a kind of NGO triumphalism at the end of the Cold War that has long since evaporated. Maren says that "most American NGOs, just like the army and the marines, had been instruments of US foreign policy all along."[7] He says that "few NGOs have ever seen a contract they didn't like, or a problem they didn't believe they could solve." And he argues that Somalia is not a story of how a humanitarian mission became a military adventure. "It's about how the people running a humanitarian mission became so dedicated to their cause that they started to see strafing, bombing, and killing as humanitarian acts." This is an exaggeration, but Maren does make a persuasive argument that much of Somalia was relatively peaceful, that huge volumes of relief supplies had actually begun to turn the situation around before the US military arrived, and that the crisis had been exaggerated out of all proportion by the media and relief agencies. The Washington-based Refugee Policy Group concluded that in the end, somewhere between 202,000 and 238,000 people died of famine in Somalia, that 100,000 deaths were averted because of outside assistance, but that only 10,000 of those lives were saved after the arrival of the US Marines.[8]

Bulgaria and the Atrocitarians

Although part of the so-called post-modern, neo-humanitarian world, Somalia was far from unique, and it is worth recalling the story because of its similarity to earlier events. A debacle analogous to Somalia but with even greater loss of life occurred only a dozen years after the first Geneva Convention was signed. It included a media frenzy, angry politicians, outraged humanitarians, military intervention, and an utterly disastrous conclusion.

In the summer of 1876, British and Russian newspapers began to report a series of massacres in Bulgaria following a local uprising there against Ottoman rule. Popular Russian sentiment had been fueled against Turkey during an earlier clash between Christian Serbia and the Muslim Ottoman Empire. An NGO called the Moscow Slavic Benevolent Committee had subsequently raised funds to foment revolt in Bulgaria. With news of the ensuing massacres, estimated to have taken the lives of some twelve thousand people, Slavic Benevolent Committees across Russia grew in number, funding, and political influence.

As with the modern Save Darfur movement, British public outrage exploded, and newspaper estimates of the death toll grew from twelve thousand to twenty-five thousand. The British government, led by Benjamin Disraeli, was in a difficult position because of an Anglo-Ottoman defense treaty, but the pressure to act was enormous, fueled by newspaper editorials, public rallies, church meetings, and hundreds of petitions. Former Prime Minister William Gladstone came out of retirement to call for intervention, writing enormously popular pamphlets on the subject and traveling the country to speak to throngs of concerned citizen who were becoming known as *atrocitarians*.

Prime Minister Disraeli's biggest concern, however, lay not with Gladstone or even Turkey. His concern lay with Russia, where anti-Ottoman bellicosity was fast wheeling out of control. What Disraeli feared most was being drawn into a war on the side of Turkey against Russia, where press outrage had stoked popular passions. The Russian Orthodox Church had created a fundraising network for the pan-Slavist committees, and donation boxes were placed on trams, in train stations, and on ships, often invoking the name of the empress, who became an activist for the cause and an early exemplar of celebrity endorsement. The Russian Red Cross also raised funds for the Bulgarian victims, although there was, as yet, no way actually to reach Bulgaria. One of the greatest pan-Slavists was Russia's interior minister, Count Nikolai Pavlovich Ignatieff. Ignatieff had been Russia's Ambassador to Constantinople for thirteen years, and his ultimate goal, to the chagrin of many in the government—including the reforming Czar Alexander II—was Russian domination over the Bosphorus Strait.[9]

Peace talks aimed at damping down public outrage failed when the Turkish sultan rejected overblown Russian demands. Finally, in June 1877, tens of thousands of Russian troops crossed the Danube, with Constantinople as their objective. They never got there. Ottoman troops fought back, stopping the Russian army at Plevna in Northern Bulgaria. The Russian invaders were surprised and nonplussed by what they found in Bulgaria: a country whose peasants were better off than those of their would-be liberators. By the end of the year, some eighty thousand Russians had died in the effort, and the final death toll may have been double that.

In the end, Bulgaria was divided, giving Russia enough territory and influence to save face and declare victory. Bosnia was picked off by Austria-Hungary, and Britain found itself with a new colony in Cyprus. The Ottoman Empire promised to behave better in future, but for Muslims this was one more in a growing series of humiliations at the hands of forces professing Christian values and purpose. Little more was said by anyone about the Bulgarians in whose cause so many had died.

Russia, weakened and now beset by political assassination and a return to reactionary rule, would never fully recover from the Bulgarian war. World War I would begin with an assassination that might not have happened had Bosnia remained under Turkish control. Turkey, disillusioned by what it saw as British duplicity, would join Germany in that conflict and in yet another defeat at the hands of the West. British civil society had lost interest in Bulgaria before the war even began, and Russian civil society—which cannot have missed the fact of so many Russian deaths to avenge the deaths of so few—had only thirty years left before it would disappear completely under the Bolshevik boot.

There have been more recent occasions when military invasion has actually succeeded in relieving a humanitarian problem. Tanzania's 1978 invasion of Uganda rid that country of the murderous Idi Amin. A simultaneous invasion of Cambodia by Vietnam put an end to the Khmer Rouge regime. But neither of these invasions was humanitarian in its primary motivation, and neither was provoked by the kind of humanitarian chorus that accompanied the Russian operation in Bulgaria and the American operations in Somalia.

Bangladesh

Bangladesh was a bit different. Political instability and a military coup had marred Pakistan's first decade of statehood. Consisting of two provinces with a thousand miles of Indian territory between them, Pakistan was riven by political, economic, and ethnic tension. During the 1960s, as a return to civilian rule became likely, calls for greater economic autonomy by the Bengali-speaking East Pakistan grew more strident. The demands were resisted in West Pakistan, and Bengali nationalists were harassed and jailed.

The final straw, perhaps, was the government's desultory response to one of the greatest natural calamities of the century. On November 12, 1970, a cyclone of unparalleled intensity roared northward out of the Bay of Bengal, pushing a massive wall of water ahead of it. Everything in its path was washed away. When it was over, animals, crops, and houses were gone. As many as half a million people died. A newspaper headline read, "Do Not Send Children's Clothing to Cyclone Affected Area. No Children Remain."[10]

In the aftermath of the disaster, the Bengali nationalist leader, Sheikh Mujibur Rahman, spoke to massive throngs of "criminal neglect" in Pakistan's dilatory humanitarian response. Ill-timed national elections three weeks later became a de facto plebiscite on greater provincial autonomy. When the ballots were counted, Sheikh Mujib's Awami League won 167 out of the 169 seats in East Pakistan, representing an absolute majority in the full National Assembly. But the prospect of a nationalist Bengali Prime Minister was too much for Pakistan's military. In March 1971, the martial law authorities announced an indefinite postponement in convening the National Assembly.

The reaction in East Pakistan was swift. Strikes crippled the country, and student leaders issued calls for independence. Riots, arson, and looting ensued. To counteract the growing disorder, the Pakistan army initiated one of the most brutal acts of political repression ever unleashed on a civilian population. Ostensibly aimed at quashing an insurrection, the first targets were not rioters but the East Bengal Regiment, the East Pakistan Rifles, border guards, and police, all judged to be untrustworthy. Soon the Pakistan army, manned and officered by West Pakistanis, was out of control, turning its wrath on the civilian population and a hastily formed army of freedom fighters.

The number of people killed has been estimated conservatively at a million, and it may have been as high as three million.[11] Hundreds of thousands of women are said to have been raped. By late summer a long war of attrition between the army and freedom fighters loomed, and refugees poured across the borders into India. At the height of the exodus, ten million refugees, almost 20 percent of the population, had flooded into West Bengal and Assam, placing a monstrous burden on India and turning the situation into the worst humanitarian crisis of all time.

A relief effort of unprecedented scale gathered in Calcutta and in hundreds of refugee camps dotted around the borders of East Pakistan. Humanitarian agencies around the world called for military intervention to stop the Pakistani genocide. The first-ever fundraising rock concert was organized in Madison Square Garden by George Harrison, Ravi Shankar, Eric Clapton, and Bob Dylan.

The Security Council debated but did nothing, in part because the United States, then working on its détente with China, had been using Pakistan as a go-between. In July, National Security Advisor Henry Kissinger had secretly visited Beijing, flying on a Pakistani military aircraft, and plans were in the works for President Nixon's groundbreaking trip to Beijing in February the following year. While the United States "tilted toward Pakistan"—a strong ally of China—East Pakistan burned.

In the end, however, the brutality of the crackdown accomplished the precise opposite of what was intended: it turned East Pakistan into a humanitarian *cause célèbre,* and it made independence a certainty. In December the Indian army intervened, and within two weeks it was over. *Bangla Desh*—land of Bengalis—had become an independent nation.

There were, of course, more than humanitarian purposes at work in the Indian invasion, but Bangladesh remains one of the few cases where the humanitarian call for military action was heeded,[12] where humanitarian need was a major and justifiable factor for the intervention that ensued, *and where the results were actually positive.*

Governments Using Humanitarians

Humanitarianism may have been the most frequently stated reason for Russian intervention in Bulgaria and for American intervention in Somalia, and it may have been prominent in Indian thinking about Bangladesh. But for each of these cases, there are a dozen where humanitarians called for action and were met with one of two things: silence or money. In many cases the governments that might have acted—whether for humanitarian or other reasons—simply threw money at a relief effort, and humanitarian action became a substitute for efforts needed to resolve the crisis. Descriptions of three prominent twentieth-century examples follow: the Armenian genocide, the Italian invasion of Abyssinia, and Biafra.

Genocide: The Twentieth Century's Exemplar

To the extent that the Somalia debacle is blamed for US inaction on Rwanda (and Samantha Power does a pretty good job of it in *A Problem from Hell*), there are two rhetorical questions. The first is whether there were, in fact, differences that might have made intervention in Rwanda possible and more successful had Somalia not frightened the United States off. And the second relates to the context of the Somalia intervention: widespread criticism about the neglect of Africa (i.e., racism), a US presidential election, a media circus, and what looked like a relatively risk-free "humanitarian" military opportunity.[13] Rwanda had none of those features, and it can be argued that no force on earth will move a government to act militarily for humanitarian purposes unless there are very compelling strategic reasons. If these do not exist, humanitarians will wind up pounding sand or serving as fig leaves to cover naked inaction on other fronts.

If there is an exemplar for the non-intervention that has been evidenced most recently in Rwanda and Darfur, it is probably the 1915 Armenian genocide in Turkey. Armenian Christians had lived a precarious existence in the Ottoman Empire until 1894, when a small-scale Armenian tax revolt was used as the pretext for massacres that left more than 300,000 dead. With the advent of World War I, Russia urged the Armenian population to rise against the Turkish government, now an ally of the Central Powers. A Russian victory over the Turkish army in January 1915 was blamed by the Turkish government on Armenian treachery, and, when Armenians in the city of Van resisted enforced conscription, a massacre ensued. It was the first in what became a genocidal bloodbath aimed at ridding Turkey of all Armenians. Estimates of the final death toll range between one and one-and-a-half million people.[14]

Western outrage was quickly galvanized. Britain and France, already at war with Turkey, promised war-crimes trials for the perpetrators, and in the United States, then a neutral power, public opinion was also enflamed. The US ambassador to Turkey, Henry Morgenthau, was stunned: "I am confident that the whole history of the human race contains no such horrible episode as this," he said.[15] The story was carried for months in the American media, and huge public sympathy and support were engendered for Armenian victims. A Committee on Armenian Atrocities was formed to raise funds for humanitarian assistance, and large amounts were raised from churches, from institutions such as the newly formed Rockefeller Foundation, and from the general public.

President Wilson, having already sent troops to occupy Haiti and the Dominican Republic, was not disinclined to use American soldiers where he saw a case. But the Armenian genocide did not beckon. His greatest fear, if he provoked Turkey, was being drawn into a war with the Central Powers, most notably Germany. But the pressure on him from the media, public opinion, and American civil society was relentless. He became the target of withering attacks from former President Theodore Roosevelt, who turned Wilson's own formulation on neutrality back on him, saying, "It is dreadful to think that these things can be done and that this nation nevertheless remains 'neutral not only in deed but in thought,' between right and the most hideous wrong, neutral between despairing and hunted people, people whose little children are murdered and their women raped, and the victorious and evil wrongdoers."[16]

Roosevelt contributed one thousand dollars of his 1906 Nobel Peace Prize money to the Armenian Relief cause, but he had little patience for relief as a substitute for military action. "To allow the Turks to massacre the Armenians," he said, "and then solicit permission to help the survivors and then to allege the fact that we are helping the survivors as a reason why we should not follow the only policy that will permanently put a stop to such massacres is both foolish and odious."[17] He might well have been speaking about Darfur, where now as then, the fig leaf of humanitarian action covers a steely political resolve to stand back on the part of those with the power to step in.

In the end, the United States did enter the war, not because of the Armenian genocide or even because of Turkey, but because of German U-boat attacks on American lives and shipping and because the United States at last became convinced of the need for an Allied victory. At the end of the war a halfhearted effort at war-crimes trials for Turkish *génocidaires* was blocked by the United States, and the Allies simply handed most of Armenia over to the Soviet Union, leaving the rest with Turkey.

Abyssinia

In October 1935, Italy invaded Ethiopia, then known as Abyssinia. The invasion, justified on the basis of fabricated provocation, had its roots in a battle forty years before. In 1896, an earlier Italian invasion had been halted at the Battle of Adowa, when superior Ethiopian forces annihilated an Italian army. Mussolini's invasion, therefore, was as much about retribution as it was about territorial expansion. But the world had changed since Adowa and the European scramble for Africa. "Mussolini's designs upon Abyssinia were unsuited to the ethics of the twentieth century," wrote Winston Churchill, not without irony. "They belonged to those dark ages when white men felt themselves entitled to conquer yellow, brown, black, or red men, and subjugate them by their superior strength and weapons."[18]

There was an added complication: now there was a League of Nations. And Abyssinia was a member of the League, whose Covenant required its members to halt aggression against a fellow member. The League had already been tested and found wanting in 1935, when Hitler began to rearm Germany, breaking the peace treaties on which the League of Nations had been founded. When the invasion of Ethiopia began, the League responded with outrage, condemnation, saber rattling, and sanctions. The export to Italy of aluminum, scrap iron, and iron ore was banned, and there was heightened British fleet action in the Mediterranean.

But the sanctions stopped short of oil, the only thing that might have made a difference. Italy was a net exporter of aluminum and had little use for iron ore and scrap, not least because steel billets and pig iron had not been embargoed. As Churchill put it, "The League of Nations proceeded to the rescue of Abyssinia on the basis that nothing must be done to hamper the invading Italian armies."[19]

In fact, despite the appearance of high-level political action, the only real assistance to Ethiopia came from humanitarian agencies, and they, like the Ethiopians, paid a heavy price. The Red Cross acted quickly, mobilizing health workers, medical supplies, trucks and field ambulances, and League of Nations states were happy with the diversion of attention to humanitarian issues. Members of flying clubs pressed light aircraft into action, and at the height of the effort, twenty-six different Red Cross societies were involved. They soon discovered, however, that the Italian Air Force had as little respect for humanitarians as it did for Ethiopian civilians, or the Ethiopian army, which had fought on horseback with rifles manufactured in the previous century. A Swedish Red Cross camp was bombed in December 1935, then a British field hospital two months later. Mustard gas and phosgene became weapons of choice against the helpless Ethiopians in direct contravention of the Geneva Convention.

As in Biafra, Rwanda, Darfur, and other instances, the international community was unprepared in the case of Ethiopia to take the well-defined and well-understood steps required to halt the Italian invasion and its accompanying horrors. The inaction of the League and of those countries that could have made a difference—Britain, France, and the United States—was veiled by a large and well-reported humanitarian effort. International public outrage was directed against the Italian Air Force rather than the League of Nations and the member states that might have prevented the war in the first place. As would be the case in later situations, interest in the political challenge was diverted by the humanitarian disaster, and debate about an oil embargo was drowned by outrage over attacks on relief hospitals.

Biafra: Savage War of Peace

> *Take up the white man's burden—*
> *The savage wars of peace—*
> *Fill full the mouth of famine*
> *And bid the sickness cease.*
>
> —RUDYARD KIPLING

The first great modern humanitarian emergency began in the southeast corner of Nigeria in 1967. A coup and two horrific pogroms in the north resulted in the deaths of at least thirty thousand Igbos, and by the end of the year, a million people living in Nigeria's Igbo diaspora began flooding back to their eastern homeland. A second murderous coup further destabilized a tenuous political situation, and a federal government decision to divide the country's four regions into a dozen states suddenly became a political watershed. Fearing destruction of the predominantly Igbo-populated Eastern Region as a power bloc, the region's military governor, Colonel Odumegwu Ojukwu, announced its secession from the Federation in May 1967. Thus began the short, violent life of the Republic of Biafra.

The Nigerian government anticipated a brief police action. But a combination of bungling, lengthy supply lines, and fierce Biafran resistance turned the effort into a siege that, by early 1968, was becoming a crisis of starvation. Initially, the United Nations Children's Fund (UNICEF) and the ICRC were able to fly food and drugs to Biafra, supplying the same amounts to the Nigerian side as well. Impartiality was the watchword, as both organizations—dependent upon donor governments for their survival—required the permission and goodwill of the Nigerian government. Permission and goodwill, however, did not last. The United Nations, still reeling from a disastrous peacekeeping experience only four years earlier in the former Belgian Congo, was unprepared to involve itself in another "internal" African affair, and in the end it never did play a role of any importance. The ICRC saw itself as the best possible coordinator for urgently needed relief flights into the besieged enclave and managed to persuade first Oxfam and then a number of church organizations to hold back their own efforts until it could obtain federal government approval for access.

By August 1968, however, the ICRC had become embroiled in negotiations with the Nigerian government and the British government, both of which hoped and believed the war would end within weeks. They also believed that any relief might serve to prolong the war, and so blocking the ICRC became a matter of policy. As with UNICEF and Oxfam, the churches had at first been willing to wait for an ICRC airlift. But as time dragged on, their frustration and anger grew. Tens of thousands of people were starving to death. Finally, tired of waiting, they began their own airlift from the Portuguese Island of São Tomé. Known as Jointchurchaid, the airlift brought together thirty-three European and North American church agencies.

The ICRC's own airlift ultimately began in September 1968, but from the outset, strenuous efforts were made by the Nigerian government to derail it: pressing fickle Western governments to withhold money; tying the United Nations and its ambivalent secretary general, U Thant, in legalistic knots; persuading the newly independent government of Equatorial Guinea— where the ICRC airlift originated—to halt flights; and finally, in June 1969, shooting down a Red Cross plane.[20] Flights were immediately suspended. Months of futile negotiations ensued, during which the ICRC—constrained by its legal mandate—became more and more entangled in technicalities and debates about the finer points of national sovereignty. Its planes never flew to Biafra again.

For the churches—which kept flying—it was a matter of conscience and of very real human need. Estimates of the death toll from starvation rose as high as twenty-five thousand a day, and the word *genocide*, not as loosely used then as it is today, became a common characterization of events as described in the editorial pages of newspapers around the world. In the end, of the 7,800 relief flights into Biafra, 5,310 were operated by Jointchurchaid, providing 66,000 tons of food and supplies, valued at an estimated US$116 million.[21] It was a historical feat rivaled in volume only by the Berlin airlift, and it is probably still unrivalled anywhere for bravery.

But the airlift and the broader relief effort did something else. It prolonged the war for eighteen months, because the relief agencies believed—incorrectly, as it turned out—that an unrestrained Nigerian government would unleash a genocidal bloodbath against Igbos, should Biafra collapse. This was a willing suspension of disbelief. By mid-1968, half of the Eastern Region, along with a large number of Igbos, had already been retaken by Nigerian forces. Large areas of the Midwest State, liberated in the early days of the war, were also Igbo speaking. There had been no massacres in any of these areas.

After the war a great deal of effort went into refuting the charge that the churches and NGOs prolonged the conflict. If it was true, they must also have prolonged the suffering, contributing to the deaths of 180,000 people or more. Other numbers, however, tell the story. Although the Biafran pound was worthless, relief agencies still exchanged hard currency at the official rate established before the war: £1 = US$2.80. As long as they accepted this rate—and it never changed—they contributed directly to the Biafran war chest. For example, the World Council of Churches representative in Orlu, one of ten Biafran provinces, reported local purchases worth US$140,000 a month in November 1968. A German agency reported spending US$1.25 million between March and October 1968.[22] In addition to purchases, most distribution costs were borne by relief agencies. Nordchurchaid, for example, spent US$50,000 renting cars and trucks in August 1969 alone. And before September 1968, the British and Irish Catholic churches alone spent more than US$400,000 on special projects—to build clinics, hospitals, and camp facilities.[23] Relief agencies built Biafra's Uli airstrip (which was also used for arms flights), providing planking, navigational equipment, and lighting, and paying hundreds of dollars in landing, parking, and take-off fees for every one of the 7,800 relief flights.

In all, the best estimate of the cost of the relief effort is US$250 million, a considerable sum in 1970 dollars.[24] If as little as 15 percent of that was spent inside Biafra, it would have provided the regime with as much foreign exchange as was spent by Nigeria on arms throughout the war.[25]

While the rapid escalation of relief activities helped Biafra to survive the late summer and early autumn of 1968, it essentially transformed a potential country into little more than an object of pity. Interpreted largely through the eyes of relief agencies, Biafra became a humanitarian rather than a political problem, excusing the United Nations and virtually every Western government from direct involvement. Unlike the spate of rapid diplomatic recognitions that followed the political breakup of the Soviet Union and Yugoslavia two decades later, the emphasis on Biafra's suffering—used by relief agencies for fundraising purposes—perhaps damaged its chances for recognition and for the international political support that might really have saved it.

Biafra is worth remembering because of the salience of its lessons to the situation in Darfur. In a detailed and compelling history of that region, Mahmood Mamdani argues that what has happened in Darfur is nothing like genocide, and that humanitarians—like the atrocitarians before them, clamoring for military intervention—have not only grossly exaggerated the death toll, but have transformed an extremely complex political and ecological disaster into a convenient war-on-terror construct in which "good" African farmers are being destroyed by the "bad" Arab/Muslim *Janjawiid*. The Save Darfur Coalition, Mamdani says,

> does not seek to end the civil war in Darfur; rather it calls for a military intervention in the civil war without bothering to address the likely

consequences of that intervention. "Out of Iraq and into Darfur," says a common Save Darfur slogan. . . . At best, Save Darfur was a romance driven by a feel-good search for instant remedies. At worst, it was a media-savvy political campaign designed to portray "Arabs" as race-intoxicated exterminators of "Africans."[26]

Neutrality and the Eye of the Beholder

If the facts don't fit the theory, change the facts.
—ATTRIBUTED TO ALBERT EINSTEIN

It is obvious in almost all of these cases that the basic elements of so-called classical humanitarianism—neutrality, impartiality, and independence—were patchy, weak, or simply nonexistent. Humanitarians may have professed neutrality for as long as it suited them, but in case after case most of the major agencies, often backed by prominent (and usually opposition) politicians and supported or egged on by the media, became proponents of one side or the other. They were used as an excuse for war, as in the case of the Bulgarian atrocities, or as an alternative or even a justification for inaction, as in the Armenian genocide, Abyssinia, and Biafra.

China, Japan, and the Protection of Civilians

In October 1934, delegates from fifty-seven national Red Cross societies gathered in Tokyo for the fifteenth International Red Cross Conference. It was a stellar gathering, bringing together more than 250 international delegates. No expense was spared by the Japanese government in making it a grand and well-publicized affair. There were concerts and banquets aplenty. Commissions were established to discuss membership, relief work, health, and other pressing topics of the day, and the Red Cross Society of the Soviet Union was at last admitted to the fold.

The most difficult subject, however, had to do with the protection of civilians, a category of war victim hitherto excluded from the Geneva Conventions and the Red Cross mandate. Here was a vast swathe of humanity, ranging from refugees and deportees to stateless people and those persecuted by their own governments. The topic had been discussed in Red Cross circles for years, to little avail. In Tokyo, a weak draft on the subject was finally accepted but not officially approved, and it was restricted to civilians in enemy and occupied territory. Even this was regarded as something of a breakthrough.

The conference and the draft, however, served primarily as fig leaves to cover up the reality of Japanese aggression. Japan had invaded Manchuria in 1931, setting up the "independent" state of Manchukuo the following year. When the League of Nations responded to a request from China to investigate atrocities and the bombing of Chinese cities, Japan promptly withdrew from the League. None of this was discussed at the Tokyo conference, nor was the fact that Japan had not even ratified the second Geneva Convention of 1929—"for the amelioration of the condition of wounded, sick and shipwrecked members of armed forces at sea."

The inability of Red Cross members to agree on a meaningful protocol for the protection of civilians would haunt it for years to come, but the first embarrassment came less than three years after the grand Tokyo conference, when, on a pretext, Japan attacked China. Soon there were 100,000 Japanese soldiers in China, and within three weeks, Peking and Tientsin had fallen. Japanese bombers attacked cities, targeting hospitals, missions, refugee camps, and other civilian targets. More than half a million refugees crowded into Shanghai, while Japanese attention turned toward Nanking, a city that would soon become a sordid symbol of Japanese brutality.

There, foreign civilians had set up an organization they called the International Red Cross Committee of Nanking, establishing a "safety zone" for civilians and caring for 100,000 displaced people. While many civilians were undoubtedly protected, an estimated 300,000 people were killed in what later became known as the rape of Nanking, and the city was virtually destroyed. Official Red Cross delegates never did gain access to Nanking.

The Red Cross's decade-long debate about civilian protection, the subject of endless meetings, studies, and drafts, had come to naught. It did nothing for Chinese civilian victims of Japanese aggression, and it would do nothing for civilians in the conflict that loomed in Ethiopia. Some insiders saw the lack of clarity as a kind of strength that allowed the Red Cross to traverse more easily the vague boundaries of its official mandate. Judging from what was to come, however, this was not just rationalization, it was delusional.

The high cost of procrastination became evident in the lead-up to World War II, when the ICRC found itself faced with what seemed like an impossible situation. Because the Conventions under which it operated, and which gave the Red Cross its legitimacy, did not cover civilians subjected to brutality by their own governments, the ICRC had no mandate to intervene on behalf of Jews, gypsies, homosexuals, political prisoners, and others who were being gathered into German concentration camps during the 1930s, and later, across Europe.

Because international humanitarian law was silent on political prisoners, the ICRC had to act with caution, if the neutrality that gave it access to its standard wartime clientele—prisoners of war—was to be preserved. The influence of the Swiss government was not insignificant. In the autumn of 1942 there were thirty-five hundred Swiss nationals working for the ICRC, and 55 percent of its Sfr33.5 million budget was provided by the Swiss government.[27] Second, the ICRC feared that a public condemnation might cause Germany to repudiate the Geneva Conventions, making life much worse for prisoners of war and others to whom the Red Cross had access behind German lines. Its public position on the plight of the Jews was that it "did not currently possess enough information," or that it was "a very tragic situation and we cannot do anything about it."[28]

Where the Holocaust is concerned, history and hindsight have been hard on the Red Cross. Although the ICRC saw the victims of concentration camps—or rather *extermination* camps—as worthy of interest, compassion, and support, it never saw them as a distinct category. In any case the ICRC saw, and still sees, its mandate stemming from law rather than morality. Even so, in an important work on the Red Cross and the Holocaust, Jean-Claude Favez says that "attempts at intervention rooted in humanitarian law tended to leave [the Jews] on the sidelines whereas, of all war victims, their fate was the most tragic."[29]

"In the practice of international humanitarian law, faced with appeals from victims who were juridically innominate, the ICRC habitually sought not ways of getting things done, but instead reasons for doing nothing, so as not to undermine the missions carried out under the auspices of the Conventions on which, in its eyes, its very existence depended."[30] The importance the ICRC attached to its credibility, Favez argues, took it down a road that led to a loss of that very credibility and of the authority of the Red Cross in a wider world.

Double Standards: Of Forests and Trees

Perhaps World War II caused the ICRC to take its responsibilities for neutrality, impartiality, and independence more seriously in the decades that followed. Barbara Rieffer-Flanagan unpacks the ICRC effort in an essay entitled "Is Neutral Humanitarianism Dead?" She examines the almost impossible case of Korea, where the ICRC bent over backward in its efforts to support POWs and civilians both north and south of the 38th Parallel. The sticking point was a North Korean charge that the United States had used biological weapons. When the ICRC offered to investigate, it was rejected by China as a most vicious and shameless accomplice and lackey of American imperialism. The purpose behind its eagerness to investigate is obviously to find out the effectiveness of the American aggressors' unparalleled, brutal crime, and to try and whitewash the perpetrators of the crime with a worthless report.[31]

Clearly China and North Korea were not going to allow an investigation of what was likely a trumped-up charge. But the issue at hand is not so much whether the Red Cross could have handled the matter differently (it could have); it is that neutrality is very much in the eye of the beholder. And Rieffer-Flanagan makes the point that "the difficulties associated with navigating neutrality are not a phenomenon of the post–Cold War or of 9/11 or the war on terrorism. The ICRC has been trying to walk the tightrope of neutral humanitarianism, sometimes more successfully than others, for a number of decades."[32]

The Boer War

Historically, however, in many of the conflicts already described, the bulk of those engaged in the humanitarian apparatus took few pains to be neutral. And in many cases humanitarians did not even notice—as with the Red Cross in Japan in 1934—that there was something else going on that should have caught their attention. Such was the case during the Boer War.

When the Boer War broke out in 1899, the British Red Cross Society rallied with fundraising drives that soon resulted in the dispatch of large quantities of medical supplies, surgical dressings, food, newspapers, and other relief goods. The British assistance was complemented by aid from the German, Italian, and other Red Cross societies, and by societies in southern Africa. A special railway carriage shipped from Britain to South Africa was used extensively to pick up casualties and drop off surgeons.

Someone once said that Bosnia was the first war to which volunteer relief workers could hitchhike. But the amateur humanitarian phenomenon is far from new. As the Boer War continued, droves of would-be nurses and relief workers boarded steamers bound for Cape Town. Soon there were hundreds of British women, as one journalist put it, "pottering about the wards in flounces and furbelows, hindering the nurses and irritating the patients."[33] Queen Victoria disapproved and asked the governor of the Cape Colony to issue an edict saying (in vain) that volunteers were not wanted.

But something more sinister was also going on. By mid-1900, the promised quick end to the war was nowhere in sight, and British casualties were mounting, thanks to successful Boer guerrilla attacks. In retaliation and as a way of ridding areas of all resistance, the British began a "policy of punishment," clearing land of anything that could sustain the guerrillas, including farms and families. The justification was that "no woman on a lonely farm was safe amid a black population" and that "the British Nation would have indeed remained under an ineffable stain had they left women and children without shelter on the veldt."[34]

Huge numbers of civilians were rounded up and placed in "camps" where living conditions were deplorable.[35] By the end of 1900 there were eight camps in the Transvaal and four in the Orange Free State. These camps, soon known as concentration camps from the *reconcentrado* of the 1895 Cuban uprising, became centers of disease, starvation, and death. In May 1901, 550 civilians died in the camps; in June, 782; and in July, 1,675.[36] The British Red Cross, which was the leading humanitarian agency in South Africa, had nothing to say about the matter and provided little in the way of humanitarian assistance.

The issue came to public attention only when a British woman named Emily Hobhouse visited the region. Hobhouse was honorary secretary of the South African Conciliation Committee, and she was one of the first to provide any kind of emergency assistance in the camps. Hobhouse returned to Britain and raised a furor over the situation. Although she and her allies were labeled agitators and traitors, and dismissed as "a few unsexed and hysterical women," they turned the camps into an international outrage, and conditions improved somewhat. Nevertheless, by the end of the war, an estimated twenty-six thousand Boer civilians had died in the camps, twenty thousand of them children under the age of sixteen, and another sixteen thousand blacks had died as well, as a direct result of the concentration camp policy.

Red Cross societies had been quick to provide succor for wounded combatants, serving as a kind of auxiliary to the British army. But the Red Cross avoided any response to the "policy of punishment," and as a prominent Red Cross historian put it, "Nowhere, at any time, was anything actually said about the concentration camps."[37]

Colonial Wars and Unremembered Emergencies

Colonial wars predate the modern humanitarian era by as many millennia as there are in the history of organized human conflict. A brief examination of humanitarian action in the post-Solferino colonial world, however, is revealing for the double standard that was in play through the last colonial wars of the 1970s.

Britain was not a signatory to the first Geneva Convention of 1864, which called for, among other things, the impartial reception and treatment of all combatants and the protection of civilians providing aid to the wounded. The protocols did not apply, therefore, when British forces reacted to a small uprising in Jamaica. In October 1865, a rag-tag army of Jamaican insurgents, frustrated by poverty, taxes, and poor government, left forty-eight dead after an attack on colonial authorities in the town of Morant Bay. The governor, Edward Eyre, feared the beginning of a Haitian-style revolution, and he was determined to suppress it. There followed a month-long reign of terror. An elected member of the House of Assembly was court martialed and hanged, and the assembly was dissolved. A thousand homes were burned, an estimated five hundred Jamaicans were killed, and equal numbers were flogged and tortured.

What makes the Jamaican "uprising" so striking as a war is that despite widespread rumor of rebel armies, British troops never met any organized opposition, and there was not a single British military casualty. The event might have slipped quietly into history had groups in Britain—humanitarians of a sort—not protested. For liberals, radicals, and those seeking wider suffrage and governmental reform, the Jamaican massacre was symbolic of larger questions. John Stuart Mill, the great Scottish philosopher, joined the fray. "The question was," he wrote, "whether the British dependencies, and eventually perhaps, Great Britain itself, were to be under the government of law, or of military license."[38]

Governor Eyre was relieved of his position. He and several of his administrators returned to England, where they were subjected to legal prosecution, paid for by subscriptions raised from outraged citizens. The massacre became a *cause célèbre,* and the matter dragged on in the courts for more than three years until a series of grand juries dismissed all charges. In the eyes of his supporters, Eyre was vindicated as a hero, and his pension as a "retired" colonial governor was reinstated. In the House of Commons, however, MP Peter Taylor called Jamaica "a case of cowardice which magnified a trumpery riot into a widespread insurrection, and then drowned the phantom it created in an ocean of murder, anarchy and blood."[39]

In some ways the Jamaican massacres set the stage for further cases of colonial murder, anarchy, and blood. Still to come were the Maori, Zulu, Matabele, and Ashanti Wars, wars in the Sudan, Afghanistan, the Northwest Frontier, and the final British colonial wars in Kenya (1952–56) and Malaya (1948–60). If humanitarians were present at all during these conflicts, their work—as in South Africa—was almost exclusively in the service of the colonial power. The same was true of French colonial wars, latterly in

Madagascar, Cameroon, Algeria, and Indo-China. The public outcry in Europe and America over Belgian atrocities in King Leopold's Congo was fueled by humanitarian sentiment, but formal humanitarian organizations were largely absent from the colony, except for those with a Christianizing mission. The modern humanitarian apparatus and the full panoply of humanitarian law were readily available during the Portuguese colonial wars that raged in Africa between 1961 and 1975, but humanitarian action was limited mainly to refugees on the periphery.

These were the precursor of today's "forgotten" emergencies, crises where politics trumps humanitarian action, where the media is absent, where consolidated UN appeals fall on deaf ears, and where principles of humanitarian proportionality simply do not apply. Humanitarian emergencies cannot, of course, be "forgotten"; they may be ignored, underfunded, or placed off limits by warring factions, but the world's humanitarian community is well aware of them and always has been. The awareness, however, can be likened to peripheral vision, something at the edges of the field of view, a state conditioned by arcane definitions of vulnerability, vague models of humanitarian need, access, and the availability of cash. Such is the nature of humanitarian instrumentality—or, one might say more politely, the political economy of humanitarian assistance—that today even the largest of humanitarian situations, such as Chechnya or the one that has festered in the Congo for the past decade, are unremembered if not forgotten.

Perhaps the most flagrant examples of willing instrumentalization took place during the Vietnam War, described in the following chapter. The parallels today in Iraq and Afghanistan are not manifestations of a new paradigm brought about by the end of the Cold War or the new War on Terror. The same tendencies have been evident at least since the Boer War, when British humanitarians failed to notice what their government was doing to Boer women and children. The absence of humanitarian neutrality was evident in the hue and cry over the Bulgarian atrocities and the positions humanitarians took in Biafra. Thousands of "humanitarians" went to war in Spain.

The obverse of humanitarian attempts to push governments into military action, from Armenia to Darfur, is the many times when governments have used humanitarians as an excuse for complete inaction. Colin Powell told a dismayed audience of American voluntary agencies in 2001 that "NGOs are such a force multiplier for us, such an important part of our combat team."[40] He can perhaps be excused for his surprise at the vehemence of the reaction from organizations that denied what was so obviously true, at least to someone in his position. Fractious, fickle, and often contrary, NGOs had nevertheless been available to US foreign policy as "force multipliers" in Europe after World War II, in Korea, throughout Southeast Asia, and in

Central America, where they dispensed lashings of US government funds under failing dictatorships in Guatemala, Nicaragua, and El Salvador.

A tiny handful of European NGOs have perhaps been more independent of governmental foreign policy, but they too have often acted as "force multipliers." German NGOs were quick to take on housing projects in Bosnia when the German government saw this as the answer to waves of Bosnian refugees flowing north. In fact the cooptation of the UN High Commissioner for Refugees and the wider humanitarian community in Bosnia was so profound that the idea of keeping it separate from governmental imperatives was—as David Rieff puts it—"a pipe dream."[41] Norwegian NGOs were everywhere in Sri Lanka when a negotiated peace settlement was the Norwegian government's signature piece in the country. British NGOs paid close attention to government wishes and proscriptions in Afghanistan before (and after) 9/11. And when mostly ignored emergencies in Sierra Leone, Liberia, the Congo, and Angola were being forgotten by governmental donors, NGOs too became forgetful or went into low-altitude holding patterns.

Conclusions

Several conclusions about instrumentalization and humanitarian action can be drawn from the cases described in this chapter.

First, history appears to demonstrate that Western donor governments have always manipulated humanitarian sentiment and action. They did it before the Cold War, during the Cold War, and they do it today. What's more, the rank and file of humanitarian agencies have been willing pawns, if not partners in this manipulation, often for their own humanitarian ends. Classic humanitarianism has not changed in its basic tenets, but it is applied by so many humanitarian organizations on such a sporadic and situational basis that it is difficult for manipulators to take it seriously. Or rather, it becomes easier for manipulators to ignore it.

Second, instrumentalization is not something restricted to Western donor governments. Humanitarians have always had to look the other way when the occasional truckload of emergency supplies went missing as a kind of informal or unspoken tribute to one faction or the other in a conflict setting. But the Biafran war demonstrates that recipients can also be major manipulators of humanitarian assistance, humanitarian organizations, and humanitarian sentiment.

Third, just as governments and combatants manipulate humanitarian assistance, so do humanitarian actors attempt to manipulate governments and combatants. The demand for a powerful government to step in and

right a perceived humanitarian wrong echoes consistently down the generations, from the Bulgarian atrocities to Darfur. As an aside, it cannot be lost
on Islamic scholars that many of these calls for intervention, from Bulgaria
and the first and second Serbian wars against the Ottoman Empire through
to Darfur today, have had a decidedly anti-Muslim flavor. The long history
of explicitly Christian humanitarian zeal may have contributed directly to
some of the more complicated humanitarian and political dilemmas that
exist in the world today.

Fourth, instrumentalization can be an act of omission as well as one of
commission. The many "forgotten" emergencies of the past 150 years—in
reality, *ignored* emergencies—are testimony to a consistent and willing
disregard for a wide range of humanitarian plights. Two described in this
chapter, the British concentration camps for Boer civilians and the Jamaican massacres, were ignored for political reasons, but many other reasons
can prevail: an inability to raise funds; too many concurrent emergencies;
emergencies hidden behind iron curtains or caste systems; the absence of
media attention.

Fifth, the media are a key part of the instrumentalization nexus and
have been from the moment the first Geneva Convention was signed. The
media have been used as much to enflame as to inform public opinion,
while their absence can mean the difference between life and death for
tens of thousands of people. Newspapers were essential to the Bulgarian
atrocitarians' campaigns in Russia and Britain. Newspapers gave voice to
Gladstone, Theodore Roosevelt, and John Stuart Mill—the Bono, Geldof,
and Clooney of their day. The media turned the Ethiopian famine from a
forgotten emergency into a *cause cèlèbre*, made Biafra a household name,
and turned the Asian tsunami into the best-funded humanitarian response
of all time. Without the media, however, humanitarian appeals can fall on
deaf ears. In the mid-1990s a World Vision fundraising effort for Sierra
Leone—at the time one of those ignored, "forgotten" emergencies—failed
to raise enough money to cover the cost of newspaper ads.

"Some of them want to use you, some of them want to get used by
you." The lyrics ring true. Part of the problem may be that the classical
ideas of humanitarian neutrality, impartiality, and independence always
had limited circulation. As the champion of these principles, the Red Cross
movement—primarily the ICRC—found itself amid a bewildering array of
humanitarian NGOs operating in the aftermath of the Rwandan genocide,
at a time when principles of every kind were being tested. The Red Cross
proposed a Code of Conduct that articulated some of these principles and
others, and they were agreed to by eight of world's largest disaster-response
agencies in the summer of 1994.[42] As of May 2011, 472 agencies had

signed the code. That 472 agencies are even available to sign such a code raises questions of its own, whether or not it is even remotely possible that all actually adhere to it. One theory is that the rush to proclaim principles of neutrality, independence, and impartiality is an effort by humanitarian agencies to clear space for themselves in a world where they have become increasingly dependent upon states and institutions for their funding.[43]

This is not to say that the standards set by the code are unattainable. Principles will always be challenged by events. For many humanitarian organizations, however, application of the "fundamental principles" falls considerably short of what might pass for "fundamental."

Chapter 3

Humanitarian Action and Politicization

A Review of Experience Since World War II

LARRY MINEAR

Much has been written about the interactions over the years between humanitarian action and politics. Many practitioners of the humanitarian craft and the public that supports their endeavors often portray humanitarian assistance and protection as devoid of political considerations. In reality, however, humanitarian action, on the giving and receiving ends alike, takes place in the context of political frameworks and is rarely, if ever, totally free of political impetus or effects.

This chapter examines the political dynamics surrounding humanitarian action during the Cold War era (1945–90). It compares these with developments during two subsequent political eras: the post–Cold War years (the decade of the 1990s) and the Global War on Terror (GWOT) since September 11, 2001. It builds on the previous chapter, which examined the pre–1945 years as well. Because the humanitarian enterprise and the wider public are less familiar with the Cold War than with subsequent experience, this chapter provides more detail for the 1945–90 period. The country case studies included in this volume themselves provide more attention to the post–Cold War and GWOT periods.[1]

The goal is to ascertain the extent to which the politicization of humanitarian action is a recurring fact of life in each of these periods. Is it more prevalent at some times than others? Is the level of instrumentalization—that is, the pressing of humanitarian action into the service of political objectives—steady-state or variable over time? The focus of this chapter is on the conduct of humanitarian action by the US government, the preeminent Western aid donor across these periods, and of American NGOs, the major

implementing agencies with occasional comparisons to European governments and agencies and the UN system. In each era most humanitarian
initiatives and actors nested comfortably within the conceptual and operational framework provided by the US government.

One source of information and analysis for this inquiry is provided by
interviews conducted with officials who helped formulate and manage
humanitarian policies and programs during the Cold War and thereafter.
A list of these "Elders" is found at the end of this chapter. A second source
comprises historical reviews of the Cold War and a score of country studies conducted over the post–Cold War years by the Feinstein International
Center and the Humanitarianism and War Project.[2]

The Cold War

The roots of the Cold War lay in World War II. Some historians see the
beginnings of the Cold War in the Yalta conference of February 1945, half
a year before the war's end. Discussions of post-war arrangements among
Roosevelt, Churchill, and Stalin exhibited signs of the future bifurcation
between East and West that would evolve into the Cold War.

In the final years of World War II and the decade that followed, new
international and regional institutional arrangements were put in place that
reflected the emerging divisions between East and West, separated by what
Winston Churchill called an "iron curtain." In 1944, the Bretton Woods
institutions—the World Bank and the International Monetary Fund—were
created, and in 1945 the United Nations itself. In January 1947, the Truman
Doctrine committed the United States to contain communist expansion.
The Marshall Plan, announced in June 1947 in a Harvard commencement
speech by General George C. Marshall and continuing through June 1952,
provided the framework for US-led assistance by Western nations in Europe's
post-war reconstruction. In 1948–49, the USSR imposed a blockade of
Berlin, to which the United States and its allies responded with an airlift.
In 1949, NATO was founded to resist communist advances; the Eastern
Bloc countries responded with the formation in 1955 of the Warsaw Pact.

East-West political and institutional divisions deepened with the Korean
War, pitting South Korea and the United States against North Korea and
China (June 1950–July 1953). With the founding of the Southeast Asia
Treaty Organization (SEATO) in August 1955, new security arrangements
sought to deter communist expansion in Southeast Asia. There was also
friction within the communist bloc between the Soviet Union and China.
On the development side, President Kennedy in 1961 launched the Peace
Corps to counter anti-Americanism, and in the same year the United States

and other Western hemisphere nations joined in creating the Alliance for Progress.

The decades following World War II saw an acceleration in the process of decolonization. When the United Nations was established in 1945, some 750 million people lived in non–self-governing territories; the figure is now about two million, with eighty former colonies having gained their independence.[3] Many newly independent states during the Cold War became members of the nonaligned movement, which was formally launched in 1961, positioning itself between East and West and seeking to influence both.

Many nonaligned or so-called Third World countries endorsed the creation of a "new international economic order" and strongly supported efforts of the UN Conference on Trade and Development (UNCTAD) to promote more just terms of trade for poorer countries. "Developing" countries also played an active role in a series of international and regional UN conferences and follow-up meetings on issues such as food and hunger (1974), population (1974), human settlements (1976), health (1978), environment and development (1992), human rights (1993), and women (1995). Such international and regional institutional arrangements provided the political framework within which US and other Western assistance was provided during the Cold War period.

Indo-China

Indo-China was one of the flashpoints of Cold War confrontation. The former French colonies of Vietnam, Laos, and Cambodia gained independence after a bitter war ending in 1954. In the 1960s, the United States joined with the Army of the Republic of Vietnam to wage war against the Vietnam People's Army, or North Vietnamese Army, and the Viet Cong, or National Front for the Liberation of South Vietnam, a South Vietnamese communist army.[4] In addition to mounting aid activities before US troops withdrew in 1975, humanitarian organizations faced the challenge of responding to genocide and starvation in Cambodia under Pol Pot (1975–79) and to the needs of Cambodians under Vietnamese occupation in Cambodia and in refugee camps in Thailand (see Chapter 11). The complex landscape for assistance and protection work in Indo-China offers parallels to the challenges faced by humanitarian organizations in conflicts elsewhere in later years.

The humanitarian situation in Vietnam was highly charged as US officials saw developments there (alongside the Korean War and the Berlin Wall) as evidence of a global political-military assault on the world's democratic governments by the forces of communism. Leaders in the region had their own agendas in which humanitarian needs did not figure prominently. Observations in case studies by academic analysts and by the Elders provide useful perspective on the humanitarian-political dynamic.

Most US NGOs—and most of the NGOs involved in Indo-China were American—positioned themselves as extensions of US policy, working "in close partnership with the US government in promoting America's Cold War policies. . . . America's longest and most divisive war subjected this partnership to enormous strains."[5] Throughout the war the US government was involved in an extended push-and-pull with humanitarian organizations. Review of the experience of four major NGOs—Vietnam Christian Service (VNCS), CARE, International Voluntary Services (IVS), and Catholic Relief Services (CRS)—demonstrates the thoroughgoing penetration of humanitarian activities by political agendas.

VNCS, a coalition of the Mennonite Central Committee (MCC) and several other faith-based Protestant organizations, waged an ongoing battle against US efforts to "assume operational control" of its personnel and programs. The fact that VNCS and its members were motivated not by politics but rather by Christian love was lost on US military officials and Vietnamese military groups on the ground. In a briefing by the Mennonites, one newly arrived US colonel responded to the MCC presentation with the comment: "Now let me tell you what I do. My job, to put it starkly, is to kill the enemy. The more Viet Cong we kill, the better. We are also here to win the hearts and minds of the Vietnamese people. And that is where you come in. . . . We are glad you are part of the team." In another exchange, US Ambassador Ellsworth Bunker warned aid staff against activities that might benefit the Viet Cong. "If you're helping the VC, that is treason," he said. "You know the penalty for treason."[6]

Maintaining operational independence from US political-military policies and actors in Vietnam was difficult and ultimately proved impossible. The Mennonites accepted transport for personnel and relief supplies from the US military, utilized military postal and commissary services, occasionally bunked at military facilities, and allowed soldiers to provide services in MCC clinics to civilians. Over time, more and more MCC staff sensed a fundamental contradiction between their day-to-day aid work and their protestations of political neutrality. Many came to agree with MCC worker Pat Hostetler: "We came to Vietnam as naive Mennonites. We wanted to do service. Then we discovered that service cannot be non-political." A reflective piece by MCC staffer James Metzler was titled "Vietnam: I Wouldn't Do It Again."[7]

CARE was far less troubled by its linkage to US policy. In fact, "in the organization, publicity, and execution of its aid projects [it] meticulously tailored its objectives" to those of the US government and the South Vietnamese authorities.[8] CARE workers in Indo-China "firmly believed that their activities were non-political and their 'people-based' programs available to all." In fact, at a global level, "the more Americans feared the communist threat, the more actively CARE sought to use humanitarian aid to combat it." CARE's own historian describes its role as "an effective instrument of foreign policy . . . in breaking down barriers between nations and creating everywhere a feeling of friendship for America and Americans." In addition to privately donated funds, CARE's Vietnam program received ample resources from US government agencies, including the Central Intelligence Agency (CIA), and the organization served as an active advocate of US Vietnam policy with the American public. The experience, concluded analyst Delia T. Pergande, demonstrated "how private citizens and beneficent institutions helped serve Cold War objectives and implement US foreign policy."[9]

CRS, the humanitarian arm of the US Catholic Conference, was also a major US government ally in Vietnam. The Catholic Church itself was "a particularly important partner in America's global humanitarian outreach," with CRS a key point of entry to Catholic institutions around the world. "Because of its willingness to work closely with the US government, CRS became the largest voluntary agency in the world, dwarfing others in budget, scope, and size. In 1967 it operated in 77 countries with a budget of 158 million dollars." Catholic theology and social teaching "viewed the Cold War as a competition between Christianity (or civilization) and communism," which was seen as "anarchistic, violent, and dangerously atheistic."[10]

CRS's work in Vietnam dated from 1952, with the agency stepping up services to meet the needs of refugees arriving from the north following the departure of the French in 1954. Activities were expanded further still in response to an appeal to NGOs by President Johnson in mid-1965 at a time of heightened US and South Vietnamese military pressure. CRS's food distribution to South Vietnamese Popular Forces, publicized in articles in the *National Catholic Reporter,* created a major controversy. Its involvement was soon phased down, with food distribution taken over by the US military itself. The Popular Forces controversy "served as a brake to the optimistic assessment that, by mixing bombs and bullets with food and schools, the Vietnam War could be won. Humanitarian aid remained a US interest, but its broad application as a Cold War strategy in the developing world was severely muted."[11]

IVS, whose work in Vietnam began in 1956, deployed more than 160 volunteers in 1967. By the time it closed operations in 1971, some 400 volunteers had served there. As with VNCS, several IVS staff lost their lives in carrying out their work. IVS's experience demonstrated some of the operational and associational pushes and pulls felt by VNCS, CARE, and

CRS, but with a different institutional response. In September 1967, three senior field staff tendered highly publicized resignations, "the first protest [against the war] from within the American community in Vietnam." Concluding that "the only way to help Vietnam was to change American policy," the trio decided "to give up their positions in protest and hope their action would have a positive impact."[12] "The resignation letter gave the former IVS volunteers a means to influence the American decision-making process that they would never have had." Other IVS staffers joined in an open letter to President Johnson, their action drawing widespread support from the IVS board.

None of these four NGOs remained unchanged by the experience, although the extent to which each became more wary of cooperation in the humanitarian sphere with the US government varied. There is little to suggest, however, that their ongoing approach to humanitarian action in the post–Cold War and GWOT periods was significantly altered to take on board the Cold War experience. Perhaps the most changed was CRS, where the debate on Vietnam policy "signaled the end of close cooperation between state and private interests in the delivery of humanitarian services."[13] The MCC, too, became considerably more circumspect in its collaboration with the US government.

The Reagan Years

Reflecting divisions that had been hardening since the closing months of World War II, the height of the Cold War in the 1980s is remembered by many Americans as a time when global forces of freedom and democracy, led by the United States and backstopped by NATO, sought to rebuff the territorial ambitions of expansionist communism, led by the USSR and drawing on the resources of the Warsaw Pact countries. The 1980 Republican Party Platform, the year in which Ronald Reagan was elected president, embraced the dominant Cold War narrative that "the premier challenge facing the United States, its allies, and the entire globe, is to check the Soviet Union's global ambitions."

International programs to assist people around the world—in the Soviet bloc, Africa, Latin America, and Asia, and those seeking refuge in the United States itself—took place on this Manichean landscape. As a result of deference to the assertion of sovereignty by the Soviet Union, people in East Bloc countries were not reached by international assistance and protection efforts, while within the "Third World" itself humanitarian initiatives were situated within and subservient to the larger East-West confrontation. Developing ("Third World") countries became an arena for confronting communism. Aid activities were an extension of the Cold War, with political goals often pursued without reference to their consequences for civilian populations. Assistance programs were typically mounted along borders where persons fleeing communism congregated, not inside communist countries themselves.

The Reagan Doctrine, articulated in the president's 1985 State of the Union message, affirmed that the United States must not "break faith with those who are risking their lives on every continent, from Afghanistan to Nicaragua, to defy Soviet-supported aggression and secure rights that have been ours from birth."[14] Earlier in the year Secretary of State George Shultz had associated the United States with popular insurgencies that were seeking to topple communist regimes. US Ambassador to the United Nations Jean J. Kirkpatrick was outspoken in her criticism of the Carter administration for not having provided more forceful assistance to the Shah in Iran and the Nicaraguan regime under duress from Marxist guerrillas. As she saw it, US policy should support anti-communist efforts, even if it required alliances with autocrats who were themselves serious human rights violators.[15]

Against the background of Cold War antagonisms, the reality remembered by the Elders interviewed for this chapter is surprising. The centerpiece of US humanitarian policy was not the view that assistance and protection should go only to people in "friendly countries" or only to people fleeing hostile regimes. Rather, it was that responding to appeals for succor should be insulated from political calculation. That policy was articulated as the result of a trip by Republican Senator John C. Danforth to Africa in late 1983.

In an effort to see firsthand the effects of famine, Danforth and his entourage visited villages in Somalia, Mozambique, and Senegal. In Mozambique, Danforth found a village where, he recalls, he took "the picture that needed no caption."[16] Acknowledging the extremity of the situation, President Samora Machel, who was hosting Soviet troops and had applied for membership in the Council for Mutual Economic Assistance (COMECO), agreed to accept food assistance and logistical help from the West.[17] Back in Washington, Danforth shared his photos with President Reagan, who agreed that starving people should not be penalized for the ideology of their government. Danforth's report to the president on his Mozambique trip, recalls then–USAID administrator M. Peter McPherson, was "key to establishing that the United States would give assistance to the people of a Soviet-aligned country. I was at that meeting and I remember it well. While the president knew of the politics of the country, there was no real discussion of them." Reagan later received Machel at the White House; Reagan and his wife, Nancy, and daughter, Maureen, also became personal friends of Machel's wife, Graça.

The policy of assisting starving people irrespective of political ideology took on wider application in 1985 when Ethiopia, under the Marxist dictator Mengistu Haile Mariam, experienced widespread famine. Quoting the president's words, McPherson announced as administration policy that "a hungry child knows no politics."[18] While Danforth's Mozambique trip laid the foundation for what would become US policy worldwide, writing the policy large was the subject of fierce debate within the administration. Resistance from the State Department, the National Security Council, and the CIA was overcome only by invoking the expressed wishes of President Reagan himself. Conservative pundits, think tanks, and Republican regulars joined the fray.

"When the president got personally involved," recalled one senior official, "there was no moving him off it, even though the entire right wing in the District of Columbia was telling him otherwise." "We relentlessly pushed the President's interest," he recalls. "We always knew we'd have Reagan's backing on the humanitarian issues involved." One State Department official traveled to New York in 1984 without the knowledge of the US ambassador to the UN to promote the creation of a new UN Office of Emergency Assistance to Africa in response to the widening food crisis. At the height of the Cold War, the three largest African recipients of US aid were Marxist governments in Mozambique, Ethiopia, and Angola.

The Hungry Child policy outlived President Reagan to become a fixed point on the nation's moral compass. "The Hungry Child policy is now incorporated into the body politic of this country," explains McPherson. Although not codified as such in the Foreign Assistance Act, it is understood and respected, he says. "Six words from a president can go a long way. Most drafters of policy papers can only hope to be so lucky." Acknowledging that the approach is not what one would expect to be Cold War policy during a conservative administration, McPherson says that the notion has served as a brake against the recurring temptation to harness humanitarian programs to short-term political objectives.[19]

That said, some humanitarian organizations had serious problems with other Reagan administration policies. At a meeting with senior State Department officials in December 1986, for example, private aid groups challenged the designation by the United States of military supplies provided to the Contras seeking to unseat the Sandinista regime in Nicaragua as humanitarian. "Anyone who examines the historical record of communism must conclude that any aid directed at overthrowing communism is humanitarian aid," one conservative newspaper editorialized approvingly at the time.[20] Others countered that the loose use of the term *humanitarian* undermined the integrity of bona fide humanitarian action in Central America and beyond.

NGOs also expressed concern about the growing involvement of the Department of Defense (DOD) in the humanitarian sector. DOD had established an Office of Humanitarian Assistance and was expanding a program to provide excess material and transport to private aid agencies, including some agencies not registered with USAID. An increase in civic action and other aid activities carried out by military personnel was seen to sow confusion and put legitimate NGO programs and personnel in jeopardy. As noted later, the role of the military in the humanitarian sphere continued as a concern in the post–Cold War and, particularly, GWOT eras.

Discussions such as the one in December 1986 were relatively rare during the Cold War years. Only in exceptional circumstances and generally behind closed doors did NGOs challenge US policies. That dynamic would change somewhat during the post–Cold War years as NGOs became both more significant actors by virtue of the range and scale of their programs and also more active participants in public debates on US policy. The necessity of engaging in dialogue with governments to protect the integrity of humanitarian action had already been established during the Cold War.

US policy toward the admission of refugees to the United States also bore the marks of prevailing pervasive Cold War thinking. "Since 1945, well over 90 percent of those admitted to the United States have fled Communist countries," concluded one review. "Guided for a generation by the view that 'each refugee from the Soviet orbit represents a failure of the Communist system,' successive administrations have sought to induce more defections and have consistently sought to transform each new arrival into a symbolic or literal 'freedom fighter.'"[21] During the regime of Ronald Reagan, "a cold warrior of the old school, vague humanitarian pieties . . . have been subordinated to strident anti-Communism."[22] The figure of 90 percent includes refugee admissions well after the end of the Cold War. During the GWOT era, the number of refugees resettled was decimated by US security concerns.

Despite the avowedly dualistic worldview that characterized the Cold War years, humanitarian and political values were frequently not of a "zero sum" nature. Political benefits accrued to the United States as a result of its international aid work while, conversely, political negotiations in Washington, at the United Nations, and overseas contributed to expanded access for humanitarian actors. Similarly, while the Reagan Doctrine was the banner under which efforts at containing communism were pursued in countries such as Afghanistan, Angola, Cambodia, and Nicaragua, US-funded humanitarian work did not grind to a halt in those locations, although its neutrality may have been affected by the prevailing geo-political context.

Alternative Approaches: Sweden, Canada, and the Southern African Liberation Wars

Humanitarian action during the Cold War had different strands, only one of which was its dominant East-West preoccupation. Thus, although NGOs in the countries of major East-West protagonists faced major constraints as a result of high-profile political agendas, these constraints were not always universal. Other actors from other donor countries on occasion enjoyed more humanitarian space. Responding to human needs generated by the wars of liberation in Southern Africa offers a case in point.[23]

The start of those wars can be dated from the Sharpeville Massacre of March 1960, when sixty-nine demonstrators were shot down by South African police. Resistance to apartheid and what remained of colonial rule—Rhodesia, Southwest Africa, and the Portuguese colonies of Mozambique and Angola (and, farther north, Guinea-Bissau)—gradually escalated into a series of armed insurrections characterized by violent guerrilla warfare, brutal suppression, and, in the case of Southwest Africa (now Namibia), the direct and overt involvement of prominent Cold War protagonists: the United States, Britain, the Soviet Union, and Cuba. To complicate matters, the liberation movements all evidenced strong socialist overtones and attracted growing Soviet and Chinese support, with Western investors frequently the targets of their rhetoric and sometimes their military action.

Cold War climate notwithstanding, the governments of both Sweden and Canada supported humanitarian action channeled through their respective NGOs and carried out by the liberation movements. The roles of those two countries contrast with those of the major Western players—Britain and the United States—but in ways quite different from one another.

Historically, Canada likes to think of itself as a prime mover at key points in the South Africa story. Prime Minister John Diefenbaker was instrumental in having South Africa removed from the Commonwealth in 1961 because of apartheid. Canada opposed Britain's resumption of arms sales to South Africa in 1970, and by the late 1970s Canada was providing limited humanitarian assistance through NGOs to South African liberation movements. But the Canadian starting point in the region was based on strong ties forged through two world wars and the Commonwealth connection, and Canada's position was always nuanced by considerations that went beyond issues of independence and majority rule.

Diefenbaker saw the Commonwealth connection as an important buffer in Canadian relations with the United States, to which he had always been cool. His primary objective in the expulsion of South Africa was preservation of the Commonwealth, increasingly populated by independent African nations. And his attitude toward racism in South Africa had distinct Cold War overtones. "Communism," he said, "marches on the application of discrimination."[24] Ending discrimination would strengthen the Commonwealth and help thwart growing communist ambitions in Africa.

Although throughout the 1960s and 1970s Canada often spoke out against apartheid—in sharp contrast to the United States and Britain—it was slow to act on sanctions and trade embargoes and until the 1980s played an ambiguous role with regard to liberation movements and demands for majority rule in South Africa. According to analyst Linda Freeman, Canada's championship of independence and self rule was always limited and self-serving: "The Canadian state served less as a neutral or 'honest broker' and more as a broker for British interests. . . . Canadian diplomats were able to help the Commonwealth survive the crises that successive British governments precipitated in their accommodation of white interests in southern Africa."[25]

The Swedish story is very different. After World War II, Sweden took an aggressively neutral stance on Cold War issues, remaining aloof from international military alliances such as NATO and becoming a major thorn in the side regarding US intervention in Vietnam. Between 1953 and 1961, the period of greatest African decolonization, Dag Hammarskjöld, a Swede, served as UN secretary-general, and relations between Sweden and Africa grew dramatically. More than ten thousand Swedes served in the Congolese peacekeeping operation that began in 1960, and more than 10 percent of the UN's combat deaths in that operation were Swedish. With the Holocaust a living memory, colonialism and apartheid were, for most Swedes, seen as crimes against humanity.

Swedish trade with southern Africa was limited, and its investments tiny. Because there had been so many positive exchanges between Sweden and Africa during the 1950s and 1960s—organized by Swedish civil society, trade unions, universities, and political parties—support for humanitarian action through the liberation movements and for majority rule was seen not as a radical departure but as a logical evolution of relationships. ANC leader Oliver Tambo visited Sweden for the first time in 1961, years before his first visit to the Soviet Union, and almost twenty-five years before his first direct discussions with high-level British and American officials.

Many years later, in 1988, Tambo would describe the relationship that had developed with Sweden as "a natural system of relations . . . from people to people." It was not based on "the policies of any party that might be in power in Sweden at any particular time, but on . . . a common outlook and impulse."[26] In short, the prevailing Cold War paradigm notwithstanding, Sweden, like Canada, found ways of responding to urgent assistance and protection imperatives. Like Canada, Sweden provided sanctuary for American draft dodgers and deserters who did not want to serve in Vietnam, although Sweden went farther, providing direct humanitarian assistance to North Vietnam in response to American bombing.

Central America

Central America represents another region that evidenced a distinctive humanitarian "counterpoint." Kees Biekart has written at length about the long and painful transition to democracy and the distinct difference in roles played by American NGOs on the one hand and European and Canadian NGOs on the other.

Between the mid-1970s and the mid-1980s, civil wars and insurgencies were devastating Guatemala, Honduras, and Nicaragua, with vast displacements of people and the movement of large numbers of refugees into Mexico and Costa Rica. The Reagan administration made the rollback of revolution in the region a top priority, and the creation of a "political center" became a focus of attention. Biekart describes an American "top down" approach that channeled economic and military assistance to quasi-democratic regimes, supporting specific groups in civil society to counterbalance revolutionary movements. These included political parties and conservative labor unions— funded by USAID through the National Endowment for Democracy—as well as business associations, policy research centers, and the civil society sector, resulting in a boom in new development NGOs. While NGOs, peasant groups, and human rights organizations that were linked to the left, along with any left of center–left political parties, were excluded from US benefactions, they received funding from Canadian and European governments, often channeled through Canadian and European NGOs.

European development aid to the revolutionary Sandinista government started in 1979 and towards El Salvador, Europe took a position opposite to that of the United States:

The European Community gave humanitarian aid to Salvadorian refugees in Honduras, the French government legitimized the role of the FLMN, while the European Parliament condemned the un-democratic nature of the Salvadorian elections. . . . It was the flow of information [from European and Canadian NGOs] on human rights abuses, refugees and increasing poverty that had an impact on public opinion in their home countries. . . . The international attention boosted the Central American budgets of private aid agencies, especially when they were directly dependent on official funding, such as the German, Dutch, Swedish, Danish, Norwegian and later also the Spanish private aid agencies.[27]

As large US NGOs such as CARE and CRS pulled out of Nicaragua, they were replaced by German organizations (Brot für die Welt, Terre des Hommes), British organizations (Oxfam, Christian Aid), Dutch organizations (ICCO, CEBEMO, NOVIB), and others. This led, Biekart says, to intense polarization and profound antagonisms within the Central American NGO sector between USAID-supported NGOs loyal to right-wing governments and "popular" NGOs working with the political opposition and supported by European and Canadian groups. Clearly, the role of European and Canadian NGOs in this situation was very different from that of their American counterparts, although some US NGOs benefited from political intelligence derived from Canadian and European counterparts and some received funding from those governments as well. European NGOs also tended to be more focused on human rights and protection issues, whereas most US NGOs were preoccupied with assistance programs.

The United Nations and Political Cross-Currents

During the Cold War years the work of the United Nations and its agencies bore the marks of the dominant politicization of international relations. Discussions during the 1970s of the need for a "new international economic order," for example, pitted developing countries against the West, with East Bloc countries often siding with the countries of the South. At the World Food Conference in 1974, discussions of the "right to food" proved contentious. However, governments were able to agree on a resolution on food aid and trade committing donor and recipient governments alike to eschew the use of food as a political weapon. Similarly, at the 1978 International Conference on Primary Health Care at Alma Ata, participants from all 134 countries present agreed that "primary health care would be the key strategy that countries would use to achieve health for all of their people."[28]

Despite occasional breakthroughs across the East-West divide, the UN system was not sufficiently independent of its major donors to undertake urgent human needs–related initiatives or to make country allocations of resources that offset the disproportionality evident in many bilateral undertakings. With respect to Afghanistan, for example, the United Nations had difficulty maintaining programs in Kabul during the Soviet occupation. Serious disproportionality existed between the levels of assistance available for people in need under the Soviet-supported regime of Najibullah and those who had fled the country and were accessible to aid agencies in surrounding areas. The office of the United Nations High Commissioner for Refugees (UNHCR) reportedly registered as refugees from Afghanistan only those affiliated with Afghan resistance parties.[29]

The Post–Cold War Era

The Cold War was succeeded by the post–Cold War and GWOT eras, each with its own particular humanitarian/political dynamic. The political framework that characterized the post–Cold War era (1990–2001) had two major new features, each affecting the context and nature of humanitarian action.

First, with the fall of the Berlin Wall and the breakup of the Soviet Union, international humanitarian actors gained access to regions that had formerly been off limits. These included the newly independent states of the former Soviet Union, many of them with large Muslim populations. Second, the relaxation of bonds of authority that had provided order and stability for generations—for example, across the diverse republics of the former Yugoslavia—made the newly accessible areas fraught with danger for humanitarian organizations unschooled in local cultures and mores. The task of assisting people in refugee camps outside of their own countries gave way to the more formidable challenge of assisting people within their own national borders. As humanitarians ventured into *terra incognita*, the generally sacrosanct status that had protected humanitarian actors and activities during the Cold War gave way to increased institutional and personal vulnerability.

These geo-political changes were reinforced by changes in the concept of national sovereignty. Regularly invoked by host governments during the Cold War to fend off international humanitarian action in "internal affairs," sovereignty became infused with more widely accepted humanitarian obligations. Regimes that failed to deliver might face pressure from outside governments.[30] In September 2005, the UN General Assembly affirmed that "each individual State has the responsibility to protect its populations from genocide, war crimes, ethnic cleansing and crimes against humanity." Those failing to exercise their "responsibility to protect" opened themselves up to collective action.[31]

These newer elements are illustrated in the experience of Fred C. Cuny, a high-profile Texas-based aid analyst and practitioner. In a 1992 article that would prove clairvoyant, Cuny wrote:

The international relief system is facing a major increase in the numbers of areas in need, governmental entities, and people in the relief caseload [many of whom are Muslim]. Before 1991 emergencies in the Soviet Union were, with a few exceptions, the exclusive domain of the Russians; now more than half of the newly emerging states are likely to be seeking international relief within five years. Many of the new states are unstable and beset with the same problems that faced African and Asian countries when they emerged three decades ago from years of colonial domination.[32]

Cuny, a front-line aid practitioner of uncommon resourcefulness and courage, was killed on a 1995 mission to Chechnya, his death reflecting the emerging realities he described.

Looking back on the Cold War years, the Elders warned against assuming that global humanitarian action would necessarily benefit from a more diverse world. They noted that the Clinton administration—avowedly more disposed to problem solving through international institutions—did not present the anticipated golden age for needs-based humanitarian action. To cite but a single example, the Clinton administration used food assistance as a lever to ensure North Korean participation in the four-party talks among the two Koreas, China, and the United States on nuclear nonproliferation.

The existence of widespread famine in North Korea in 1995–96 was known to US, UN, and NGO officials, despite the secretive nature of the Pyongyang regime. At NGO conferences in December 1996 and January 1997, State Department officials confirmed the Clinton administration's carrot-and-stick strategy: "If the North Koreans were cooperative in the negotiations, then the United States would be cooperative with food aid. If they were not, the United States would not be either."[33] The linkage was unapologetic; food-aid shipments in modest amounts were made by the United States to North Korea shortly before each session in the four-party talks.

In 1997, NGOs mounted an effort to generate pressure on the administration to cease the use of food as a political weapon against North Korea and to respond at a scale commensurate with the need. Andrew Natsios, a senior World Vision official who had directed USAID's Office of Foreign Disaster Assistance in the George H. W. Bush administration, observed that "successive presidents had insulated humanitarian food aid from the geopolitical strategic interest of the United States, so that the humanitarian imperative could operate relatively unimpeded." The administration's approach regarding North Korea, he argued, was not only unethical but also unlikely to succeed. "Punishing the common people in a totalitarian regime as a means of forcing their government to change its behavior has seldom been successful."[34] The administration eventually increased its levels of food assistance, though arguably for political rather than humanitarian reasons.

During the post–Cold War period the connection between assistance programs and US national security interests seemed less direct and dispositive. "With the end of the Cold War, the United States no longer has any substantial geopolitical interests that require military or political intervention in Africa," wrote analyst Michael Clough.

> The outcome of the many ongoing struggles for political supremacy in Africa will not threaten the security or welfare of the United States. I may prefer Nelson Mandela to Chief Buthelezi in South Africa, or Amos Sawyer to Charles Taylor in Liberia, or John Garang to Mohamed Beshir in Sudan, or Joaquim Chissano to Aflonso Dhlakama in Mozambique, but I strongly doubt that US national interests will be much affected over the long run by which, if any, of these leaders eventually triumph.[35]

Linkages between humanitarian action and other policies and programs also became more apparent during the post–Cold War years. The international focus shifted from states as members of East, West, or nonaligned blocs to states as political entities confronting a range of domestic challenges, including economic development, human rights, good governance, and improved accountability. The "interface" issues loomed particularly large. During the post–Cold War era the challenge of working with regimes in places like Haiti, Rwanda, East Timor, and Bosnia came to be seen as a far more complex task requiring a far wider array of policy instruments. In many settings bilateral and multilateral military and peacekeeping forces played hitherto unaccustomed roles.[36]

In engaging countries such as Cambodia, Liberia, Somalia, El Salvador, Georgia, Rwanda, and the former Yugoslavia that were experiencing or recovering from crises, the UN system and its member governments struggled with how missions, objectives, and personnel in specific countries could best be "integrated."[37] As noted earlier, the presence of international organizations and personnel within countries experiencing crises, rather than simply on their borders, added new elements of complexity as well as new creative possibilities. Figure 1–1 identifies some of the prototypical tensions at the interface between humanitarian action, political agendas, and human rights and justice.

Assistance and protection agencies wrestled with their own relationships to this wider array of policies and actors, many of them highly political in nature. Thorny issues of coherence or integration have been more effectively addressed in some settings than others. In general terms, however, "rather than giving politics and diplomacy a humanitarian dimension," comments long-time aid worker Joel Charny, "'integration' has resulted in the politicization of humanitarian action."[38] Given the tendency to define *humanitarian* in overly broad terms, several Elders urge retention of a narrow focus in the interest of minimizing such politicization.

The experience in Angola is instructive. "The lack of international aid until the early 1990s," concluded one review, "is not explained by a dearth of needs, but rather by the aid community's focus on other emergencies, by the reticent position of the government of Angola with regard to aid, and by the Cold War conditions that determined Angola's international relations." Similarly, the upsurge in aid agency involvement after 1992 reflected not an increase in the scale of need but rather the fact that "many agencies had established themselves in the country during the post–Cold War mini peace." Yet by 2005, agency involvement had decreased, again without reference to the continuing incidence of human need.[39]

In sum, management of humanitarian affairs during the post–Cold War period lacked the clarity afforded by the conceptual model of a world divided neatly into spheres: communist and democratic. Policymakers and aid practitioners were hard pressed to design programs more reflective of global human need rather than of political calculations. The peace dividend anticipated as a result of the easing of Cold War tensions was conspicuous by its failure to materialize.

The Global War on Terror

The political framework accompanying the GWOT has similarities to both the Cold War and the post–Cold War eras. Like the Cold War, the GWOT framework, articulated by President George W. Bush, divided the world into those "for us" and "against us." Responding to the 9/11 attacks by al Qaeda on the United States, the president "put into motion a simple and direct policy: Terrorists were to be pursued relentlessly and given no safe haven; those who harbored or tolerated terrorists were also the enemy."[40] The principal legal vehicles were Executive Order 13224 (September 23, 2001) and the USA Patriot Act (enacted in October 2001 and reauthorized in 2005). Organizations were forbidden to provide services, personnel, training, and expert advice and assistance to enumerated terrorist organizations and individuals.[41] "Given the Patriot Act's expanded reach and stiff penalties, nonprofits and grant makers should be on notice," warned one analysis. "The prohibitions specifically include certain acts that may otherwise be regarded as humanitarian efforts."[42]

Efforts by a coalition of more than seventy groups to negotiate an easing of the Treasury Department's anti-terrorist financing guidelines, which the agencies found unworkable and unnecessary, broke down. The government proved unwilling, the groups said in opting out of further discussion, "to recognize the important role of global philanthropy in increasing national security through funding to address poverty, inequality, disease, and other pressing needs."[43]

An earlier study by the Feinstein Center examined GWOT impacts on the work of humanitarian organizations in thirteen crisis countries including Afghanistan, Iraq, Colombia, Liberia, Northern Uganda, and Sudan. The review concluded that to one degree or another in each of these settings

> terrorism and efforts to counteract it had specific, discernible, recur-
> ring—and largely negative—impacts on the humanitarian enterprise.
> These include increased unwillingness on the part of belligerents to
> allow organizations to carry out their assistance and protection man-
> dates, stepped up efforts at manipulation and control of aid institutions
> and personnel, and reduced space for advocacy.[44]

The case studies in the present volume provide additional data and analysis.

The temptation to attach political conditions to US humanitarian assistance, a fact of life throughout the history of US foreign aid, has proved
if anything more seductive during the GWOT. One of the proposals considered early in the Obama administration was to prohibit assistance to
anyone in Gaza who had voted for Hamas. In response, NGOs mobilized to
familiarize officials with the Hungry Child policy, which would be violated
by such a restriction. In April 2011, the chair of the House Foreign Affairs
Committee threatened to cut off economic assistance to the Palestinian
Authority in response to its rapprochement with Hamas in Gaza. Hamas,
which had refused to recognize the right of Israel to exist, was one of the
regimes on the US list of terrorist entities with whom US aid agencies are
forbidden to interact.

The GWOT period also witnessed an increased role played by DOD
resources and personnel in the humanitarian sphere. "Since 9/11, an increasing proportion of US foreign aid has been channeled through the US
military," notes one recent study. "In Africa, over 20% of US assistance is
reportedly controlled by the military."[45] In the two principal theaters of the

GWOT, Afghanistan and Iraq, many observers noted a loss of space for neutral and impartial humanitarian action.

Planning for the war in Afghanistan also subsumed humanitarian assistance under US political and military objectives. Douglas Feith, a senior DOD official in the George W. Bush administration, recalls:

> Humanitarian assistance had been a component of the planning from the start, emphasized by President Bush and [Defense Secretary Donald] Rumsfeld. . . . I suggested that we should take care that our humanitarian aid wasn't distributed at cross-purposes with our strategy. We wanted to reward initiative and encourage southerners to fight on our side, but we didn't want our aid appearing to reward unhelpful action, which could happen if we put provisions in the hands of leaders working for the Taliban.[46]

US-based humanitarian organizations carried on an intensive dialogue with military actors on their role in the humanitarian sector during the GWOT years. From the perspective of the NGO professional association InterAction, relationships with international military forces had been generally positive in northern Iraq during Operation Provide Comfort following the Gulf War. The collaboration became less productive following 9/11, first in Afghanistan and then in Iraq, where, in the words of one of the Elders, "The lines between military and NGO activities were transgressed by military units which, with their members disguised as civilians but carrying weapons, looked for opportunity to engage in humanitarian activities."[47]

After two years of negotiations, NGOs and the US military reached agreement in mid-2007 on guidelines to "mitigate frictions between military and humanitarian personnel over the preservation of humanitarian space in places like Afghanistan and Iraq."[48] In both theaters NGOs found themselves investing increasing time in dialogue with US, NATO, and UN military forces on humanitarian issues, even producing a DVD to assist in the challenge. NGO activities included

> lecturing on humanitarian values and principles at military academies and schools, participation in seminars, role-playing humanitarian workers in command post exercises, and on a few occasions actually participating in field exercises. We also help write and edit military policy documents related to peacekeeping and disaster response.[49]

Humanitarian agencies waged numerous battles to protect their ability to function as independent humanitarian actors. Early in the conflicts the invitation to have representatives of UN organizations, the ICRC, and NGOs co-located with the US Central Command in Tampa drew mixed responses. At an operational level, US NGOs resisted DOD's requirement that US NGO personnel not talk to the media in the absence of military officials. The question of collaborating in Afghanistan with the Provincial Reconstruction Teams (PRTs), which contained military and intelligence personnel as well as humanitarian and development staff, proved vexing, recalling earlier tensions with the US government in Vietnam. Although many US NGOs initially resisted collaboration, some acquiesced over time. Meanwhile, reflecting the counterpoint observed during the Cold War, European NGOs for the most part kept their distance.

While some US humanitarian actors have labored to safeguard their independence from US policy, others welcome a close convergence with US foreign policy objectives. The late John C. Whitehead, deputy secretary of state in the second Reagan administration and long-time board member of the International Rescue Committee (IRC), explains that the IRC by charter and tradition "concerns itself with refugees fleeing from countries where their rights are being constrained." This emphasis, he says, distinguishes it from other NGOs engaged in humanitarian relief and in resettlement work not specifically linked to "the cause of freedom."[50] Founded in 1933 and playing a high-profile role during World War II and the Cold War, its focus has broadened beyond refugees to include "other victims of oppression and violent conflict around the world."

The United States has often been in the forefront of international aid efforts. Its identification with food assistance, the Marshall Plan, and the Peace Corps are widely known and supported by the American public. That said, US aid allocations have often lacked the desired element of proportionality. Already a reality in the Cold War and post–Cold War periods, the problem may be even more acute in the GWOT era. "The financial commitments of the United States and its allies in the war on terrorism" comments Joel Charny, then with Refugees International, "make a mockery of the principle of proportionality because they intend to bear any burden to defeat the enemy in a global struggle that may last for decades."[51] Disproportionately generous funding to high-profile countries contrasts with smaller amounts for nations with equally if not more serious assistance and protection needs.[52]

At this writing in late 2011, it is too early to determine what particular imprint the Obama administration will put on issues of humanitarian action as it relates to US national security objectives. The Obama approach has initially evidenced greater continuity than change regarding the predecessor administration. It remains to be seen whether, "when the story of

America's post–9/11 wars is written, historians will be obliged to assess the two administrations together, and pass judgment on the Bush-Obama era."[53]

Concluding Reflections

Several conclusions emerge from the experience recounted. First, the Cold War, post–Cold War, and GWOT eras demonstrate that political frameworks make up the unavoidable context within which humanitarian actors function and programs of assistance and protection take place. The three eras evidence a growing complexity of contexts, actors, and interactions over time. Whereas states were the prime movers during the Cold War, the humanitarian landscape in subsequent years has become increasingly populated with state and non-state actors, including military forces, counter-insurgency operatives, private contractors, diasporas, and the social media.[54] Faced with positioning themselves in relation to this far larger galaxy, humanitarian organizations find the task of "stakeholder mapping" at once more essential and more complex.

Second, while the three frameworks have differential impacts on the ability of humanitarians to function, some frameworks are more conducive to effective humanitarian action than others. However, "conservative" administrations should not be assumed to provide more constricted humanitarian space than "liberal" ones. The Reagan Doctrine, aimed at rolling back the advance of communism, did not result in the denial of emergency assistance to Ethiopia, where the policies of Soviet protégé Mengistu were creating famine and fear. Nor was the doctrine applied to Mozambique in support of "freedom fighters" seeking to displace a left-leaning regime. Conversely, liberal internationalists are not necessarily superior stewards of the humanitarian imperative. Clinton administration officials on occasion showed themselves to be just as punitive and small-minded as their more conservative counterparts.

Third, efforts to minimize instrumentalization and/or to harness political interest to advance humanitarian goals are aided by institutional memory. The protection of humanitarian action from political penetration requires constant vigilance. The specificities of individual situations call for a diverse playbook. The conversations with the Elders underscore benefits that accrue when aid officials and sympathetic government policymakers are familiar with what has and not worked in the past. The fact that during the Cold War US aid agencies were warned against treason in assisting people in North Vietnam and that during the GWOT period they have been kept on a short leash under the USA Patriot Act underscores the reality that the rationale for humanitarian work cannot be nested comfortably within political frameworks.

The word *humanitarian* itself is prone to recurring abuse. The US decision in 2010 to allow "humanitarian" items such as chewing gum, popcorn, food colorings, and cake sprinkles to be shipped to Cuba recalled a more egregious politicization of humanitarian action in the 1980s, when the Reagan administration authorized the shipment of boots and radios to the Nicaraguan Contras under the "humanitarian" pass-through provision of the then-existing law.[55] Spanning a quarter of a century, the two incidents underscore the perennial seductiveness of instrumentalizing humanitarian action and the need for political acumen and institutional memory. "The older I get," muses one of the Elders, "the more sharp are my recollections of events that never took place."

In sum, the major take-away from our three-era review is that the prevailing political frameworks need not irretrievably or permanently trim the expression of core humanitarian impulses. The humanitarian enterprise still has lessons to learn and protective changes of policy and institutional configuration to embrace. The vitality and viability of the humanitarian enterprise in the post-GWOT years may indeed hinge in large measure on its understanding and selective appropriation—to date, unevenly savored and applied—of its own experience in the Cold War, post–Cold War, and GWOT eras.

Persons interviewed for this chapter and the organizations with which they have been associated.

James Bishop, US Foreign Service, InterAction
Landrum Bolling, Mercy Corps International
Joel Charny, Oxfam-US, Refugees International, InterAction
Chester Crocker, Africa Bureau, US State Department
John C. Danforth, former US senator from Missouri
Eugene Dewey, Refugee Bureau, US State Department
Hunter Farnam, USAID
Elizabeth G. Ferris, The Brookings Institution
Princeton Lyman, USAID
James MacCracken, Church World Service
Flora MacDonald, former Canadian foreign minister
M. Peter McPherson, administrator, USAID
Andrew Natsios, director, AID Office of Foreign Disaster Assistance, WorldVision
Jonathan Moore, US coordinator of Refugee Affairs, US Department of State
Cornelio Sommaruga, former president, International Committee of the Red Cross
Brian Walker, Oxfam-UK
John C. Whitehead, deputy US secretary of state

Part Two

NEVER-ENDING CRISES: TAKING A LONG VIEW

Chapter 4

Afghanistan

Back to the Future

ANTONIO DONINI

This chapter looks at the tension between principles and politics in the response to the Afghan crisis and, more specifically, at the extent to which humanitarian action has been instrumentalized, and by whom, along the arc of a thirty-year conflict. After a brief historical introduction, it focuses first on a few emblematic examples of manipulation of aid. It then examines tensions around the issue of *coherence*—the code word for the integration of humanitarian action into wider political designs of donors, the United Nations, and of the UN-mandated military coalition that has been operating in Afghanistan since late 2001. The chapter ends with some conclusions on the humanitarian-political relationship and what the experience of instrumentalization in Afghanistan tells us for the future of humanitarian action.

The international community's response to the Afghan crisis spans a thirty-year period that saw the end of the Cold War; the ensuing disorder and reshuffling of political, military, and economic agendas in Central and South Asia; and the putative emergence—and now the likely decline—of a hegemonic order built around globalization and securitization. Thirty years of failed interventions, civil war, and aborted nation-building attempts have resulted in unprecedented levels of human suffering and volatility in Afghanistan with significant implications for the region and beyond. The high hopes of peace and stability raised by the US-led intervention after the 9/11 attacks in the United States have given way to widespread despondency, disillusionment, and the evaporation of the mirage of a *pax americana*.

Humanitarian action has been a constant in Afghanistan's troubled recent history—and so has its instrumentalization. Humanitarian action has of course been affected by the structural changes in the nature of the conflict and by the wider developments in the international community's approaches to conflict and crisis. Relief efforts have waxed and waned, depending on the vagaries of the local and international political contexts. There have been periods of extreme politicization and manipulation and times where humanitarian principles were relatively easier to uphold. The political and military vicissitudes that shaped the crisis in turn gave rise to massive humanitarian needs. As in other crises, the manner in which the international community understood and responded to these assistance and protection needs, as well as the fluctuations of the response over time, was heavily influenced by political agendas that were often anything but humanitarian. From the start, as in most complex emergencies, the space for humanitarian action was determined by politics. This intrusion of the political has ranged from the relatively benign to the overt manipulation of humanitarian action for partisan purposes. This intrusion has come from external political and military actors, successive Afghan governments and warlords, the media, and aid agencies themselves.

As we shall see, there are two important lessons. They are quite obvious and commonsensical but all too often disregarded. The first is that there is a negative correlation between direct superpower involvement and the ability of the humanitarian enterprise to engage with crises in a relatively principled manner. In Afghanistan, the "highs" in politics (Cold War and post–9/11 interventions) corresponded to "lows" in principles. Conversely, superpower dis-attention to the Afghan crisis, as in the 1992–98 period of factional fighting, allowed more space—but much less financial support—for principled approaches and for significant innovations in how the United Nations and other relief actors could do business in a crisis country. The corollary to this law is that when great power interest is high, the political players in the donor and UN bureaucracies take over policy and decision making, including on humanitarian and human rights issues, undermining principles and displacing humanitarian actors who often have a better understanding of realities on the ground.

The second lesson is that the instrumentalization of humanitarian assistance for political gain, in addition to constituting in itself a violation of humanitarian principles, rarely works. Subordination to the "higher" imperatives of *realpolitik* may allow short-term gains, but in the long run the chickens come home to roost. And in Afghanistan, blow-back from the politics and the manipulations of humanitarian assistance of the 1980s continues to this day.

It is useful, for analytical purposes, to separate the humanitarian response to the Afghan crisis into four distinct phases:

1. *From the Soviet invasion to the fall of Najibullah (1979–92)—or the Cold War period and its immediate aftermath.* In humanitarian terms there were two distinct phases to this period: the NGO cross-border solidarity phase during which UN humanitarian agencies operated, by necessity, only in neighboring countries; and the arrival of the UN agencies on the scene, which was accompanied by the first attempt to set up a robust UN humanitarian coordination mechanism while simultaneous UN attempts to broker peace followed a formulaic Cold War script.

2. *The civil war and the triumph of warlordism (1992–96).* The volatility of the situation in Afghanistan, which included the devastation and complete breakdown of institutions, hampered the provision of assistance and provoked great soul searching in the assistance community—What are we doing here? Are we fueling the war?—as well as growing disillusionment in a UN peace process that was increasingly reduced to "talks about talks."

3. *The Taliban period (1996–mid-November 2001).* The rise of the Taliban regime triggered a resurgence of interest in humanitarian principles and was coupled with a second attempt at robust coordination among, at least in theory, the assistance, human rights, and political dimensions of the international response. The Taliban restrictions on aid agencies and attempts to manipulate aid to their advantage were paralleled by the limited funding and huge constraints placed on humanitarian action by influential donors.

4. *Post–9/11:* From "nation-building lite"[1] to back to the future. The heavy engagement of the international community in Afghanistan since 2001 has, again, been characterized by politics trumping principles in a vain quest for a durable peace. This period comprises an ascending phase, where post-conflict rhetoric ruled and the need for humanitarian action was dismissed, and a descending (into chaos?) phase, resembling in many ways the end of the Soviet occupation, where principles again are struggling to regain some currency.

Each of these periods corresponds to a shift: from weak unitary state to fragmenting state; from fragmenting to failing state; from failing to rogue state; and from rogue to a corrupt and fissured "protégé" state.[2]

Humanitarian action in Afghanistan has always been subject to varying degrees of instrumentalization. In fact, it is safe to say that all parties to the conflict and all the players involved have used the humanitarian enterprise as a tool to achieve non-humanitarian objectives. As such, Afghanistan constitutes a laboratory of the humanitarian/political relationship that straddles the Cold War and post–Cold War eras from which much can be learned. The agents and types of instrumentalization have included:

- ***belligerent states***, the Soviet Union and its allies who denied access or interdicted militarily the work of humanitarian agencies (ICRC) or agencies claiming to be humanitarian (a variety of more or less politicized NGOs) during phase 1; the US and other coalition forces that attempted to incorporate humanitarian players in their political/military strategies in phase 4.
- ***external formally non-belligerent states*** such as the Western and Arab states that supported the Afghan "freedom fighters" and provided funds and other support to solidarity groups and NGOs working inside Afghanistan during phase 1.
- ***regional powers,*** Pakistan and Iran in the first instance (but also India and to a lesser extent Central Asian states) typically by facilitating, denying, or manipulating access to particular areas or groups. The Pakistani Inter-Services Intelligence (ISI) has been the essential gatekeeper and manipulator par excellence.
- ***the successive host governments*** who have variously provided or denied access based on political considerations (for example, the Taliban attempts to use the acceptance of foreign aid agencies as a way to promote international legitimacy and the denial of acceptance when legitimacy was not forthcoming).
- ***Afghan non-state actors/warlords/druglords*** that employed a vast panoply of methods to take advantage politically and economically of humanitarian aid ranging from denial of access, or in some cases egress (that is, holding NGOs more or less captive), various types of conditionality ("if you want to work there, you also have to work here"), thievery, and abuse.
- ***donors*** who have exerted pressures on NGOs and the United Nations to work or not to work in certain areas by providing or withholding funds, disregarding proportionality of need and politicizing the aid environment.
- ***international organizations***, in particular the United Nations, which after 9/11 abandoned any pretense of equidistance and actively promoted the subordination of humanitarian assistance to the political/military agenda of the US-led coalition through the integrated mission modality that has limited the independence and agency of humanitarian players.

- *NGOs and solidarity groups* that have accepted at times to be the willing tools of political designs during the phase 1 cross-border operations but also in phase 4. On occasion, agencies have also distorted or exaggerated needs for purposes of institutional survival.
- *human rights, advocacy groups, and the media* who, particularly in Taliban times, often resorted to one-sided or black-and-white statements and policies that made humanitarian work on the ground more difficult.
- *affected communities themselves,* who naturally took advantage of sloppy programming and naive agency operators.

The "Cross-Border" Years

During the mid- to late 1980s, humanitarian assistance was used by the United States and its allies as a tool serving political and military objectives to give the Soviet Union "its Vietnam." The context was the Cold War, and overt manipulation was *de rigueur*. This was a very messy environment in which an array of NGOs sponsored largely by the United States and other Western governments provided so-called humanitarian assistance to mujahideen commanders.[3] The stage for the politicization and manipulation was set in the refugee camps that dotted the Northwest Frontier Province and Balochistan border areas, where the UNHCR and the UN World Food Programme (WFP) and their NGO implementing partners provided assistance to more than three million Afghan refugees under extraordinarily constrained conditions dictated by the Pakistani authorities. In order to receive assistance, refugees had to be affiliated with one of the resistance political parties. UNHCR failed in its attempt to enumerate refugees and ensure that individual families received the assistance directly. It had to accept that assistance be provided through more or less legitimate tribal leaders, or "ration maleks," who controlled the food distributions and siphoned off a portion both to feed mujahideen combatants sheltering in the camps and to increase their power to distribute favors.[4] Beneficiary lists were inflated: ration maleks could control several hundred ration books.[5] Working in tandem with the Pakistani camp managers, the maleks and their political patrons developed an effective system for creaming off international assistance. Given the Cold War context and the presence of Soviet troops in Afghanistan, donors, NGOs, and even the United Nations were not too concerned with the diversion of aid.

A cottage industry of international NGOs financed by a maze of grants from bilateral Western donors and UN agencies grew around the refugee camps.[6] Many NGOs started with refugee programs and then extended cross-border. Others were created for the purpose of providing assistance inside Afghanistan and mostly operated under a veil of secrecy. The inept often combined with the unscrupulous: cash was taken across the border and liberally handed out; compromises with unsavory commanders were made from which it became very difficult to disentangle. Not all NGOs were incompetent or indifferent to principles and the importance of needs-based programming. Some did good technical work, particularly medical NGOs. But by and large, they had taken sides in support of the mujahideen cause.[7] While there was some concern for impartiality, solidarity and saving lives trumped neutrality. In the NGO community in Peshawar and Quetta, the rear bases of the "cross-border" effort, *neutrality* was a dirty word. Access to the border was controlled by the ISI, which had gained ample experience in manipulating UN and NGO assistance to refugees in Pakistan. It was difficult if not impossible to work with groups that were not "blessed" by the ISI. This meant that Pashtun commanders and the political parties that represented them received the lion's share of NGO assistance—to the detriment of Tajik or Hazara groups that were inimical to the ISI's command and control objectives.

The encounter between well-meaning but amateurish outsiders and local communities in tribal Afghanistan was not always easy. Different logics and universes of obligation were at play: NGOs arrived with Western mental models of access to services and social change that clashed with the patronage inherent in tribal structures, where the *khan* privileged the well-being of his own people rather than the needs of the wider community, and the commander drew his legitimacy from the resources, including relief, that he could attract—or pilfer. Naive outsiders with grand ideas of territorial coverage for health clinics or vaccination programs had to contend with power relations and allegiances based on a leopard-skin patchwork of tribal or political networks. Providing services for all tribes in a particular valley was not necessarily acceptable to all local commanders as they vied for the presence of an NGO base in order to attract resources and increase legitimacy. The relief provided could easily become a stake in competition with neighboring commanders, and to a lesser extent among NGOs. In the Pashtun tribal patchwork of eastern Afghanistan, where, because of ease of access, most of the cross-border assistance was concentrated, instances of commanders stealing one another's relief supplies, much as they did with weapons, were common. NGO staff were frequently taken hostage or forced to work in particular areas, regardless of actual need.

Matters were complicated by the fact that commanders sent their representatives to Peshawar and Quetta to proposition NGOs, and later UN agencies, with assurances of the agreement of the local shura (council) and guarantees of security if they opened up shop in their area. It was often difficult for inexperienced outsiders to judge the veracity of such claims, which if readily accepted could lead to unsavory consequences. In one such instance, upon the invitation of the Paktika Shura, the United Nations agreed to establish a base in Urgun to initiate mine action and other humanitarian programs. All seemed fine until, after a few weeks on the ground, the UN team was stopped at a checkpoint and forced to have an extended tea-drinking session with an angry commander who was incensed that the United Nations had set up a base "with those miscreants up in Urgun." *He* was the leader of the *real* Paktika Shura, and the United Nations should be dealing with him, or so he claimed. The United Nations learned the hard way that overlapping shuras were the norm in many areas. This incident, fortunately without consequence, illustrates the lack of understanding of local culture that many outsiders displayed, a fact compounded by the rapid turnover of aid workers and the absence of collective memory.

In some cases the outcome was more serious. Attracting an aid presence was often a vector for commander expansionism. In Wardak province, for example, in the mid-1980s, a senior commander—Amin Wardak—utilized the presence of an NGO vaccination program to intrude into the political space of a commander from another armed group. The NGO vaccinators were accompanied by Wardak's armed guards as they entered areas controlled by a rival commander. This led to a number of violent incidents, and the program had to be aborted.[8] A similar incident, which resulted in the assassination of an MSF medical worker, occurred in Badakhshan province in 1990.

NGOs were caught in a double instrumentalization trap. They were subjected to the manipulation of the commanders they worked with, and of their Pakistani ISI minders, but they also promoted instrumentalization by their own political alignments. NGOs were jockeying for position to get into the "good areas" under the "good commanders" who might be more effective as implementing partners or have access to a good public-relations network extending beyond Peshawar to Paris, London, or New York. The actual result was often questionable. NGOs, even the most reputable ones, were heavily infiltrated by resistance party agents (and by the ISI). Most agencies concealed this, although it was understood by all that certain NGOs were in hock to specific political parties. The fundamentalist Hezbi-Islami and the more moderate Jamiat party were particularly adept at placing their men in NGOs, and later, the United Nations. Thus, cross-border assistance projects and the offices of the NGOs in Pakistan suffered at a minimum from political pressures and often from what can best be described as Mafia terror tactics. Such pressures led to frequent "tribal" squabbles among NGOs. As one commander put it, mirroring what the NGOs said about the resistance parties: "It's so hard for the mujahideen to deal with the NGOs, because there are so many different ones. They are so fragmented, and they are always fighting among themselves."[9]

With the benefit of hindsight, even some of the most reputable NGOs now recognize that their activities were partisan. MSF, for example, rationalizes this a posteriori as an "anti-totalitarian" stance.[10] Other NGOs—and key donors such as the United States—had a clear "anti-communist" position that in some cases went as far as embracing the Islamist mirror image of the communists represented by Gulbuddin Hekmatyar's Hezbi Islami, which was "totalitarian" in its own right. These nuances aside, the consequence of the politicization of the cross-border effort was that ideology trumped accountability. Donors were not particularly concerned with cost effectiveness since one of the major objectives of their support was to assuage public opinion back home and embarrass the Soviets. Certain countries, the United States in particular, prohibited their citizens from traveling inside the country, and some donors discouraged cross-border missions. These were difficult to organize and sometimes dangerous, given the risks of land mines, internecine mujahideen conflicts, and Soviet or Afghan army offensives.

As a result, project activities were seldom monitored, and when they were, it was often by Afghan staff who could not go on record as being critical of local commanders. Delivery was affected by conflicts among groups and by widespread corruption both in Afghanistan and Pakistan. Food aid, medical supplies, and agricultural equipment often were looted or hijacked for ransom. One observer estimated that "less than half of the overall assistance designated for Afghanistan is believed to have gotten through to the intended recipients."[11] While this figure is impossible to verify, it is true that the complicated web of complicity that united resistance party leaders, the ISI, Pakistani border guards, *bona fide* mujahideen, and nondescript bearded bandits resulted in siphoning off large quantities of commodities, especially food aid, which was easier to "monetize." This writer can attest that spot checks in Kandahar province in the summer of 1989 showed that several education projects financed by a major Western donor existed only on paper.

When the UN humanitarian agencies, which had been confined to assisting refugees outside the country, appeared on the Afghan scene after the 1988 Geneva Accords that resulted in the eventual withdrawal of Soviet troops, they tried, with difficulty, to introduce a more principled approach and reduce the one-sidedness of the assistance effort. The special UN coordinator, Sadruddin Aga Khan, negotiated a "humanitarian consensus" with all parties to the conflict, including all the neighboring countries. The consensus implied that assistance should be provided on the basis of need and not politics or geography. In order to appear more equidistant and reduce the stranglehold of Pakistan-based NGOs (and their ISI minders) on the assistance market, the United Nations opened offices in and set up assistance activities from Iran and the then Soviet Union as well as in Kabul and other Afghan cities.[12] It thus was able to operate cross-line from government-held cities to territory controlled by the mujahideen in addition to cross-border. NGOs remained essentially Peshawar-based and Quetta-based, and considered the very thought of opening offices in Kabul anathema. For them, there was a "good UN" based in Pakistan and a "bad UN" in Kabul. Accusations of partiality flew both ways. Donors had no qualms about imposing their political agenda on the NGOs they funded and attempted to do so with the United Nations.[13]

Feeding chickens . . . that come home to roost

A personal recollection of strong-arm tactics

In the fall of 1989, forces led by Jallaludin Haqqani had laid siege to the city of Khost in eastern Afghanistan. The US embassy in Islamabad requested UNOCA (the then UN office for the coordination of humanitarian assistance to Afghanistan) to pre-position food outside the city so that the civilian population could be "drawn out" and the mujahideen could step up their offensive. According to the ambassador, internally displaced persons (IDPs) were fleeing toward the border with Pakistan and required assistance. The United Nations was reluctant but agreed to do an assessment. With a WFP colleague (and an ISI escort) we drove to the border where we were met by Haqqani and his mujahideen and then to his base in the hills above Khost, from which he was rocketing the town. We asked to interview some IDP families, but there were none at hand. We interviewed some kuchis (nomads) who were smuggling timber into Pakistan, and they had seen none. Haqqani showed us the caves where he was planning to store the food and produced freshly thumb-printed lists of prospective beneficiaries. On that occasion we declined to help, but subsequently the United Nations agreed to send a few truckloads of wheat to the Haqqani base. As a senior UN colleague explained, "This is a ticket we have to pay to keep the United States and the ISI happy. If we don't, they will block our cross-border access to Afghanistan." Twenty years later, Haqqani is still around and allegedly still benefiting from ISI largesse; with his sons he runs the Haqqani Network, which is known for its ruthlessness and is responsible for much of the insurgent activity in eastern Afghanistan and in and around Kabul.

Principles and Pragmatism: Civil War and the Taliban

When the Najibullah regime collapsed in April 1992, Afghanistan dropped off the international radar screen. There were no longer any ideological stakes for which to fight. Afghanistan became an orphan of the Cold War, and the political patrons of the cross-border NGO cottage industry suddenly lost interest. Commanders lost their aura and became "warlords." Donors became more wary of how their funds were being spent. Also, some of the more shady characters at the margins of the NGO world, such as those who had mixed assistance and intelligence gathering, left the Afghan circuit. Paradoxically, it became easier for the United Nations and humanitarian NGOs to advocate for a more principled approach. Mainstream INGOs with proven track records, which had eschewed the Afghan crisis during the cross-border period, were now on the scene. As mentioned previously, Afghanistan confirms the rule that when major political players are not present, humanitarian principles have a better chance of being respected.

Mujahideen unity, such as it was, quickly collapsed in Kabul and throughout the country. As intense factional fighting with frequently shifting alliances replaced the anti-communist struggle, massive soul searching spread through the humanitarian community. What had the assistance effort added up to? Had it prolonged the war? Were aid agencies part of the problem or part of the solution? The field-based quest for more effective and principled action was helped by emerging processes at UN headquarters aimed at improving overall UN performance in intractable crises in accordance with the "unitary approach" that was articulated in the UN secretary-general's *Agenda for Peace*. As a result, in 1998 the Strategic Framework for Afghanistan was born of the frustrations of agencies in the field with a seemingly unending war in which the manipulation and impact of humanitarian action was questioned, and of an overarching concern at headquarters for a more coherent, UN system-wide response to complex crises. The key assumption was that by reducing the disconnects among the political, assistance, and human rights pillars of UN action, overall effectiveness would improve and so would the prospect of peace. This was both the strength and, in the end, the indictment of the Strategic Framework.

The objective of the Strategic Framework was to provide a stronger voice, or at least equal billing, to humanitarian and human rights concerns in regard to the UN's political initiatives, and thus to reduce the risk of instrumentalization of assistance. Principles and modalities for common programming were agreed across the assistance community—including the vast majority of NGOs—and functioned much in the same way as the "cluster system" does today. Coordination on the ground was boosted, as was the ability of the aid system to present a relatively united front in its difficult negotiations for access and acceptance with the Taliban, who had emerged victorious from the bloody civil war (they had taken Kabul in 1996 and controlled upward of two-thirds of the country by 1998). A measure of coherence and greater integrity was injected within the assistance community. It was facilitated by the fact that donors were limiting their involvement in Afghanistan to humanitarian assistance; capacity building of Taliban institutions was proscribed for fear of legitimizing the regime. In effect, the humanitarian system created its own parallel structures to the Taliban regime to respond to a deepening crisis for which resources were scarce and international support was weak.

The Strategic Framework was criticized by some for the alleged subordination of humanitarian and human rights concerns to the UN's political agenda. Some organizations, particularly MSF, claimed that humanitarian action was being compromised by the Strategic Framework because it provided a single umbrella for the three components of UN action in Afghanistan—political, humanitarian, and human rights. In fact, quite the opposite happened, at least during the period between 1999 and mid-2001; because the Strategic Framework contained a clear set of principles and objectives to which all segments of the United Nations and the vast majority of the NGOs had subscribed, the humanitarian voice tended to be the strongest and had a better chance of being heard. This was facilitated by the fact that no major power had strategic political stakes in Afghanistan, that humanitarian action was the main form of UN engagement on the ground, and that the peace process was mostly reduced to talks about talks with no substantive discussions among the belligerents.

The Strategic Framework facilitated the search for common approaches in the aid community on how to deal with restrictive Taliban policies and on issues such as negotiations for access to vulnerable groups, particularly to "internally stuck people" (ISPs) blocked behind the front lines or too poor to move to safer areas. Negotiations with the Taliban were never easy because their expectations and agendas changed over time, as did those of the international community. Initially, both sides sought to manipulate the other: the Taliban viewed engagement with aid agencies and their reluctant acceptance of international assistance as a way to gain legitimacy and recognition, while donors and UN agencies used the promise of assistance to try to force the Taliban to lift restrictions on girls' education and women's access to health care. There was much talking *at* each other rather than *to* each other. Each side used its principles instrumentally: international humanitarian law (IHL) on one side, and purist Islamic precepts on the other. Over time, positions hardened and both sides were seen to renege on prior agreements. The West effectively punished the Taliban by denying their regime any development assistance and by portraying as black a situation that contained many shades of gray. The Taliban responded in kind by restricting access and accusing aid agencies of spreading immorality. Those on both sides—moderate Taliban and humanitarian agencies—who favored principled engagement were lambasted as accommodationists or worse.[14]

Issues of principles and attention to protection issues got a hearing because of the relatively strong degree of unity in the humanitarian community and because the Strategic Framework allowed the humanitarian voice to be heard at the political UN and donor levels.[15] In the end, there was little integration between the assistance and the political pillar of the Strategic Framework. While it is true that the Strategic Framework was based on the assumption that assistance activities should "advance the logic of peace," because the Taliban were ostracized and the peace process was going nowhere, aid-induced pacification was more virtual than real. If there was instrumentalization, it was by the humanitarians who had to fight hard to keep the plight of Afghan civilians on the agenda and used the access and information they had to pressure reluctant donors.

Principles Under the *Kilim*

All this changed utterly after 9/11. The coherence and unity that the Strategic Framework had engendered within relief circles was shattered by the political and military hurricane that followed. Humanitarian and human rights concerns were pushed aside. They were swept under the *kilim*.

First, the nature of the crisis was radically changed by the US-led intervention. The Bonn Agreement, and the UN Security Council resolutions that endorsed it, resulted in a process of taking sides by the United Nations and the assistance community. This was not immediately apparent to aid agencies that were benefiting from the sudden windfall of donor largesse, but it was to the "spoilers" and "losers"—the remnants of the Taliban and other groups who had temporarily gone underground but were already planning their comeback. Humanitarian actors who had been part of the Afghan landscape for many years, and who had been broadly accepted by all parties to the conflict, were now being viewed with suspicion by the losers, if not as legitimate targets in their war effort. This was because the humanitarian agencies in the post–Bonn Peace Agreement euphoria accepted the conventional wisdom that peace was in the offing and that their erstwhile interlocutor, the Taliban, was no longer a player with which a dialogue needed to be maintained. The Karzai government had been legitimized by its Western backers. Donors urged the United Nations and NGOs to work with the government. To be fair, few needed prodding. This, in turn, broke the social contract of acceptance that normally allows humanitarian agencies to operate in volatile environments. To aggravate matters, the situation was defined and accepted by all except a handful of analysts as "post-conflict" and therefore no longer requiring a humanitarian response.[16] Of course, humanitarian needs did not disappear; the post-conflict designation warped the analysis. As a consequence, the strong UN humanitarian capacity that existed in the country up to 9/11 was summarily disbanded.

Second, the fulcrum of international intervention shifted from the humanitarian to the political arena—and the former increasingly subordinated to the latter. The United Nations Assistance Mission in Afghanistan (UNAMA) was established as the most integrated UN mission until then.[17] All UN political, assistance, and human rights functions were brought under the stewardship of a single official. The mission's operating system revolved around the twin mantras of "support the government" and "nothing must derail the peace process." In other words, politics—in this instance to strengthen the Karzai government—ruled. These features of UNAMA had a number of consequences for humanitarian action. Because of the lack of decisiveness in the UN assistance pillar, into which the previous humanitarian coordination structure had been folded, and the Klondike-style rush of aid agencies attracted by the sudden availability of funds, coordination essentially collapsed. Donors set up shop in Kabul and privileged their own bilateral channels and implementing agencies. This undermined multilateralism and defeated any attempt at coherence in the assistance realm. NGOs distanced themselves from the United Nations, either because they distrusted the politicization of UNAMA or because they were now flush with funds. The myriad new reputable or fly-by-night players that appeared on the scene simply ignored it.

At the same time the UN humanitarian efforts that had been a driving force—and the vehicle for coordination—in Taliban times came to be seen as antagonistic to the peacebuilding agenda by the political side of UNAMA. It thus became much more difficult to raise protection concerns within and outside the mission. In the winter of 2001 and the spring of 2002 there were massive abuses in the north of the country—including reprisals against Pashtun communities perceived as being pro-Taliban, forced displacement and press-ganging, as well as killings and rape of aid workers—but while these abuses were carefully documented by UN humanitarian staff, there was little interest or traction by the UN leadership and the coalition either to acknowledge or to take action to curb theses violations.[18]

The Dangers of Integration

In early 2002, the UN offices became "integrated." This meant that the field offices, which until then had been essentially humanitarian hubs, where NGOs had easy access for information and meetings (and as a courtesy could send or receive messages from the radio room), became "no-go" spaces for non-UN staff. Political staff, hitherto only present in Kabul, were appointed and in most cases headed these field offices. Integration had immediate effects on the ability of ordinary Afghans to come and interact with humanitarian and human rights staff. Collecting confidential information became difficult: outsiders had to leave their name at the door; coalition personnel, some bearing arms, and Afghan officials were in and out; there was no space for private meetings. In one particularly unnerving incident, in Mazar-e-Sharif, a UN protection officer was interviewing a group of women whose sons had been forcibly recruited into a local militia when her political colleague walked into the meeting room with the commander of the said militia. Needless to say, the women covered their faces and left as soon as they could, and never returned.

The assistance community came to be perceived by the Taliban and other insurgent groups as having taken sides in a "Western conspiracy" and as providing a prop for the corrupt Kabul administration, whose legitimacy was increasingly questioned and whose writ outside the capital remained weak. Aid agencies had been by and large accepted, sometimes grudgingly, by all parties in earlier phases of the conflict. All of a sudden they were perceived by the Taliban, and the communities that supported them, for what they were: deeply embedded financially, politically, and culturally in the West. Their status shifted "from that of benign infidels to agents of Western imperialism."[19] Even ICRC, the paragon of neutral and principled humanitarianism, did not escape this labeling and was one of the first agencies to suffer from the deliberate killing of one of its staff,[20] shattering the assumption that neutrality continued to have a protective value for aid workers in Afghanistan. While ICRC subsequently worked hard to reestablish its *bona fides* with the insurgents, most aid agencies opted for more, rather than less, alignment with the US-led coalition agenda, calling, for example, for an expansion of the presence of the International Security Assistance Force (ISAF)—until then based only in Kabul—to the entire country.[21] Moreover, NGOs had been traditionally state-avoiding during the previous decades; now many were working as government-implementing partners or even in the Provincial Reconstruction Teams (PRTs) set up by the US-led coalition, further adding to the blurring of the lines between humanitarian action and military-led initiatives.

As the insurgency progressed, access by aid agencies to many parts of the country became more difficult, if not impossible. Programs had to be managed by remote control from government-held towns thereby reinforcing the perception of taking sides and transferring the security risk to local staff. Civilians have borne the brunt of the alignment and instrumentalization: villages where aid agencies had been working were targeted for "collaborating with the enemy," NGO clinics perceived as harboring wounded insurgents have been bombed or raided by coalition forces, and the quality of and access to health services have generally declined in the growing expanses that escaped government control.

In sum, the incorporation of humanitarian aid in the strategies implemented by the coalition and the United Nations had a triple negative impact: it marginalized humanitarian action and subordinated it to a partisan political agenda, it made it more difficult for aid agencies to access vulnerable groups, and it put the lives of aid workers at risk. The charitable explanation is perhaps that the post–9/11 enthusiasm clouded the vision of the main actors in the UN leadership, Western donors, and aid agencies. Peace seemed within grasp. Nonetheless, there were and still are good reasons to be skeptical of the integration/coherence agenda whether writ narrow— that is, limited to the United Nations—or writ large across the joined-up approaches of the NATO military coalition and its civilian appendages.

Humanitarianism Unraveled

If we fast forward to 2012, we find humanitarianism in Afghanistan in a parlous state. The optimism of 2002 has been replaced, within and outside the aid community, by growing despondency and foreboding. Many, in Western establishments saw Afghanistan as a laboratory for new approaches to conflict resolution, if not world ordering. Some, on the heels of Kosovo, and later Iraq, even waxed about a new and benign imperialism.[22] For the past ten years Afghanistan has been a testing ground for "joined up," "comprehensive" or coherent approaches to conflict resolution. We will look briefly both at the UN and coalition versions of "coherence" and how they have resulted in a quantum leap in the instrumentalization of humanitarian action.

While the United Nations has had an integrated mission since early 2002, the integration of coalition efforts, where political, military, and civilian activities fit into a single strategy, came later. Both Afghanistan and Iraq (and now Kenya/Somalia) were laboratories where different types of military/political/assistance hybrids have been tested by the United States and its partners.[23] These can be grouped under the moniker of "stabilization" operations and covered approaches ranging from the relatively indirect—where civilian assistance activities were delivered from more or less militarized PRTs—to the direct involvement of the military in assistance activities.[24] Examples of the latter included the direct delivery of "humanitarian assistance" by the military as described in the following box.

Giving "Humanitarian" a Bad Name

A NATO/ISAF press release reads: "Humanitarian operations are helping both the people of Afghanistan and coalition forces fight the global war on terror. Under a strategy known as 'information operations,' coalition mentors assigned to Afghan Regional Security Integration Command–North are developing humanitarian projects for even the most remote villages in the Hindu Kush Mountains. During a recent mission in both Faryab and Badghis Provinces, the Afghan National Army [ANA] and their coalition mentors . . . provided relief to the Afghan people. . . . In return for their generosity, the ANA asked the elders to provide them with assistance in tracking down anti-government forces."[25]

"Stability operations are humanitarian relief missions that the military conducts outside the U.S. in pre-conflict, conflict and post-conflict countries, disaster areas or underdeveloped nations, and in coordination with other federal agencies, allied governments and international organizations. Such missions can include reestablishing a safe environment and essential services, delivering aid, transporting personnel, providing direct health care to the population, mentoring host country military medical personnel and helping nations rebuild their health infrastructure. Improving local medical capacity can in turn help stabilize governments and produce healthier populations. The new policy elevates the importance of such military health support in stability operations, called Medical Stability Operations (MSOs), to a DoD priority that is comparable with combat operations."[26]

In the language of the military, the objective of counter-insurgency and stabilization was to "shape, clear, hold, and build."[27] Essentially, these activities involved a concerted set of actions in "swing" or "critical" districts that were recaptured from or might otherwise have fallen to the insurgents. Once the district is secured, the theory goes, the United Nations and its agencies, the government, and the NGOs come in, first with quick-impact projects and then with more durable initiatives, to transform physical security into more durable human security. This is based on the postulate that "hearts and minds" and other assistance activities can actually "deliver" durable security, an assumption that has been increasingly questioned.[28] Understandably, agencies and NGOs, particularly those with long histories of work in Afghanistan, have been reluctant to jump onto the stabilization bandwagon despite strong donor pressure to do so. New assistance subjects—private contractors or for profit "quasi NGOs" like Development Alternatives Inc. (DAI)[29]—have been much more ready, willing, and able to take the plunge.

In post-2001 Afghanistan all major aid donors—with the exception of Switzerland and India—were belligerents. This was unprecedented. Unsurprisingly, the militarization of aid and its incorporation into political agendas reached unheard-of levels. One of the consequences of such "coherence" was that, because "post-conflict" was declared by the international community in 2002, there was very little interest in and funding for humanitarian activities from bilateral donors. Until 2009–10, there was much denial as to whether the deepening crisis had generated humanitarian needs. Apart from the European Commission Humanitarian Office (ECHO) and the USAID Office for Disaster Assistance (OFDA), the relatively principled humanitarian branches of the European Commission and USAID, there were no officials with humanitarian portfolios in donor embassies in Kabul in 2010.[30]

The United Nations and Humanitarian Action: The Gold Standard of Instrumentalization

While donors' support for coherent agendas and disregard for humanitarian principles were somewhat understandable given the reality of being active belligerents, the posture of the United Nations was not. In the ten years after 9/11, Afghanistan was the only complex emergency where the United Nations was politically fully aligned with one set of belligerents and did not act as a honest broker in "talking peace" or interacting with the other side.[31] It was also the only complex emergency where the UN's humanitarian wing—the Office for the Coordination of Humanitarian Affairs (OCHA)—was neither vigorously negotiating access with the insurgents[32] nor openly advocating for the respect of humanitarian principles with all parties to the conflict. This represents a failure of mandate[33] and of leadership. The UN humanitarian coordinator acted also as DSRSG (deputy special representative of the secretary general) in charge of the assistance pillar and as UN resident coordinator and deputized for the SRSG as required. This conflation underscored the consequences of integration from a humanitarian perspective; it was difficult if not impossible for the same person to be an advocate for humanitarian principles and impartial humanitarian action and at the same time act as the main interlocutor on reconstruction and development issues with the government and coalition forces. The government—as well as major donors and the coalition forces themselves—was not keen to acknowledge the depth of the conflict-related humanitarian situation because this undermined the rhetoric of post-conflict nation-building. Nor did it encourage the United Nations to step out of the relative comfort of government-held cities to assess the humanitarian situation on the ground.

Unlike the United Nations, the ICRC nurtured its relationship with all the belligerents. It provided services like caring for wounded combatants, the repatriation of mortal remains, and facilitating contacts between families and their loved ones detained in Bagram or Guantanamo that were valued by the insurgents and the communities that supported them. Thus, ICRC was the only humanitarian agency able to develop a modicum of trust with the other side—to the extent that, for example, WHO needed to rely on ICRC's contacts for its immunization campaigns in areas where the insurgents were present.[34] Following its return to Afghanistan in 2009, MSF has followed the same approach.[35]

The one-sidedness of the United Nations stemmed from the various UN Security Council resolutions establishing UNAMA and supporting the US-led coalition. These resolutions repeatedly referred to "synergies" and strengthening cooperation and coherence between the UN's special representative, the foreign military forces, and the Karzai government.[36] This meant that the United Nations was joined at the hip with the international military intervention and the Karzai government. Moreover, the public messaging of the UN bureaucracy from its top level down singularly lacked equidistance. Both the UN secretary-general and his SRSG publicly and repeatedly welcomed the military surge and the prosecution of the war.[37] The SRSG was often seen in public with ISAF commanders, visiting ministers from belligerent countries, and assorted dignitaries. Many aid workers, UN and NGO alike, felt that the UN secretary-general's remarks to the press expressing "admiration" for ISAF, after the October 2009 insurgent attack on a Kabul guest house in which five UN staff were killed, were particularly insensitive and unhelpful.[38] Such statements allowed the armed opposition to underscore the lack of impartiality of the United Nations as a whole for not acting "as per its responsibilities and caliber as a universal body" and for "calling for more brutality under the leadership of USA."[39] More generally, the level of trust of ordinary Afghans in the United Nations was deeply fractured.[40] While as of 2008 the United Nations had became more vocal in documenting the impact of the war on civilians and in recognizing more openly the need for negotiated humanitarian access, its posture—an integrated mission in support of the government, aligned with the coalition, ensconced in government-held towns—and its credibility remained weak.

From a humanitarian perspective, OCHA's capacity to maintain a principled position remained uncertain and its ability to negotiate humanitarian access and acceptance untested. This was compounded by the absence of reliable data and analysis on the depth and breadth of the humanitarian caseload—a task that would normally be undertaken by OCHA. The failure to put together a credible picture of the humanitarian implications of the war, rising insecurity, and lawlessness in wide swathes of the country was particularly serious as it fed donor reluctance to acknowledge that a robust humanitarian response was necessary.[41] As such, this constituted a serious form of passive instrumentalization.

More broadly, the aid community suffered from the confusion faced by ordinary Afghans, not to mention the armed opposition, in distinguishing humanitarians from other aid and political actors. The perception that the aid enterprise had taken sides was of course reinforced by the fact that aid agencies were only present in increasingly securitized compounds in government-held towns.

In the fraught urban geography of Kabul and other major cities, there was little to distinguish UN compounds from those of the coalition or of private security companies, thus reinforcing the perception that the United Nations and the foreign militaries were parts of a joint enterprise. Bunkerized behind blast walls of seemingly ever-increasing height,[42] the beleaguered aid community was cutting itself off from the Afghan population it was meant to assist. This was particularly true of the United Nations, whose international staff could only move around, with crippling restrictions, in armored vehicles. But access was rapidly shrinking for the NGOs as well; long-standing relationships with communities were fraying because of the impossibility of senior staff visiting project activities. Remote management and difficulties in assessing changing needs and monitoring projects were affecting program quality. Responsibility and risk were transferred to local staff, and the risk of being associated with the government or the coalition was one that, understandably, many were not prepared to take. In short, the one-sidedness of aid agencies was affecting both the reach and the quality of their work. Undoubtedly, acute vulnerabilities requiring urgent attention were not being addressed. With the exception of the ICRC and MSF, mainstream international agencies, UN and NGO alike, who claim to have a humanitarian mandate were becoming more risk averse and loath to rethink their modus operandi. As a result, they were allowing their universe of responsibility to be defined by political and security considerations rather than by the acuteness of need and the humanitarian imperative to save and protect lives.

Back to the Future

As this book went to press, Afghanistan was entering its thirty-third year of war with an ever-rising death toll and unimaginable levels of suffering. The West's might, its ever-changing strategies, and billions of dollars of treasure had exacerbated rather than mitigated the country's problems. Nation-building had unraveled. Injections of cash had fueled massive corruption and unsustainable projects that had benefited Afghan elites and foreign contractors. Modest gains in education and other social indicators had been recorded but had limited prospect of being sustained if, as anticipated, the war economy fractures and aid budgets collapse with the withdrawal of foreign military forces in 2014. Externally supported development had fueled urbanization and urban misery, while livelihoods in rural areas remained precarious. Peace remained elusive, if not illusive. If anything, the country was more polarized than ever. The return to a multi-sided civil war was a looming and dreaded possibility. In many ways the situation resembled that of the Soviet withdrawal: a weak central government on life support, a weakened but defiant insurgency, dire levels of structural violence, widespread impunity, and daily reminders of new and old injustices including gender discrimination, a general feeling of desperation, and much packing of bags among the educated or kleptocratic elites.

From a humanitarian perspective the ability of the international community to provide assistance and enhance protection for communities endangered by crisis and conflict was patchy at best. With the exception of ICRC, MSF, and a few other principled humanitarian agencies, most agencies were ill equipped conceptually and practically for the likely challenges ahead. The consequences of the decisions taken in late 2001 to use humanitarian infrastructure to advance the West's political/military world-ordering agenda were significant and would continue to add to the country's woes.

What do we learn from the long litany of crossed instrumentalizations of humanitarian action in Afghanistan? Perhaps the first thing to say is that the international community does not learn, and apparently does not wish to do so. Despite ample evidence of the risks and consequences, the temptation to use humanitarian action to achieve political or military objectives—or, more broadly, to incorporate humanitarian action in grand political designs—has been a recurrent theme in Afghanistan's recent troubled history. Views differ greatly on the pertinence of such integrated or coherent approaches that seem to have become the orthodoxy both in the United Nations and most Western governments. So far, the debate on the effectiveness of such approaches has been largely ideological, pitting those who believe that integration is a good thing against those who advocate more independence and insulation of humanitarians from partisan agendas. The evidence from Afghanistan, however, shows the perils of integration and instrumentalization in stark relief. One can only hope that donors and the UN leadership will take notice to avoid the pitfalls of similar strategies elsewhere.

Second, principles matter. Afghanistan—and the same applies to Darfur and Somalia (see Chapters 5 and 6)—shows that while in the short run people in need may not really care whether a sack of wheat is delivered from the back of an ICRC or a military truck, endangered communities do understand the importance of a clinic that is able to function in the midst of a war zone and appreciate policies that reduce rather than increase the risks they face. Attaching strings to life-saving assistance ("We'll give it to you if you tell us where the bad guys are") or linking it to the security strategies of the PRTs, tends to backfire over time. As an anti-government tribal leader explained to an ICRC delegate, "Just as we do not expect you to support our religious, social, political views and actions, so we expect you not to support—in any way—our enemies. Know when so-called humanitarian action becomes a sword, or a poison, and stop there."[43] Core humanitarian principles are no guarantee of safety or access but are the only tools available to *bona fide* humanitarians to negotiate the space and the trust needed to undertake humanitarian action in contested and contentious environments.

Neutrality is not an end in itself; it is a means of fulfilling the humanitarian imperative. The abuse of the term *humanitarian* for stabilization activities that are not based on need but on a political-military agenda dangerously muddies the waters. The same applies to the many NGOs that perform a variety of relief and/or development functions and receive funds from belligerent nations and/or work as government implementing partners, if not for military/assistance hybrids such as the PRTs. The perception of being associated with a belligerent carries potentially deadly consequences for aid workers. Those who work with one set of belligerents put in jeopardy the work of those who try to affirm their neutrality and independence. Unlike other conflict situations, there are few NGOs with a humanitarian track record in Afghanistan. As for bilateral donors, they see "their" NGOs as force multipliers for their political and military objectives. Therefore, stabilization operations affect humanitarianism because that is where the money is, and NGOs are forced to balance principle with institutional survival.

In sum, there are good practical reasons for separating or insulating principled humanitarian action from integrated missions or stabilization activities. An even stronger theoretical argument points to the flaws of incorporating humanitarian action in the "coherence" agenda. Humanitarian action derives its legitimacy from universal principles enshrined in the UN Charter, the Universal Declaration of Human Rights, and international humanitarian law, not to mention universal compassion instincts. Such principles do not sit well with Security Council political compromises; politics, the art of the possible, is not usually informed by principle. Incorporating a function that draws legitimacy from the UN Charter (or the Universal Declaration of Human Rights) within a management structure born of political compromise in the Security Council is questionable and, in the case of Afghanistan, has proven to be deleterious for humanitarian agencies, and, more important, for those they strive to assist and protect.

On balance, the experience from Afghanistan shows that the integration/coherence agenda has not served humanitarianism; it has blurred the lines, compromised acceptance, made access to vulnerable groups more difficult, and put aid workers in harm's way.[44] Restoring the *bona fides* of a humanitarian enterprise weakened and discredited by decades of manipulation is an uphill task that will require better insulation from partisan political agendas and a clearer separation between principled humanitarians and other forms of relief, legitimate, perhaps, but not humanitarian.

Chapter 5

Diminishing Returns

The Challenges Facing Humanitarian Action in Darfur

HELEN YOUNG

From its eruption in 2003, the conflict and crisis in Darfur has evolved dramatically. At the time of writing in late 2011, the protracted humanitarian crisis had no end in sight, and despite a massive international humanitarian presence in the region there remained serious unmet humanitarian needs. Before the expulsion of thirteen INGOs by the government of Sudan in 2009, Darfur was regularly in the press, but developments after the expulsions largely went uncharted and unremarked. Despite the continuing peace processes, a wide array of international actions, and massive inputs of resources, the capacity of the international humanitarian community had declined dramatically. In the early days of the conflict and crisis, international humanitarian capacities were very weak to nonexistent. They became increasingly stronger and well established from late 2004 to 2006 following the signing of a humanitarian ceasefire agreement and rapid expansion of international humanitarian operations. But after the partial signing of the Darfur Peace Agreement in 2006, security worsened, humanitarian access contracted severely, and humanitarian response was seriously weakened. The overnight expulsion of the INGOs in April 2009 led to dramatic changes, compounded by the further increase in insecurity, car-jackings, and hostage-takings targeting the international community. At times the international community could no longer assess or respond adequately to newly emerging humanitarian needs. There was both a general lack of information and analysis and also a lack of international acknowledgment or accountability for the changing state of affairs.

This chapter explores how different actors, including donors and national government, media and human rights groups, UN agencies and INGOs,

the International Criminal Court (ICC), and even local agencies and affected communities, used, manipulated, or influenced humanitarian arguments and action in order to promote their own agendas. Following from
the conceptual framework introduced in the Introduction to this volume,
Figure 5–1 illustrates the main actors, processes, and agendas at play in
the Darfur context. The crisis-affected people of the Darfur region are not
homogenous, and only three different groups are identified in Figure 5–1,
although this masks the complexity and differences that are to be found in
Darfur. Similarly, only four broad categories of national and international
actors are included in the framework, including Western media, donors,
non-state actors, and state actors. Humanitarian action is the point of interest
and is broken down between the wider protracted crisis response and the
more acute humanitarian action aimed at saving lives. The multiple agendas
that are thought to have influenced humanitarian action are shown in the
light gray circles and include early recovery, local peacebuilding initiatives,
wider peacekeeping initiatives, and internationally supported peace talks,
human rights activism, and the judicial processes of the ICC. Figure 5–1
shows that the potential for instrumentalizing humanitarian aid is always
present because it is inevitable that these multiple and often-competing
agendas will have an impact on peace and security, humanitarian access,
and the longer-term vulnerability of the people of the Darfur region.

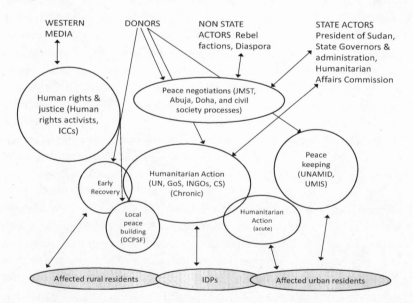

**Figure 5–1. Main actors and their influence on the multiple
modalities for response in the Darfur crisis.**

The chapter starts with a background to the Darfur conflict, associated peace processes, and failed peace agreements. Against this backdrop the chapter reviews specific examples of the instrumentalization of humanitarian aid by different actors. Finally, the chapter reviews the implications and outcomes of the combined effects of these multiple pressures on humanitarian action.

Background to the War:
Peace Processes and Failed Agreements

The Darfur civil war between armed rebel groups, the Sudanese Liberation Movement (SLM) and Justice and Equality Movement (JEM), and government forces erupted in 2003 as a result of long-held grievances about the marginalization of Darfur, a crisis of development, and increasing social and resource-based conflicts. Darfur's transnational links with the people and governments of Chad, Libya, and Central African Republic were an added complication. For more than thirty years various Chadian and Libyan groups fought proxy wars in and from bases in Darfur.

Early successes in 2003 by the armed resistance groups were quickly overtaken by the now-infamous government counter-insurgency strategy. Following similar approaches adopted in southern Sudan, government strategy took advantage of the existing ethnic rivalries in Darfur, as it fostered and supported the new militia known as Janjaweed, largely composed of Arab groups from Darfur and the region. The Janjaweed, with support from government air and land forces, attacked and destroyed villages, causing mass forced displacement of civilians and a protection crisis of epic proportions.[1] The violence and tactics employed also devastated livelihoods and created much wider food insecurity.[2]

Since 2003, different phases of the civil conflict have evolved, as have patterns of displacement. Following the rapid escalation of forced displacement in 2003 and 2004, it began to level out in 2005 and then in 2006 increased marginally as a result of ongoing conflict. Despite reports of small numbers of returns by the government, the mass displacement of more than 1.5 million in 2003 and 2004 had not been reversed by the end of 2011. Instead, the demographic map of Darfur has been strategically redrawn as a result of displacement and the restricted mobility and access for different groups, particularly for the sedentary farmers who were displaced to more urban areas. Different groups or factions control access to rural areas and therefore control civilian movements and people's access to markets, farms, pasture, forestry, and so on, all of which are essential for livelihoods.

The generic term *displaced* hides a complex diversity of experiences, losses, and ongoing grievances. The forced displacement linked to the counter-insurgency was strategic, following political aims of depriving the insurgents of their perceived support and impoverishing their resource base. For those former rural farmers who were forcefully displaced, humanitarian needs for assistance and protection were strongly linked to the promise of restitution and reparations. Alternatively, there were those driven to migrate by fears for their safety (rather than by actual attacks) and also by their loss of liveli-hood. Not all the displaced migrated to towns or to IDP camps; for example, groups of Arab pastoralists were also displaced from their former homes as a result of conflict and moved to safer rural areas occupied by allied groups.

A shaky humanitarian ceasefire agreement was brokered in early 2004 between the government and the two rebel factions at the time (SLM and JEM). They also agreed on the deployment of African Union (AU) inter-national observers, which was the start of the peacekeeping operations.

Mediated by the AU, a long process of peace talks followed in Abuja, Nigeria, between the two rebel movements and the government. By the final round of the talks in 2006, the SLM had split into two factions; one led by Abdul Wahid Nour (SLM/AW) and another led by Mini Minnawi (SLM/MM). Both were committed to one common negotiation platform. Finally, the Darfur Peace Accord was signed on May 5, 2006, by the govern-ment of Sudan and the SLM/MM, but the other rebel groups, the JEM and the SLM/AW, rejected the deal and called for more concessions from the Khartoum government. The pressures of deadline diplomacy also played a role, with global leaders attending the meeting and instigating unworkable deadlines. Several members of the SLM/AW delegation broke with their leader and declared their support for the agreement. This partial signing of the peace agreement sparked violent protests among supporters of the non-signatories in Darfur.

From this point the Darfur rebel movements were not only divided in terms of who signed and who didn't, but even the non-signatories began to break into innumerable groupings and factions, creating instability on the ground and generalized disunity and in-fighting, thus severely disabling subsequent international efforts to get the non-signatories on board with the peace process and also exacerbating localized insecurity. Insecurity led to ever-decreasing humanitarian access. For example, in mid-2006, OCHA and the AU had to withdraw altogether from the IDP camps in Zalingei for a period of several weeks.

In 2006, the UN Security Council voted to deploy a force of more than seventeen thousand peacekeepers across Darfur and a hybrid African Union/ United Nations Mission in Darfur (UNAMID[3]). The Security Council also created a unique body called the Joint Mediation Support Team (JMST) to support the efforts of the joint mediators of the UN and AU.

Since the partial signing of the Darfur Peace Agreement in 2006, there have been periods of intense international support and efforts to bring together the divided rebel groups, but their lack of unity generally thwarted international efforts to bring them together to reach a common negotiating position. In the first seven months of 2010, peace talks between the Sudanese government and Darfuri rebel groups took several new turns. Efforts by Qatar, Egypt, and the Arab League to encourage negotiations continued, not only among the parties to the conflict but also with representatives of Darfur civil society.

The international community heralded the signing of preliminary peace agreements in early 2010 (for example, between the government of Sudan and the JEM) as a significant breakthrough. This was despite the lack of a unified negotiating position of all armed movements and the continuing accusations by JEM and government of ongoing attacks in Darfur. Efforts to bring in a newly formed umbrella group of ten movements—the Liberation and Justice Movement—was opposed by JEM, thus creating further tension and even outbreaks of violent protests in some IDP camps in west and south Darfur. Often these high-level conciliatory moves on the part of government to get traction on peace agreements coincided with other crucial national events, such as the Sudan presidential and parliamentary elections in April 2010.

Developments at the end of 2010 perhaps signaled the last nail in the coffin of the 2006 Darfur Peace Agreement, with the declaration by the government that ex-rebel forces loyal to Mini Minnawi had become "hostile forces." By the end of 2010, it seemed that despite wide-ranging international efforts, the various Darfur peace processes had failed to establish inclusive or lasting peace agreements. Little had been achieved by pursuing peace at this level, and long-term observers argued that the mediated peace prospects were over.

Rhetoric of "War Is Over": Government Strategy and Donor Stabilization Agenda

In the months preceding the national elections in April 2010, there was a growing affirmation from government and others that the Darfur conflict was over, despite considerable evidence to the contrary. In August 2009, General Martin Agwai, the UNAMID military commander, announced that the Darfur war was over and that fighting had subsided as the Darfur rebel groups had split into factions—all that remained, he said, were low-level disputes and banditry. After signing the ceasefire with the JEM rebel group in early 2010, President al-Bashir also declared that the war was over. Such claims continued throughout the summer with statements in July from Minister of Defense Abdel Rahim Hussain.[4]

At an international donor's conference focused on development and reconstruction of Darfur, in March 2010,[5] the general tone was that the situation had stabilized. The UN humanitarian and resident coordinator even talked about overall improvements, and many broadly concurred that it was time for recovery, reconstruction, and development in order to give impetus to the peace process and transition away from relief. Yet crucially, neither the indicators of conflict,[6] nor security, nor the humanitarian indicators supported this rhetoric of improvement. Essentially, there was no evidence at that time to support the notion that war was over, the situation stabilized, and the humanitarian situation improving. These statements were driven by the government's strategy for Darfur, on the one hand, and the donor's stabilization agenda, on the other; both were conveniently ignoring the reality on the ground.

Several different levels of conflict continued unabated in parts of Darfur, including inter-tribal fighting, ongoing fighting between the government forces and SLM/JEM, fighting along the disputed north-south border between the Sudan People's Liberation Army (SPLA) and Darfuri Arab tribes, rampant banditry and generalized insecurity, and continuing clashes between Chadian and Sudanese forces along the Chad border.[7]

By the end of the 2010, the international community tentatively acknowledged the deteriorating security situation but continued to ignore the humanitarian implications. For example, a humanitarian update by UN OCHA (the first of its kind available online since March 2009) reported that security developments had a significant impact on the ability of humanitarian partners to provide assistance but concluded, "The humanitarian situation remained stable in many parts of Darfur, as shown by comparing several major sector indicators from the third quarter 2010 with the same time last year."[8] This contradiction between the "degraded operating environment" and the apparently stable humanitarian context highlights the inconsistency with which a humanitarian emergency is presented. Usual practice is to prioritize the most acute humanitarian needs, rather than generalizing based on the wider protracted crisis.

Shifts From Relief to Early Recovery:
A New Panacea

Humanitarian action was one of multiple modalities for international intervention in the Darfur crisis in 2011. The setup was confusing and represented diverse and sometimes overlapping interests. UNAMID was specific for Darfur and was headed by the Joint UN-AU special representative for Darfur, Ibrahim Gambari, who reported to the Sudan representative of the secretary-general. The UN resident coordinator/humanitarian coordinator had specific responsibilities for Darfur, although he worked within the United Nations Mission in Sudan (UNMIS) and did not report formally to the Joint UN/AU special representative for Darfur. This made collaboration somewhat difficult.

At that time early recovery was a relatively new modus operandi, intended to pave the way for intervention strategies aimed at laying the foundations for future peace and stability. Early recovery was conceived as a transition to a more stable era, in which humanitarian needs could be reduced and peacebuilding, reconstruction, and development could start. What determines when this happens? In Darfur, it seemed to be triggered by wider political events rather than a response to conditions on the ground. For example, elements of early recovery were first introduced following the partial signing of the Darfur Peace Agreement, as part of the Darfur Joint Assessment Mission and associated Darfur Community Peace and Stability Fund (DCPSF).[9]

In Darfur, early recovery was synonymous with an overly optimistic view in the international community regarding the peace process, while at the same time the early recovery agenda complemented the government's strategy of returns and resettlement as a solution for the displaced. However, early recovery as a strategy ignored local realities, particularly the practical and security challenges of IDP returns to areas under the control of potentially hostile groups; the ongoing processes of urbanization, which meant many did not want to return; and the already overstretched humanitarian programs that were focused on more urban areas and unable to support a more diverse set of early recovery programs.

Initially in 2007, there was strong resistance by several INGOs (including some of those subsequently expelled—see later discussion) to the "early recovery" agenda, which was seen as an externally driven agenda that contributed to the normalization of the crisis and was therefore based on limited local analyses and possibly threatened to undermine humanitarian action and budgets. Even the DCPSF subsequently acknowledged that the initiative was conceived "on the anvil of optimism that preceded the peace talks in Sirte in October 2007."[10] Ever hopeful of a peaceful resolution to the crisis, the DCPSF focused on incentivizing peace through early recovery activities. But locally the challenges to recovery and peacebuilding remained, with ongoing conflict of all types and with a significant deterioration in security.

A premature early recovery agenda potentially undermines humanitarian action because it competes for donors' attentions and funding. Furthermore, it often involves programs that are more developmentalist in approach, with a blurring of humanitarian principles of neutrality and independence. Early recovery also has implications for overstretching or monopolizing agency capacity to implement recovery projects.[11] Capacities of civil society organizations (CSOs) are not sufficient to implement large million-dollar projects,[12] and the administration and technical support does not exist to service and build capacity in local organizations. New tools and approaches are desperately needed to address vulnerability in the context of protracted complex crises, but these should complement rather than undermine humanitarian action.

Early Politicization of Humanitarian Action: Distrust, Divisions, and Partiality

Humanitarian action was highly politicized in Darfur long before it was fully established. Could it have been otherwise? The intense media coverage of Darfur in 2004 was based on the widespread human rights reporting[13] and not the limited humanitarian assessments that were available. The media gave voice to the human rights testimonies and concerns of IDPs, who had been forcibly displaced by the counter-insurgency tactics, many of whom were closely aligned with the rebel groups. It was impossible to have an interest in the Darfur region and not be exposed to these compelling and disturbing narratives.

The Western media were further influenced by the public relations of rebel movements supported by diaspora groups. In time, elements of the diaspora were closely allied to the newly emerging Darfur activist campaigns in the United States and Europe (the ENOUGH project and the Save Darfur coalition) that mobilized celebrity activists and public support throughout the Western world.

In contrast, humanitarian assessment reports were few at that time.[14] Partly this was a result of restricted access—the World Food Programme's (WFP) annual needs assessment in 2004 was only able to reach 25 percent of the selected sites. Also, it was because most humanitarian agencies focused on addressing the highly visible and immediate needs of displaced people. Only in late 2004 and early 2005 was relief extended to crisis-affected rural groups. Apart from the highly politicized nature of the civil conflict, the other politicizing factor was the high-profile genocide debate. Humanitarian assessments were the only source of hard evidence on mortality, although no mortality surveys were completed covering the period of the most intense violence from mid- to late 2003.

Following usual practice, agencies recruited international personnel to manage their programs, almost all of whom had no previous experience in Darfur, or even Sudan. With more than one thousand internationals with little or no experience of Darfur, except what they had read or seen and heard in the media, the lack of trust among agencies, government, and civil society was immediate. Many international staff, including those of long-established agencies like Oxfam, did not trust even their own national staff or long-term local partners.

As in many crises (see, for example, Chapter 4 on Afghanistan in this volume), inexperienced relief workers naturally developed sympathies with their beneficiaries—who represented one side in the conflict. This combination of local sympathies and the profound international demonization of the Arab groups associated with the Janjaweed inevitably meant that most humanitarian actors were not impartial and either ignored Arab groups or actively discriminated against them—only referring to Arab communities by shortcut pejorative terms such as "JJ" (Janjaweed). This was in part because of genuine fear of these groups—fear generated by Western media and the narrative around the conflict at that time. But it was also a result of the belief among some humanitarian actors that their assets and staff were being attacked by "government supporting" elements or Janjaweed.

There were exceptions, including a small number of INGOs (including Danish Refugee Council, Triangle, Samaritan's Purse, Catholic Relief Services, Save the Children US) who pioneered humanitarian programs in rural areas and among Arab groups. Also by 2005, the WFP had included many rural pastoralist groups in its food distributions, for pragmatic reasons rather than based on needs assessments.

Moreover, the INGO public information and programming strategy was driven by INGO headquarters staff. Research on agency coordination and decision making has shown that the staffs with the best knowledge about the situation in Darfur were often not making decisions on how to handle it.[15] Some technical agency staffs complained that headquarters was ignoring their reports. Communications between the field and headquarters made it difficult to reach a common understanding. The centralized decision making of INGOs, combined with the lack of assessments and availability of reports, meant that INGO public information closely echoed the widely available human rights reports and the international Darfur activist campaigns and media coverage. Newspapers have subsequently been accused of sketching "a pornography of violence" that reduced the crisis to a morality tale whose effect was to obscure the actual politics of violence.[16]

There was distrust between the humanitarian agencies and the government authorities, with both sides accusing the other of hidden political agendas. The government believed that the agencies were passing on information to human rights groups, and later to the ICC investigators. For many INGOs, ingrained distrust of potential government-aligned groups spilled over into them mistrusting local Darfuris and local Sudanese organizations. This severely impeded the recruitment of national staff, with many being drawn from the same tribal groups as the displaced population, which further isolated the INGOs from a broader perspective on the Darfur crisis. That said, there were risks to national staff in fronting the humanitarian operations, with reports of imprisonment of INGO staff and challenges of dealing with daily bureaucratic impediments (referred to as *BIMPS* among the INGOs).

Since 2004, parts of government and some of the groups in Darfur did not see international humanitarian operations in the Darfur region as neutral and impartial. This was manifested by the expulsions of INGOs in 2009, which is taken up later in this chapter. Several factors contributed to the politicization of humanitarian action in the Darfur region, including the international human rights reporting, which fed the international media campaign, which was used by the humanitarian agencies as part of their strategy for raising public awareness and fundraising; the late arrival of INGOs after April 2004 and lack of completed and published humanitarian assessments that presented a broader picture of humanitarian suffering across the region; the centralized decision-making processes of INGOs and poor coordination between their headquarters and field staff that undermined a wider and deeper understanding of the crisis; and the ingrained distrust between the INGOs and the government that spilled over into distrust of local staff and local organizations.

Merging of Humanitarian Claims of IDPs With Political Entitlements

The partial signing of the Darfur Peace Agreement in 2006 by only some of the parties, the subsequent implementation failures and delays, and the floundering peace process had lasting repercussions in Darfur and left large IDP populations in limbo in terms of finding a political solution to the crisis and to their displacement. The majority of IDPs were displaced for more than five or six years, and from the beginning, the IDP claims on humanitarian assistance were intrinsically linked to their need for protection and to their political grievances and perceived political entitlements. The crisis was widely referred to as a protection crisis,[17] in which the need for security often outweighed the need for relief food, water, shelter, and so on.[18] In presenting the crisis as a "protection crisis," the media, human rights advocates, and INGOs not only reinforced but also sanctioned these links—and so the provision of humanitarian assistance was inevitably linked to a promise of protection and eventual restitution.

Few symbols of these links were as tangible as the general food distribution ration card that entitled the owner to a monthly food basket of cereals, oil, and pulses. The ration cards were linked to an international food distribution program with more than three hundred distribution points, costing in excess of US$800 million per year, and a logistical infrastructure that delivered on a regular basis to more than three million people. These ration cards were the only UN-endorsed evidence of IDP or other conflict-affected status and represented an entitlement to food aid. They were also symbolic of the IDPs' conflict-affected status, their political grievances, and their claims for restitution. This has made it increasingly difficult for humanitarian agencies to assess the need for humanitarian assistance and challenge this claim in any way, as evidenced by the resistance to re-registration of the beneficiary population.[19] To remove the IDP card was not only a threat to the humanitarian resources that IDPs received but, more fundamentally, undermined their wider political claims.

The IDP humanitarian claim or "right to food" became closely interwoven with IDPs' claim for protection. This meant that while protection needs remained unaddressed, IDPs would continue to demand a full entitlement to humanitarian food assistance, irrespective of their food security status. The right to humanitarian food assistance has become strongly embedded within the IDPs' individual narrative and IDP identity, which for the more politicized IDPs was linked to their political grievances as represented by the insurgency, the ongoing protection threats, and higher-level peace processes. A study in 2008 concluded that if the IDP ration cards were withdrawn, this would challenge not only the right to food assistance, but also their status as IDPs, which for many was linked to their political identity.[20] The scale and efficiency of the food distribution system also served to demonstrate the serious intent of the international community in addressing Darfur's problems and by association the injustices of the Darfur conflict.

The INGO Expulsions and Processes of "Sudanization"

On March 4, 2009, the government announced its decision to expel thirteen INGOs operating in Northern Sudan and revoke the licenses of three national aid organizations. The order came within half an hour of the ICC's news conference that announced the decision to issue an arrest warrant against President al-Bashir for war crimes, genocide, and crimes against humanity. The Sudanese authorities initially accused the aid groups of passing information to the ICC on alleged atrocities in Darfur. Although no formal accusation was ever made against the INGOs, it was widely thought that at least some staff were providing information to the ICC. Later, in a government communications release, it was stated that the expelled INGOs were removed for involvement in political activities and not respecting their humanitarian mandates. Within twenty-four hours, humanitarian capacity in Darfur was significantly reduced. This was immediately followed by announcements by the president himself that he had ordered the Ministry of Humanitarian Affairs to "Sudanize" humanitarian operations completely within one year to close the gap in the humanitarian work.

The decision was a bolt from the blue. While the government had reassured the international community that, in the event of an ICC decision, the international community would be safe, the idea of INGO expulsions was beyond imagination.[21] The lack of forewarning and the direct strike at the heart of the Western international humanitarian establishment created a complete and utter shock for all involved, including more than six thousand national staff members who lost their jobs.

The expulsions were followed by intense media coverage and an international furor voicing both outrage and serious concerns. Hundreds of thousands of lives were thought to be at risk, based on the claim that 40 percent of the aid was provided by these same agencies. Internationally, a clear priority was to reinstate the expelled agencies, which represented core elements of the humanitarian establishment (including the three INGO representatives on the UN humanitarian country team). American and British donors, in particular, lost several of their INGO implementing partners. Overnight their programs were shredded and their assets confiscated by the government of Sudan.

One tactic used by the UN humanitarian coordinator to justify the INGOs' reinstatement was to emphasize the expert and professional expertise residing within these agencies.[22] Taking the moral high ground (attributing expert status to the INGOs and presenting local capacity as "quick and dirty") was unlikely to persuade the government of Sudan, given its stated commitments to nationalizing humanitarian operations. Neither was there international acknowledgment that many humanitarian INGOs had largely ignored or even shunned local capacities before the expulsions, except when it suited them. That WFP, UNICEF, and other UN agencies were able to continue their relief operations and fill a large proportion of the gaps left was largely because they could work directly with national and local organizations, including the state-level Ministry of Health and local community bodies, such as the food relief committees. Without this local capacity, very little humanitarian relief would have been delivered in Darfur even before the expulsions.

Following the expulsions, efforts were immediately directed at filling the gaps in service provision, with the United Nations and the government conducting a joint assessment of the humanitarian impact of the departure of the INGOs and of the capacity to meet emergency needs.[23] This only looked at the situation in thirty-eight communities and therefore did not reflect the wider regional context. The initial predictions had underestimated the capacity of local relief committees and the ability of WFP and UNICEF to ramp up their operations, which included hiring the recently sacked national personnel of the expelled INGOs and the direct implementation of programs. Remaining INGOs "mopped up" the programs of other agencies and quickly expanded into new geographic areas and sectors, with new "lead" agencies in different sectors. On the surface, at least, it appeared that humanitarian capacities had been restored.

The government process of "Sudanization" of humanitarian action also took immediate effect, with two broad elements affecting the remaining INGOs. First, they were required to take on and work through national partners; and second, they had restrictions placed on them as to how many international staff they could employ, and they had to involve the national Humanitarian Aid Commission in the recruitment and selection of new staff.

In addition to these government measures, the greatest force for Sudanization was the increasing and widespread insecurity that forced agencies to pull their international staff out of the field locations to the regional centers (see the following section on security). These field programs continued to operate but increasingly under "remote control," sometimes with weekly field visits from national staff by helicopter, but increasingly rarer were visits by international humanitarian professionals.

In the post-expulsion environment, the remaining agencies found themselves considerably overstretched, with many taking on multi-million dollar programs as the norm. Increasing coverage and scale meant focusing on maintaining essential services and relief distributions while having to cut back on more innovative but intensive livelihoods programming. There was little remaining capacity to expand into the new areas suggested by an early recovery agenda. Another casualty, in name at least, appeared to be protection. Protection was now rarely if ever referred to in program strategies and had been stripped from any UN and NGO information materials or websites, presumably because of the need to sanitize assistance programs and remove all associations with human rights advocacy of the type that might be associated with information of relevance to the ICC.

In June 2009, after much negotiation, the government of Sudan authorized four aid agencies expelled from the country in March to return to
Darfur, provided they registered under slightly changed names and logos.
Agencies on the ground, for example in Zalingei, explained that in terms of
service delivery many of the gaps still remained. According to one informant:
"Some government departments have tried to help, but there is always a
stand-off between the IDPs and anything to do with the government. It's
a classical stand-off; they [the IDPs] would rather go to a private service
provider than the government."

In retrospect, a certain arrogance among some INGOs and trends in
their behavior almost certainly contributed to the government's decision.
For example, agencies continued humanitarian operations and adopted
the narrative of the displaced groups they were helping, while at the same
time they contributed to the stigmatization of pro-government groups
involved in the conflict. Before the expulsions INGOs tended to mistrust
and shun local capacity and failed to develop a nondiscriminatory employment policy. Initial predictions of imminent deaths among the affected
population as a result of the expulsions underestimated the capacity of
local relief committees and the ability of WFP and UNICEF, and the
remaining agencies, to ramp up their operations and also to operate in
closer partnership with government ministries. The increased role for
state-level ministries, such as the Ministry of Health, and local NGOs has
been positive, although significant gaps in service delivery and problems
with timely release of information remained.

The Evolving and Exponential Deterioration in Security

By 2010 insecurity was spiraling and appeared to target the international
humanitarian community in addition to the wider insecurity affecting IDPs
and local residents. The targeting of humanitarian assets and personnel
evolved from relative stability in 2005 (despite the deaths of two Save the
Children UK workers in that year) to an epidemic of car-jackings in 2008,
and, more sinister still, the spate of killings of UNAMID personnel and
the plague of kidnappings and hostage-taking in 2010 and 2011. At the
same time, there appeared to be a deliberate government strategy to deny
humanitarians access to areas where hostilities continued. Thus security was
the overarching determinant of humanitarian access—whether directly, or
indirectly as a result of government edicts.

The kidnapping started just before the arrest warrant was issued in
2009, but following that there were at least five kidnapping occurrences

(not all are reported publicly, especially attempted kidnappings), usually by armed gangs demanding a ransom. The time taken for hostages to be released has gradually increased with each incident, from a few days to a few weeks to more than five months. The kidnapping of ICRC aid workers was of particular concern given ICRC's exemplary record of work in the Darfur region, which covered large rural areas and a range of protection and assistance activities.

Since the most recent kidnapping and ongoing hostage incidents, which involved hostages being taken from their compounds in Nyala, the capital of South Darfur state, and al Fasher, the capital of North Darfur state, several INGOs have withdrawn their international staff to Khartoum, thus isolating the humanitarian programs from international involvement even further. Before this most recent incident, those who were directly affected had scaled back their sub-offices, suspended movements outside towns (for those who previously traveled outside), and pulled their international staff and many of their national staff out of their field offices.

The effect on aid workers of such conditions also needs serious attention. Some individuals have been held up at gunpoint and "jacked" several times while in Darfur. This undermines their judgment and sends out an implicit message to observers that they are prepared to continue to work in Darfur under any circumstances. The alternative strategy is to "go to ground" and run activities remotely, relying on local groups—relief committees and community-based organizations—to do the best they can without direct support or supervision. The job of humanitarian workers in Darfur has changed from a field- and people-focused role to an urban desk-based administrator weighing up risks versus benefits of particular activities. Making life-or-death decisions is no longer just about the people they are helping, but also concerns their own lives, those of their colleagues, their partners, and the people with whom they work at a distance.

To sum up, the security situation took a particularly sinister shift, from soft looting and attacks on humanitarian resources (convoys, premises, stores) to direct attacks on personnel, with kidnappings, hostage-taking, and killings of humanitarian personnel. This has directly affected the presence of international personnel and ways of working, with staff being pulled back to state capitals and in some cases to Khartoum. This diminishing humanitarian presence inevitably has had effects on the capacity to assess, respond, and monitor humanitarian programs. This changing security context has evolved over a relatively short period of time and has shaped humanitarian programming dramatically, with few questions asked about the implications for accountability and quality control.

Muffled Information and Lack of Analysis

Attention and media coverage of the humanitarian crisis in Darfur waned following the INGO expulsions, with a switch in focus to the 2010 elections, instability in the south, and the 2011 referendum and secession of South Sudan. This was in part because there were fewer INGOs on the ground, but also because UN reporting on the humanitarian situation in Darfur dried up. First to go was the "Darfur Humanitarian Profile," published on a quarterly basis from October 2004 to March 2009 by the UN Humanitarian Coordinator's Office, which provided a crucial overview of humanitarian operations. UNICEF also stopped publishing online its "Sudan Humanitarian Action Update"—the last one available on the Web was March 13, 2009—just before the expulsions. In 2010, online humanitarian action reports from UNICEF on Darfur were only available as part of broader Sudan updates or updates from the region. The UN agencies were clearly taking a different tack from the pre-expulsion era, keeping a low profile and not drawing attention to either ongoing acute humanitarian needs or issues of protection.

This decline in availability in information and analysis in 2009 and in 2010 coincided with UN claims that the situation was stabilizing. In a report on May 5, 2010, Ban Ki-Moon claimed, "The humanitarian operation in Darfur has succeeded in stabilizing the situation with regard to food security, health, nutrition and water."[24] Yet available evidence pointed to a different reality both in terms of the war and the humanitarian indicators.

The "UNICEF Nutrition Update for Darfur" in January 2010 had limited circulation but showed prevalence of global acute malnutrition almost double the emergency thresholds in several surveys, despite humanitarian operations reaching these same populations.[25] Between June 2009 and the update published in January 2010 more than twenty-one surveys had been completed, but only seven had been formally released and approved by the government's Humanitarian Affairs Commission, of which five reported malnutrition rates from 15 percent to 29 percent.[26] There was also a problem with the way UNICEF presented this crucial data. While technically competent, the updates lacked any analysis of what the figures meant—either for the communities affected or for response strategies. The crucial summary statements were ambiguous and did not convey the seriousness of the nutrition results, while the main narrative was intended for the technically dedicated, not the generalist reader. UNICEF did make complaints about the Ministry of Health blocking the release of nutrition survey reports, which was yet another impediment to understanding the severity of the humanitarian crisis.

Crucial information and analysis of the humanitarian situation were lacking. There were serious problems with the release and proper review of the nutrition survey reports—without such information and analysis humanitarian actors cannot properly understand the severity of the humanitarian situation or the efficacy of the response. Navigating a crisis without a compass leaves it liable to be driven by a wider politicized agenda.

Discussion and Conclusions

From 2003 to 2010 the power dynamics among national, international, and local actors in pushing their different agendas have oscillated, with varying implications for humanitarian action. By mid-2010, the government had the upper hand, and thus humanitarian action was out of vogue, in Khartoum at least. The government's implicit vetoing of the "h" word was met with ambivalence by the international community. On the one hand, humanitarian needs were still evident; on the other, the remaining agencies were struggling to cope with various challenges to humanitarian action, including the immediate threats of insecurity to staff, threats of expulsion by the Darfur regional authorities if agency activities were not in accordance with government plans, and the daily bureaucratic impediments of working in Darfur, where growing insecurity had forced agencies to withdraw, leaving "remote programming" as their only option for responding in most cases.

The ongoing instrumentalization of humanitarian aid by all parties has resulted in serious outcomes for both the people of Darfur and for the capacity of the international humanitarian community to respond. It has affected the scale, duration, and severity of the humanitarian crisis. Over time, the Darfur conflict has changed, and so have humanitarian needs and responses. The scale of the crisis has grown to include not only the displaced but also rural and urban residents throughout the region. The humanitarian crisis has become protracted, with no end in sight, and most seriously, the protracted crisis has contributed to increasing and chronic vulnerability, combined with humanitarian hotspots—areas of acute crisis, many of which are inaccessible to the humanitarian community. The unending nature of the conflict and crisis has contributed to a chronic vulnerability of the long-term displaced, whose livelihoods were far from sustainable. In urban areas the combined effects of high population, competition for limited livelihood opportunities, increasing pressures on accessing water and other natural resources (firewood, cultivable land, and so forth) have deepened the chronic vulnerability of IDPs and the urban poor.

Acute and protracted humanitarian needs also persisted as a result of the failure of international peace processes to secure durable higher-level peace agreements or to secure the engagement of key opposition groups. The attempts to promote unity among the factions and the inclusion of large sections of civil society at the actual peace talks in Doha were accompanied by further bloodshed within the IDP constituencies.

At the same time that vulnerability became more entrenched, international humanitarian capacities were seriously eroded and impaired to a point that left Darfuris in a more vulnerable position in 2010 than at any other time since the counter-insurgency operations and forced displacements in 2003 through early 2004. This weakened capacity of the aid community was in part a result of the tactics of instrumentalization employed by the government of Sudan, but it was also the result of the tacit endorsement by parts of the humanitarian community of the politicization of aid, which eventually backfired and got many of them expelled and caused fundamental damage to unhindered humanitarian access. Following the expulsions, the government of Sudan exerted almost complete control over international humanitarian actions and humanitarian agencies in the Darfur region, including control of humanitarian access and information (such as humanitarian indicators). This was further demonstrated by the announcement by President al-Bashir on August 7, 2010, that if any agency exceeded its authority, it could be expelled on the same day by the authority of the state governors—which was shown to be true in the months that followed with many "soft" expulsions that were not even noted in the media. At the same time, government policies of Sudanization of humanitarian response have controlled whom agencies can hire and also enforced a system of partnerships with local agencies. While initiatives to strengthen and build on local capacities were long overdue, the government strategies failed to acknowledge or address the weak capacity and limited coverage of local CSOs.

International attention frequently focused on the manipulation of aid by the government of Sudan, while there was little critical self-examination within the humanitarian community of how international actions had directly and indirectly affected the people of Darfur, including their current vulnerability and future resilience. It is within this domain of international responsibility that there is potentially the most room to maneuver in terms of addressing the humanitarian challenges. This chapter has identified certain trends in international response that may have also contributed to the increasing risks and vulnerability of some groups in the Darfur region, including,

- The early politicization of humanitarian action and failures of the international community to promote actively a more impartial and balanced response to the crisis. This in turn raised expectations among some IDP groups regarding an internationally brokered political settlement and the protection offered by the international peacekeeping forces.
- Failures to develop strategically and support local partnerships with civil society from the beginning and address the lack of trust between international and local organizations.
- The employment policies of international organizations, which included a high turnover of international staff, who were often recruited internationally from rosters and therefore lacked local knowledge and personal networks; plus the discriminatory recruitment of national staff who were not broadly representative of tribal groups in Darfur.
- The accommodation and sometimes endorsement of the government position that war was over and uncritical moves toward early recovery.
- In 2009 to 2010, the failure to provide objective and up-to-date assessments and analysis of humanitarian needs. Over and above the problem of delayed and blocked reports by the Ministry of Health, what little data was available was subject to "spin" and obfuscation.
- The decrease in general information, clear commentary, and leadership on the humanitarian situation, particularly by the United Nations and donors.

Of more universal concern than these specific trends witnessed in the Darfur region are the humanitarian challenges that fundamentally stem from humanitarian response to protracted crises, particularly where lives are no longer at imminent risk. A simple switch to early recovery fails to address chronic vulnerability or recognize the implications of a protracted political and protection crisis. The region has experienced unprecedented levels of humanitarian assistance, and humanitarian action has become institutionalized and part of local governance. These issues cannot be addressed until a deeper analysis of the political economy of conflict and humanitarian response informs response strategies.

Once past the first phase of humanitarian response, humanitarian actors become local players and inevitably their work influences and almost becomes assimilated as part of the local political economy. Sustaining an impartial, independent, and neutral humanitarian operation becomes increasingly difficult and possibly less relevant. This phenomenon of "humanitarian diminishing returns" suggests that to continue after a certain level of performance has been reached will result in a decline in effectiveness, despite the continuing application of effort and in some cases increasing input of resources. This has been seen in Darfur, where humanitarian indicators reached their peak (best levels) in 2005—only one year after the humanitarian operation started—but regular high rates of acute malnutrition have stubbornly refused to come down since. This has also been witnessed in a number of other protracted humanitarian crises where maintaining the status quo becomes an ever-increasing challenge. At this stage new or different approaches and tools are needed to address the problems of protracted crises and chronic vulnerability, while reserving the short-term acute humanitarian model of response for newly emerging and most severe crises. This involves multiple shifts. The tried-and-tested, top-down, and inherently technical approach to saving lives in acute emergencies needs to give way to a broader, more community-based approach to livelihood adaptation and recovery. Supporting local efforts inevitably means a shift in power among international, national, and local institutions. Whoever is calling the shots or setting the agenda, at all times the politics of instrumentalization of humanitarian aid will continue—and all actors need to consider their roles as both instrumentalizers and instrumentalized.

One last question is whether, in the case of Darfur, instrumentalization worked for the instrumentalizers. This is difficult if not impossible to answer without clarity on the objectives of instrumentalization. It is also complicated because most actors were both instrumentalizers and also were instrumentalized by others. On the surface, the INGOs' short-term goals of instrumentalization were met, in that by actively promoting an intensive international media campaign they were able to generate unprecedented levels of international support for their own Darfur humanitarian programs (joint appeals were met in full, which is rare). But there was little apparent thought or analysis of the wider or future implications—including relations with civil society and national parties, or implications for the wider unmet humanitarian needs and the contribution of humanitarian action to further marginalization and inequities within the region. For the government of Sudan, on the surface it also appears that its objectives were met with the expulsion of the agencies and the reclaiming of authority and control over humanitarian action. Both examples characterize instrumentalizers' objectives as being in their self-interest and connected with claiming the moral high ground. From this point of view, instrumentalization works well for the instrumentalizers. However, successful instrumentalization is usually at the expense of more important humanitarian goals. A focus on the politics of instrumentalization can help us learn more about the adverse affects and costs of instrumentalization; how they evolve over time; and how they could be avoided, or at least minimized.

Chapter 6

When State-Building Fails

Famine, Counterterrorism, and the Politicization
of Humanitarian Action in Somalia

MARK BRADBURY AND ROBERT MALETTA

"US extends drone strikes to Somalia"[1]

"The UN declares famine in Somalia"[2]

In June 2011 the United States conducted the first drone strike in Somalia against leaders of the militant Islamist movement al-Shabaab. At the time thousands of Somalis were crossing into Kenya fleeing a severe drought and conflict that turned Somalia into one of the world's worst humanitarian disasters, a position it had held two decades earlier. While the US drone was able to find its target with pinpoint accuracy, humanitarian aid agencies had experienced a disastrous decline in their ability to reach civilians affected by the drought and food shortages.

The first part of this chapter reviews the ways in which international politics has shaped humanitarian action in Somalia. The second part examines how, in the wake of 9/11 and the global war on terror (GWOT), international state-building, stabilization, and counterterrorism policies compromised the ability of humanitarian aid organizations to assist and protect people in Somalia and helped to create a famine.

This chapter draws on the Briefing Paper *Statebuilding, Counterterrorism, and Licensing Humanitarianism in Somalia* by Mark Bradbury, published by the Feinstein International Centre (September 2010), available on the tufts.edu website.

How Aid Has Been Instrumentalized in Somalia

In March 2010, the UN Monitoring Group on Somalia, a body originally established to monitor compliance to the 1992 UN arms embargo on Somalia, revealed there had been substantial diversion of food aid to support the efforts of armed groups. The report was a stark reminder that humanitarian assistance has long been part of Somalia's political economy and throughout two decades of state collapse it has been manipulated and fought over by belligerents and instrumentalized by foreign governments and international aid agencies.

At different periods over the past thirty years humanitarian aid has been instrumentalized by foreign governments and the United Nations in pursuit of strategic interests in Somalia. This is apparent in the waxing and waning of assistance, the conditions placed on assistance at one time and the lack of accountability at another, and a willingness to undermine humanitarian principles and to ignore protection needs. Those in power in Somalia, whether the predatory military regime of Mohamed Siyad Barre, the "warlords" and military factions in the 1990s, Somali business people, the successive transitional governments since 2000, regional and district authorities, clan authorities, Somali NGOs and, most recently, militant Islamists have all sought to manipulate humanitarian assistance either to project their authority or to enrich themselves through multiple forms of taxation, direct diversion, and in some cases the creation of localized crises and "people farming" to attract assistance. International aid organizations are also far from blameless. In response to the war and famine in the early 1990s the INGOs that rushed into Somalia were accused of exacerbating the conflict by fueling a war economy, dividing local communities and efforts to restore local order by bypassing or substituting for local authorities, while at the same time enriching themselves.[3] Two decades later questions over accountability, transparency, and independence from foreign donors continue to affect humanitarian agencies. The actors and their influence has varied at different times; Table 6–1 on pages 133–35 summarizes examples of instrumentalization in different periods.

The Cold War

International political and security interests have always shaped humanitarian assistance in Somalia. In the last decade of the Cold War, Somalia, as a strategic ally of the West, became the largest per capita recipient of foreign aid in Africa, and well before the state collapsed humanitarian assistance had become an integral part of its political economy. For over ten years Somalia received substantial humanitarian assistance for hosting refugees from the 1977–78 war with Ethiopia over the Ogaden. During this period donors tolerated the falsification of refugee numbers, their recruitment into the army to suppress the Somali National Movement's rebellion in the north, and what was described as the worst example of food diversion in the history of the US Food for Peace program.[4] As the Cold War thawed and Somalia's strategic importance declined, conditions were placed on Western aid, justified by human rights reports that revealed the brutality of the government's military campaign in the north.[5] As the international community began to disengage from Somalia, the regime's authority dissipated and the state collapsed. The links between aid and the violent warlord politics that plagued Somalia after the state collapsed were laid in the pre-war international aid programs to Somalia.

Civil War and "Military Humanitarianism," 1991–95

The internecine war that followed the overthrow of the Barre regime in January 1991, characterized by mass forced displacement and an economy of plunder, created one million refugees, two million IDPs, and a famine that killed over a quarter of a million people.[6] The international response to the crisis, while ostensibly driven by a humanitarian imperative to relieve the famine, also reflected the new spirit of interventionism after the Cold War and changes in the structures of global governance to manage the humanitarian fallout from the shifts in global power—the so-called complex political emergencies.[7] This included the creation in 1992 of the UN Department of Humanitarian Affairs. The United Nations Operation in Somalia (UNOSOM) created in 1992 was one of the first multi-mandated humanitarian and peacekeeping missions that became a feature of international management of crises in the 1990s. The "armed humanitarian intervention"[8] was shaped by numerous interests and agendas. Somalia thus became a testing ground for international institutions and mechanisms for managing global crises.

For the outgoing administration of George H. W. Bush, US leadership of UNOSOM, following the allied victory in the first Gulf War, was an opportunity to project its role as a global policeman in what the president had defined as the "new world order." The original drafts of the UN Security Council Resolutions 794 (December 3, 1992) and 814 (March 26, 1993), authorizing the US-led UN task force (UNITAF) and the expanded mission of UNOSOM II, were written in the Pentagon and reflected the concerns of US Central Command.[9] UNOSOM therefore reflected the close link between international security and humanitarian operations in Somalia.

Somalia in the early 1990s was also an experimental arena for an expanding privatized nongovernmental humanitarian system. Under the media spotlight, INGOs flooded into Somalia, while Somali NGOs multiplied in the absence of government and in response to the massive infusion of aid.[10] Some INGOs flexed their newfound power by lobbying for military intervention. In Somalia the growing power of a globalized media also became apparent. Global coverage of the war and famine helped to influence opinion in favor of a military intervention, which was captured in the prime-time landing of US forces on the beaches of Mogadishu.

Some credit the intervention for alleviating the famine and temporarily stabilizing the conflict. Others argue that the famine had already peaked, and while warlords and other "gatekeepers" were variously guilty of aid diversion, the poorly conceived intervention and the vast sums of money spent on armed protection fed a war economy and prolonged the conflict by shoring up the power structures of the warring factions.[11]

The nature of intervention changed in March 1993 when UNOSOM's mandate was reinforced with the powers of peace enforcement and broadened to include state-building. This brought the United Nations into conflict with faction leader General Mohamed Farah Aideed, and it crossed the line from a neutral intervention force to a participant in the war. The loss of nineteen US soldiers and three Black Hawk helicopters in a battle with Aideed's forces in October 1993 ended the US military engagement, and UNOSOM's mandate expired in 1995, having failed to restore a national government.

Relief to Development and the Normalization of the Crisis, 1995–99

After the failures of UNOSOM the model of international engagement in Somalia changed. Western powers disengaged and diplomatic management of the crisis was regionalized through the Intergovernmental Authority on Development (IGAD) and regional states who initiated a series of peace talks that reflected their own geopolitical interests.[12] With no acute emergency, no peacekeeping forces, and no geo-political interest, Western aid to Somalia sharply declined.[13] Humanitarian assistance raised through the UN Consolidated Appeal Process (CAP) fell from US$200 million in 1993 to less than US$50 million in 2000.[14] Without the security infrastructure provided by UNOSOM, many aid agencies withdrew or relocated to Kenya, from where they ran cross-border programs.

With the emergency deemed over, Somalia's crisis was redefined in developmental terms to reflect both a diminishing conflict within Somalia, new forms of economic activity[15] and functioning autonomous administrations,[16] and international disengagement. The shift to recovery and development was institutionalized with the creation of the Somalia Aid Coordination Body (SACB), chaired by the European Commission,[17] and the UN Development Office for Somalia, both of which gave strategic weight to the transition from relief to development. As strategies switched from external intervention to supporting "local solutions," aid was made conditional on security and good governance.[18] Cost recovery and public-private partnerships were adopted as strategies to create sustainable service provision and avoid "relief dependency," despite the fact that people were no more able to pay for these services than they previously had been.

UNDP's Somalia program, which aimed to "integrate Sustainable Human Development into the relief to development continuum," was typical of this approach. The 1996–97 UN CAP for Somalia[19] sought to resolve the difficulty of formulating a unified aid strategy in a country with varying political and security environments by grading the country along a continuum from "zones of crisis" to zones of "transition" and "recovery." The transition from crisis to recovery was to be encouraged through "peace dividends," while the SACB imposed sanctions on areas that failed to comply with its code of conduct on security and development.

The policy shift from relief to development was not matched by increased donor funding to address Somalia's structural vulnerabilities. By most standards Somalia remained in a state of chronic disaster, but one consequence of this internalization of the causes and solutions to the war was a creeping "normalization" of the crisis.[20] Levels of humanitarian need that at one time would have provoked an emergency response were treated as normal. In 1997, El Niño–induced floods in southern Somalia, which caught the international community unprepared, demonstrated how vulnerable the country was and how far the international humanitarian response capacity had been eroded.[21]

"Failed States" and the "Global War on Terror," 2000–2005

Two events ended Somalia's period of incremental recovery and isolation and forced it back onto the agenda of Western governments: the formation of the Transitional National Government (TNG) in August 2000, which became the first internationally recognized government of Somalia since 1991, and the 9/11 attacks on the United States a year later. In the wake of 9/11, the 2002 US National Security Strategy concluded that the biggest threat to American security came from "failing states." Somalia, without a functional government for a decade and in a state of chronic humanitarian distress, was identified as a potential haven for al Qaeda and a breeding ground for transnational terrorism. The presence in Somalia of al-Itihad al-Islamiya, a militant Islamist organization whose members had links to al Qaeda, and the fact that Somalia had been a conduit for materials and personnel involved in the US embassy bombings in Nairobi and Dar es Salaam in 1998, lent credibility to this thesis.[22]

Seizing on the renewed interest in Somalia, some analysts suggested that counterterrorism could now provide the "door through which longer term international re-engagement in peace, reconciliation and state reconstruction . . . should take place."[23] This idea has proven highly problematic. It changed the premise for international engagement in Somalia from one of humanitarian protection to one of international, specifically American, security.

State-Building, Counterterrorism, and Humanitarian Catastrophe, 2006–11

After 2001, state-building in Somalia, as in Afghanistan and Iraq, became part of the strategy to counter the threat of international terrorism. International security and development policies coalesced around a view that internal stability and international security could only be ensured by the existence of a state that was capable of addressing problems of porous borders and emigration, weak law enforcement and surveillance systems, and poverty and lack of social services, all of which were thought to make "fragile states" vulnerable to exploitation by transnational terrorists. The coalescing of state-building and counterterrorism strategies also led to renewed international military engagement in Somalia, involving military intervention by Ethiopia between 2007 and 2008, US air strikes against Islamist leaders and al Qaeda operatives, the deployment of the African Union Mission to Somalia (AMISOM) to support the transitional government, the training of Somali security forces by foreign governments and private military companies,[24] and an international naval armada to protect commercial shipping from Somali pirates.

In 2004, the TNG was replaced by the Transitional Federal Government (TFG), following a two-year national reconciliation process in Kenya facilitated by IGAD and sponsored by the European Union. Once the TFG was ratified by the international community, the United Nations took the lead in supporting it. Donor funds were channeled to UNDP to coordinate assistance for state-building through a reconstruction and development plan that would build the legitimacy and viability of the TFG with the support of political, development, and humanitarian actors.[25] Support for the state-building project was reflected in revived levels of aid, which grew from US$36 million in 2000 humanitarian funding through the CAP to over US$429 million in 2008.[26]

The TFG that emerged from the internationally sponsored peace process commanded little support in Somalia. Unable to access Mogadishu, it established interim bases in Baidoa and Jowhar. It was also unable to counter the growing influence of Islamist groups in south central Somalia, which coalesced in 2006 as the Islamic Courts Union (ICU).[27] The ICU succeeded in removing a US-financed warlord alliance[28] from Mogadishu and brought some security to the capital for the first time in fifteen years.[29] Within a year Ethiopia, which was concerned about the irredentist rhetoric of some ICU leaders and Eritrean backing for it, intervened militarily. Backed by US air power, it routed the ICU and installed the TFG in Mogadishu in January 2007. The United Nations and foreign governments sought to capitalize on the situation by extending support to strengthen the TFG's capacity and legitimacy. AMISOM was deployed to protect government institutions in advance of an envisaged UN peacekeeping mission, but with no civilian protection mandate.[30] Humanitarian agencies came under pressure to seize the "window of opportunity" and respond to the humanitarian and development needs.[31] For humanitarian agencies it was the beginning of an inexorable path to a humanitarian disaster and to a reassessment of the way they operated in Somalia.[32]

In April 2007 attempts by the TFG to disarm Mogadishu ignited a conflict with elements of the former ICU and clans outraged at the Ethiopian "occupation." The worst fighting in fifteen years displaced some 700,000 civilians from Mogadishu and catalyzed the rise of Harakat al-Shabaab al-Mujahideen (Mujahideen Youth Movement), which emerged from under the umbrella of the ICU to become a dominant force in Somali politics. It also served to radicalize Somalis in the diaspora. In an environment polarized between those who were "for" or "against" it, the TFG described the displaced as "terrorists" and condemned international and Somali NGOs for aiding the enemy.[33]

This was a time when the international community could have tried to reinforce humanitarian principles. Instead, the Ethiopian invasion (unsanctioned by the United Nations), the US air strikes, the rendition of suspected Islamic militants from Kenya, the closure of the Kenyan border to Somali refugees, the indiscriminate shelling of civilian neighborhoods in Mogadishu by Ethiopian forces, the mass displacement of civilians, and the assassinations and arbitrary detentions all elicited little condemnation from foreign governments and multilateral agencies. The muted response illustrated the extent to which GWOT was driving policy. In March 2008, al-Shabaab was designated as a terrorist organization by the US administration and in

May its leader, Aden Hashi "Ayro," was killed by a US missile. Al-Shabaab subsequently declared all Western organizations and UN officials to be legitimate targets. The participation of foreign forces in Somalia, including AMISOM, internationalized the conflict to a level not seen for two decades and produced the most severe humanitarian crisis since the 1990s famine.

UN diplomatic efforts to stem the conflict led to the withdrawal of Ethiopia in 2008 and the reformation of the TFG in January 2009, with a moderate leader of the ICU, Sheikh Sharif Sheikh Ahmed, selected as president. But it failed to halt the conflict. Supported by AMISOM and armed by the US government, the TFG survived an offensive by al-Shabaab and Hizbul Islam in May 2009, but it was unable to stop al-Shabaab from extending its control over south central Somalia. Its northwards advance was halted by a third military force—Ahlu Sunnah Wal Jama'a—backed by Ethiopia, but bombings in Kampala in July 2010[34] demonstrated al-Shabaab's regional reach.

The TFG's failure to expand its support within Somalia brought another change in international policy in mid-2010, when the United States announced its readiness to deal with the TFG and sub-state actors, like Somaliland and Puntland and other stable areas, as a "dual track" policy to advance peace and development. Other donors followed suit, although critics asserted that it would exacerbate clan divisions and further balkanize Somalia. At the same time, support continued to the TFG to strengthen its capacity to fight al-Shabaab, with training of TFG forces and an expansion of AMISOM from eight thousand to twelve thousand troops in December 2010. This enabled the TFG and AMISOM to launch a counter-offensive against al-Shabaab in Mogadishu, coordinated with Ahlu Sunnah Wal Jama'a in parts of south central Somalia. By early 2011, this had weakened al-Shabaab's control in Mogadishu and places in south central Somalia. It had also led to further population displacements.

The Humanitarian Fallout

If the intention behind the internationally sponsored state-building project in Somalia was to restore internal order, it had the opposite result. Renewed conflict from 2006 turned Somalia's chronic emergency into what humanitarian agencies began to refer to as a humanitarian catastrophe. Between 2006 and 2011 over eighteen thousand civilians are estimated to have been killed in fighting in Mogadishu alone. During the same period the numbers of displaced people rose from 500,000 to 1.46 million,[35] of whom an estimated 410,000 moved to the Afgooye corridor, northwest of Mogadishu, one of the most dense concentrations of displaced people in the world. By March 2011, 680,000 Somalis were refugees in neighboring countries,[36] the majority in Kenya, where Africa's largest refugee camp, Dadaab, housed 314,000 Somalis.[37] Between 2007 and 2010, UN estimates of the number of people in need of humanitarian assistance in Somalia rose from 1.5 million to 3.2 million. By mid-2011, conflict, a drought described as the worst in sixty years, and deteriorating food security caused by global food prices, hyperinflation, and a reduction in remittances caused by the global financial crisis combined to create famine conditions in south central Somalia.[38]

Humanitarian organizations had warned about the severity of the crisis in Somalia since 2008[39] and did not stand idle in the face of the humanitarian needs, as successive CAPs since 2006 attest to.[40] But from 2006 their ability to respond to the emergency in Somalia declined in inverse proportion to growing needs. The rest of this chapter examines some of the factors that led to the 2011 famine, in particular the loss of humanitarian access.

Diminishing Access

The decline in humanitarian access is illustrated by the limited presence of humanitarian agencies and foreign aid workers in Somalia. In 1995, there were reported to be approximately fifty INGOs operating in south central Somalia, in addition to multilateral agencies. Following UNOSOM's departure many withdrew to Kenya, and as funding declined and insecurity persisted, the number of INGOs operating in south central Somalia diminished. By 1997 there were reported to be twenty-six INGOs in south central Somalia,[41] and only fifteen in 2010, with no international aid workers permanently based south of Galkaiyo.[42]

The presence of UN agencies in south central Somalia has similarly been minimal and declined after 2006. Successive SRSGs to Somalia optimistically announced plans to rectify this and take the United Nations "back to Somalia." While numbers of international aid workers deployed in Somalia did increase in 2010, according to the UN's own figures, in early 2011 only 23 percent of the 364 international staff working on Somalia were based full time in-country and up to 44 percent of national staff were stationed outside Somalia.[43] Furthermore, the European Union was the only donor to have a permanent and limited presence in-country (in Somaliland), with other donor governments placing strict conditions on staff travel to Somalia. Presence was weakest where the need was greatest, and where agencies were present, their staffs were often bunkered behind blast walls and restricted from traveling. In November 2010, the United Nations described humanitarian access in central and southern Somalia as "fleeting, limited, and variable," and said that it was not possible to meet international Sphere standards of assistance.[44] One humanitarian agency reported that conditions meant it had changed its approach from "needs-based programming" to "constraints-based programming," responding only to those needs that were feasible to address. The constraint was not a shortage of funding, but "the disappearance of 'humanitarian space.'"[45]

The loss of humanitarian space in south central Somalia meant that humanitarian agencies resorted to various forms of remote management of their programs through national staff or local partner organizations. Making use of new communication technology and money transfer systems; recruiting Somalis from the diaspora; and involving the communities in program design, implementation, and monitoring, agencies managed to overcome some access difficulties. However, analysis, accountability and transparency, and quality assurance were more difficult, and the approach also transferred the risks of negotiating access to Somali staff and partners.

The decline in humanitarian access and the erosion of humanitarian space was symptomatic of an operating environment that had been radically altered by the rise of militant Islamist movements and the internationalization of the conflict as a result of GWOT, a combination of operational and political factors that accounted for the erosion of humanitarian space and decline in humanitarian access.

Operational Constraints to Humanitarian Action

Violence Against Aid Workers

South central Somalia has always been an insecure operating environment for aid agencies, which have employed armed guards to protect their operations since 1991. But the direct targeting of aid workers was uncommon. Between 2005 and 2010, however, Somalia ranked third, after Afghanistan and Iraq, for attacks on aid workers,[46] and in 2008 two-thirds of the aid workers killed worldwide died in Somalia.[47] Although the attrition rate declined thereafter, due to a lighter presence and tighter security measures, Somalia became one of the most dangerous countries in the world for aid workers.[48] There were several reasons for this. Ransoms paid by donor governments for the release of foreign nationals had created an internal market for hostage-taking. Aid workers had also become victims of the conflict between Islamic militants and Western governments. After US air strikes killed al-Shabaab leader Aden Hashi "Ayro" in 2008, aid workers were accused of collaborating with foreign forces and given notice that they were legitimate targets. In 2009, such threats led to the withdrawal of the two main food agencies, CARE and WFP, and the closure of the food pipeline. The possibility to mitigate this through humanitarian dialogue was limited by the proscription of al-Shabaab as a terrorist organizaton.

Attacks against aid workers also appeared to be linked to political processes in Somalia, with the highest number of attacks occurring in 2008 during the Djibouti peace talks, when old scores were being settled by the warring factions. Another contributing factor was the silence of donor governments and the United Nations about human rights abuses perpetrated by the TFG and Ethiopian forces in 2007 and 2008, which created an "accountability-free zone."[49]

Bureaucratic Restrictions on Humanitarian Action

Efforts by local authorities to control aid operations, whether by warlords, the TFG, or al-Shabaab, have been a perennial issue in Somalia. Both al-Shabaab and the TFG made demands on aid agencies to register and pay tax. The lengthy negotiations required to overcome these bureaucratic restrictions could delay the delivery of assistance. As al-Shabaab extended its control over territory, it imposed new regulations that restricted agency access, which often varied from one district to the next.[50] After 2009 the ascendancy of an uncompromising al-Shabaab leadership introduced stringent regulations on hiring female staff, the sharing of compounds, and direct communication with communities. In places, national staff were intimidated into resigning.

Checkpoints and Taxation

The use of checkpoints to assert territorial control and raise revenue has been a persistent obstacle to the delivery of assistance. Islamist authorities have generally opposed their use, and during their brief administration in Mogadishu the ICU cleared most checkpoints from the city. When the TFG took over, checkpoints multiplied again; some 336 were recorded in south central Somalia, with fifteen on the 9.3-mile Afgooye corridor alone, where the displaced from Mogadishu were concentrated.[51] As al-Shabaab gained territory in 2009 and 2010, many checkpoints were removed, easing the movement of aid and trade, but in 2011 reports from areas controlled by al-Shabaab indicated that it was restricting the movement of civilians affected by drought.

Attitudes Toward Humanitarian Agencies

Since 2006, aid agencies in Somalia faced increased antipathy from both the TFG and Islamist authorities that affected humanitarian access and the delivery of certain types of assistance. The TFG accused Somali CSOs of being terrorists and INGOs of assisting the enemy and of working in cohort with Western intelligence agencies. In 2010, al-Shabaab ordered eight international organizations to cease their operations because of their relations with the United States or for propagating Christianity, accusing some of delivering contaminated food and expired drugs. An assertive nationalism was also apparent in the rhetoric of some al-Shabaab statements. After rejecting WFP assistance, for example, it declared that "communities from South of Somalia should wake up and start helping themselves to avoid dependency on humanitarian support."[52]

Managing public perceptions in this politicized environment therefore became an important element of risk management. The international agencies who were able to maintain an operational presence in south central Somalia claimed that demonstrating impartiality and neutrality was crucial for maintaining access. For some this meant maintaining a public distance from UN agencies and AMISOM, and not taking US funding. Some aid workers argued that multi-mandate agencies that combined humanitarian, development, and public advocacy were more vulnerable than those with a singular humanitarian focus, such as medical assistance.[53] The evidence for this is difficult to substantiate because medical agencies also experienced threats, attacks, and killings, while some multi-mandate agencies managed to remain operational. A common feature of those NGOs who were able to maintain their operations in south central Somalia after 2008 was their independence from US funding.

Political Constraints to Humanitarian Action

The events of 9/11 restored international interest in Somalia, as this collapsed and "ungoverned" state was identified as a threat to international security. International political, economic, and military resources have been deployed to reestablish a Somali government. In the view of many aid agencies the erosion of humanitarian space in Somalia and the operational constraints faced by them are directly linked to the instrumentalization of humanitarian assistance to meet this security agenda. This has several aspects: the failure of donors to hold warring parties accountable under international humanitarian law (IHL); the integration of humanitarian assistance with political processes; the use of aid to support military strategies; the licensing of humanitarian aid; the centralization of humanitarian funding; the lack of robust humanitarian diplomacy; and the absence of humanitarian accountability.

The Failure of Protection and Erosion of International Humanitarian Law

Throughout two decades the warring parties in Somalia have shown a disregard for humanitarian principles and IHL. The TFG has violated its own charter to protect civilians, and foreign forces, including UNOSOM, Ethiopia, and AMISOM, have also been criticized for violating IHL. Reports by Human Rights Watch and Amnesty International, detailing violations of IHL by the warring parties during fighting in Mogadishu in 2007,[54] elicited little response from international bodies and donor governments.[55] In defending the TFG and the peace process that created it, and by failing to put in place any practical protection measures, the United Nations and donor governments prioritized protection of the political process over the protection of civilians.[56]

In pursuing their political and security objectives, donors, regional governments, and the United Nations in Somalia, as in Afghanistan, became belligerents in the war. The United States took unilateral military action against targets in Somalia, while other donors funded the training and salaries of TFG security forces, even when there was clear evidence of their abuse of civilians. Donors also avoided criticism of Ethiopian forces in Somalia, and they rarely called for a ceasefire between the TFG and its opponents. International condemnation of assassinations of members of the government and attacks on AMISOM by insurgents were not balanced by holding the TFG and AMISOM to account. Retaliation by the latter involved the collective punishment of civilians through the indiscriminate use of force in Mogadishu. Donor governments were criticized for being complicit in war crimes for their silence on violations of international humanitarian and human rights laws by the belligerents.[57] The lack of civilian protection facilitated civilian displacement, created a climate of impunity, and contributed to the shrinking of humanitarian space.

Humanitarian Assistance and Political Processes

As the situation in Somalia became more polarized, aid agencies were pressed by the United Nations and donor governments to support the TFG. In January 2007, for example, when the TFG was installed in Mogadishu the UN humanitarian coordinator called on humanitarian agencies to seize the "window of opportunity" to reengage in Mogadishu.[58] In the wake of the Ethiopian and US military action in support of the TFG, INGOs declined, insisting that "humanitarian aid must be solely based on the needs of the population and strictly guided by humanitarian principles, especially impartiality and independence" and that OCHA and the humanitarian coordinator should "strengthen the necessary distinction between humanitarian activities and any political agenda."[59] Coincidentally, Somalia had been identified as a pilot country to roll out the UN humanitarian reform program. Humanitarian agencies were therefore also concerned that the alignment of political, military, and aid objectives risked breaching the humanitarian principles of independence, impartiality, and neutrality.[60]

Again, in 2008, humanitarian agencies came under pressure from the SRSG for Somalia to support peace talks between the TFG and the opposition Alliance for the Re-liberation of Somalia. Some Somali and INGOs did engage, while others restated the need to maintain a clear separation between humanitarian aid and political agendas.

Nevertheless, attempts by the UN political office to integrate political and humanitarian agendas continued, and in 2010 the United Nations and NGOs became embroiled in a debate over the benefits of establishing an integrated UN mission in Somalia. The UN Department of Political Affairs (UNDPA) argued that bringing the UN political, security, development, and humanitarian offices under the office of the SRSG would improve the coherence and efficiency of the mission by aligning aid activities around state-building and stabilization objectives. INGOs and the UN humanitarian coordinator and some donor governments opposed the move, arguing that bringing humanitarian assistance under the control of the office of the SRSG would politicize the role of the humanitarian coordinator and affect his ability to negotiate access and advocate for humanitarian principles. Humanitarian NGOs (many of whom were accepting contracts from the United Nations) were also concerned that field-based staff of NGOs associated with the United Nations could be targeted by armed groups, a fear founded upon the experiences of aid agencies who had lost local staff members and seen their programs close in the aftermath of counterterrorism air strikes.

The UN political office, however, continued to try to incorporate humanitarian assistance in its political strategies. A "concept note" drawn up by the UNDPA in January 2011 for an African Union summit, proposed a communiqué on Somalia that committed participants to, among other things:

> Additional efforts on the part of humanitarian relief and development actors to provide a coherent support for the political process and stabilization efforts, including in south central Somalia.[61]

The concept note also supported the use of humanitarian assistance to win hearts and minds by stating:

> The TFG continues to lack the necessary backing of humanitarian and development assistance that can critically enhance its efforts to reach-out and broaden its political space and legitimacy.

Humanitarian agencies' refusal to engage in such an undertaking was often received by diplomats as unhelpful and obstructionist. But, from a humanitarian perspective, providing assistance on the basis of assessed need alone was not only morally correct, but also pragmatic. Mixing political, military, and humanitarian objectives would leave them open to attack and further erode access.

At the same time, some agencies raised concerns about the donor preference for pooled funding mechanisms administered by the United Nations, such as the Humanitarian Response Fund (HRF) and the Central Emergency Response Fund (CERF). Given the UN's political stance and its listing of al-Shabaab, some NGOs questioned whether they should seek funding through UN common funding pools. As one aid worker remarked: "Are we selling our souls to cover our core costs? If you are a partner with the UN you compromise your right to say anything."[62]

Humanitarian Assistance, Military Strategies, and Stabilization

The international project to establish a Somali government that would stabilize the country and provide a bulwark against forces that are considered a threat to regional and international security has included military assistance to the TFG, the training and arming of TFG security forces, backing the Ethiopian intervention, and support to AMISOM.[63] A key element of this support has been the training of TFG security forces since 2004, despite persistent criticisms of this approach to security sector development by analysts and aid organizations as well as concerns over the lack of transparency and accountability of the assistance.[64] There is no accurate record of the total number of TFG security forces that have been trained since 2004.

Mogadishu has been the epicenter of conflict in Somalia since 2006. Although internationally brokered peace talks have countenanced the option of establishing an administrative capital elsewhere, assisting the TFG to secure Mogadishu has become an international objective since 2007 in order to demonstrate the government's authority and establish a viable administration. In 2010, the SRSG made little secret of his support for a counteroffensive against al-Shabaab[65] and with donors encouraged aid agencies to prepare quick-impact projects to win "hearts and minds" in areas that would be secured by the government. The view that humanitarian assistance should be part of the military strategy was apparent in an AMISOM press release in 2011, in which the deputy head noted that "with greater security developing in the city, we can start to deploy more assistance and support to both the Transitional Federal Institutions and the civilian population, especially on the humanitarian front."[66] In this they were following a well-established counter-insurgency model in use in Afghanistan and Iraq.

Some donor governments rationalized support for a counteroffensive on the grounds that it would expand humanitarian access to populations in need. However, by supporting the training of TFG security forces, on the one hand, and, on the other, using anti-terrorism legislation to prevent the delivery of assistance to opposition areas, donors became belligerents in Somalia. In doing so they ignored the OECD/DAC principle "do no harm," one of the principles for good international engagement in fragile states and situations.[67]

Humanitarian agencies, for their part, were acutely aware of the potential impact that foreign military support for the TFG could have on their access. Some European NGOs were fearful about the effect that the training of TFG soldiers by their governments would have on their operations. Others publicly distanced themselves from the UNDP because police forces that it trained through the Rule of Law program were implicated in human right abuses.

For humanitarian agencies the situation was further complicated by the increasing presence of for-profit aid actors and private military companies in Somalia. Although commonplace in Iraq and Afghanistan, their engagement in developmental and nation-building activities in Somalia was a new development. These organizations do not aim to be impartial but rather to win hearts and minds through aid provision, elevating stabilization above humanitarian principles. As such, they can affect local perceptions of humanitarian actors and compromise their programs and access.[68]

A Fragile Humanitarian Framework

The erosion of humanitarian space and loss of access was also a function of a weak humanitarian framework for Somalia. For two decades there have been sporadic attempts to create a common humanitarian framework in Somalia through various organizational arrangements, joint programs, common funding mechanisms, and common operational policies and principles. The political and security concerns of donor governments, the dual political and humanitarian role of the United Nations, multiple mandates, and market competition among NGOs have made this difficult to achieve. Attempts by the United Nations and donors to integrate humanitarian assistance into political and military strategies in Somalia were indicative of the primacy given to stabilization and counterterrorism and the fragility of the humanitarian framework. In its support of the TFG, the humanitarian, military, and political objectives of the United Nations became blurred.

A report co-authored by former UN emergency relief coordinator, Jan Egeland, explains the risks that such positioning by the United Nations can create to delivering life-saving assistance in contested environments like Somalia, where the UN's political role and position in the "Western camp" has made it a "legitimate and prominent target."[69] In Somalia the United Nations was denounced as the enemy of Islam by al-Shabaab because it supported the TFG and by extension the Ethiopians. The targeting of the UNDP compound in Hargeysa in October 2008 by a suicide bomb (along with the residence of the Somaliland president and the Ethiopian trade delegate) was clear evidence that the agency was viewed as a political player.[70] In this context the UN resident and humanitarian coordinator faced a difficult challenge of mediating a political agenda that was seemingly irreconcilable with the notion of humanitarian impartiality. How, asked NGOs, could the office that trains government security forces be independent and impartial? The political position of the UN humanitarian agencies left little room to maneuver in negotiating humanitarian access. As one aid worker commented: "The UN is seen as biased. It is unable to lead on humanitarian negotiations, side with the humanitarian community and advocate for humanitarian principles in a more robust way because of the political process."[71]

The fact that the United Nations in Somalia was not an integrated mission did help to preserve some distance between the UN technical agencies and the UN Political Office. But from the perspective of humanitarian NGOs, the UN's political stance prevented it from developing a robust humanitarian leadership role, which contributed to the erosion of humanitarian space after 2006.

In response, the United Nations argued that the real problem lay with the warring parties, that the TFG was in no position to impose discipline, and that ideologically motivated groups like al-Shabaab, with a global agenda, were uninterested in dialogue. According to the humanitarian coordinator this prevented the humanitarian community "at the highest levels" from engaging with them on humanitarian principles and humanitarian operations.[72] Thus, in the view of one UN employee, there was less possibility to promote humanitarian principles in Somalia than anywhere in the world.[73]

Establishing agreement on a common set of operational principles among humanitarian agencies has proven to be difficult in Somalia.[74] In the mid-1990s, for example, the SACB drew up a code of conduct that made security for aid agencies a precondition for assistance, but its application was inconsistent. Ground rules were developed to assist with access negotiations during the 1997 floods in Somalia but were rarely applied. After 2006, in response to the escalating crisis, agencies sought to address access constraints by reasserting humanitarian principles and agreements on operational standards. In 2009, the United Nations produced the "IASC Ground Rules: Advisory Note on Practical Considerations for Negotiations" as a step toward shared principles on access negotiations. However, INGOs could only agree to a series of "red lines" beyond which they were not prepared to continue working in the country.

One of the underlying difficulties to achieving a common humanitarian framework was a lack of shared analysis among humanitarian agencies and political actors on the nature of the crisis and what to do about it. This was both a reflection on the operational environment and the different interests and perspectives of humanitarian and political actors and aid agencies themselves on the issue of access. Much analysis was localized, and there was a disjunction among the analyses of operational agencies, Nairobi-based offices, and donor capitals. Even with sophisticated analysis, mapping, and tracking units that exist for Somalia (such as the Food Security and Nutrition Unit), which are among the best in any emergency, it remains hard to gauge the scale of the humanitarian crisis. Without a shared analysis the possibilities of identifying common workable strategies are slim.

Licensing Humanitarian Assistance

One of the most challenging developments for humanitarian agencies in Somalia in this period was the impact of anti-terrorism legislation on humanitarian action. After 9/11, a series of anti-terrorism resolutions in the United Nations and legislation in member states changed the legal context within which aid agencies had operated. For example, since 1992, USAID grantees have had to certify that their monies do not "purposefully or inadvertently" assist entities or individuals deemed to be a risk to national security.[75] When al-Shabaab was designated as a terrorist organization by the US government in March 2008, aid agencies receiving US funding were confronted by the dilemma that food distribution and other assistance in regions controlled by al-Shabaab was illegal.[76] Any individual, including the USAID administrator, could, in theory, be held accountable for assistance that benefited al-Shabaab. This also applied to sub-contracting partners of humanitarian agencies.

In 2009, US humanitarian assistance to Somalia fell foul of the legislation. On the orders of the US Treasury Department's Office of Foreign Assets Control (OFAC), over US$50 million of US humanitarian assistance programmed through USAID and OFDA was suspended out of concern that it might benefit al-Shabaab.[77] The informal taxation and diversion of aid that had been tolerated by donors and aid agencies for years as the "price of doing business" in Somalia suddenly came under scrutiny.

The suspension had the hardest impact on WFP, the largest recipient of US funds, and left a funding gap for the United Nations that threatened to undermine humanitarian relief efforts more broadly.[78] In January 2010, WFP suspended food distributions in much of south central Somalia, citing as its reason threats and attacks on its staff and unacceptable demands by armed groups.[79] Al-Shabaab rejected the claim that WFP left for security reasons or that it had been ordered to leave, asserting that it had simply asked WFP to purchase grains locally. It did subsequently ban WFP and advised its national staff to resign.[80] However, some aid workers were convinced that WFP's suspension was the consequence of a US government strategy to weaken al-Shabaab by withholding food from areas it controlled. As one UN employee commented: "The view among hawks in the [US] administration is that humanitarian assistance is part of the war economy, and if you cut aid you deprive al-Shabaab of income. This is an economic war against al-Shabaab."[81]

The designation of certain parties as terrorists is a political decision and the UN humanitarian coordinator for Somalia pointed out that OFAC regulations politicized humanitarian assistance by restricting the delivery of assistance provided by the US government to populations in areas controlled by its allies.[82]

One reason this became such an issue in Somalia was due to the unique sanctions regime that already existed. One of the first acts of the UN Security Council in response to the war in Somalia was to pass Resolution 733 (1992), which imposed an arms embargo and established a Monitoring Group on Somalia to oversee its implementation. In 2008, the group's mandate was extended by UN Resolution 1844 (2008) to deal with individuals and groups perpetuating the war, by investigating the political economy of armed groups and acts that "obstruct the delivery of humanitarian assistance to Somalia, or access to, or distribution of, humanitarian assistance in Somalia."[83] In March 2010, three months after WFP suspended its operations, the Monitoring Group on Somalia reported to the Security Council that substantial quantities of food aid delivered through a cartel of local contractors had been diverted. One of the contractors was accused of having links to Hizbul Islam, a group fighting the TFG and proscribed by the US government.[84]

In March 2010, UN Security Council Resolution 1916 responded to the report by condemning "the misappropriation and politicization of humanitarian assistance by armed groups in Somalia and called upon all Member States and United Nations units to take all feasible steps to mitigate such practices."[85] It introduced a twelve-month waiver on humanitarian assistance but required the UN humanitarian coordinator in Somalia to report every 120 days on the delivery of humanitarian assistance, to reassure the UN Security Council (UNSC) that it was not being misused or misappropriated or benefiting listed parties; the implication was that if this is not the case, humanitarian assistance could be suspended.

A month later, in April 2010, the US president signed an executive order blocking the assets of parties considered a threat to US interests and introducing sanctions against them. The UN designated al-Shabaab as a threat to peace and security in Somalia and urged member states to establish sanctions against it.[86] Attacks on the TFG and AMISOM were deemed to be an attack on the Djibouti Peace Agreement and the peace process that, according to the United Nations, represented the will of the international community and was "the basis for a resolution of the conflict in Somalia."[87] The British and Canadian governments had already proscribed al-Shabaab in early March 2010, following similar actions by Australia, Norway, and Sweden, and Canada suspended humanitarian assistance to Somalia. Aid agencies became fearful the licensing regime on humanitarian assistance would tighten further if it became subject to the domestic terrorist legislation of other European states.

Impacts of Licensing

Humanitarian agencies reacted differently to the UN resolutions and OFAC restrictions. Some accepted that donor money raised from US taxpayers should not benefit anti-Western groups and negotiated new contracts with USAID. Others declared it was impossible to work with the enhanced due diligence conditions of USAID grants. They chose to assert their independence by not taking US funds, arguing that it was impossible to work in many areas of south central Somalia without negotiating with al-Shabaab and that urgent needs outweighed US concerns over collaboration with proscribed groups.[88]

The new regulations did affect humanitarian access. They reaffirmed WFP's suspension in south central Somalia, which had an impact on other humanitarian actors who relied upon it for supplementary food, UN air services, and the security infrastructure it managed. In the first 120-day report to the Security Council, the humanitarian coordinator[89] noted with concern that the resolution had politicized humanitarian operations and that "confidence in impartiality of humanitarian action has waned because populations where humanitarian aid can be delivered are selected not only according to their needs, but also on the basis of who controls the territory they live in."

The letter also noted that affected populations were being treated unfairly for reasons they did not comprehend and that this "affected the working relationships and trust between the humanitarian organizations and the affected populations."

The impact of the OFAC legislation and UN resolutions on funding was more equivocal. Aid flows to Somalia rose substantially from 2000, reaching a peak in 2008 of US$429 million.[90] In this period Somalia was among the top ten recipients of humanitarian aid and the subject of eight successive CAPs, more than any other country. Although the CAPs were never fully funded and never matched the level of assessed need, this had not been an impediment to access. From 2008, the amount of new funding received through the CAP had begun to decline. By 2011 the United Nations was reporting that Somalia was receiving less humanitarian funding in absolute terms than it was in 2008, which was partly attributed to the global economic crisis and the emergencies in Haiti and Pakistan.

The cut in US funding to WFP did, as noted, have an impact on access. The United States is one of the few high-volume donors to Somalia. An 88 percent cut in humanitarian funding between 2008 and 2010 (from US$237.4 million in 2008 to US$28 million in 2010[91]) affected not only WFP operations but also other agencies that depended on it for air services and security. The "waiver" on humanitarian assistance in UNSC Resolution 1916 was no guarantee against donors applying domestic legislation to humanitarian assistance, so there was a concern that other donor governments would follow the United States and Canada in placing political conditions on humanitarian assistance to Somalia. Although there may not have been a direct link between the UN resolutions and the drop in funding, it was clear that at a time when the number of people in need of humanitarian assistance was increasing, humanitarian funds were diminishing. The first two 120-day reports by the humanitarian coordinator to the UN Security Council therefore expressed concern that a significant decline would affect the aid community's ability to maintain programming proportionate to humanitarian needs.[92]

Anti-terrorism legislation affected other sources of assistance for people in Somalia, including overseas remittances and assistance from Islamic charities.

Remittances from the Somalia diaspora, estimated to be over US$1 billion a year, have been as critical for sustaining livelihoods as humanitarian aid, particularly in times of acute humanitarian stress when the flow of remittances increased. But previous US sanctions against Somali remittance companies, and the possibility that remittances could inadvertently benefit armed groups like al-Shabaab, or be perceived as support for them, had reportedly made Somalis more cautious in remitting money to Somalia.

When WFP suspended its operations, some 3.2 million people were projected to need food aid in 2010. WFP's suspension followed the earlier withdrawal of the US NGO CARE, leaving ICRC as the only agency distributing food aid in south central Somalia, and in much smaller quantities. Better-than-expected harvests in 2010 appeared to offset the loss of food aid in the short term, but a hike in food prices and an increase in children in feeding centers were indicative of a deteriorating situation.[93] At the same time, very little assistance was going into TFG-controlled areas because there were few people living there. By early 2011, following another failure of rains, the numbers of people projected to be in need of food assistance began to rise again. During the famine of 1991–92, malnutrition rates among Somali children were among the highest ever recorded. By early 2011, rates of malnutrition in Somalia were again among the worst in the world, with one in four children in south central Somalia acutely malnourished and one in seventeen severely malnourished.[94] The numbers of Somalis crossing into Kenya to escape the drought was also increasing, an indicator of an escalating emergency. In July 2011, the United Nations declared there was famine in Somalia for the first time in twenty years.

Whether a direct link can be made between the suspension of WFP operations and the famine should be a subject of future inquiry. What is clear is that the famine was preventable. The deterioration in humanitarian access due to the war and the instrumentalization of humanitarian assistance by the warring parties and the international community certainly compromised the ability of humanitarian actors to respond and mitigate it.

Humanitarian Accountability

The misuse, misappropriation, and obstruction of humanitarian aid in Somalia have a well-documented history. In the early 1990s, aid—and the intended beneficiaries of that aid—became resources that were fought over by rival factions, leading to criticisms that humanitarian agencies were fueling a war economy. Two decades later the UN Monitoring Group on Somalia exposed how foreign aid remained entwined with the conflict.[95]

Its investigations concluded that humanitarian assistance had been diverted and used to support armed groups opposed to the TFG.

The group's findings were refuted by the UN humanitarian coordinator in Somalia, who argued that the suspension of US assistance to WFP was politically motivated and would affect the "humanitarian lifeline to central and Southern Somalia at a time when there are increasingly high levels of child malnutrition."[96] While WFP was singled out for investigation, the report raised questions about the entire humanitarian system in Somalia and illustrated how resource capture could also compromise humanitarian space. As one aid worker commented: "For NGOs the arms Monitoring Group [the Monitoring Group was originally established to monitor an arms embargo on Somalia and is still sometimes referred to as that] has broken the shell of presumptive accountability that agencies are operating honestly in Somalia. . . . It is incumbent on us to explain what we are doing."[97]

The UN Security Council chose a soft target when it decided to investigate aid diversion. Since the arms embargo was established in 1992, it has had little or no impact on containing arms flows to Somalia. Suspending humanitarian assistance is easier for member states to do. One aid worker lamented, "Humanitarianism as an abstract concept of compassion is in tatters in Somalia and the monitoring group report is the latest shot at that."[98] While aid agencies will need to improve on their monitoring and management of aid, the UN Security Council and member states will also need to reflect on the impact they have had on humanitarian action in Somalia.

The "shot" may have had two positive outcomes, however. First, agencies responded to the criticisms by putting in place new mechanisms to monitor assistance and improve upward and downward accountability and to be more transparent in their ways of working.[99] OCHA also commissioned an evaluation of humanitarian assistance to south central Somalia between 2005 and 2010. Second, the requirement of the humanitarian coordinator to report every 120 days meant that the UN Security Council could be regularly kept abreast of the humanitarian needs in Somalia.[100]

Conclusions

The return of famine to Somalia in 2011 attests not only to the culpable failures of internal governance, but also to the failure of the system of international governance and politics. For two decades international policy in Somalia has revolved around the provision of humanitarian assistance to meet recurrent humanitarian need and establishing a viable government to restore internal order and address international security concerns.

These objectives have often been in contradiction to each other. Having failed to restore a government in the early 1990s, international interest in Somalia was revived after the 9/11 attacks, when as a "collapsed state" it was considered a regional and international security threat. The restoration of a Somali government became part of a counterterrorism strategy, rather than a way to deal with the root causes of state collapse and conflict in Somalia. In defending the TFG and the peace agreement that created it, the UN and donor governments became belligerents in a war that created a severe humanitarian crisis. The neutrality of humanitarian agencies was compromised as humanitarian assistance was used to further political and security agendas. And, as humanitarian needs inexorably rose, humanitarian agencies experienced a decline in humanitarian access.

In response to diminishing humanitarian space, the UN and INGOs sought to reaffirm the principles that underlie their work, establishing common operating procedures and advocating for the clear separation of humanitarian operations and political strategies. They also sounded early warnings on the dire consequences of prioritizing international security and state-building over civilian protection and the delivery of humanitarian assistance. Failure to heed those warnings, coupled with the suspension of food aid on the grounds that it might benefit the "enemy" at a time when 3.2 million Somalis were in need of assistance, contributed to the famine that developed in 2011.

By coopting humanitarian assistance in support of political security agendas, the United Nations and donor governments in Somalia lost sight of the principles that guide humanitarian assistance and donor engagement with fragile states. Having signed up to them, they appeared unable to recognize the harm their policies were doing. Ultimately, the causes of famine in Somalia in 2011 remain the same as those that produced famine twenty years earlier, in 1992: they are political. Preventing another famine will require an approach to state-building that addresses the causes of prolonged state collapse in Somalia. But it needs to be one that also preserves space for humanitarian action when state-building fails.

Table 6–1. How Aid Has Been Instrumentalized in Somalia

Period and Key Features	Policy Context	Key Actors	Examples of the Instrumentalization of Aid
1977–1990 Siyad Barre dictatorship. Ogaden war produces long-term refugee population in Somalia.	Cold War The West and the Soviet Union vie for influence in the Horn of Africa.	Foreign donors	Foreign donors overlooked the Somali government's manipulation of aid.
		Somali government	Refugee counts were manipulated to attract more aid.
		Aid organizations	NGOs were complicit in aid diversion by the government and silent about government human rights abuses in order to remain in Somalia.
1991–1995 State collapse results in civil war, famine, warlords, and "military humanitarianism." US-led UN-authorized armed, humanitarian intervention and peace-keeping.	Post–Cold War In a "new world order," the primacy of state sovereignty was eroded and global institutions were prepared to intervene in the affairs of states. The US, as the sole superpower, leads the allied forces to liberate Kuwait from Iraq, then projects itself in the role of global policeman in Somalia leading the UN humanitarian and peacekeeping mission (UNOSOM).	Warlords, military factions, clan-based authorities	Armed factions multiplied to gain seats in political negotiations. They enrich themselves through aid diversion and act as "gatekeepers" of aid.
		Foreign donors	Donors were embarrassed by media coverage and domestic pressure into responding to the "poor man's" war in Africa; humanitarian assistance became a substitute for political engagement.
		United Nations	Aid was used as an incentive to draw factions into political talks.
		International NGOs	International NGOs flooded into the country as part of an expanding privatized non-governmental humanitarian system. Some lobbied for military intervention to protect humanitarian space and allow safe aid delivery. Aid money spent on armed protection fueled a war economy and helped shore up the power structures of the warring factions.
		Somali NGOs	Local NGOs multiplied overnight in the absence of government and in response to the massive infusion of international aid.
		Somali businesses	Somali entrepreneurs profited from the economy of plunder and aid.

(continues)

Table 6–1 (continued)

1995–1999	International disengagement	Foreign donors	EC, the largest donor and chair of SACB, exerted influence on aid policy. Aid was tied to compliance with the SACB "code of conduct" on security and development, which meant that some regions experienced sanctions on aid.
Diminishing conflict and incremental recovery in parts of the country, chronic and perennial emergency in other areas.	Overall assistance declined and switched from "relief" to "development," and from external intervention to support for "local solutions to local problems."		
High levels of humanitarian distress were treated as "normal" to Somalia.	Relief-to-development and "peace dividend" approaches made the provision of aid conditional on security and good governance.	United Nations	The country is graded along a continuum from "zones of crisis" to zones of "transition" and "recovery." Aid was used to support communities to transition from crisis to recover and development through a "peace dividends." "Local solutions" were encouraged through cost-recovery.
Decline in international humanitarian response capacity and preparedness.		Warlords, factions, and clan-based authorities	Continued to act as gatekeepers for aid agencies and extract revenue through various forms of taxation on aid.
		International NGOs	With the security infrastructure provided by UNOSOM dismantled and fewer funds, many NGOs ended their operations or relocated to Kenya.
2000–2005	"Failed states," "ungoverned spaces," and the post-9/11 GWOT drive policy.	Foreign donors	International security concerns drive policy in Somalia. Aid was directed toward supporting the capacity building of the TNG and TFG. Donors set "good governance" bench marks but fail to enforce them.
International re-engagement			
Revived conflict over control of the state.	Counterterrorism objectives linked to state-building and development.	Regional governments	Internationally sponsored IGAD-led peace process results in Transitional Federal Government (TFG), which has little legitimacy or support inside Somalia.
The influence of Islamist groups was growing and viewed as a greater threat than warlords.		United Nations	UNDP takes a lead in supporting state-building with the TNG and TFG by formulating a reconstruction and development plan. UNDP benefited from increase in donor funding, but was criticized for management of aid to the TNG and TFG.
International community take sides again.		TNG/TFG	Once established, the governments assumed a gatekeeper role over foreign aid.
		Somali NGOs	NGOs seek legitimacy as "civil society" organizations and compete for seats in the peace talks.

2006–2011		Foreign donors	Global war on terror gained priority over humanitarian principles, human rights and international law. Donor assistance provided virtually unconditionally to the TFG to strengthen its capacity and legitimacy, with little condemnation of its behavior. Pressed NGOs to do the same.
Renewed international military engagement, to counter terrorism, in support of the TFG and against growing the influence of militant Islamists and piracy.	State-building, accountable governance, development, and counterterrorism strategies linked.		Legislation and sanctions is used against individuals and parties listed as terrorists.
	Deployment of an African peace-keeping force (AMISOM) to protect transitional institutions.		Legislation and sanctions is used to regulate humanitarian assistance.
The worst fighting since 1990 leads to high numbers of civilian deaths, massive internal displacement, diminished humanitarian access, and famine.	Integrated mission promoted by the UN to improve coherence and efficiency.	Regional governments	Ethiopian intervenes militarily to protect its own security interests. Eritrea supports militant Islamist factions against Ethiopia. Kenya closes its border to refugees fleeing the conflict. Uganda uses its role as head of AMISOM to overcome international criticisms of its own domestic politics.
	Mid-2010 international policy changed from a single to "dual track" approach to security and state-building.	United Nations	UN attempts to incorporate humanitarian assistance into political strategies in support of the TFG.
		International NGOs	Under pressure to seize the "window of opportunity" and respond to humanitarian and development needs. Remote management adopted in response to security threats.
		TFG	TFG attempts to impose controls on aid accusing displaced of being "terrorists" and NGOs of "aiding the enemy." Revenue is raised through various forms of taxation on aid, at check-points and though visas, etc.
		Al-Shabaab	Aid workers are targeted. Various forms of taxation are imposed on aid. Businesses associated with Islamists are accused of diverting aid to pay militia. Foreign aid to communities under their control is blocked by expelling aid agencies.

Chapter 7

Palestine:
Sixty Years of Instrumentalization

*A Conversation With Peter Hansen,
Former Commissioner-General of UNRWA*

Diana Buttu

In December 1947, following the UN's resolution to partition Palestine just a few weeks earlier, Zionist forces began their campaign to expel Palestinians from their homeland. Within a month of the passage of the UN partition resolution, the first Palestinian village was wiped out, followed by a full operation to drive Palestinians from their homes. By March 1948, more than seventy thousand Palestinians had left Palestine, seeking refuge in the neighboring countries of Lebanon, Syria, and Jordan. By May 1948, that number rose to one-third of the Palestinian population and by the end of hostilities in 1949, Zionist forces had expelled three-quarters of a million Palestinians (amounting to 75 percent of the Palestinian population), turning them into refugees.

Facing an unprecedented refugee crisis, the international community was at a loss as to how to provide relief; there was no UN body in existence at the time that was capable of providing assistance to the floods of refugees leaving Palestine for safety. By the winter of 1948, international charity organizations and the Red Cross stepped in to provide humanitarian assistance, including shelter in the form of tents, food, and medical aid. Armed with the UN General Assembly's Resolution 194 (1948) enshrining the right of Palestinian refugees to return to their homes, Palestinian refugees—and likely the international community—believed that the Palestinian refugee crisis would soon be over. Despite resolutions by the international community, however, the Palestinian refugee crisis continued, and the UN stepped in to provide relief.

That relief came in the form of the United Nations Relief and Works Agency for Palestine Refugees (UNRWA) established pursuant to UN General Assembly Resolution 302 (IV) of December 8, 1949. UNRWA's mandate was to carry out direct relief and works programs to "prevent the conditions of starvation and distress among [Palestine refugees] and to further conditions of peace and stability." UNRWA became operational on May 1, 1950, when it began responding to the humanitarian needs of an estimated 800,000 Palestinian refugees. Originally envisaged as a temporary organization, UNRWA has gradually adjusted its initiatives to meet the changing needs of Palestinian refugees. A year following the launch of its operations, UNRWA published its first publication, *From Camps to Homes,* describing the challenges faced by the agency:

> Three years ago, the Palestinian conflict forced into exile just under a million Arabs from the region which has become Israel. They were completely destitute. They lived as best they could in unorganized and insanitary camps, or under trees in makeshift shelters, under bridges, in caves or, sometime, just in the holes they dug in the ground. . . .
>
> They were saved from starvation by the United Nations International Children's Emergency Fund (UNICEF) and the United Nations Relief for Palestine Refugees with the assistance of the Red Cross Societies and the American Society of Friends. (1)

By 1951, with no political solution in sight, the UNRWA began advocating for new programs to assist the growing refugee population:

> The Agency provides supplies and services for a population equivalent to that of Washington DC, or Brussels. This population is scattered over 100,000 square miles in five different countries. UNRWA distributes 11,000 tons of food each month. But relief alone leads nowhere. It is demoralizing and wasteful at a time when the Arab states have their own social problems. A rising standard of living demands economic development, labour and technicians. The refugees can play a part far from being a burden they can become an asset. (10–11)

Today, the agency has grown to be among the largest UN programs, with nearly five million Palestinian refugees under its mandate and with thirty thousand staff members serving as the main provider of basic (and in Lebanon, secondary) education, comprehensive primary health care, emergency relief and social interventions, microfinance, housing, and infrastructural support in the areas of its operation—the occupied Palestinian territory,

Jordan, Syria, and Lebanon. UNRWA remains unique among UN agencies in its long-standing support to four generations of Palestinian refugees. It is also the only UN organization dedicated to a specific geographical population in need.

With the signing of the Oslo Accords in 1993 between Israel and the Palestine Liberation Organization (PLO), many questions were soon raised about the future of UNRWA and its relationship to the newly formed Palestinian Authority (PA) and the host countries of the refugee population. The negotiations that commenced under the Oslo Accords deferred for "final status" negotiations a number of vague, yet broad, topics including the issue of "refugees" and their future. For each of the two sides the ultimate outcome of such negotiations had very different meanings, particularly for the fate of millions of Palestinian refugees. For Palestinians, the negotiations would result in the return of refugees to their homes in Israel after decades of languishing in camps. For Israel, however, Palestinian refugees would need to give up their right to return and resettle instead in other countries and with that, UNRWA would be dismantled in order to put a definitive end to the phenomenon of Palestinian refugees.

At the same time the PA, owing to its unique status as a government in an occupied territory, had little ability to set policies that would influence economic growth and development. Rather, from its inception and to the modern day, the PA remains largely dependent upon foreign assistance to operate. External actors who, at times, exert great influence over the programs, direction, and composition of the PA government provide an estimated 50 percent of the PA's operating budget. The establishment of the PA and the concomitant international mechanisms designed to coordinate and facilitate international assistance also had significant financial implications for UNRWA and consequently for the provision of essential humanitarian services.

It is in this trying and difficult period that Peter Hansen served as UNRWA's commissioner-general. Beginning his career with the United Nations in 1978 as assistant secretary general for Programme Planning and Coordination, Hansen, from 1985 to 1992, served as assistant secretary-general and executive director of the United Nations Centre on Transnational Corporations. In March 1994, he took over the post of Undersecretary-General for Humanitarian Affairs and Emergency Relief Coordinator.

From his appointment in 1996 to 2005, Hansen was the longest-serving UNRWA commissioner-general, with others serving, on average, four years. He was, by his own admission, the most controversial, owing in large part to his vocal criticism of Israel's actions against Palestinian refugees and his questioning of the neutrality and independence of humanitarian assistance as provided by governments through UNRWA. In 2005, Hansen's offer to remain commissioner-general was rejected by UNRWA's single largest do-nor—the United States—following an aggressive Congressional campaign for his removal.

Witnessing the international euphoria surrounding the start of nego-tiations and the formation of the PA through to the collapse of the peace process followed by the start of the Palestinian *intifada* in September 2000 and the extreme violence that ensued, Hansen reflects upon the impact of these changing political circumstances on UNRWA's operations and the wider meaning of the experience.

Q: In addition to being the longest-serving commissioner-general in UNRWA's history, you served UNRWA during a very interesting and politically volatile period. During this period, did you see a change in the nature of the humanitarian assistance provided to the Palestinians?

Humanitarian assistance should always be conceived and delivered in full cognizance of the political framework within which it functions. But during this period clearly the political framework changed so much and so quickly that the functions of UNRWA and the role of UNRWA changed with it. The first change in political context came in the warm afterglow of the signing of the Oslo Agreements when it was assumed that UNRWA was supposed to be phasing itself out and handing over all its functions and responsibilities to the soon-to-be sovereign PA. Very early on—before taking the office of commissioner-general—during one of our many conversations, I asked President Arafat, with the prospect of an agreement and negotiations coming to a conclusion in the late 1990s, when we could think of winding down UNRWA. He said that we could *begin* talking about the winding down of UNRWA ten years after the signing of an agreement and not be-fore. So, the PA was unlike all the other parties that were looking forward to the winding down of UNRWA but rather wanted UNRWA to continue to operate and stay. My understanding of this reasoning was because the PA saw UNRWA not just as a provider of medical care, food, education, and so on, but as a manifestation of the international community's com-mitment to the solution of the refugee problem. President Arafat thought that achieving a solution might not be as easy or mechanical as the optimists may have believed it to be when Oslo was first signed. This different take between how the PA looked at this issue and how the donors looked at it shows you the different expectations of what was the role of UNRWA, or, if one uses the instrumentalization metaphor, how differently the various parties instrumentalized UNRWA.

The donors came with different demands of what UNRWA "should be," even though the mandate did not encompass all of their demands. The donors, created, as it were, the images of how they wanted to see UNRWA, and these images were not always based in the political reality in which we were operating.

Q: With this political framework in mind, were the programs of UNRWA in any way adapted to meet the demands and expectations of the donors?

It is difficult to speak of the donors as a monolithic group. The donors come to this issue with very different perspectives, ranging from, for example, the United States that has stood shoulder to shoulder with Israel and its positions and, at the other end, Sweden, which has taken the issue of Palestinian refugees as a strong humanitarian and political commitment in the best traditions of Swedish neutralism and activism. Donors, accordingly, had very different perspectives and different wishes as to what should happen in the future. For some, UNRWA was a sort of magic cover to place over the Palestinian refugee problem implying that the nonexistence of UNRWA would make the Palestinian refugee problem go away. These individuals and groups wanted to see the winding down of UNRWA as soon as possible because that would mean somehow that the refugee problem could be seen to be "solved" or a "question of the past." Others looked at UNRWA as an emanation of the international community's understanding of, and responsibility for, the fate of the refugees and did not want to do anything that would prematurely put UNRWA out of existence. In between these two, there were different shades of donors' perspectives, with some hiding under and succumbing to the pressures of the some of the more extreme donors.

Q: During this period, did the agency face pressure to change its mandate? Specifically, there was a debate surrounding the issue of UNRWA and its protection of Palestine refugees. Did the role of UNRWA change? And, if it did change, how did UNRWA change?

Yes, the role did change. The discussion about protection is a confused one because the term *protection* can mean different things. Some of those who were looking for a protection mandate pointed to the UNHCR's protection mandate as an example to show that refugees that came under the ambit of the UNHCR were afforded protection. But this was a protection mandate that is irrelevant to the Palestinian refugee situation, which is, in most respects, very different from those issues that UNHCR deals with by way of protection of rights of non-*refoulement* of refugees. When Palestinians speak of protection, and this was particularly during the second *intifada*,[1] they were looking for protection from Israeli violence against them and not the type of wishy-washy consular protection that is afforded under international diplomatic law. There, the Palestinians wanted, as I heard them mention many times, *physical protection* from Israel, and this was something that simply wasn't on the cards, as no international agency would ever have been willing or able to step in, for all sorts political reasons, most of all the Israeli and American determination that this was never going to happen. But, when you speak of physical protection, this may not mean simply putting counter violence to Israeli violence; it could mean being present in ways where the agency would bear witness to what happened. This is a significant step for a humanitarian agency.

In the first *intifada*, before my time, there was a very weak provision in a Security Council resolution that the agency should observe what was going on with a view to seeing how Palestinian rights could be protected. This is the first and only wisp of a protection mandate in UNRWA. This was later used to establish the refugee affairs officer function in UNRWA and as a way of inserting a protection function without a clear mandate. Then, during the outbreak of the second *intifada*—which was a different type of confrontation between Palestinians and Israelis—I took the initiative to establish a follow-up institution to the refugee affairs officer now called *refugee protection officers*. Whereas the refugee affairs officers very often could go out or be present when the Israelis were committing acts of violence against unarmed Palestinians and interpose—and they did this often and effectively—the new institution could not, because the much higher level of armed violence on both sides in the second *intifada* put its staff in the line of fire and counter fire. The protection officers still went out with great courage and effectively ameliorated situations where they could. The donors as a group never called for protection and among the donors, some—such as Sweden and Norway—were willing to support such a program. The Americans, ironically, became interested in these special refugee officers because they saw them as a means by which they could appease Israel's supporters in Congress by making sure that they would observe that the Palestinians were not doing all of the things that they were accused of doing! So the picture of protection and how we were using it was a muddy and complex one. It was intended to serve as a mechanism to protect Palestinians, but some donors saw it as a way for them to exercise control over the refugee camps or the UNRWA institutions. For example, if there were graffiti on an UNRWA school, it became the task of the refugee protection officer to hinder that, in the US perspective. Yet for other donors, it was supposed to be a mechanism to protect Palestinian refugees.

Q: In addition to the basic changes taking place politically, did the provision of aid change? For example, was the assistance now conditional or were there demands that the funds be channeled to the PA?

In order to assess the concept of instrumentalization, it is important to examine UNRWA's resources in a historical perspective. When UNRWA started, 97 percent of its resources were for immediate, emergency relief—food, tents, and so on. UNRWA then was a classical emergency humanitarian aid agency. It morphed over the years so that the relief budget of UNRWA, which is basically for hardship cases, went down to 5–10 percent of the overall budget, whereas 70 percent of the overall budget was now directed for education and the health budget. UNRWA morphed from a classical emergency humanitarian relief organization into what really had become in terms of its program expenditures a human development organization. But you could not say that too loudly because neither the donors nor the Palestinians were interested in seeing UNRWA as a development organization because that would mean, politically speaking, that you were working on the unspoken premise that UNRWA was no longer a refugee organization. Donors felt they needed to have a special humanitarian dimension to support UNRWA to keep its appearance properly depoliticized. This was a type of false labeling, so to speak, which had to do with the fact that the different parties wanted to see the agency and its activities doing or representing different things. For the Palestinians, they wanted to see UNRWA as a political organization giving international legitimacy to the Palestinian refugee cause, whereas the donors wanted a humanitarian flavor to be seen as doing "something" for the refugees.

At the same time, the PA was always in need of resources, and we offered to scale down UNRWA's programs and to transfer resources and installations to the PA.[2] The PA opposed this vehemently, first because they understood the quality of services that were being provided and did not want to impact negatively on those services. The PA also opposed it because they did not want the refugee situation to be seen as having lost its standing as a basic international issue and reduced to an issue between the two parties. Some of the donors, however, took the opposite view and wanted to see all of UNRWA's funds transferred away from UNRWA to the PA for the very same reason.[3]

Q: Was humanitarian assistance used or abused by the various actors, such as UNRWA's donors, the various Palestinian political factions, the host countries, or the Israeli government?

Not in the classical sense, but in a different manner. While I cannot make statements generalizing all of the donors, for the most part they overwhelmingly sought to depoliticize the issue of Palestinian refugees because they did not want to face the fact that the Palestinian refugee issue and the issue of Palestine was a political one. A political issue can only have a political solution and the donors did not want to face this fact or address it as such. Even after the start of the Oslo negotiations, there was an evasiveness surrounding the final status issues on the table—Jerusalem, refugees, borders, and so on—and especially as regards the refugees. The donors were happy dealing with the refugee issue as a humanitarian issue because they could continue to use UNRWA as a band-aid to show that something was being done for the refugees. But nothing was done to face the fact that a political issue, such as that of the refugees, required a political solution. Applying humanitarian solutions was a make-believe act that might have deceived some (though not many Palestinians) and bought some feeling of good conscience in the donor community.

Donors did not want UNRWA to speak out and put the political issue on the table. Rather, they wanted to keep it as a pure humanitarian mission, ignoring the political causes and the need for political solutions. For example, with the exception of its creation, all of UNRWA's transitions—whether the movement was away from tents to cinder-block buildings, from emergency relief to education, or from emergency health to primary and secondary health—were driven not by any particular mandate change but by UNRWA's ability to adapt to the changing needs of the refugees and the willingness of donors to continue to serve these needs as long as they were not politicized or focused on the right of return or any other political message that would create difficulties in their relationship with Israel over the years. Moreover, there was the perception among many Palestinians that UNRWA served Israeli and US interests by keeping conditions for Palestinian refugees just barely tolerable so as to avoid the situation from exploding further.

In addition, some of the host countries also politicized UNRWA. Syria played a role in attempting to politicize UNRWA, as did Lebanon; but as far as the donors were concerned, UNRWA was not to be politicized but to remain humanitarian. Palestinians wanted to—and continue to want to—make the connection between UN Resolution 194 [enshrining the right of return] and UNRWA, but this was strongly resisted at every turn by the donor community.

In addition to the donors, the host countries also instrumentalized UNRWA in their own way. For example, Syria, early on in my tenure, took the position that UNRWA was not an international institution and therefore indicated that UNRWA was not entitled to the special exchange rate for the funds that go into its account, with the resulting effect that Syria skimmed about half the value of donor funding into Syrian coffers. It viewed UNRWA as a cash cow, and while we put an end to this, it was an example of instrumentalization.

In Lebanon the refugees up until recently have had a difficult time with the Lebanese authorities, who did not treat them well. Similarly in Jordan, the government has always demonstrated tension in terms of how to view

UNRWA's role with the refugees and with the Jordan First program that the Jordanian government unveiled during my tenure. Different people need to give different meaning to the activity they undertake in a humanitarian context, and often it has little to do with impartiality and neutrality and independence. Apart from a few countries—Sweden, Luxembourg, and Norway—that protect these principles, many countries have used unrelated agencies as tools for their own political purposes. In the case of Palestine, for the most part, it is a case of instrumentalization in the extreme.

Q: What methods were used by the donors? Specifically post-negotiations, when it became clear that UNRWA was not winding itself down, did the donors follow a different path?

Each of the donors behaved differently. For example, for Sweden and Norway, the late 1990s and early 2000s was the time of financial crisis, and in Sweden the government cut down on a number of domestic social programs. At the same time, they kept up their commitments, and increased them to UNRWA, and never put any conditions on the aid that they gave. They put their full trust in the agency and simply asked that we continue to provide quality services. At the other end, the United States took advantage of these years to follow up with various political campaigns against UNRWA. One campaign, which I refer to as the so-called textbook issue, attempted to erroneously show that Palestinian textbooks promoted violence. I use the term *so-called issue* because it was no issue at all; Israel had used the *exact same* textbooks, and the Palestinian textbooks were not at all offensive. To the contrary, as George Washington University Professor Nathan Brown has pointed out in his writings, Palestinians were extremely cautious and took great care not to offend or step on any sensitive issues. But, the Americans—and here, I cannot use this term to generalize, as there were various American actors, such as the State Department, who were more empathetic—had to respond to Congress and pursue many of these spurious claims against UNRWA. This was done to twist UNRWA in ways to ensure that UNRWA was hostage to whatever accusations you could make against it. Another campaign surrounded the continued Israeli breaches of the word and spirit of the Geneva Conventions. When I raised these breaches, I was hushed up as being "unhelpful" to the peace process. In other words, I was expected to ignore the broader political context in which UNRWA was operating.

That said, other donors had different views. For example, I was invited as the first non-state party to the 1999 conference in Geneva on the Geneva Conventions to look at the issues that were raised in the Middle East. The US boycotted the meeting, and Canada also took a hard-line stance. It was clear that the purpose of the meeting was not to be too specific about the violations of the Conventions but to take note of the issue, in the mildest possible form, without any hint of actual breaches of obligations, and to kindly draw attention to the need to respect the Conventions.

Responding to these fires ironically helped define the UNRWA's mandate and direct it also towards Palestinian rights and not simply focus on providing services. It must be kept in mind that UNRWA's mandate, as set out in the embodying UN resolution, is virtually nonexistent. It is a mere three lines that set out that the agency should provide relief provided that there are resources to do so. There is nothing in the mandate that defines what the organization should do and how its programs should be composed. Rather, this is a matter that is discussed every year in light of UNRWA's own proposals. UNRWA is a major program of the General Assembly like UNDP, UNHCR, and UNICEF. However, unlike these three other programs, which all have elaborate constitutions that define their purpose, their objectives, and means of action, UNRWA has nothing. This means that it is left up to UNRWA to improvise through the various pressures, crises, and agreements that it has with donors and host countries in order to keep the organization going.

Q: Did the commissioner-general play a role in defining the mandate?

As time passed, it became obvious that this was not a short-term humanitarian emergency crisis. Early commissioners-general could put their head in the sand and hold firm to the belief that the Palestinian refugee crisis would be resolved, and each of them left after three years. It became a dilemma during my time, and to some of my predecessors, to realize that we were in a protracted political situation with negotiations that turned into a series of protracted violent confrontations. In these circumstances, UNRWA could not just ignore this situation by focusing on sacks of wheat flour or the number of students in the classroom and so on. But on the other hand, as I was repeatedly reminded, there was no political mandate for UNRWA. The General Assembly gave the political mandate to the UN Conciliation Commission for Palestine, and this mandate was never exercised. Accordingly, there was a vacuum that UNRWA could not constitutionally fill. But I felt that there was a context to the needs of a people who had been robbed of all dignity, hope, and recognition, and that this needed to be understood by all parties. This is because the needs of Palestinians—if we were going to address their needs—had to do not only with food, health care, or education but were at least as much centered on the recognition of their dignity, their fate, and the injustices they had suffered. Unfortunately, the international community was not particularly interested in confronting those who needed to be confronted during the period of negotiations.

Q: Could you ignore the political situation?

UNRWA was repeatedly told to lie low, organize the delivery trucks, the food distribution, forget about the real situation on the ground, and leave the rest to the "parties" to negotiate. But, when thirteen UNRWA staff members were murdered and 220 schoolchildren that attended UNRWA schools were killed and other children maimed by the Israeli army, I could not simply shrug my shoulders and say "stuff happens." I was assured that the killings would be investigated, but no one was ever held responsible for any of breaches of the Conventions or the breaches of the agreements under which a UN agency is supposed to operate.

Q: How do you think things are now regarding instrumentalization?

I don't often find reason to rejoice in things moving forward or getting better. I no longer feel constrained to put on as optimistic a face as I had to when I was representing a UN agency. I've become increasingly pessimistic about where things are now and the lack of movement and prospect to see the process moving towards any solution offering hope of justice and peace for both parties.

Public opinion is shifting in Europe, and perhaps in the United States too, which means that perhaps the Palestinians will hopefully receive a more fair and balanced approach to how the international community deals with their political and humanitarian plight. I hope that the international community can move forward and have the strength to take the necessary steps to put forward solutions that are based in justice and international law. The pace that public opinion is moving at is glacial, and I am afraid that it will take longer than we can afford if we are to reach a peaceful solution.

Chapter 8

Politics, Rhetoric, and Practice of Humanitarian Action in Pakistan

MARION PÉCHAYRE

> *Furious aid workers say the CIA's reckless use of aid work as a cover by spy agencies has threatened the safety of genuine aid workers and endangered multimillion-pound programmes to help Pakistan's poor.[1]*
>
> —DECLAN WALSH, THE GUARDIAN,
> SEPTEMBER 28, 2011

Since the early 1980s, Pakistan has played a key geo-strategic role in international politics. It has served as a proxy for the United States' fight against communism during the Soviet invasion of Afghanistan in the 1980s. It was subjected to economic sanctions by the United States during the 1990s because of its program to develop nuclear capacity. And Pakistan was again mobilized as a strategic ally by the United States immediately after 9/11 to assist in the GWOT. It has also been accused of being too close to the Afghan Taliban movement[2] and the Haqqani network,[3] leading to significant tensions between Islamabad and Washington in the latter part of 2011 and beyond.

This chapter draws on the briefing paper *Humanitarian Action in Pakistan 2005–2010: Challenges, Principles, and Politics* by Marion Péchayre, published by the Feinstein International Center in January 2011 (available on the fic.tufts.edu website).

Since 2004, Pakistan has additionally been at war with home grown militants. Attitudes and activities by both sets of warring parties reached a turning point in 2007 when a wave of attacks escalated across the country after a government crackdown on militants who had taken over the Red Mosque in the heart of Islamabad. The increase in acts of terrorism was phenomenal, with attacks growing by 43 percent in 2008 and 48 percent in 2009.[4] Pakistani citizens in the Federally Administered Tribal Areas (FATA) and Khyber Pakhtunkhwa[5] (KPK) have since been living with the threat of attacks by militant groups, fighting between Pakistani military and militants, US drone attacks, extrajudicial killings by Pakistani military and militants, as well as sectarian violence.[6]

At a time when the US Senate declared it wanted "strengthened restrictions on assistance for Pakistan by conditioning all funds to the government of Pakistan (GoP) on co-operation against the Haqqani network, al Qaeda and other terrorist organizations,"[7] it is important to examine the form, role, and consequences of the use of humanitarian action for purposes other than assistance to crisis-affected people. In other words, what are the nature and consequences of "instrumentalization" in the context of humanitarian action in Pakistan?

Taking a short historical perspective, this chapter examines major events shaping humanitarian action in Pakistan commencing with the Afghan refugee situation in the 1980s, the 2005 earthquake, a dramatic upsurge in fighting that began in 2008 between the Pakistani military and militants, and the 2010 floods. For each of these crises, I examine how aid has been instrumentalized, by whom, and with what consequences. Examples of instrumentalization, specific to different crisis events, are presented in Table 8–1 at the end of the chapter.

A Complex Environment

A useful starting point for a review of instrumentalization in Pakistan is the country's dominant narrative on existential threats to its territorial integrity, the ubiquitous role of the military, poor socioeconomic indicators, and years of fraught relations with its neighbors and major Western backers.

Concerns about threats to Pakistan's territorial integrity have been engrained since independence in 1947, as disputes emerged with India over Jammu and Kashmir,[8] and with Baloch nationalists over the province of Baluchistan in the first year of the state's existence. These disputes remain unresolved. The Afghan-Pakistani border brought its lot of contentious history as the "Durand line" imposed in 1893 by the government of colonial British India on Afghan Amir Abdur Rahman Khan has never been officially recognized by Afghanistan, and certainly not by the Pashtuns, whose nation was effectively cut in half by this border. Pakistan's sense of nationhood has also been shaped by its defeat in its war with India in 1971 and the loss of East Pakistan (where a Bengali majority was ruled by western Pakistan elites), which resulted in the emergence of the independent state of Bangladesh.

Pakistani state formation and the country's psyche have been very much shaped by the ubiquitous role of the military and security apparatus. Since the country's first constitution in 1956, there have been three military coups. Pakistani generals have governed directly for more than half of the country's history. Even Zulfikar Ali Bhutto, who was a declared social democrat and was elected in 1971 as the country's president after fourteen years of military dictatorship, was obsessed by India's nuclear progress and famously said: "If India builds the Bomb, we will eat grass or leaves, even go hungry, but we will get one of our own."[9] This set the trajectory of the Pakistani nation, which prioritized its nuclear capabilities over many pressing needs. Today, the country has the fastest-growing nuclear arsenal in the world and will soon be the fifth biggest nuclear power.[10] With 617,000 active personnel in a country of some 180 million, the Pakistan Armed Force is the seventh largest in the world. While the 1973 constitution clearly affirms the primacy of the democratically elected civilian government over the country's armed forces, in practice the military establishment exercises considerable influence over major national policy decisions and their implementation. Whether the dominant role of the military in a wide range of economic and other activities, including relief, reconstruction, and development work, is the result of an incompetent or poorly developed political and bureaucratic system, or whether it can be attributed to the self-interested leverage constructed by the military, remains an open debate.

Pakistan has experienced a constant increase in its per capita income over the past decade, but indicators such as infant mortality and literacy remain among the worst in the world; only 2 percent[11] of Pakistan's GDP is spent on public health.[12]

Pakistan does not have a long tradition of working with international humanitarian partners outside its role as host to millions of Afghan refugees who first arrived in the early1980s. However, between 2005 and 2010 Pakistan experienced three major crises affecting millions of people. The nature and scale of these catastrophic events were different. The crises included the 2005 earthquake, which affected 3.5 million people and resulted in the loss of 73,338 lives,[13] and the 2010 floods, which affected more than 18 million people. An upsurge in fighting during the 2008–10 period resulted in an "IDP crisis" involving some 4.2 million people[14] from the KPK and FATA. An estimated 35,000 people[15] were killed between 2004 and 2010 as a result of armed clashes, drone attacks, and extrajudicial killings.

Afghan Refugees in the 1980s:
A Tool of Cold War Politics

Although Pakistan was not a signatory to the 1951 Convention relating to the Status of Refugees, beginning in the 1980s the country was host to millions of Afghan refugees. ICRC, numerous NGOs, and UN humanitarian organizations provided assistance, while Pakistani authorities maintained tight control over the overall relief system (see Chapter 4). As noted by Fiona Terry, "Aid [played] a complementary, though in no way determinant, role in the conflict."[16] Terry also documents how the GoP and Afghan opposition political parties based in Peshawar benefited greatly from the legitimacy that flowed from international humanitarian action. General Zia-ul-Haq, notorious for his use of Islam to tighten his hold on power, was determined that Pakistan have an Islamic ally on its Western border in order to counter or diminish the influence of India. Support to refugees operated in concert with the support given to military training camps for the Afghan resistance. The anti-Soviet *jihad* helped justify the state of emergency, which allowed Zia to ban internal political opposition. At the same time, Pakistan's public image improved significantly, and Pakistan benefited from an important US financial package.[17]

Pakistani authorities introduced systems that favored the legitimacy of Afghan political opposition parties settled in Peshawar; all refugees had to be politically affiliated with one of these parties to have an identity card and therefore be entitled to registration as a refugee and to receive assistance. Since international financial support to Afghan political parties was proportional to the representation they claimed, refugees were instrumental for these parties to gain influence and accumulate resources. "With military means, General Zia and the Peshawar-based political parties were empowered, and with humanitarian means they were legitimized."[18] Without question, humanitarian agencies were part of an instrumentalized system that helped set the scene for future humanitarian activities in Pakistan. At the same time, relief agencies were happy to benefit from the political dividends associated with the Afghan refugee situation, as most of them fully supported the anti-communist agenda as a "just cause."

2005 Earthquake:
Humanitarians Hand in Hand With the Military

International humanitarian agencies that had worked with Afghan refugees had a history of working closely with Pakistani authorities and had little inclination to do otherwise in the aftermath of the 2005 earthquake. Such collaboration is widely seen to have benefited the earthquake response and thus the affected population.

Until 2005, the experience of most aid agencies in Pakistan was limited to Afghan refugees or dedicated to development work. Most Pakistani NGOs were created in the 1980s and the 1990s and were development organizations working at grass-roots level, mainly on structural, social, economic, and health issues.[19] When the 2005 earthquake struck, regardless of their previous expertise, organizations working in Pakistan mobilized to assist those affected. Traditional international relief organizations stepped in alongside Pakistani development organizations, benefiting from their knowledge of local networks and culture. Pakistani civil society also played a major role in the response, which was considered "the largest philanthropic response by Pakistanis that the country had ever experienced."[20]

Pakistani state institutions, with the exception of the military, were ill prepared for major emergencies; the army rapidly took the lead, giving rise to what was rated[21] one of the best examples of international civil-military cooperation in a major disaster.[22] Major General Farooq Ahmad was appointed to head up the newly established Federal Relief Commission (FRC) in charge of coordinating the emergency response. Looking back, two officials involved in the response—one Pakistani and one from the UN—summarized key features of what they called "non-interfering coordination" as follows:

(1) Share an open and honest assessment of needs with the NGO and humanitarian world, including the United Nations. (2) Allow humanitarian actors to choose what operations they will undertake, rather than dictate activities. (3) Ask NGOs to inform central commanders of the choices made. (4) Central commanders can then identify unmet gaps in humanitarian delivery, which can then be back-filled with the Army and other government agencies.[23]

According to the authors, military and humanitarian actors were complementary:

The military has assets, mobility, means, organization and wherewithal, and can provide national, district and local coordination infrastructure for NGOs, civil society and international support to "plug in to." Most importantly, they can work in distant areas, hard-to-reach and perhaps "insecure" regions.[24]

The authors noted, however, that humanitarian actors were better equipped than the military to assess vulnerabilities of the affected populations and prevent certain groups from being marginalized.

The response to the disaster provided the United Nations with an opportunity to pilot newly adopted humanitarian reform mechanisms, including the "cluster system" for assigning responsibilities to key actors in disaster response. Far from clashing with military initiatives, some have even argued that, ironically, "the military found it easier to adapt to the new Cluster system than did the humanitarian world."[25] An evaluation conducted in February 2006 recommended improvements, based on the Pakistan experience, but overall assessed the clusters as having "successfully provided a single and recognizable framework for coordination, collaboration, decision-making and practical solutions in a chaotic operational environment."[26] UNDP funds were used to set up the FRC, which used the clusters to facilitate the overall coordination of national relief efforts. As a result, Pakistan is one of the rare cases where national and international coordination mechanisms were perceived as complementary and mutually beneficial.

Two major legacies of the earthquake response included the development of Pakistani infrastructure to deal with disasters and the dynamics that shaped relations between humanitarian actors and the Pakistani military. In the aftermath of the earthquake the Pakistani government created institutions responsible for disaster preparedness and response at national, provincial, and local levels. The National Disaster Management Authority (NDMA) was defined as responsible for policymaking and coordination at the national level. Provincial Disaster Management Authorities (PDMAs) were "mandated to effectively set up a system to look after disasters and calamities whether natural, man-induced, or accidents."[27] PDMAs were to become the backbone of emergency responses at the provincial level.

The earthquake response was considered one of the best ever implemented in the context of a natural hazard event of such a scale. Close cooperation between relief agencies and the Pakistani armed forces was a significant issue, and humanitarian actors came to accept this arrangement as the most effective way of addressing urgent needs, including the organization of camps and providing them with basic medical, water, sanitation, and food assistance. Notwithstanding widespread reports of relief efforts by militant organizations in the aftermath of the earthquake, a study published in 2010 showed that "the presence of militant organizations at the village level was extremely limited even in villages close to the fault-line—of all organizations, these had the lowest coverage and even at their highest point right next to the fault-line, not more than ten percent of households reported receiving assistance from such an organization."[28]

The 2005 earthquake response provides a case where instrumentalization of aid was minimal because the interests of relief actors and of the Pakistani authorities converged. Swift and effective rescue and relief efforts were also seen as an important sign of the country's disaster response capability and sovereignty. It is worth noting that, at the time, Pakistan was one of the main staging areas of the GWOT, but major tensions among political, security, and humanitarian agendas did not emerge. As a result, aid actors developed (in the case of Pakistan) and tested (in the case of international aid actors) effective institutions whose objective was to govern people in times of disaster. The 2005 earthquake response was, in a sense, a laboratory for developing new national and international technologies of humanitarian governance. The use of aid to test new technologies of governance could be seen as a form of instrumentalization, but in this case it did not prevent affected people from receiving relatively effective and proportional assistance.

2007–8: "Early Recovery," an Anesthetic for Humanitarian Actors

Within two years of the onset of the disaster, the relief period had come to an end and the majority of INGOs that had arrived in Pakistan to help in the aftermath of the earthquake had left the country. Such departures were a natural consequence of the reduction of funds available for relief work; in some cases humanitarian organizations decided that their mandate no longer applied to recovery and reconstruction needs. Clusters were put on hold. NGOs that remained staffed their teams with development-experienced personnel and pursued strategies geared to addressing structural issues and long-term recovery.

The Pakistani authorities, who considered the cluster experience to be a successful model of coordination, volunteered to participate in the One UN approach when this initiative emerged in 2007. The One UN concept is geared, primarily, to post-conflict situations and is concerned with "more coherent programmes, reduced transaction costs for governments, and lower overhead costs for the UN system."[29] Even though Pakistan had been confronted with numerous armed conflicts that had intensified since 2004, it was selected to pilot the Delivering as One approach, that is, one leader, one budget, one program, and one office for the UN. The same year violence escalated between the Pakistani army and militant groups. When the conflict triggered important population displacements in 2008–9, the post-earthquake early recovery mood acted as an anesthetic on the humanitarian community; it was not positioned or mobilized to react swiftly and had little sensitivity to the risks faced by some affected populations when relief was organized in cooperation with one of the parties to the conflict.

2008–10: Humanitarianism Compromised

The conflict between Pakistani forces and militants worsened throughout 2008 and by the end of 2009 had triggered the displacement of up to 4.2 million people. Although Pakistani army operations against militants in South Waziristan had started as early as 2004 and caused significant displacement, before 2008 the humanitarian community did not, for the most part, investigate whether humanitarian action was required in the KPK and FATA areas. One possible explanation is that international organizations working in Pakistan considered these areas inaccessible for reasons of security stemming from the fact that Pashtuns in these more traditional areas had a long history of rejecting Western influence. This may also have been compounded by the fact that the conflict did not attract much international media attention.

In 2008, after counter-insurgency military operations in FATA had displaced more than half a million people, the humanitarian community started to react. The ICRC, which until then had been mostly assisting Afghan refugees, expanded its programs to include Pakistanis affected by the conflict. It opened offices in Karachi, Lahore, Mingora (in the Swat valley), and in the FATA. Its budget grew from approximately US$20 million in 2008 to US$100 million in 2009 and US$130 million in 2010 (before the floods); the number of its employees grew from two hundred in 2008 to thirteen hundred in 2010.[30] Many NGOs also scaled up their presence to assist conflict-affected communities.

When Pakistani military operations intensified, and especially when the Swat "stabilization"[31] initiative started in April 2009, the international humanitarian apparatus was mobilized again. Humanitarians were requested to assist by the GoP in what appears to have been an attempt to find greater coherence among its different spheres of intervention. As a result, humanitarian agencies were embedded in the GoP's stabilization strategy. The Pakistani army's counter-insurgency operations in the Malakand division in the KPK in April 2009 had triggered more than 2.8 million IDPs, and in July the Pakistani military initiated a mass return of the displaced.

By mid-August, the government announced that 1.6 million IDPs were back in their areas of origin, sending the message that it had accomplished a successful security operation. The GoP also made it clear that it expected aid actors to help returnees reconstruct their lives.

Throughout the crisis the GoP called for international assistance for the IDPs and then for the returnees. Once again, the emergency response was mostly coordinated by the Pakistani military. Surprisingly, little advocacy was made by aid agencies to prevent or denounce the circumstances in which IDPs were sometimes forced to return to their area of origins: Pakistani authorities would cut electricity and water in camps, for instance, so that people would have no alternative but to leave. Additionally, collaboration with the Pakistani military meant most actors, consciously or unconsciously, accepted the risk that relief could in some instances discriminate against families suspected of supporting the militants.

Many international actors relied on local NGOs to implement their programs. Those who had experienced the 2005 earthquake pursued the same "hand-in-hand with the military" approach, to the extent that beneficiary lists were sometimes shared with, or even provided by, the military. Several aid workers interviewed by the author underlined their concern that beneficiary lists were used as a tool for the counter-insurgency strategy of the military by denying assistance to civilians suspected of supporting insurgents.

When the Swat valley assault started, there was a certain level of trust between the aid community and the Pakistani military, and a low degree of vigilance on how to maintain an acceptable level of impartiality in assisting a population affected by a conflict. One of the first critical papers on the topic was published in September 2009 and spoke about "a clash of principles,"[32] arguing that "humanitarians [had] not spoken out against the conduct of hostilities and the politicization of the emergency response" and "that aid agencies [were] faced with the dilemma of engaging with and supporting government efforts to promote stability or maintaining a principled approach." Indeed, protection issues associated with the armed conflict, including civilian casualties, were not a critical feature of the humanitarian agenda.

The issue of access was at the center of the compromises humanitarians were to make. The GoP restricted access to KPK and FATA in general. INGOs wanting to implement programs in Pakistan had to submit an application to the Economic Affairs Department (EAD) of the Ministry for Finance and Economic Affairs for each project and obtain a "No Objection Certificate" (NOC). This process officially was supposed to take seven days, but in practice it took up to several months and could be "used to control access to pressure NGOs to accept instructions about providing assistance to particular beneficiaries."[33] For example, access to areas bordering South Waziristan (Dera Ismael Khan and Tank) was denied to humanitarian actors for months when hundreds of thousands of people had been displaced and there was limited understanding of the impact of the war on these displaced civilians. When access was eventually permitted, it was restricted to Pakistani personnel, thus preventing organizations from involving expatriates who would have been less exposed to local pressure. Humanitarian actors developed ad hoc strategies of sub-contracting their response or sending their key local staff to implement programs in order to reach the 428,000 people who had fled South Waziristan to Tank and D.I. Khan. Pakistani staff were under very high pressure from the Pakistani army to operate under its umbrella. The Mehsud tribe was specifically accused of attacking Pakistani military personnel and infrastructure all over the country, and was targeted in the war effort by the military.[34] Mehsudi families who had managed to flee conflict-affected areas of South Waziristan were mostly denied assistance.

In May 2009, the GoP military established a headquarters structure known as the Special Support Group (SSG) for IDPs with the responsibility for logistics, health, administration, and assistance in registration.[35] According to a member of the SSG, its role was to mediate between the military and humanitarian actors. In reality, it was responsible for security clearances and ultimately had the power to refuse access and thus assistance to at-risk groups in KPK/FATA. As one observer noted, "The Pakistani armed forces not only decide where, when and how to conduct anti-Taliban operations, but also—primarily through the civil-military Special Support Group—largely dictate the terms of the humanitarian response."[36]

When interviewed, most INGOs relied on the rhetoric of principles of independence and impartiality to explain their work; however, facts proved that very few could pride themselves with working proportionally for conflict-affected people from both sides of the conflict.

Access to areas controlled by the militants was not easy. Pashtuns living in the tribal areas where the militants were located had long been suspicious of, or hostile to, contacts with the Western world. The cooption of humanitarian agencies by the Pakistani military did not improve the perception of Western-dominated relief agencies. Moreover, public statements by the UN special envoy for assistance to Pakistan and other senior officials that "aid must follow Pakistan military gains" and efforts to eradicate insurgents in the FATA did not help.[37] Comments associating humanitarian actors with a post-crisis peacebuilding agenda made it more difficult for humanitarian actors to present themselves as neutral and impartial and therefore to have a chance to access war-affected people in areas controlled by the militants.

In the face of such a highly politicized environment, some humanitarian agencies developed protective and deterrent measures, to the extent of sending implicit signals of exclusion to local populations in some instances. These decisions were taken on the assumption that threats were diverse and coming from different groups whose dynamics were very difficult to grasp. Without being the primary targets, humanitarians were indeed targeted several times.[38] This evolution could be observed in Islamabad as well as in Peshawar, where massive prison-like buildings have mushroomed, separating expatriates from the "undocumented surplus-life" existing outside the walls of agency compounds.[39] Such "fortified aid compounds"[40] designed to keep the local world out are intimidating and symbolic of the recent militarization of security management in the aid sector that is counterproductive and undermines efforts to secure acceptance and the building of trust as a basis for access to vulnerable populations.

Humanitarian actors' lack of access to areas controlled by the militants cannot be attributed *only* to the instrumentalization of humanitarian action by the GoP. Indeed, the lack of advocacy by humanitarian actors to reduce instrumentalization and their association with a particular party to the conflict did not put them in a favorable position to negotiate access with the militants.

The UN humanitarian agencies provided an illustration of how siding with the GoP prevented them from accessing conflict-affected people on the other side of the front line. In 2010, the very existence of a UN special envoy for assistance in Pakistan, in addition to a resident coordinator (RC) and a humanitarian coordinator (HC), illustrated the ambiguity and in-built tensions within the UN's coordination machinery and the leadership challenges it faced. On the one hand, UN agencies belonged to the One UN arrangement and were therefore expected to support Pakistani institutions. On the other hand, the UN humanitarian reform initiative had entrusted the humanitarian country team (HCT) with the responsibility to coordinate the response and in doing so to uphold principles of neutrality and impartiality. Some UN officials interviewed described this as a "clash between the two reforms."

Historically close to the GoP, the United Nations was blamed for not wanting to "confront the government and acknowledge the scale of the problem,"[41] that is, to uphold the humanitarian imperative for IDPs from FATA/KPK. The long-established UN agencies in Pakistan were wary of jeopardizing their good relationship with Pakistani authorities. Similar criticisms about the UN's behavior at a later stage of the response were formulated as follows:

Instead of advocating for a more needs-based registration criteria or overcoming exclusion errors by supplementing government beneficiary lists with agencies' own lists of vulnerable individuals (as was done, for example, by the ICRC and several NGOs), most members of the HCT simply continued to base their response on what they knew to be flawed registration lists [provided by the government].[42]

A view supported by several people interviewed by the author was that, in 2008–9, the UNHCR and the UN WFP, by working closely with the GoP, which was a party to the conflict, largely contributed to making negotiations with the GoP very difficult for other humanitarian actors. Some humanitarian agencies were striving to operate more independently, for instance without armed escorts, and to deploy expatriate staff to locations of greatest concern. The ability of the HC to support humanitarian principles was generally rated as very low, whether for personality or structural reasons. The HC was sometimes blamed for not being strong enough in defending principles in HCT meetings;[43] he was seen as having his hands tied, given the leverage of agencies that controlled the largest humanitarian UN budgets in the country and that tended to align with the government.

Reported tensions within the HCT reflected a lack of unity and the struggle to make different responsibilities coexist. Several aid workers referred positively, however, to the role of the UN Office for the Coordination of Humanitarian Affairs (OCHA) as the main entity that had invested in efforts to resolve problems associated with access, protection, and impartiality of assistance, through negotiations with authorities at the national and provincial level. For example, in February 2010 OCHA managed to push the issue of the sharing of beneficiary lists onto the agenda of the joint GoP/UN Policy and Strategy Committee and to have the committee agree "that nominal lists of beneficiaries (i.e., beneficiary names) [would] not be shared with the civil or military authorities."[44] In order to try to improve civil-military coordination in Pakistan, OCHA drafted guidelines and, while waiting for the Pakistani military to sign them,[45] circulated them within the humanitarian community. OCHA also launched a pilot vulnerability assessment of people affected by the Swat displacement aiming at addressing exclusionary errors. This eventually became a multi-agency (NGOs as well as UN) effort to refine the targeting of beneficiaries by the humanitarian agencies after the Swat crisis.

Attempts to solve the problem of access were probably the least successful; as an illustration, OCHA managed to obtain authorizations to send expatriates, under armed escort, to monitor assistance in Dera Ismael Khan and Tank. Unfortunately, their convoy was stopped at the entrance to the district, and the mission was aborted.

The UN experience in 2008–10 shows that its decision to stand by the Pakistani government compromised the UN's impartiality and, by extension, its ability to help all in need of assistance. However, the example of OCHA's efforts to uphold the principle of impartiality shows that it is possible to minimize the negative effects of instrumentalization through commitment and negotiations.

A few other humanitarian actors attempted to avoid passive instrumentalization. MSF and the ICRC[46] both made explicit efforts to avoid association with the United Nations and other NGOs. In Pakistan, MSF and ICRC shared a similar approach that minimized instrumentalization in order to help communities in politically sensitive areas, that is, the districts of KPK, FATA, and Baluchistan. They explicitly and consciously affirmed their independence and neutrality as a means to provide protection and assistance on both sides of the conflict.

While the ICRC is funded by donor states, they do so on the basis of a total independence in the use of these funds. The credibility the ICRC has built over the years with its own donors in order to operate freely is constantly challenged and maintained thanks to a proven record and recognized quality of work.

Similarly, MSF insists on its financial independence. In Pakistan it did not accept funds from any government donor. MSF uses its financial independence as one of its arguments to prove the consistency of its acts with its intentions when negotiating access in the field; the absence of funding by Western or other government donors minimizes the perception that MSF is manipulated for ends at odds with its humanitarian objectives. This stance is considered by MSF as a necessary condition to demonstrate its independence.

In order to be useful, principles need to translate into concrete actions, and this starts with a clear understanding of principles by agency field staff (national and international). MSF, for instance, had a strong policy of briefing its staff on its mission statement and operating in compliance with humanitarian principles; dedicated efforts to this effect occurred routinely in the context of the emergency response.[47] In addition, MSF developed a communication strategy specifically for Afghanistan and Pakistan, which conveyed the message that MSF was an independent medical humanitarian association—purposely eschewing the NGO acronym—in order to avoid confusion with other NGOs that had different mission statements and to shape perceptions of its independence from the rest of the humanitarian community. In a similar vein, the ICRC differentiated itself by, among other things, using a high-profile strategy in terms of visibility on the ground.[48] In 2009, the ICRC was one of the very few organizations that had stickers and flags on its vehicles.

Nonetheless, it is important to note that both organizations would argue that this approach alone is not sufficient to build a trustful relationship with a party to a conflict. The ability to also understand, discuss, and negotiate with parties to a conflict is a crucial element in order to gain access to sensitive areas and have the leverage and capacity to operate impartially. Negotiation entailed the search for common interests and acceptable compromises. One characteristic of this kind of approach was that it took time and consumed a lot of resources and was not seen as cost-effective compared to programs embedded in the stabilization strategy of the GoP. For example, it took MSF more than six months to negotiate access locally to work in a hospital in Hangu, after it had received the provincial authorities' green light. MSF requested that the hospital be weapons free. Long negotiations resulted in a compromise, whereby local authorities requested that MSF set up strict security measures at the entrance of the hospital (including high walls and sand bags) to maximize people's safety. For the MSF team, it was urgent to start treating patients, but it was equally important, in the long term, to secure a weapons-free space; therefore, the decision was made to invest time and resources to secure a real "operational space," translating into better access to patients, better treatment, and greater trust from the local people.

Neither MSF nor ICRC would claim that it had an exclusive recipe for negotiating and maintaining access; however, trying to escape instrumentalization by Western donors and the GoP was part of the strategy of both organizations in order to reach war-affected people in areas where militants were present at a time when most of the assistance community was focused on government-held areas.

2010 Floods:
A Natural Hazard Event or a Complex Emergency?

The floods—a slow-moving and insidious disaster—did not strike Pakistan in one day but unfolded over several weeks starting on July 22, 2010, in Baluchistan. The floods then hit KPK, which ended up with the highest figure of casualties, and flowed down to Punjab, Pakistan's breadbasket. Finally, they reached Sindh, where evacuations were better organized, and the impact less disastrous than elsewhere. Tremendous habitat and infrastructure damage, however, could not be avoided. On August 14, the World Bank estimated that crops worth one billion dollars had been destroyed, threatening to cut the country's economic growth by half.[49] The floods swamped villages stretching from the Himalayas to the Arabian Sea, affecting more than 18 million people, injuring more than 2,900, and killing 1,985 people.[50]

The 2010 floods were a catastrophic experience for the Pakistani people, many of whom were already struggling to survive in precarious circumstances. The scale of the flooding and attendant devastation was unprecedented. Even though the disaster was widely seen as an unfortunate natural event, both its impact and the speed of the emergency response were also understood as a statement of the nature of politics in Pakistan. While the response was, in many respects, a race against time to rescue and provide succor to the stranded and homeless, it was also a competition to win "hearts and minds." Arriving on top of the crisis associated with the military's counter-insurgency and stabilization efforts, the floods were an opportunity for Western donors and the GoP to enhance their image in Pakistani society and in the media as the biggest providers of relief. The rhetoric surrounding relief efforts served this purpose while also actually helping people. Humanitarian actors, confronted with the unprecedented nature of the flooding, coupled with security restrictions, had to make choices about whom to assist, and whether fighting potential instrumentalization by Western donors and GoP was a priority.

"Army Zindabad!"[51] *and the Underlying Stabilization Rhetoric*

The Pakistani military played a critical and dominant role in orchestrating the provision of relief. It used this role to try to improve its public standing by "winning the hearts and minds" of the people of Pakistan with the support of Western donors. Even though the Pakistani government was widely blamed for being slow in responding to the catastrophe, its military institutions were at the fore of the response: sixty thousand troops were deployed in rescue and relief operations, and as of August 27, they had rescued 800,000 people and set up over one hundred Army Relief Camps across the country.[52] As one of the main actors on the ground in the south of the country, the Pakistani military took part in UN coordination platforms. NATO[53] and other international military forces provided resources as well as logistics support to the Pakistani authorities. Never before 2008 had the United States provided so much foreign assistance to Pakistan during a period of civilian rule. Such assistance, apparently, was not focused on buying Pakistan's support for US foreign policy but rather "to help stabilize Pakistan itself."[54] There is no proof, however, that Pakistani hearts and minds were won over.

Simultaneously, the GoP enforced a restricted-access policy to conflict areas, especially in the FATA. Even when the GoP issued an NOC waiver in mid-August for certain parts of the KPK to speed up the international response, the most sensitive districts of FATA and KPK remained practically "no go" areas for security reasons. Access for expatriates to Dera Ismael Khan and Tank remained blocked, even as the response needed to be scaled up swiftly and some INGO emergency surge protocols required the presence of expatriates. Similarly, the GoP did not authorize the United Nations Humanitarian Air Services (UNHAS) to deploy helicopters in KPK/FATA, where the use of Pakistani aircraft by humanitarians was the most problematic.

Local organizations linked to Islamist groups and political parties[55] moved quickly, and their relief efforts benefited from their proximity to local communities. Although there should not be anything surprising about Islamic organizations working at the grass-roots level in a Muslim country, once again, this phenomenon raised concerns in the media[56] as to whether the actions of such groups would spread support for Islamist extremists. At the time of writing, there was no solid proof for such concerns. However, the fear that Islamist groups would instrumentalize assistance was used widely in the media to mobilize donations: "Unless we act decisively, large parts of flood-stricken Pakistan will be taken over by the Taliban,"[57] wrote Ahmed Rashid in the *Telegraph*. This line of argument became so pervasive that, even when trying to advocate for the "depoliticization" of humanitarian aid, Marvin Parvez, the director of Church World Service, used the same underlying argument of stabilization strategies:

> If the international community does not come up with support at this time of need, the flood-survivors' children will go in droves to the *madrassas* because they have food there. If you don't send aid to where the need is, people will be more vulnerable to the militant organizations that believe in violence. They have nothing left, so we will be pushing them into the arms of these militant groups whose humanitarian wings are providing help.[58]

As mentioned earlier in this chapter, the stabilization agenda had been an underlying rationale for the overall international aid strategy in Pakistan at least since 2008. The floods did not escape this logic and along these lines, the US administration's special representative for Afghanistan and Pakistan at the time, said: "If we do the right thing, it will be good not only for the people whose lives we save but for the US image in Pakistan. . . . The people of Pakistan will see that when the crisis hits, it's not the Chinese. It's not the Iranians. It's not other countries. It's not the EU. It's the US that always leads."[59] This logic attracted substantial resources for the response, and the United States was the swiftest to react after the start of the floods and eventually contributed approximately US$630 million. It was by far the largest donor, accounting for 33 percent of the total amount of donations recorded by the United Nations. However, it is not so clear whether agitating the Islamist "straw man" helped to mobilize public opinion or even further reinforced prejudices against Pakistanis.

Humanitarian Choices

In such a compound crisis, international humanitarian actors were faced with a set of choices that shaped their positioning and therefore the scope of their response. Choices about the kind of funding used and whether a partnership with military forces would be established influenced the scope and nature of the response.

Most of the international funds that were allocated to international humanitarian actors for the floods response came from institutional donors. Despite their scale, the 2010 Pakistani floods attracted very little international public attention, and therefore very little in private donations outside Pakistan. As an element of comparison, a Red Cross campaign in the United States raising funds through mobile phone raised US$31 million for Haiti and only about US$10,000 for Pakistan later in the same year.[60] The vast majority of humanitarian actors depended on institutional donors. Even if the Good Humanitarian Donorship principles required donors to "support humanitarian action that is explicitly neutral and impartial in its intent,"[61] the perception in Pakistan seemed to be that Western funds often came with an agenda attached. As more than 64 percent of the funds allocated for the floods came from countries involved in the war in Afghanistan,[62] most humanitarian actors were concerned with issues of perception. On one hand, funds were needed to assist flood-affected people. On the other, donor funds exposed the humanitarian imperative to a political dependency that may have prevented humanitarian agencies from gaining the trust of Pakistani people in certain areas, or over time. Eventually, most humanitarian agencies provided assistance financed by Western donors. In conflict-affected areas, however, reports of people not trusting assistance from states supporting the Pakistani authorities[63] showed that the ability of a humanitarian actor to demonstrate financial independence was crucial to gain trust and access.

The other major question humanitarian actors had to answer was whether they would cooperate with the military. As described in the first section of this chapter, working hand in hand with the military had in the past enabled complementarities and enhanced effectiveness. However, in 2010 such collaboration could distort humanitarian priorities in favor of the military's agenda. Logistics and access were two critical issues shaping the timeliness and effectiveness of the emergency response. Logistics were a major challenge, with millions of people isolated on strips of land, unable to move to assistance points, and very difficult to reach. The humanitarian response was especially slow in Sindh, Punjab, and Baluchistan for two main reasons: access to certain areas was physically impossible, and most humanitarian organizations had no pre-flood presence in Punjab and Sindh. As a result, some humanitarian actors used Pakistani military assets at the onset of the emergency, invoking the "last resort" principle of the guidelines on the use of foreign military and civil defense assets in disaster relief.[64] At least until September 2010, WFP used military assets[65] to deliver food in remote areas of Punjab and Sindh. The issue was discussed in an HCT meeting, and WFP obtained an exceptional validation from the HC on the grounds of "last resort" until UNHAS was able to take over. Together with the military rescue operations, the bulk of the response was provided by WFP, which in October 2010 was reaching 6.5 million people across the country and by January 2011 was providing food for more than 5 million people a month.[66]

There was a lively internal debate among UN agencies on whether to use the NATO air-bridge requested by the GoP, considering the role of NATO in neighboring Afghanistan and the US use of drones in Pakistan. The HCT finally ruled out the option of using the NATO air-bridge on the basis that this was not a last-resort situation because non-military alternatives were available.[67]

ICRC and MSF, in line with their previous positions, decided that they would not use any military assets to deliver assistance. They also declined any kind of funds associating them with donor governments or the United Nations. They also refused to be mentioned in any UN public reporting, such as "who? does what? where?" data, in order to maintain control over their image.

The scale of the floods certainly put an enormous amount of pressure on humanitarian actors. Facing the volume of needs and the complexity of the political background, organizations had to make choices about their operational positioning. Some decided that their priority was to reach as many people as quickly as possible, which often meant taking donor money, and sometimes using military assets, although respecting the Pakistan civil-military guidelines in order to mitigate the risk that aid would be perceived as taking sides. Others considered that in the age of the "citizen reporter," information on what agencies do and data on the origins of their funds traveled fast. For these actors, preserving an impartial space for assisting people in the long run required financial independence and not using military assets even if this resulted in helping fewer people. Considering the size of the 2010 catastrophe, not giving priority to resisting instrumentalization in the short term was legitimate, although it was fortunate that other actors prioritized affected groups who were politically less accessible.

Conclusions

This chapter shows that instrumentalization of humanitarian action can materialize in various ways. Conditioning registration of refugees to political affiliation is a form of instrumentalization, as is blocking assistance that deprives conflict-affected people suspected of supporting the militants, or using humanitarian rhetoric to attempt to win "hearts and minds," or even using aid to test technologies or institutions that reinforce state power over the people.

However, the Pakistani case shows that instrumentalization is not always negative and does not always work for the instrumentalizers. Humanitarian action almost always has side effects that serve purposes other than those of helping disaster-affected people. The 2005 earthquake response showed how institutions designed to be responsible for people in time of disasters expanded their power. This is nothing other than the expression of state responsibility. Institutions set up to coordinate assistance did play a positive role in helping earthquake victims, but, as a side effect, assistance was instrumental in establishing institutions reinforcing asymmetrical power relations. Since these government institutions have facilitated a timely humanitarian response, all side effects should not automatically be considered negatively.

Another way instrumentalization works for the instrumentalizer but plays out negatively for certain affected people is in situations in which actors involved in a conflict block humanitarian action. When the GoP used a security rationale to block access to certain war-affected communities, it was difficult for humanitarian agencies to counter this line of argument. The 2008–9 period showed that in such a situation, there were several kinds of reaction for humanitarian actors: either they accepted the GoP conditions without realizing they were being manipulated, and hence risked contributing to discrimination against their will, or they negotiated to provide assistance on humanitarian terms within the framework of nonnegotiable restrictions (OCHA, MSF, ICRC). This last option was the construction of a compromise that often involved reducing the scope of organizations' ambitions in terms of volume of aid and areas covered.

The 2010 floods provide empirical evidence that a third way is possible: humanitarian actors can consciously decide to accept the instrumentalization by one of the parties to the conflict because it serves their humanitarian strategic positioning. In the case of the floods, since the GoP controlled the vast majority of the territory affected by the floods, making an alliance with it in order to reach out to as many people as possible was a legitimate option. However, in this precise case it was also good that other humanitarian actors decided that their policy was to reach groups that were politically marginalized by the GoP and therefore took measures to avoid alignment with the GoP strategy of assisting some and not others. The coexistence of both policy positions proved positive as long as they remained clearly stated and monitored.

Finally, there is no evidence that the type of instrumentalization that was dominant during the floods, namely, the use of humanitarian rhetoric to win "hearts and minds," had the expected impact.

That actors engaged in armed conflict attempt to instrumentalize humanitarian action should not surprise anyone. It is, rather, the attitude of humanitarian actors that needs to be looked at. The Pakistani case shows that different humanitarian actors made different decisions according to their own strategic positioning. The lesson here is that as long as they do not let instrumentalization happen to them passively, aid actors should be able to determine when instrumentalization is an unavoidable trade-off that allows them to implement their own strategy.

Table 8–1 Pakistan: Examples of Instrumentalization of Aid

Event and Key Features of the Period	Policy Context	Key Actors	Examples of Instrumentalization of Aid
	Cold War and Western anti-communist agenda	Pakistani government	General Zia ul-Haq was determined that Pakistan have an Islamic ally on its western border to make sure no alliance would be made with India. Refugee camps acted as a shield for military training camps for the Afghan resistance and also to justify the state of emergency, which allowed Zia to ban internal political opposition.
1979–92 Soviet invasion of Afghanistan. Pakistan supports the Afghan opposition in exile.		Afghan mujahideen	Used refugee camps as their constituencies and as means to accumulate resources from international powers like the United States or Saudi Arabia. Manipulation of NGOs.
		The United States	The largest donor of "nonlethal" aid in Pakistan uses its leverage over humanitarian assistance within Afghan refugee camps in Pakistan as well as over cross-border aid activities to implement its Cold War anti-communist foreign policy.
		Saudi Arabia	Funds from Saudi Arabia to the Afghan resistance.
		INGOs	INGOs were willing instruments. Most of them took up the cause of the Afghan opposition and saw support to mujahideen as a just cause.
2005 Earthquake	Since 2001 Pakistan has been involved in an ambiguous relationship with Pakistani-based Islamist networks, both fighting them and allegedly supporting Afghan Taliban. UN humanitarian reform and the clusters are piloted in Pakistan.	Pakistan army/ government	The earthquake in 2005 provided opportunity for the Pakistani government to prove it is capable of effective disaster response. Disaster management institutions are created. Assistance acts as a tool to channel and consolidate state power.
October 2005 earthquake of 7.6 magnitude affects Gilgit-Baltistan and Khyber Pashtunkwa.		International humanitarian apparatus	The international humanitarian apparatus chooses Pakistan to pilot the UN humanitarian reform and the cluster system.

(continues)

Table 8–1 (continued)

2006–8 The stabilization process in Afghanistan progressively proves unsuccessful.	INGOs	Most INGOs involved in earthquake response leave because of lack of institutional funding. The development agenda is used by some INGOs to maintain a presence in Pakistan.
	The Pakistani Government	The GoP applies for "ONE UN" status and benefits from the successful response to the 2005 earthquake and positive cooperation with the UN while piloting the humanitarian reform.
2008–10 Fight between the Pakistani military and militants intensifies, triggering up to 4.2 million IDPs. Internal conflict and displacement.	PoG/Military	Pak military controls assistance to people displaced by the conflict: - Denial of assistance to groups suspected of supporting militants through control of beneficiary lists - Security clearance to conflict affected areas often denied and/or conditions imposed on assistance (armed escorts, no expatriates, etc.) - Assistance used by the Pakistani military to weaken its enemy.
	Western donors	Donors clearly support own GWOT agenda through regional attempt "to win hearts and minds." USAID following the Swat Valley massive displacement openly involved in a stabilization strategy that subsumes assistance to the political agenda.
	Most international assistance actors	Beneficiary lists are shared with and sometimes provided by the military. Some humanitarian actors de facto contribute to instrumentalization of aid by the Pakistani military (party to the conflict). Most UN (development) agencies align with GoP policies and war effort.
2010 Floods NATO announces reduction in troop levels in Afghanistan as of 2011 and intensifies stabilization strategy through regional "hearts and minds" approaches.	GoP/Military	Pakistani government uses assistance to show its ability to protect its population as well as mobilize people in a "hearts and minds" campaign that helps it fight the militants.
	Western donors/aid agencies	Western countries need Pakistan in their fight against terrorism and have an interest in improving their public image in Pakistan. They use the assistance to increase their visibility in the field.

Chapter 9

Haiti's Bitter Harvest

Humanitarian Aid in the "Republic of NGOs"

MARK SCHULLER

A Haitian proverb states *Kabrit ki gen anpil mèt toujou mouri nan solèy.* Literally translated, this means, "The goat with many caretakers always dies in the sun." With too many helpers, no one takes responsibility for making sure the goat has food or water. This wisdom is unfortunately very appropriate for the post-earthquake situation in Haiti. Even before the January 12, 2010, earthquake, Haiti was already called a "republic of NGOs," not only because there were so many—in 2009, UN Special Envoy Bill Clinton estimated them at ten thousand—but also because of the way that many NGOs have sidestepped the government.

There is no question that the world shared an outpouring of goodwill toward Haiti following the tragedy that according to the government claimed 316,000 lives. The international community responded with generosity. According to the *Chronicle of Philanthropy*,[1] US$1.3 billion was contributed by private US citizens to NGOs within six months. At a March 31, 2010, UN conference, donors pledged US$10 billion for the long-term response effort, with US$5.6 billion for the following eighteen months.

Unfortunately, these good intentions and generous promises did not translate into success commensurate with the relief effort. By the end of September 2011, only 43 percent of pledged funds had been disbursed; the two largest donors, Venezuela and the United States, had only disbursed 12.7 and 18.8 percent, respectively.[2] Of the over 382,000 houses in the Port-au-Prince metropolitan area evaluated by engineers, 99,000 were marked "yellow," in need of serious repair, and 78,000 "red," slotted for demolition. Twenty months after the earthquake, repair or new construction had been conducted on five thousand houses. An estimated 600,000 IDPs still lived in camps. While the overwhelming majority of camp dwellers (92 percent according to one study,[3] 94 percent according to another[4]) preferred to leave these temporary settlements, there was simply no viable alternative. The residents—one-fifth of the population of Port-au-Prince—were trapped in an emergency phase long after emergency funds and contracts for life-saving water, food aid, and sanitation services ran out.

To many, most important to the residents themselves, the camps had become symbols of frustration and lack of progress in the aid response. While the emergency medical response immediately following the earthquake saved thousands of lives and was a model of collaboration between the government and NGOs such as MSF and Partners in Health/Zanmi Lasante (PIH), services within IDP camps remained patchy. For example, in October 2010, when cholera spread from a UN military base, many camps lacked any water and sanitation services. The cholera epidemic, which had killed 6,300 and infected 240,000 by the end of August 2011, remobilized emergency interventions. However, progress was minimal except in one particular municipality. Both this selective success and collective failure shed light on the way in which instrumentalization of aid shaped the effectiveness of the relief effort.

This chapter distills lessons learned from this situation. The failures in both prevention and response to the cholera epidemic are symptomatic of a long-standing pattern of instrumentalization. Primary among the problems were an ineffective coordination system, a reward structure imposed by donors but adopted by NGOs themselves that worked against collaboration and local participation, and a long-standing dismissal of any role for the Haitian government.

Context: The Earthquake

It should be acknowledged at the outset that the conditions of the disaster itself rendered the humanitarian task extremely difficult. Haiti's heightened vulnerability to disasters both amplified the earthquake's destructiveness and presented additional challenges to the humanitarian community. Its urban nature complicated the response, as did its enormous scale.

Much of Haiti's death toll can be linked to the extreme density of Port-au-Prince and lack of quake-resistant housing. The capital's population had exploded as a direct consequence of neo-liberal push-and-pull factors. As Haitian social theorist Alex Dupuy notes, 732,000 people lived in Port-au-Prince in the 1980s, growing to three million by 2008.[5] Unplanned, uncoordinated *bidonvil* (shantytowns) sprang up to accommodate the two million people who were pushed off their land and pulled into low-wage factory jobs or urban unemployment.

Even the lucky few who made a steadily declining minimum wage lived in square, seven-by-seven-foot cinderblock dwellings with patchwork tin roofs that barely kept out the pouring rain or scorching Caribbean sun; these structures offered no privacy, were not connected to any water-supply or sanitation system, and thus had no toilet or shower. With state services privatized under neo-liberal policies, families (especially mothers) had to pay for their children's education (40 percent of a minimum wage salary for one child) and health care, on top of high housing costs and increasing food costs. Most tenants had to build their own houses on land they rented. Predictably, given the nature and level of poverty, many dwellings were built as cheaply as possible. When the earthquake struck, these structures were reduced to rubble and crushed those underneath. Of the homes destroyed, 86 percent were built after 1990, according to Haitian development expert Yolette Etienne.[6]

The earthquake shook the very foundations of the country's economic and political apparatus. In large part because of the neo-liberal policies just noted, and a policy of centralization begun during the 1915–34 US occupation, Port-au-Prince was not only home to one-third of the country's population but also housed nearly all of Haiti's administrative functions, NGO offices, banks, and industry.

Typically, humanitarian agencies operate in rural settings and were poorly equipped for an urban disaster. Haiti did not fit the model that many aid workers that arrived in-country attempted to use. According to an IOM staff member, "In rural disaster situations, it's easy to find land on which to relocate people. In Port-au-Prince, that was simply not the case. We could not control access, on top of a very volatile situation regarding land ownership."[7] Said another, "We just don't have a model for this."

The scale of the destruction stretched the local economy, certainly the job market, beyond its limit. There simply weren't enough offices, rental cars, equipment, and computers to support the multi-billion dollar relief effort. To some humanitarians, the scale lent a sense of hopelessness. To others, it justified the practice of flying in aid workers who were nominally trained but notably young and inexperienced, and lacking an understanding of Haiti's particularities or urban-disaster settings, not to mention the local language. According to the chief diplomat of the Organization for American States (OAS), Ricardo Seitenfus of Brazil, in a December 20, 2010, interview with the Swiss paper *Le Temps:*

The age of aid workers who arrived after the earthquake is very low; they came to Haiti without any experience. And Haiti, I can tell you, is not appropriate for amateurs. . . . Because of a massive recruitment, the professional quality is much diminished. There is a sinister or perverse relationship between the strength of NGOs and the weakness of the Haitian State. Certain NGOs wouldn't exist except because of Haitian misfortune.

As the intermediaries of billions of dollars in aid programs, these newcomers held the purse strings and the decision-making power.

Key Players

To understand the story of the manipulation of aid in Haiti, it is first necessary to take account of the various actors in the earthquake response. Apart from the thousands of newly arrived aid workers in a ballooning NGO response, many actors were already on the ground. These aid agencies had histories and relationships with one another before the earthquake that shaped their interaction with the newcomers. In an earlier work I argued that Haiti's history is usually told in a binary lens: the mainstream liberal discourse of the "evil Haitian state oppressing the people" has been dominant but has been increasingly challenged by another, that of a "Haiti oppressed by the world system."[8] Employing binary frames that do not even discuss the same sets of actors, these discourses talk past one another. At least a tripartite framework is required for understanding the interplay among the Haitian people, the state, and foreign powers. As the following discussion demonstrates, these sets of actors are diverse; they include the Haitian people, the government of Haiti, the United Nations, donor countries, and finally the NGOs. By briefly sketching their history and the roles they played following the earthquake, we can assess how aid was used, by whom, for what purpose, and to what effect.

Haitian People

The first responders to the earthquake were the Haitian people. Haiti had been ripped apart just six years prior to the earthquake in a prolonged conflict over the rule of president Jean-Bertrand Aristide, a former leftist priest overwhelmingly elected in 1990 but deposed eight months into his presidency by a military coup. Aristide's second forced removal in February 2004 followed five months of daily clashes among armed groups, the government, and putatively independent protesters. Aristide's ouster exposed the many cleavages within Haitian society. Most visible were Haiti's vast income disparities: in 2006, Haiti topped the list of income inequality in the Western hemisphere, second only to Namibia in the world.[9] Whereas 80 percent of Haiti's people lived on US$2 per day or less, with just under a half with an average income of US$1 a day, Haiti also had the most millionaires per capita. It is estimated that eight to ten families in Haiti owned over half of Haiti's wealth. This lighter-skinned mercantile elite is distinct from the black military elite that ruled under the Duvalier dictatorships. Traditionally, both elite groups competed for control of the state apparatus, oppressing and exploiting the poor majority in the process. The earthquake also exposed tensions based on religious lines, as growing and increasingly powerful Protestant evangelicals blamed the earthquake, and later the cholera outbreak, on Vodou, or as televangelist Pat Robertson put it, a "pact with the devil."

These divisions—political, economic, and religious—were largely set aside in the immediate aftermath of the earthquake in a common cause for survival and an expression of Haiti's tradition of solidarity, *youn ede lòt* (one helping the other). Since the port and airport were damaged, and the Dominican Army had shut its borders with Haiti, the only aid people had for survival was what was already in the country. Neighbors helped one another out of the rubble, pulling out dead family members and sharing emergency rations. Makeshift clinics were set up in the middle of the street, where people slept side by side, middle class and *pèp la*, Haiti's poor majority. Committees sprang up, making lists of household members, those dead, injured, or handicapped, elderly, infants, and pregnant women. They also shared water and pots to store it, foodstuffs, medicine, and first-aid materials. People put away their differences and unified to survive. Those who found the trauma, the rubble, and the stench of thousands of cadavers decomposing too much to bear left Port-au-Prince. These 600,000 displaced were greeted with open arms by their cousins *andeyò*, in the countryside (literally "outside"). Family members shared what little food they had on hand, in many cases sacrificing the next summer's crop to feed their urban cousins.

This life-saving contribution by Haiti's people was immediate and significant but went without recognition or compensation by the Haitian government, foreign agencies, or the media. Household or salvaged stocks were running out as the first emergency aid arrived from outside the country. Almost as soon as external aid arrived, social divisions returned with great force.

Government of Haiti

As Haitian anthropologist Michel-Rolph Trouillot and many commentators have noted, Haiti's state has traditionally aligned against the nation.[10] The two elite groups—the black military and the lighter-skinned merchants—differed primarily in their strategy.[11] Both received justification if not open support from foreign powers. The merchant class made its livelihood by monopolizing the trade between Haiti and the outside world. Its interests were thus directly aligned with foreign capitalists, and it did little to promote national production. The military drew its strength and justification from the threat of foreign invasion, partially abated in 1825 when France demanded 150 million francs in indemnity for its recognition of Haiti's independence.[12] Much later, at several key moments in Haiti's history, the military received foreign munitions and financial support. For example, the modern Haitian army was a creation of the 1915–34 US occupation, and the Cold War provided the opportunity for dictator François Duvalier (1957–71) to build a vast military and paramilitary terror apparatus using hundreds of millions of US dollars in foreign aid.

While dutifully paying its foreign debt obligations, the Haitian state plundered the peasantry. Development aid in the Cold War context provided new opportunities for government leaders to enrich themselves. For example, according to the International Monetary Fund's (IMF) own records, Jean-Claude "Baby Doc" Duvalier (1971–86) took all but US$2 million of a US$22 million December 1980 IMF loan for the paramilitary (*tonton makout*) and his personal accounts.[13] Duvalierist Haiti, and the military juntas that followed, became known as a "kleptocracy."[14]

The 1990 elections surprised many when the people brought Aristide to power by a landslide with a very high turnout. During the eight months he was in office, Aristide promised radical social change and to undo centuries of exclusion. The fast pace of change and his fiery rhetoric earned him the ire of reactionary forces: Haiti's two elite groups and the CIA.[15] He was ousted on September 30, 1991. A bloody three-year dictatorial period ensued. Under immense pressure and facing the death of tens of thousands of supporters, Aristide promised to support neo-liberal measures in exchange for his return. Aristide returned in 1994 after a UN-brokered accord, under US military occupation, and was forced to reverse his campaign promises.

Aristide was a contradictory and controversial figure. Many in the aid community were enraged when Aristide attempted to renege on past agreements, and many pointed to his kleptocratic tendencies.[16] Others pointed to the fact that he was never allowed to serve out his term, and by any index his administration performed better than the interim regimes chosen by the international community.[17]

Aristide's late-chosen successor, René Préval, had a quiet and unassuming persona and was a technocrat. He was the only president elected in Haiti to ever serve a full term of office—and he did so twice, 1996–2001 and 2006–11. During the interim regime following Aristide's second ouster, Haiti topped the list of countries on Transparency International's "Corruption Perception Index." Préval received praise internationally for making progress on this and other measures. Préval rejected the minimum wage increase in 2009, soon after former US president Clinton was named special envoy to Haiti, made the last financial reforms required by international financial institutions to cancel Haiti's debt, and pushed through constitutional reforms favored by Clinton, the United Nations, and the international business community.

While Préval's low-key persona may have explained his longevity in office, after the earthquake it provoked criticism from the international community and the Haitian population alike. The world waited for days for Préval to make his first public pronouncement. He eventually asked Parliament, at the behest of the international community, to dissolve itself and be replaced by the Interim Haiti Reconstruction Commission (IHRC). According to a high-level government official, "Préval almost single-handedly blew the best opportunity Haiti ever had. You had Clinton—both Clintons, actually—finally talking about Haitian sovereignty. In the end, Préval's actions—or should I say inactions—exposed once and for all just how irrelevant the presidency is." Given the centuries of kleptocracy, and that the only leaders ever chosen by the people were either forcibly removed by foreign intervention or allowed foreigners to take over completely, many Haitian people simply gave up hope that the Haitian government would ever do anything useful for them.

The Haitian government is more than just the presidency; tens of thousands of personnel worked in the public sector. The Haitian government had already lost many qualified technicians to the NGO sector because of the pull of higher salaries, and it lost many others in the earthquake, since the government complex was in one of the worst-hit areas of Port-au-Prince. But many qualified and hard-working personnel remained.

The United Nations

The United Nations has had an ambivalent relationship with the country, owing in part to its multiple mandates. While many citizens distinguish the

UN's development and humanitarian branches from UN military contingents, the role of MINUSTAH—the UN Mission for the Stabilization of Haiti—was particularly visible in recent times. Following Aristide's 2004 forced departure, actively supported by the United States and France, the so-called Friends of Haiti deployed a Multinational Interim Force. This was replaced a few months later by MINUSTAH. Following the earthquake, MINUSTAH comprised 12,249 soldiers and police officers from fifty-five countries. Crucially, this mission was headed by Brazil, governed by the left-leaning president "Lula," who in 2004 capitalized on the popularity in Haiti of the Brazilian soccer team to promote goodwill.

This goodwill did not last. Many Haitians came to see the presence of foreign troops as an occupation and an infringement of Haitian sovereignty. The force has been called various things, including "touristah," because of the troops' frequenting of the beaches, hotels, and nightclubs—while not spending money on local merchants—and "vole kabrit," because of repeated allegations of troops confiscating peasants' goats. Goodwill collapsed with the cholera epidemic that began in October 2010. Two independent studies have concluded that UN troops stationed just outside Mirebalais were the source of the cholera epidemic that proved devastating for Haiti.[18]

Donor Countries

When it was a colony of France, Haiti (then called Saint-Domingue) generated more wealth than any other colony before or since. France's loss of the "pearl of the Antilles" led Napoleon to give away Louisiana, allowing for US expansion and hegemony in the region. The Haitian Revolution of 1804 convinced wavering British parliamentarians to end the slave trade three years later. Its independence—won from a slave revolt—isolated Haiti in a sea of sugar plantations. As many scholars have argued, dominant powers punished Haiti for this "unthinkable" act,[19] not least for the example it offered to slaves in Virginia and Cuba, among others.

With the end of chattel slavery and the enormous profits wrested from it, the Caribbean lost much of its geo-political significance, but Haiti remained a strategic site for dominant powers. Haiti's independence debt—dutifully serviced by Haitian governments with the majority of ever-dwindling tax resources—represented a cash cow for the creditor, France. The United States seized the island nation in 1915, when the European powers were at war with one another, justified by long-standing German banking interests that had established ties in Haiti.

As noted previously, the United States supported the Duvalier dictatorship on Cold War grounds. Across the windward channel from Cuba, Haiti cast a decisive vote to exclude the Castro regime from the OAS. After Aristide's return in 1994 from three-year exile, formal ties with Cuba were established. Since then, Cuba has provided large-scale medical assistance: one-third of the doctors working in Haiti are Cuban, and another third are Haitians who received medical degrees in Cuba.

Aristide's 2004 ouster provided an opportunity for France to mend relations with the United States, soured after the latter had unilaterally invaded Iraq. French president Jacques Chirac was the first world leader to call for Aristide's ouster. France had other "internal" matters to think about since Aristide had raised the issue of compensation for the 1825 debt that had drained Haiti's productive resources for over 120 years. Eying French overseas departments in the Caribbean that maintained ties with the former colony and that had racially charged union unrest brewing of their own, Chirac called Aristide's US$22 billion demand for restitution "preposterous." France promoted Brazil, which had publicly aired ambitions for a permanent seat on the UN Security Council, to lead Haiti's peacekeeping forces. According to my interviews with officials in Washington, France's proposal served US interests in several ways. One in particular was that MINUSTAH's failures could serve as proof that Brazil—or India, or any other Southern country for that matter—was ill equipped to handle the responsibilities of leading UN missions, and hence of permanent Security Council membership.

Nonetheless, with MINUSTAH's presence, Cuba's medical aid, and the rise of the "Bolivarian alternative" of Venezuelan president Hugo Chávez, which subsidized low-cost petroleum products, the United States saw its dominance weakened in Haiti. According to a report by the right-wing Heritage Foundation, the earthquake presented an opportunity to restore US influence.[20] The March 2010 UN Donors' Conference was an opportunity for countries to compete for leadership in the provision of largesse; topping the list of pledges was not the United States (US$1.15 billion) but Venezuela (US$1.34 billion). Former colonial power France was outdone by Spain and Canada.[21]

NGOs

The political climate under the Duvalier dictatorship, particularly Papa Doc, was hostile to NGOs; however, a handful of foreign humanitarian agencies and NGOs worked in the country. Most, such as Catholic Relief Services and the American Friends Service Committee, were faith-based. During a 1969 visit to an ailing François Duvalier in which the United States pledged support for a transition to the dictator's teenage son, US vice president Nelson Rockefeller negotiated a space for US evangelical groups.

The ouster of Jean-Claude Duvalier in February 1986 also provided an opening for foreign agencies—international financial institutions as well as bilateral agencies such as USAID—to implement neo-liberal policy reforms of trade liberalization, floating the currency, and privatization.[22] Duvalier's ouster, supported by the United States, was also an opening for NGOs. According to official records, only forty NGOs were legally registered and recognized before 1971, when Baby Doc took over upon the death of his father. By contrast, from 1986 (when Duvalier fled) to 1990 (the first democratic election), at least thirty-one NGOs opened offices in Haiti.[23] By 2005, the Ministry of Planning and Foreign Cooperation had officially recognized 343 national and international NGOs,[24] inching up to 400 just before the earthquake.

Critiques of what some analysts called the NGO invasion abounded from across the political spectrum in Haiti. Leftist academics Sauveur Pierre Etienne and Janil Lwijis had a public argument, each trying to outflank the other in terms of whose critique of NGOs was more radical.[25] Both were also vocal critics of Aristide. Aristide supporter Paul Farmer offered a note of caution about NGOs, saying that they "aren't necessarily more democratic than *elected* governments."[26] Haitians on the right are similarly critical. A general mistrust is reflected in the two foundational regulatory documents of the NGO system: Jean-Claude Duvalier's decree on NGOs of December 1982, and military dictator Henri Namphy's revised decree of September 1989. The preamble to both decrees declared the legislation necessary to "protect national sovereignty."

Ordinary citizens were also critical of what they saw as corruption, as NGOs were perceived as getting rich from people's misery. Said one, "When they come to give the country aid, only the bigwigs see it. They only give us a coating of dust." Many people began speaking of an insular, privileged "NGO class" that acted as intermediaries for foreign interests.[27] Since the earthquake, these critiques have only gotten louder. Graffiti denouncing NGOs have become a common occurrence in Port-au-Prince, particularly following the cholera outbreak in October 2010. NGOs appear to many to lack the will to help. One frustrated youth said, "NGOs know the problems to resolve, but they want you to be in misery; before they give to you, they make you suffer." And another: "They have the means to help. If they don't help, NGOs wouldn't exist. And it's because of these problems that they exist. If all problems were resolved there would never be NGOs."

This was obviously not true of all NGOs, but the public's perception was based on the fact that they saw NGOs playing a significant role in under-mining Haitian sovereignty and the ability of the state to manage its own affairs. Haitians had concerns about NGO actions and funding streams, and as institutions of power presiding over the continued slow pace of progress. How well-meaning NGOs ended up being part of what one UN expert called "the biggest boondoggle in the history of humanitarian aid" requires an understanding of how aid was instrumentalized on many levels.

Long-Term Structure of Humanitarian Aid to Haiti

Donor States

As a donor country, the United States has a long history of manipulating development and humanitarian aid to Haiti. For example, the Clinton administration provided food aid in the mid-1990s on the condition that the Haitian government lower its tariffs on rice and reduce other barriers to US trade and investment. Testifying before the US Congress in March 2010, Clinton apologized for destroying Haitian food production, saying, "It may have been good for some of my farmers in Arkansas, but it has not worked." Aid to Haiti was also tied up in the US political process; in 1995, Republicans, who had just taken over Congress, were looking to expose President Clinton's inexperience in foreign policy. Returning exiled President Aristide to power was his only perceived "success" story at that point and contrasted positively with Rwanda and Somalia. So Congress forbade USAID to fund Aristide's government development programs; all USAID funds were to go to NGOs. Other donors, such as Canada and the European Union, followed suit.

NGO influence was not limited to service delivery; several authors have detailed the role NGOs played in governance, including the ouster of President Aristide.[28] In 2003, even though USAID's overall Haiti portfolio had been halved during the previous years, funds for "democracy and governance" doubled, with the explicit goal to "develop new political leadership."[29] While there is a lively debate within Haiti about Aristide's actions as president, there is no doubt that the United States and other governments played an active role in removing him. As part of the anti-Aristide agenda, in 2001, the Inter-American Development Bank (IDB), acting under US veto, withheld US$535 million in loans that were to develop Haiti's water and public-health infrastructure.

As the largest bilateral donor, USAID set transnational trends but was by no means the only agency engaged in instrumentalization. Haitian scholars of NGOs note that French or Canadian NGOs were vehicles for marketing their country's technology.[30] In the prevailing neo-liberal policy mood of the so-called Washington Consensus, combined with a (belated) concern about corruption, donors tended to weaken governments and empower

NGOs. Weaker governments are more likely to align themselves with the agendas of their foreign benefactors, such as opening markets for US businesses or promoting French technologies. They are also used as pawns in a geo-political struggle; a WikiLeaked cable documented the lengths the US government took to kill Chavez's PetroCaribe initiative, which would have resulted in lower prices for gas and hence food as well as rebuilding the public electricity grid.[31]

The end result was that both the Haitian government and its ability to run the state were weakened: 80 percent of the schools and 90 percent of clinics were run by NGOs.[32] Many large US NGOs had budgets greater than the entire government ministry they worked with, like Public Health or Agriculture. Tellingly, donors failed to support any disaster-risk-reduction program, an area in which the Latin America region tended to do quite well.

NGOs

As the fulcrum for this massive infusion of aid, NGOs were prime agents of instrumentalization, sometimes unwillingly and unknowingly. The pressures were both external and internal. The use of NGOs as conduits for promoting foreign-policy objectives and neo-liberal policies clearly had its roots in donor governments. But NGOs were also instrumentalized by donors through reward structures that worked against collaboration, coordination, and participation. This reward structure was within the purview of international aid agencies to change, particularly by applying the collective principles of accountability that they had signed up to implement. Internal processes, including fundraising pressures and individual staff members' concerns about their careers, added to these external pressures.

INGOs—and national NGOs that receive official development aid— operate within an aid system that inhibits collaboration and partnership, and thus capacity building, of indigenous NGOs. The net effect was detrimental to Haitians in need of effective humanitarian action. I conducted a multi-year ethnographic analysis of two local women's NGOs, both working in HIV/AIDS prevention.[33] One received primarily private funding from an array of European NGOs and the other from official public sources, mostly bilateral aid. This difference in aid and donor policies resulted in marked differences in the two NGOs' management and relationship with their recipient populations. The one with public aid had more constraints on participation and autonomy than the NGO with private NGO partners. More specifically, public aid policies like "results-based" or "performance-based" management centralized decision-making authority and closed off avenues for meaningful local participation. These new accountability regimes, designed for tighter financial transparency, often had the side effect of top-down planning wherein recipients had less say on NGO activities. Genuine local participation requires flexibility in financial decisions, which are increasingly difficult in new financial accountability regimes. On top of this, pressures for upward accountability and to spend (and get more contracts from the donor) undermine the relationship with local communities. Consequently, corrections and changes made from on-the-ground experience were increasingly difficult. The reporting requirements also cut off intra-NGO communication. Staff who worked in the field and who were the direct points of contact with aid recipients were increasingly removed from decision-making authority. NGOs, like the one in my study receiving only public aid, had to follow the project cycle and do exactly as they were told, implementing donor priorities, or risk their funding being pulled. In Haiti, the reporting requirements make NGOs more top-heavy, with more resources directed toward higher-paid full time administrative staff to keep up with them, with at least one full-time accountant versed in USAID or other donor reporting requirements and software. Job advertisements—often written in English—explicitly asked for these competencies.[34] Since the earthquake this communication gap has widened, with English-speaking foreigners in decision-making roles unable to communicate with Creole-speaking Haitian field staff.

Despite much rhetoric on accountability to beneficiaries and the emergence of principles and standards such as the Humanitarian Accountability Partnership and Sphere, the reward structure actively discourages local participation, open lines of communication with aid recipients and within the office, and collaboration and coordination with the state or other NGOs. The reporting and other requirements imposed by donors reorient NGOs to be more concerned with accountability from above, not from below. If an NGO fails a community, the community has no recourse. Intended beneficiaries have no direct contact with the donors or even NGO directors. If a state-sponsored development project fails or lines the pockets of insiders, citizens would be in the streets protesting, because there is at least in theory some accountability to the citizenry and politicians can be voted out of office. But in environments such as post-quake Haiti, NGOs could not be compelled by the state to work better, or work in under-serviced areas, because they were first and foremost *private, voluntary* initiatives.

There is little incentive for NGOs to cooperate with one another. NGOs are in fact competitors with one another and the Haitian government itself.

According to a staff member at the Ministry of Planning and Foreign Cooperation, only 10–20 percent of NGOs gave their reports to the government in any given year. Donor policies can actually encourage NGOs to disregard the authority of the state. NGOs often pay employees three times as much as the equivalent government ministry, what World Bank researcher Alice Morton termed "raiding."[35]

NGO staff have some agency in the process. As actors within the system, they are behaving in a quite understandable fashion, responding to the power structure, inequality, and the rewards system of the aid enterprise. But NGOs, especially INGOs who receive the majority of their funds from official sources, tend to be concerned about greater funding streams and inflate their budgets. In pre-earthquake Haiti, many INGOs seemed comfortable in their governance roles, which displaced and often undermined the state. After the earthquake, many INGOs themselves contributed to high expectations given their fundraising appeals that pulled on people's heartstrings by reproducing the most negative and tragic images of the devastation and contributing to a narrative that projected Haitians as incapable of helping themselves. As the Disaster Accountability Project demonstrated, their promises were as exaggerated as they were vague.[36] In this way, NGOs were active agents in their own instrumentalization both passively by accepting rules of the game that failed to promote accountability to beneficiaries,and actively by unrealistically raising expectations.

Finally, it should be noted that some individual agency representatives were instrumentalizing aid through their own career aspirations. NGOs offer higher-paying jobs than the Haitian government is able to provide; in-country aid agency staff are the backbone of Haiti's small middle class. Haiti's high unemployment rate, and related intense competition for available jobs, militates against bearers of bad news or whistleblowers. Even if they could communicate with their English-speaking foreign supervisors, many field staff were fearful of sticking their necks out and risking being fired. While presumably many foreign staff had other options—though the global recession limited them—and hence chose the job of working in Haiti based on principle, there were substantial perks, such as higher salaries based on "hazard pay" and expense allowances, including housing. Given that many expatriate aid personnel tended to be young, they "tend to treat Haiti as a stepping stone. Working in Haiti is a huge notch in the bedpost for those wanting jobs in the foreign service. The result is, these ambitious young people don't rock the boat or think outside the box," said an NGO researcher with decades of international experience.

After the Earthquake

US Military

Twenty-two thousand US troops landed in Haiti hours after the quake. The US Southern Command was the closest entity with the logistical capacity to rebuild the crumbled infrastructure after the earthquake, and as an NGO country director noted, they "got their boots dirty" doing grunt work.[37] However, as military, they prioritized the issue of security above all else, delaying aid and augmenting the culture of fear that divided non-Haitian aid workers from the aid recipients. According to WikiLeaked documents, security was not on the list of Préval's priorities outlined in a January 16 communiqué.[38] Yet a day later, he requested the deployment of US troops (days after they had already been deployed) in a public-relations effort to rationalize their de facto presence. On January 20, Secretary of State Hillary Clinton issued a directive to embassies to discipline "irresponsible journalism" because it was important to "get the narrative right" about US intentions in Haiti. Most upsetting to many within the humanitarian community was that the United States used its foothold in the airport to assume the role of gatekeeper, promoting a US aid "shock and awe" to the detriment of other donors, NGOs, and aid agencies anxious to ship in supplies. The US military infamously denied landing rights to an MSF team while allowing the Pennsylvania governor to airlift out of Haiti two twenty-somethings from his state who had started an orphanage there.

The US show of force paid dividends from Washington's perspective. On July 12, 2010, six months after the earthquake, Préval awarded medals to various individuals, including several US personalities such as Anderson Cooper, Sean Penn, and Bill Clinton, at an upbeat event applauding post-quake recovery. This contrasted sharply with the growing rather than diminishing number of tent settlements and unanswered questions about the tangible effects of more than US$3 billion in aid. The next day, one day before Bastille Day, the French ambassador criticized this slight of the French effort, which included MSF and other NGOs that had been establishing community water taps with neighborhood associations even before the earthquake.

A concrete manifestation of instrumentalization that undermined Haitian authorities is the lack of support for Haiti's public infrastructure, including its relief-coordinating capacity. Only 1 percent of emergency post-earthquake aid passed through the Haitian government, and only 15 percent of the reconstruction aid was nominally destined for the Haitian government. Projects were usually "preferenced" to contractors from the donor country.[39] While funds for the IHRC that Bill Clinton co-chaired were not supposed to be "earmarked," in practice the vast majority of the funds were still "tied aid." Only 2.5 percent of reconstruction funds went to Haitian firms.

Government of Haiti

Given that the majority of aid circumvented it, the government had very little capacity to exert its authority. However, one sovereign power it still had was over customs, and some agents attempted to leverage this. Whether or not in retaliation against being shut out of the quake recovery efforts or to put a "tax" on aid assets to ensure that at least some of it went to Haitians, stories abounded of wheelchairs or medical supplies being held up at customs for several months, until duties were paid. This was certainly a source of frustration to aid agencies, but seen from another point of view, why would inexperienced humanitarians have expected not to go through customs? Only formally registered NGOs, four hundred of the alleged ten thousand, are exempt from customs duties as stipulated in Haiti's law relating to NGOs. Whether justifiable or not, red tape did slow delivery of aid following the earthquake.

Within Haiti's Population

As noted previously, the post-earthquake solidarity temporarily suspended Haiti's pervasive social division and exclusion. With the arrival of outside aid, these negative social dynamics returned stronger than ever, in no small part because of the large stakes involved. While people were still grieving for their loved ones and piecing their lives back together, news spread of billions of dollars in aid being allocated to Haiti. Predictably, people with social advantages—Haiti's lighter-skinned merchants, landowners, NGO workers, well-educated English speakers, and pastors connected to foreign mission groups—were poised to benefit from the windfall. Aided by structures favoring foreign control and the relative inexperience of the newcomers, many of these local intermediaries leveraged the aid to their benefit, doling out ration cards to members of their church, their friends, and relatives. Cases were reported of women forced to have sex in exchange for two weeks' worth of food.[40] In many parts of Port-au-Prince food distribution was implemented by evangelical groups that had little experience in emergency food aid and few relationships or local networks in Port-au-Prince. This all but guaranteed that pastors (many of whom spoke a few key phrases in English from an earlier connection to mission groups) would be empowered to make decisions on distribution.

A six-week study I conducted in the summer of 2010, in a random sample of 108 camps (one in eight in the Port-au-Prince metropolitan area, 861 at the time), underscored how lack of effective coordination and manipulation of relief efforts, aided and abetted by policies of NGOs, marginalized Haitians and worked against the participation of IDPs in programs ostensibly designed for their benefit. Many NGOs created camp committees, some of whose members lived outside the camps; 59 percent of the committees were self-selected, and an additional 10 percent were named by NGOs or others.[41] While IDPs knew the name of the leader, only about one-third of the IDPs[42] could name the strategy, plan, activities, or even the name of the camp committee. Reports—including those from NGOs—abounded of these committees using their monopoly of doling out aid to increase personal power, reward constituencies such as members of churches, and even attempt to force women recipients into having sex. NGOs were officially encouraged to work with such committees; as one agency staff put it, "to check off the box for local participation."

Landlords who were lucky enough to have their houses still standing, car rental agents, retailers of computers and other foreign equipment, restaurant and hotel proprietors, the handful of companies delivering private water and sanitation services, and other members of Haiti's elite benefited even more than these camp committees. Procurement policies and procedures that had origins in promoting donors' national interests and a concern about financial accountability all but guaranteed that the hundreds of foreign aid agencies would spend money on foreign companies, even as they needed local agents to complete transactions. In this way much of the funds were sent upward to Haiti's elites, who had not been as badly hit. Knowing about these procedures and the pressures to spend the money, it was common for landlords to charge monthly rents of US$2,500 for a studio for foreign aid workers. Knowing they had a monopoly and good political connections, private water and sanitation companies often tripled the price per gallon for water delivery within the NGO contracts.

The direct result was that—abetted by policies from donors and NGOs that may have been well intentioned—those who were most needy received under par assistance while the system redirected the aid upward and outward.

Consequences

The cholera epidemic provides a good example of how the structural deficiencies of a top-down aid system undermined an effective response. Instrumentalization had consequences and may well have contributed to the spread of cholera. Despite the evidence that UN troops were the vectors for the cholera, the United Nations consistently downplayed and denied responsibility for the epidemic. It suppressed publication of the first independent report and continued to cast doubt on its conclusions even after the second report that used genetic evidence to link the cholera strain directly to Nepal was published. MINUTSAH's preoccupation with face-saving delayed action needed to contain the crisis. The United Nations also failed to screen troops, even though half of the countries participating in the mission had had recent cholera outbreaks. More to the point of this chapter, the rapid spread of the disease was at least in part attributable to the continued gaps in prevention services and slow response efforts resulting from the way in which the aid system was set up in Haiti.

Prevention efforts had been undercut. As part of the lead up to Aristide's 2004 ouster, the IDB withheld US$535 million in needed loans, many of which were for water and sanitation. Partners in Health called this a "straight line" to cholera.[43] Post-earthquake gaps in water, sanitation and hygiene (WASH) services persisted within the camps. According to a November 2010 WASH cluster database, of 1,199 camps officially recognized nationwide, only 383, or 31.9 percent, had an NGO actor responsible for the toilets. While the larger camps were better serviced, and a much higher percentage of the population had access to toilets, of the 1,058,853 people officially registered, only 434,901, or 41.07 percent, lived in camps where an NGO offered toilet services. The database identified 187 camps across the country, 15.6 percent, with an NGO responsible for water. Given that services were concentrated in larger camps, this represented just under a quarter (24.73 percent) of the population. It is important to note that this database was compiled immediately following the October cholera outbreak.

I conducted two surveys, in July–August 2010[44] and January 2011,[45] of a random sample of IDP camps within the Port-au-Prince metropolitan area. Researchers conducted quantitative and qualitative surveys of the camps, combining interview and observational methods, in three interrelated areas: conditions and services within the camps, residents' level of understanding and involvement in the camp committees, and interviews with committee representatives. For quality control, several camps were visited by different researchers and information cross checked. I personally visited thirty-one IDP camps. The data showed persistent gaps in WASH services: seven months following the earthquake, 40.5 percent of IDP camps did not have access to water, and 30.3 percent did not have toilets of any kind. Despite the Sphere standard that a toilet should be shared by no more than twenty people, in the sample the average was 273; 26 percent of the toilets had not been cleaned in the seven months following the earthquake. Despite the millions in newly pledged aid to Haiti to combat cholera, very little progress had been made during the first several months following the outbreak. Using the same random sample of 108 IDP camps, a team of three State University of Haiti students investigated forty-five camps in January 2011 that as per the previous August 2010 study had lacked either water or toilets. The results showed a minimum of progress: 37.6 percent instead of 40.5 percent still did not have water, and 25.8 instead of 30.3 percent still did not have a toilet.

In part, instrumentalization explains these gaps: a lack of coordination, a "silo" mentality, and conflicts with landowners. The services provided in the camps varied significantly according to a range of factors. Camps in low-income shantytown Cité Soleil had almost no services, while those in traditionally well-off suburb Pétion-Ville were better managed. Camps that were far from major roads or the city center in Croix-des-Bouquets or Carrefour had little to no services. Finally, camps situated on private land were significantly worse off than those on public land.

There are many firsthand testimonies revealing that people in non-centrally located camps had been forgotten. "Maybe it's because we're hidden away inside that the NGOs have forgotten us, but we're the area that is most affected! This area, Fort-National and Pivoine, doesn't have a big road so the NGO trucks just don't see us," said Ti Georges, camp committee leader in Pivoine. The first words from Olga Ulysse, leader within the CAJIT camp in Carrefour, were gratitude that we even showed up: "People make appointments and they don't come. I don't know if it's too far or if people are afraid of the mountain." Her colleague Madame Odrigue, who is an elected member of the community council, the official local government, had another theory: "It's because the donors don't get credit for giving us water, unlike down the hill next to the Route Nationale." NGOs were significantly more likely to manage camps in central areas, where UN and NGO officers were located, than far peripheral areas.

Consistently, humanitarian agencies bowed to pressure to not provide services on private land, thus allowing Haitian elites and middle classes to assert private-property rights. Because the earthquake destroyed walls that protected private property, camps were created on private land such as the Pétion-Ville Club, a private golf club that became home to 30,100 people as of July 2010. At that time, 71 percent of camps sat on private land. With people desperately seeking shelter, this posed a fundamental conflict of interest between landowners' right to their property and residents' rights to decent temporary shelter and living conditions. Acting on the belief that people were living in the camps because of the services provided, some private owners cut off life-saving services in order to force people to leave the camps. The administration of the Saint-Louis de Gonzague School refused NGO access to distribute food and water. Camp leader Elvire Constant, who lived there at the time recalled, "The priest told the Americans to not pile up the grounds! He said there were too many tents in the compound, that the space was saturated." NGOs and the United Nations "cannot interfere when the owner does not want us there," said an official. According to several neighborhood leaders, the school director prevented the Red Cross and MSF from providing services. On one of the days we visited, a group of Cuban doctors sat sheepishly near the entrance, waiting for authorization. Human rights agencies documented at least five other locations where this same situation of starving people out of services occurred.[46] Camps that were on public land were more likely to have water (75.0 percent) than those on private land (51.8 percent), although this gap was not statistically significant. However, the differences in health provision were dramatic; 39.1 percent of camps on state land had a clinic, whereas only 12.9 percent of camps on private land did.

Consistently, camps managed by NGOs fared better; it was the most statistically significant independent variable. However, only 22 percent of camps in August 2010 were managed by NGOs. According to IOM staff, despite the availability of information on services or lack thereof, there was no mechanism to force NGOs to assume camp-management responsibilities. "It's a thankless job," said one. An NGO among the most visible and hardworking in Cité Soleil bristled at being listed as camp manager for fear of the public responsibility that this designation connoted. "Others are just plain lazy," said a development agency official on condition of anonymity. With very little capacity to play an oversight role even adequately, not to mention offering incentives to NGOs, the Haitian government had little ability to help. To sum up, according to a Haitian government WASH official, "The bottom line is we have no carrots and sticks. NGOs are private agencies and pretty much can do what they want."

Despite the promises, the UN cluster system, responsible for ensuring effective and coordinated action, generally excluded local voices; all but the WASH cluster meetings were held at a UN base where access was closely guarded, and media reports described how even high-ranking Haitian government employees were denied access. Many meetings were held in English, excluding the field staff who both needed and had vital information. Coordination and attendance in meetings depended on the willingness of NGOs to provide more services to more camps. Said an NGO manager: "I stopped going to the meetings. I don't have the time, since it takes me away from my job. I have to be accountable to funders." So in the end, no one individual agency had to take the blame for the collective failure or could be compelled to provide needed services in the camps. The one entity that could, the Haitian government, was still under-resourced despite the

billions in aid sent to Haiti. In addition, cluster meetings were also perfor-
mative, not deliberative spaces: instead of focusing on problem solving, the
meetings tended to be spaces to communicate "messaging" or promote an
NGO or for-profit service, for example. Again, the notable exception was
the WASH cluster. Problems within camps were solved one by one, with
the government official facilitating the meeting, encouraging and cajoling
NGOs to take action.

This coordinated, hands-on, inclusive approach, *led by the Haitian
government*, is likely the reason that one municipality made progress in
WASH services following the cholera outbreak. Cité Soleil is Haiti's largest
slum, made infamous as the site of clashes during the violence surrounding
Aristide's 2004 ouster and a film, *Ghosts of Cité Soleil*, that declared it to be
the "most dangerous place on earth." The United Nations declared it a "red
zone," and hence many INGOs stayed away; many car rental companies
banned their vehicles from going there for insurance reasons. As a result, IDP
camps in Cité Soleil had fewer services, despite the fact that the population
tended to be the poorest and in greatest need. Camps had less water and
toilets on average, and no clinics, compared to other, less poverty-stricken,
neighborhoods. Toilets in Cité Soleil were cleaned less often.

Following the outbreak, the government WASH agency made 100 percent coverage in Cité Soleil a priority and directed staff resources and lob-
bied for UN, donor, and INGO aid in the effort. NGOs like Médecins du
Monde-Canada and MSF-Belgium agreed to coordinate with the local and
national government staff. The minimal progress documented in my two
studies was concentrated in Cité Soleil. The 100 percent coverage goal was
reached in February 2011. The clear lesson here was that NGO coordination with the Haitian government that set guidelines and priorities—in
other words, *not* being instrumentalized—can lead to successful outcomes.

Lessons

As noted in the introduction to the chapter, the scale and the urban
nature of Haiti's earthquake, not to mention the scale of the relief effort,
undoubtedly posed serious challenges. However, as an urban disaster, it is a
wake-up call for future humanitarian action, as urban areas are increasingly
at risk for large-scale disaster events. Moreover, Haiti offers a clear view and
several cautionary lessons of the structural weaknesses of an aid system that
was instrumentalized on many levels.

Several NGOs, including MSF and PIH, led valiant efforts to bring life-
saving services to the IDP camps. There are lessons in their best practices,
such as the latter's explicit coordination with the Haitian government.

However, the failures to close the huge assistance gaps require attention and analysis to address problems such as the cholera epidemic or prevent similar problems in other disaster situations. Neither international nor national NGOs are structurally accountable to the Haitian population. They have no incentive or requirement to go outside their turf. Closing avoidable assistance gaps would require greater investment in, and more resources flowing to, the government.

As this chapter shows, the government-avoiding posture of NGOs at best does nothing to address chronic problems and more likely exacerbates them. Donors' neo-liberal ideologies and prejudices that favor private voluntary NGOs that have little accountability to crisis-affected populations have kept the one institution that has the responsibility and public account-ability—the Haitian government, both national and local—from being able to respond to this crisis, both in terms of prevention and emergency aid.[47] The progress made in Cité Soleil was in no small part due to the fact that the Haitian government led the effort and that it used a collabora-tive approach with the IOM, the United Nations, local governments, and NGOs. It is also because the government began with identifying problems and demanded full coverage.

This chapter distills lessons on the long history of instrumentalization of the aid enterprise in Haiti. It shows that NGOs failed in their mission because they were tools in the service of external political and economic agendas. The result was a patchwork of NGOs that were all beholden to donors, afraid to speak up, and removed from their purported beneficia-ries. Moreover, agencies instrumentalized their beneficiaries—and to some extent the donors as well—in order to protect their turf and expand their budgets and the prospects of future contracts. The result was a total lack of communication of local needs and priorities to those structures able to respond, and a disarticulated, individualized patchwork of private unac-countable "fiefdoms" instead of a network of agencies working together under a coordinated public response that attempts access to all.

These problems are structural, inherited by a legacy of instrumentalist policies and a reward structure that cut off local participation, intra-NGO communication, inter-NGO collaboration, and cooperation with the Hai-tian government. The scale of the disaster and its response, coupled with the rise of globalization, has increased the stakes and therefore the risks of instrumentalization. The Haitian proverb predicted the consequence of too many competing agendas and no designated, responsible authority: the goat with many caretakers dying in the sun because of a lack of water. Adequate water—and reinforcing government capacity to provide it more cheaply and to the neighborhoods in addition to camps—could have prevented thousands of deaths. It is to be hoped that humanitarian actors elsewhere can learn some crucial lessons from the Haitian experience, including the critical importance of investing in and building capacity of indigenous mechanisms that are accountable to those who are most in need.

Part Three

THEMATIC CHAPTERS

Chapter 10

"Those With Guns Never Go Hungry"

The Instrumental Use of Humanitarian Food Assistance in Conflict

DANIEL MAXWELL

Like other forms of humanitarian aid in conflict, food assistance is intended to be provided solely based on the needs of recipients and in such a way that it does not support one belligerent or another in the conflict or fulfill some other political or social agenda. Yet in case after case, humanitarian food assistance—historically most frequently in the form of in-kind food aid—sent to provide succor for the victims of conflict has been diverted, plundered, and manipulated by belligerents. It has been used to prolong the conflict, to drive the movement of civilian populations displaced by war to the strategic advantage of one party or another in the conflict, and, frequently, to try to win civilian populations over to the political agenda of one of the belligerents. Critics have noted that humanitarian food aid is seldom completely free of political considerations and often has unforeseen consequences.[1] But the form of this instrumentalization of food assistance has varied over time.

One of the most massive food aid programs of all time was support to the governments of South Vietnam and other friendly nations in the region during the Indo-China War. US officials at the time were convinced that "food for peace" was a critical plank in the overall strategy to "win hearts

An earlier version of this paper was presented at the symposium Problems, Promises, and Paradoxes of Aid: Africa's Experience, April 16–17, 2010, at Cornell University.

and minds" among the populace of Southeast Asia—and hence to prevail in the regional confrontation with communist regimes. While displacement of civilians during the war did cause localized crises of food access, the purpose of this massive food aid program was much more about buying political allegiances than it was about preventing or addressing hunger.[2] This case is clearly about the use of humanitarian food aid for strategic and military purposes by the donor (and belligerent)—a case with some parallels to the current conflict in Afghanistan. But donors aren't the only party to manipulate food assistance to their perceived political advantage. And there is, of course, the larger question of whether food aid has simply been a political tool that donors have manipulated all along—that their motives have had less to do with humanitarian assistance than with surplus disposal, market creation, or simply trying to win influence with foreign governments. With recent changes in food aid policy—even in the United States—and shrinking food aid budgets globally, much of this argument is now mainly of historical interest and is beyond the scope of this chapter.[3]

In 2010, twenty-five years after Live Aid raised millions of dollars for famine relief in Ethiopia during the great famine of the mid-1980s, the British Broadcasting Corporation (BBC) ran a report about the diversion of some of that famine assistance to purchase weapons by rebel groups in Ethiopia. The ferocity of the ensuing argument eventually led to the withdrawal of the story. Though the merits of the argument both for and against the allegations were difficult to judge twenty-five years after the fact, the allegation was a case of a rebel movement or non-state actor diverting money for food assistance to purchase arms.[4] In other words, this case was much less about trying to change the broad political parameters of an ideologically inspired conflict, and much more about trying to gain military advantage through more weaponry. But food assistance was the currency. And institutional donors were not particularly involved in this case. These were nongovernmental actors, both those who raised the resources and the rebel movements who received (and allegedly diverted) them.

Later in 2010, the *New Yorker* ran a column by Philip Gourevitch alleging that wherever they go, humanitarian agencies end up permitting their assistance to be used—sometimes deliberately, sometimes inadvertently—to prolong the conflicts whose consequences they seek to mitigate. The story Gourevitch presented included the use of food assistance—particularly in Biafra. The information was not new, and indeed his argument ignored the attempts over recent years to prevent the very phenomenon he was describing. But the implication was that humanitarians are either very easy to fool, or else not above politicizing assistance themselves—or perhaps a bit of both.

Since 9/11, international assistance of all types has become increasingly linked to security or counterterrorism objectives. This has affected both humanitarian and development assistance and is captured by the general theme of the "securitization of aid," but also "humanity as a weapon of war."[5] This trend has several important implications. Governments and donors have funneled significant amounts of assistance to affected civilian recipients through the military or military contractors rather than through traditional aid agencies. The objectives of assistance have been increasingly "securitized," even when assistance was channeled through "traditional" humanitarian agencies.[6] And, critically, this assistance has been guided by a belief that poverty and underdevelopment are key drivers of insurgency and terrorism; hence, the notion of "winning hearts and minds" has become central to the aid-allocation strategies of some donors, as it was during the Indo-China war in the 1960s.[7] This trend is broader than just US foreign assistance, but it has been most strongly manifested in US assistance.[8] In 2010, a new government took power in the United Kingdom and announced that future British aid would also be allocated subject to security considerations.[9]

Writing in the official, peer-reviewed journal of the US Army War College, Matthew LeRiche noted in 2004 that, with the end of the Cold War,

> when the United States and the Soviet Union began to disengage from the many conflicts spawned by the failure of decolonization, particularly in Africa, insurgents and governments had to find new methods of providing for the supply of their armed forces. An increasing influx of humanitarian aid from independent and even state donors, intended to help the collateral casualties of war, often has been co-opted to fill part of the void left by superpowers.[10]

LeRiche goes on to state, "The co-optation of international humanitarian aid has likely become one of the most reliable sources of funding for belligerents" in contemporary conflicts and notes, *"those with guns never go hungry."*[11]

Even these few brief examples highlight the many different actors manipulating food assistance and the many different reasons why food is particularly vulnerable to manipulation. But although examples of abuse abound, the significance of the problem is not always clear, or whether using food assistance in conflict for purposes other than to alleviate hunger actually serves those purposes. This chapter seeks to assess the evidence on deliberate usage of humanitarian food assistance to achieve political or security objectives of the many parties in conflict situations. At one level there is little difference between food aid and other assistance, but several points are worth noting.

First, the loss of access to adequate food is often one of the first consequences of conflict—food is a powerful tool, and control over food is a lucrative lever to belligerents. Many contemporary conflicts occur in resource-constrained environments, in which food is not only an important resource for human survival, but also a significant economic and political tool.

Second, food aid remains the most common form of humanitarian aid, and the biggest single category of recipients of humanitarian food aid remains conflict-affected populations.[12] Thus, while symptomatic of many of the abuses of humanitarian assistance, the sheer volume of food aid puts it in a different category from many other forms of assistance.

Third, the instrumentalization of food aid is done not just by donors. All the actors and agendas mentioned in the conceptual framework in Chapter 1 are implicated in one way or another in the abuse of food aid in conflicts: donors, national governments, non-state actors (rebel movements, militias, and warlords), the media and celebrities (in the BBC story), humanitarians themselves, and in some cases even recipient communities.

Fourth, quite apart from conflict, the history of food aid itself is a story of a resource ostensibly being provided for one purpose, while its "real" purpose may be something different—in other words, food aid has been instrumentally manipulated for all kinds of purposes. For example, over the sixty or so years that the United States has maintained an official food aid program, its ostensible rationale has usually been humanitarian and developmental, but the actual policy objectives often had more to do with disposing of surplus production, providing producer price supports, developing new export markets, providing budgetary support to friendly foreign governments, and even providing a measure of financial self-preservation for the shipping firms that transport food aid overseas and the agencies that distribute it. The manipulation of food aid in conflict is a variation on this theme and is the focus of this chapter.[13]

This chapter seeks to evaluate the evidence on these questions by reviewing a number of case studies of food aid in conflict to elucidate the different forms this manipulation has taken and the different actors involved. An earlier paper provided some initial conclusions.[14] This chapter briefly reviews the limited general literature on this topic and notes the normative guidelines governing humanitarian food assistance over the past fifty years. Case studies focus on different events at different times, but case study evidence is organized by the different categories of actors just noted, the intents of the actors, and the outcomes they achieved. The chapter concludes with several general observations, as well as suggestions for humanitarian policy, practice, and further research.

The Politicization of Food Aid and the Normative Guidance to Prevent It

In 1985, Robert Paarlberg described "food power" as exercising "political influence through the manipulation of food production or distribution" whether between or within states, and by both governments and non-state actors.[15] He examined several cases, including food aid to India in the 1960s and the attempts to restrict US commercial exports to the Soviet Union in retaliation for the invasion of Afghanistan in 1980. Paarlberg concluded that the use of "food power" was unlikely to achieve strategic objectives. Manipulating access to food is not easy to do. There are too many alternative sources of food, and too many unforeseen consequences of manipulating food supplies, to make food aid a viable policy instrument for influencing other countries. In the case of commercial food exports, there are too many alternative exporters and too much opposition from the US agriculture lobby. In brief, tying food (whether humanitarian food aid or commercial exports) to political objectives was rarely successful.

Even if food were to be used to pursue foreign policy objectives, Paarlberg suggested that little influence would be gained and the chances of the whole process backfiring were high. The evidence suggested that only poor people would suffer the consequences of sanctions, but political elites and belligerents would not, making the same point noted previously that LeRiche reiterated twenty years later. Indeed, attempts to influence recipient countries using food aid would result in the donor being blamed for manipulation, possibly leading to an effect opposite of the intended one—one of the many potential unintended consequences of manipulating food supplies. Paarlberg's 2010 book, based on more-recent examples, reconfirms most of these findings.[16]

Other research on the use of food as a weapon of war suggests that the manipulation of food assistance is a factor in contemporary famines, but one of many—it rarely stands alone as the cause. Macrae and Zwi reviewed the uses of food as a weapon of war in Africa and noted that food was used to influence conflict, indirectly through its political and economic uses, and directly through its diversion and plunder either to feed militias and armies or to sell to purchase weaponry.[17] They noted three ways in which food—or more specifically, manipulating access to food—was used as a weapon: through acts of omission or the failure to prevent abuse, through acts of commission or direct attacks on food production and distribution systems, and through direct provision of food to some groups and the active denial of food to others. The abuse of food aid falls mainly into the first and last categories.

The responses to the instrumentalization of humanitarian food aid in conflict have been twofold. Traditional humanitarian organizations have noted that this manipulation is in direct violation of humanitarian principles and international codes of conduct. From this viewpoint, subjecting humanitarian assistance to political or security objectives puts at risk not only genuinely disaster-affected populations, but also threatens the independence of humanitarian action and the normative foundations on which it is based.[18] A number of initiatives, conducted across the humanitarian community, have attempted to curb such practices, and most donors and agencies have signed on. These are outlined in the following sections. An alternative critique questions whether tying aid to political or strategic objectives actually has the intended result of promoting those objectives. This perspective focuses less on the question of principles and normative guidance, and more on the question of the impact or effectiveness of such practices.[19]

Humanitarians have long been aware of the pitfalls of providing assistance in conflict—where almost by definition, resources are scarce and any resource introduced has political consequences, irrespective of the motivations behind it.[20] Substantial international guidance exists to ensure that food assistance is not misused and that unintended consequences are minimized, monitored, and mitigated. Over the past decade and a half, numerous efforts have been made to improve this normative guidance and its application. The intent is to provide humanitarian assistance to conflict- or disaster-affected people in a manner that is somewhat insulated from the political circumstances of the conflict or disaster that caused the food security crisis in the first place. While actual practice often falls short of this norm, a number of international instruments have been designed to promote and protect the norm.

The 1949 Geneva Conventions and their additional protocols, part of the body of international humanitarian law (IHL),[21] place very clear limits on the use of food (of any type) in war. According to IHL, the state has the primary responsibility for the well-being of its population (including ensuring access to food). Starvation of civilians as a method of warfare is specifically prohibited, though IHL is largely silent on the manipulation of food aid per se, except to note that belligerents should not interfere with food convoys when people "lack essential supplies for their survival."[22] IHL applies mainly to states, and not all countries have signed up to all the provisions of IHL. NGOs at the 1974 World Food Conference drafted a strongly worded resolution warning that food should not be used as a political weapon, but the language was watered down by the formal conference, and did not appear in the Universal Declaration on the Eradication of Hunger and Malnutrition, the major document emerging from the conference.[23]

The Code of Conduct for the International Red Cross and Red Crescent Movement and NGOs in disaster relief also clearly seeks to keep humanitarian assistance insulated from politics. It states that humanitarian aid shall not promote any "religious or political standpoint" and it separates humanitarian objectives from foreign policy objectives. Aid agencies "shall endeavor not to act as instruments of government foreign policy."[24] At last count, 472 humanitarian agencies have signed the Code of Conduct, including almost all major humanitarian agencies and alliances.[25] The Sphere Standards—industry-wide guidance on how humanitarian assistance is to be delivered—reiterates the prohibition on starvation as a method of war and notes, "Where there is a risk of food aid being commandeered or used by combatants in an armed conflict, measures [should be] put in place to avoid it fuelling the conflict."[26]

More generally, humanitarian assistance is guided by a set of principles, initially adopted by the ICRC but now widely adopted by the international humanitarian community. These include *humanity*, or the humanitarian imperative; *impartiality*, or the provision of assistance solely on the basis of need; *neutrality*, or the provision of assistance in a way that avoids favoring any belligerent in an armed conflict; *independence*, or the provision of aid independent from the interference of other actors, particularly belligerents in a conflict; and *universality*, or the claim that the humanitarian imperative applies equally in all situations. While the principles have no legal force, they are widely (and formally) incorporated into the policies of agencies, donors, and the current humanitarian donor initiatives, if perhaps not the policies of other actors mentioned previously.[27]

The "do no harm" initiative of Mary Anderson and her colleagues outlines at least five different ways in which humanitarian aid can exacerbate the impact of conflict—and though not specific to food assistance, it is especially relevant to preventing the abuse of food assistance.[28] The "do no harm" idea has spawned efforts to give agencies tools to identify (and weigh) potential harms as well as potential benefits, and to monitor for and prevent the former.[29] Other codes of conduct that govern the distribution of humanitarian food assistance don't speak to the question of the politicization of food aid.[30]

The Manipulation of Food Aid

Clearly, formally, a strong international consensus exists on the normative framework for the provision of humanitarian food assistance. Agencies and donors—and to a lesser extent, national governments—have all reiterated their commitments to this consensus. Despite this formal consensus, actual practice on the ground is often very different. All these actors have, in one way or another, manipulated food assistance to achieve political, strategic, or military objectives. Although quantifying who was the most responsible is not possible, the following brief cases illustrate the widespread nature of the phenomenon. This is only a sample drawn from nearly thirty examples studied in about a dozen countries.[31]

Donors

Somalia

In 2009, the United States shut down all its food assistance to south central Somalia, even though Somalia was in a major humanitarian crisis. This was justified on the grounds that significant quantities of food aid were being diverted from humanitarian purposes in Somalia; some of it was being captured by the al-Shabaab insurgency that controlled much of southern Somalia, and which was believed to have links to al Qaeda. The shut-off of aid was cast in legal terms as simple compliance with the regulations of OFAC, set up under the Patriot Act. Much of the US food was delivered in Somalia by WFP, which at the time was investigating corruption charges against some of the local contractors hired to transport food aid.

These corruption charges provided some legitimacy to US concerns that food aid was being diverted by or to proscribed organizations. However, other motives were apparent for the shut down, and several obvious anomalies as well. First, al-Shabaab had been listed as a "terrorist organization" by OFAC for almost two years by the time food aid was shut off. And second, the diversion of food aid—by warlords, militias, and criminals—had been happening in Somalia for decades. So neither the diversion of food aid nor al-Shabaab's connections were news to anyone who knew the Somalia context. Perhaps more tellingly, the US shutdown of food aid coincided with an intended offensive by the TFG that the United States and the African Union strongly supported. Behind the scenes in late 2009 and early 2010, the United States was putting pressure on humanitarian agencies to support the offensive by providing assistance to civilians in areas recaptured by the TFG (while aid was being denied to areas controlled by al-Shabaab). The 2010 offensive never really materialized, and the US move—whether motivated by simple legal concerns or an attempt to use food aid to win support for the TFG—was, in the words of one observer, "a distinction without difference."[32] WFP's pipeline was reduced significantly, and indeed, several months later WFP was forced to pull out of most of its operations is south central Somalia altogether after increased threats from al-Shabaab, reducing even further food assistance to south central Somalia.[33] Although at the time WFP sought to downplay the impact of the US shutdown, the UN humanitarian coordinator in Somalia subsequently accused the United States of politicizing its food assistance, making it practically impossible to operate, even in places still accessible by humanitarian agencies.[34] But there were disagreements over the causes and impacts of the aid withdrawal, even within the United Nations.[35] The impact of the shutdown of aid in 2010 was blunted by the best harvest for five years in south central Somalia. The real humanitarian impact was not fully felt until 2011. Meanwhile the security situation for civilians caught in the conflict had worsened, and the likelihood of a political settlement remained low.

Afghanistan

The use of food aid by donors to achieve political and security objectives is probably nowhere better illustrated than in Afghanistan. A recent analysis of food aid notes, "The case of Afghanistan in 2001–2002 highlights the tendency of food aid donors to favor high-profile efforts in geopolitically strategic situations rather than to attend to acute or chronic emergencies, even in the same place, but at a less politically advantageous time."[36] In the initial stages of the war to overthrow the Taliban regime in Afghanistan, food aid was deemed an important tool, and after more than six years of attempts to institutionalize democratic governance in Afghanistan, food aid reemerged as an important tool in the latter part of the 2000s. In both cases, food aid was a tool of donors, but donors who were belligerents in the conflict—first against the Taliban-led regime, and later in the counter-insurgency.

The humanitarian situation in Afghanistan in 2001 was critical, even before the US-led invasion began. Twenty-two years of conflict combined with three severe drought years and a widespread rural-livelihoods crisis meant large numbers were displaced and at risk of famine. But from 2000 onward, the humanitarian effort had been shrinking, and deliveries of food assistance—critical to both the displacement crisis and the drought response—had been declining even as the crisis worsened. But in the immediate aftermath of the US invasion, the availability of food aid skyrocketed, from less than six hundred metric tons per month in September 2001, to nearly three thousand by January 2002. Food aid levels remained high throughout 2002 but dropped off significantly thereafter.[37] US policymakers believed food aid to be so important that few expenses were spared in the early part of the conflict, including for air drops that were expensive and ineffective, and—in the most famously depicted circumstance at the time—dangerous: some of the ready-to-eat meals included in the air drops looked very similar to unexploded ordnance from cluster bombs.

The similarity in appearance of food aid and bombs was a metaphor not lost on some in the humanitarian community, but the merging of humanitarian aid and security objectives in Afghanistan was to continue throughout the Afghanistan war. Colin Powell was famous for his remark that humanitarian agencies were a "force multiplier," but he was far from being the only NATO leader to express such views.[38] Powell himself, speaking at the fiftieth anniversary celebration of Public Law 480 that established the US food aid program, indicated that the early food aid effort in the Afghanistan war had been responsible for allowing the repatriation of three million refugees and had promoted the agenda of "winning hearts and minds" in Afghanistan.[39] As Pérouse de Montclos notes, "Humanitarian rhetoric was always an argument of foreign policy."[40]

Food aid reemerged as a tool in the counter-insurgency later in Afghanistan, with a highly publicized stabilization program known as FIRUP (Food Insecurity Response to Urban Populations) that highlighted the merging of objectives to address food insecurity and objectives to defeat the insurgency into one aid package. Program documentation touts the FIRUP model as "successful in providing vulnerable populations with a means of meeting their household food requirements while serving to enhance stability. . . . USAID Afghanistan would like to expand the program to serve rural areas in direct support of on-going and planned USG counter-insurgency (COIN) efforts."[41] Program documentation notes that the humanitarian agencies implementing FIRUP emphasized its food security and livelihoods-sustaining elements, while the donor emphasized its counter-insurgency elements. Elsewhere US forces were directly involved in food distributions[42] and even in using food distributions as a tool to obtain information on the whereabouts of the insurgents.

The FIRUP program has yet to be evaluated—in terms of either its food-security or its counter-insurgency objectives. However, other research on the use of humanitarian and development aid for counter-insurgency purposes in Afghanistan shows little impact on security objectives, and indeed, perhaps negative impact in some cases (that is, worsened insecurity).[43] Yet the belief that aid with both humanitarian and developmental objectives is a critical component of security strategy was underlined in the 2011 US federal budget.[44] This, of course, goes well beyond just food aid, but the role food aid plays in this strategy is central.

Recipient Country Governments

Democratic People's Republic of Korea

North Korea suffered a catastrophic famine that peaked between 1996 and 1998. Mortality was conservatively estimated at about one million, out of a pre-famine population of about twenty million—or nearly 5 percent of the population.[45] But North Korea is one of the most secretive and authoritarian regimes in the world, and one of the most closed societies. Outsiders—whether foreign diplomats or humanitarian aid workers—were unable to conduct independent assessments or monitoring, and they suspected that the authorities were manipulating them not for the purposes of addressing famine, but of preserving the regime. North Korea had long depended on the Soviet Union and China for food imports. After the collapse of the Soviet Union, the economy was in free fall for several years, and a food crisis—though not necessarily a famine—was inevitable when trade channels dried up.[46] Major flooding occurred in 1995 and 1996, which, while not the cause of the famine, provided a face-saving pretext for requesting outside assistance.

The government was fighting a political battle on two fronts. The first was internationally, not to have the famine revealed in the international press; the second was internally, to prevent conditions from turning so bad as to risk a coup or popular uprising. The government's goals were contradictory in that it needed international help to address conditions internally. South Korea and China were both deeply concerned about the implosion of the North Korean regime, with potential military consequences and an almost certain refugee crisis. They provided food aid with few restrictions; other donors tried to attach conditions of humanitarian access and monitoring to their assistance, or else used it to gain some diplomatic leverage with the reclusive government. Eventually, the United States became the biggest donor of food, but not until rather late in the crisis.

Domestic food distribution was centrally controlled through the Public Distribution System. As early as 1987, daily food rations were cut, and these cuts intensified through the 1990s, leading to food riots in some cities. When the government began to seize grain from farmers' annual retained allotment in the mid-1990s, farmers resorted to hoarding and cultivating illegal plots. Therefore, less grain was sold to the central supply mechanism, meaning that while those with some access to land were able to cope to a degree, people without farming connections began to starve.[47] Andrew Natsios, who headed the US mission to North Korea, noted that the development of private markets in an otherwise Stalinist command economy was one of the major unintended consequences of the way the famine was managed by the North Korean government—an outcome that was quite satisfactory to the United States and other Western donors.[48]

From the outset the priority of the regime clearly was to protect certain categories of people, including the military, the political elite, and some categories of workers, by diverting food aid to them. Whole areas of the country were simply "triaged" out of the survival equation by the allocation of such minimal amounts of food as to virtually guarantee starvation. Estimates of the amount of food that was diverted in this way vary from as low as 30 percent to as high as 90 percent in the accounts of refugees who managed to reach the Chinese border.[49] UN Special Rapporteur on the Right to Food Jean Ziegler made these charges official in 1998.[50] From the outset the government of North Korea clearly was not going to make any pretense about humanitarian principles, humanitarian access, or transparency. Instead, the government deftly managed to use food assistance to help contain domestic unrest and shore up political support in critical sectors of the country, even while ignoring other parts of the country.[51]

External donors had another—equally political—set of objectives. Many saw in the famine a chance to use aid to shape the behavior of the isolated regime, or even a chance to bring it down. One proposed option implied the use of food aid as a "carrot," rewarding certain kinds of behavior—most frequently participation in multi-party talks on nuclear nonproliferation—with more aid. Others intended the collapse of the regime as the policy objective of aid. Many in the humanitarian community objected to the use of food aid as a bargaining chip for anything other than access to starving populations. But external parties weren't going to pass up the chance to use any leverage possible in one of the most intractable foreign-policy dilemmas of the post–Cold War world. Some argued that food aid could be used to favor North Korean "pragmatists" over the orthodox elements of the leadership cadre and eventually pave the way for significant reforms—a process of "reform by stealth."[52] This was unofficially the US policy for five years, from 1995 to 2000, and was eventually given the tongue-in-cheek label of "food for talks." Natsios noted: "Food aid can be used as a powerful weapon in war or as a key instrument of diplomacy in negotiations. The more severe the food crisis, the greater the power of food aid to influence the behavior of those who need it."[53]

However, whether these attempts were especially successful is not clear. The regime did not collapse and did not significantly change its behavior toward the outside world, at least on certain critical issues such as nuclear nonproliferation. Internally, the regime was weakened, and the diversion of the food aid led to urban markets and unplanned privatization—objectives that the North Korean state certainly did not welcome. The famine had a destabilizing effect on North Korea, but the same regime survived in power and pursued many if not most of the same policies ten years after the famine had ended.

Sudan

North Korea was a case of a totalitarian regime manipulating food assistance. Subtler forms of manipulation by host governments were evident in other cases. In 2005–6, for example, the Sudanese government had reason to send internally displaced people in camps in Darfur back to their places of origin. Knowing it could not forcibly repatriate IDPs without invoking the wrath of donors and the international community, the government utilized a process of re-registering IDPs in camps to affect this repatriation in other ways. The agencies had rushed to register IDPs when they had finally been granted access to Darfur in 2004, nearly a year after the conflict started. By then, highly vulnerable groups of IDPs were congregating in urban areas in squalid conditions, and donors made a major push simply to start sending in assistance—mostly food in the initial response—to protect against the further loss of life. This inevitably led to poor targeting, and by 2005 the agencies were certain that some IDP leaders had become quite corrupt, holding multiple ration cards and using them to divert food aid either for their own enrichment or to various groups engaged in the conflict. The major re-registration exercise was conducted in mid-2005 to bring this diversion of aid under control. While officially the government was not directly involved in the re-registration in some areas, it was clearly pleased when the exercise resulted in a tense standoff between agencies and local leaders: the agencies stopped the supply of aid until the diversion problem was controlled. From the government's point of view, this had the desired effect of forcing the IDPs to disperse from camps, but the agencies were blamed, not the government.[54] Whether the government quietly manipulated the corruption issue to force the standoff or simply recognized that its policy objectives stood to gain from the standoff is not clear. Similar attempts to entice the agencies to cut off food assistance to bolster governing-party political objectives indirectly were noted in the case of Zimbabwe as well.[55]

Separatist Movements and Non-State Actors

Biafra

The Nigerian civil war of 1967–70 was a case in which the governing authority—whether it was called a separatist movement or a host government—deliberately played on international sympathies to finance its struggle to secede from Nigeria. And the humanitarian agencies didn't recognize that their role might prolong the war and prolong the suffering of civilians caught in the conflict.[56]

The war and the aspirations of the Igbo people in Eastern Nigeria captured the imagination of Western liberals—disillusioned with both European imperialism and the US war in Indo-China—and Christian groups who saw the Nigerian civil war as a confrontation between Islam and Christianity.[57] The war started in 1967, but by mid-1968 Biafra was cut off from the sea coast, and the Federal Nigerian army's strategy was to blockade the remaining territory controlled by the breakaway government, eventually forcing it to surrender. The pro-Biafra movement outside the country responded with an airlift into the remaining enclave. Initially for weapons, the humanitarians began sending in assistance on the same planes in 1968. The ICRC, conscious of its obligations to neutrality, attempted to assist civilian casualties on both sides of the battle lines. It negotiated with the federal authorities to begin a humanitarian airlift to Biafra, but when the Federal Nigerian air force shot down one of their planes in mid-1969, the ICRC withdrew from operations in Nigeria. This left the operation of the airlift to Joint Church Aid (JCA), bringing food and other humanitarian assistance into the landlocked enclave during the height of the famine.

The overlap between the arms resupply mission and the humanitarian mission was breathtaking by contemporary standards; many planes in the airlift carried both humanitarian and military cargo.[58] Some of the same expatriates were involved with both the humanitarian airlift and the military resistance—notably one Count Carl-Gustaf von Rosen, a Swede who headed the JCA in 1968, then built a "Biafran air force" in 1969 (whose attempted attack on federal territory prompted the shooting down of the Red Cross plane).[59] Much of the food assistance was in the form of money to buy food within the limited confines of Biafra. Allegations of food being directly diverted to the Biafran army were denied by many of the humanitarians; feeding the army, of course, was the first priority of the Biafran leadership.[60]

The humanitarian food aid effort succeeded in raising awareness for the Biafran cause where other angles had failed. An official of the Biafran Propaganda Secretariat noted that "political emancipation," "religious persecution," and even "genocide" had all largely failed to capture external interest. But starving children and "famine" brought about by military blockade were the successful selling points for garnering international interest for the cause.[61] Most important, the humanitarian operation indirectly financed Biafra's attempts to continue fighting; with nothing to export and no way of exporting it after access to the oil fields and the sea coast was cut off, the

Biafran leadership turned to the only resource at hand—the aid effort—to finance its secessionist dream.

According to Biafran sources, taxes on landing rights and profits from exchange rates with the nominal Biafran currency (when aid funds were used to purchase food locally) accounted for nearly two-thirds of total foreign currency income to Biafra during the war. A Biafran general confirmed that "financing the war was largely accomplished through private and humanitarian contributions."[62] Pérouse de Montclos notes, "The military impact of relief operations . . . helped the secessionists to continue the war for over a year after it was lost militarily."[63] The ostensible reason for this, of course, was the famine occurring inside the Biafran enclave under the tight blockade of the Federal army, and the fear that a "genocidal bloodbath" would follow a Federal victory. In fact, no major retaliatory killings materialized when the Nigerian army finally overran all remaining Biafran territory in early 1970. In retrospect, little doubt remains that the humanitarian operation helped prolong the war, and the prolonged war caused more damage than the assistance prevented. From the point of view of the separatist government, the food aid effort helped in the short term, but ultimately the long-term goal of a separate Biafra failed.

As Ian Smillie notes, after the conflict ended, NGOs and church agencies went to great lengths to demonstrate that they had not prolonged the war, "Because if it is true, they must also have prolonged the suffering, contributing to the deaths of 180,000 people or more."[64]

Humanitarian Agencies

Darfur

Humanitarians were implicated in the misuse of food aid in Biafra, but humanitarian organizations used food aid in a very different way to serve security objectives in the Darfur conflict. A recent study noted the practice of providing food aid to belligerents threatening food aid convoys or other recipient communities. In cases where food aid convoys had to pass through communities that were not included in the food aid distribution, groups of armed locals would stop convoys, demanding food for their area as well. Making payments of food to these groups was informally known to aid workers as "food for access."[65] Alternatively, armed groups would demand food in exchange for their guarantee not to attack communities that had received food aid, or "food for protection."[66] In many of these cases the parties demanding payment in food were nomadic groups seen to be associated with *Janjaweed* militias that were perceived to be the aggressors in the conflict. Nevertheless, to ensure the safety of both the food convoys and the recipient communities, some amount of food was provided to these armed groups—although exactly how it was used was never clear.[67]

While none of this was an officially condoned practice, it was the manner in which agencies dealt with (or were forced to deal with) the prevailing security situation for both themselves and their clientele in western Sudan at the time. Viewed as a "security guarantee" using food as the payment, the practice clearly undermined the impartiality of the agencies—but also reflected a view that the humanitarian community had been biased against pastoral groups (from whom the *Janjaweed* militias were mostly recruited) throughout the response to the crisis. In this case food aid was manipulated by humanitarian agencies to serve security objectives—both their own security ("food for access") and that of the intended recipients ("food for protection"). Agency staff interviewed at the time argued that they were not manipulating aid, that under the prevailing circumstances they had no choice: they could either provide for security through this kind of practice or else pull out altogether, with obvious consequences for the communities that they knew required assistance. No other party—the government, the United Nations, or the African Union peacekeeping force—could guarantee security for either the food aid transporters or the recipient communities.[68] But the practice lent support to the allegation that humanitarian agencies in Darfur used aid to promote an agenda that was generally biased in favor of the populations that were displaced by the conflict and against pastoral populations, from whom the *Janjaweed* militias were drawn in the early years of the conflict.[69]

Recipient Communities

Southern Sudan

Local political priorities are important in the management of aid in conflict, and "taxation" of food aid is common. In Southern Sudan during the civil war of 1983–2005, a taxation system known as *tayeen* ensured certain amounts of food aid would be set aside for the Sudan People's Liberation Army (SPLA).[70] During the war, the United Nations came under criticism for permitting the diversion of food aid to the SPLA, though some analysts report little direct empirical evidence to support these claims.[71] The impact of the *tayeen* system on actual food consumption is difficult to determine. A 1998 evaluation of the UN-led Operation Lifeline Sudan concluded that the system had "a negative effect on targeting the needy population who under normal circumstances would be exempted from the '*tayeen*' obligation."[72]

However, one observer noted that "ordinary people did not appear to begrudge the SPLA its share—soldiers, they argued, needed to eat too, most of them came from the area and were perceived as part of the force that was trying to protect it."[73] In the Southern Sudan case, after much experimentation with alternatives, control over local distribution of food aid during the war was left in the hands of local leaders.[74] Hence, in this case, while food was diverted away from its primarily humanitarian objectives, it was clearly done by or with the consent of much of the recipient community.

Somalia

In Somalia distribution of food aid was also left in the hands of local leaders, but in this case "local leaders" almost by definition meant clan leaders, who often excluded some groups because they were from the "wrong" clans.[75] Alternatively, to prevent local conflict, leaders were often forced to allocate food aid equally between sub-clans. In practice, this meant everyone was given the same amount, because of the threat of violence when attempting to exclude certain groups—even if they were obviously better off. Food aid was seen as a "free" gift from outside, which entitled everyone to a share.[76]

Questions and Conclusions

It should be clear by now that most—if not all—parties involved have manipulated food aid in some way or another. Table 10–1 at the end of the chapter summarizes briefly the actors, actions, and outcomes of this manipulation from the case studies.

Several questions grow out of the analysis of these cases. First, how has the instrumentalization of food assistance affected humanitarian operations? Has it led to the collapse of "humanitarian space," that is, decreased access and increased insecurity? Second, how have humanitarians responded? Has the humanitarian community been able to learn from these experiences? Third, and perhaps most important, what has been the political impact of this manipulation? Has the manipulation of food assistance served the political or security objectives of parties (whether humanitarian or otherwise) doing the manipulating? And finally, why does it matter? What are the implications for humanitarian action?

The humanitarian impact of this manipulation has been variable. It was deadly in the case of Biafra, as well as North Korea and many other cases reviewed. Elsewhere, the manipulation had less serious, short-term humanitarian consequences, but the manipulation resulted in the further constricting of humanitarian space. Governing authorities often insisted that they—not humanitarian agencies—control the targeting and final distribution of aid, making diversion or manipulation easier and more likely. Where food aid is diverted from populations genuinely at risk, the consequences have proven serious—often catastrophic—in humanitarian terms.

Humanitarians have responded in several ways. The first is the development of the normative guidelines reviewed earlier. Despite the fact that most of the parties engaged (with the exception of non-state actors) have formally agreed to the normative guidelines intended to govern humanitarian assistance, these instruments have proven inadequate to prevent manipulation or diversion of aid when important political or strategic interests lie elsewhere.

The kinds of misuse outlined here have undermined the principles set up to protect humanitarian assistance from being used to promote strategic or partisan objectives. The repeated abuse of those principles becomes a self-reinforcing cycle, making access and security more difficult, and increasing operational complexities for humanitarian actors (that is, shrinking humanitarian space or the fragile consensus intended to allow humanitarian agencies to operate in a manner somewhat insulated from the political causes of the crisis to which they are responding). But more to the point, this abuse increases the risk to groups that the assistance is intended to serve. When normative codes and guidelines do not prevent abuse, humanitarians are left to their own devices—and practices such as "food for access" or "food for protection" begin to appear. These may serve short-term purposes but probably also contribute to the shrinkage of humanitarian space in the longer term. The alternative of simply pulling out of difficult situations has its own problems—particularly for the affected population (as highlighted by the Somalia case study).

The political impact of the kind of manipulation outlined here has to be further explored. Paarlberg argued twenty-five years ago that the exercise of "food power" rarely achieved its political or strategic objectives.[77] The evidence from cases examined here tends to confirm Paarlberg's observations, albeit with an important qualification: the evidence suggests that in the long term, attempts to instrumentally manipulate food aid have not significantly affected the military or political circumstances on the ground, though such manipulation has had devastating effects on the humanitarian situation. For example, nothing suggests that subjecting US food assistance in Somalia to counterterrorism objectives has resulted in any increase in the support for the TFG or resistance to al-Shabaab. No evaluations of the FIRUP program are available, but examining similar programs across several provinces in Afghanistan, Andrew Wilder and his colleagues argue convincingly that attempts to "win hearts and minds" in counter-insurgency warfare using aid (of various kinds) has rarely had the intended effect and in fact risks having the opposite effect.[78] Most of the other cases investigated likewise suggest that the instrumentalization of aid rarely serves the policy objectives the "instrumentalizers."

The exceptions seem to be Biafra (but only in the short term) and North Korea (only to a limited degree). Of course, the instrumentalization of the humanitarian effort in Biafra only put off the ultimate defeat of the separatists, but it did serve their short-term purposes of survival. In North Korea, while the regime was weakened, it did survive—but suffered other unexpected outcomes, in particular the emergence of a private market in foodstuffs. However, these cases tend to reinforce the observation made twenty-five years ago by Paarlberg. Paarlberg noted that "food power" usually fails as a foreign policy tool because there are too many alternative options; no one country or party can control enough of these alternatives to achieve political objectives. In both Biafra and North Korea the state or governing authority controlled most if not all the means of access to food and thus was able to manipulate food aid to meet its purposes—at least for a time. These cases, as well as several others reviewed in my earlier work, imply that manipulating food aid can be made to serve political purposes of donors or governing authorities *only so long as they control all other forms of access to food*, a set of circumstances rarely genuinely achieved.

These observations lead to two possible conclusions for humanitarian actors, a pessimistic one and a somewhat more optimistic one. The pessimistic conclusion is that food aid will always be a valuable resource in resource-constrained conflict environments where humanitarian access is difficult. This implies that political concerns will always trump humanitarian concerns, and any attempt to insulate humanitarian assistance from political manipulation is simply unrealistic. Humanitarian actors must be aware of this risk—they are often in a weaker position than donors, national governments, or non-state actors.

But a more optimistic conclusion exists as well. If—as Paarlberg suggested and the evidence presented here seems to confirm—political or security goals are not really served by this kind of manipulation, then the argument is strengthened for reclaiming some humanitarian space around the provision of food assistance in conflict. The evidence summarized in Table 10–1 suggests that manipulating aid rarely works to anyone's significant political or strategic advantage. Humanitarian actors should monitor this closely. If this can be confirmed more generally, it would constitute grounds for arguing that humanitarian aid should—once again—be provided in such a way as to promote humanitarian objectives over political objectives. Further research will be necessary to verify this observation.

Table 10–1. Actors, Actions, and Outcomes: The Instrumentalization of Food Assistance

Actors	Country	Action—Goal	Outcome
Donor Agencies	Somalia	Cutting off aid—prevent diversion	• Significant humanitarian impact • Little political or security improvement
	Afghanistan	"Securitization" of aid—undermine insurgency	• Not clear—similar securitization of aid efforts have been counter-productive in security terms
	North Korea	Aid as a carrot—"food for talks"	• Famine not prevented. • No major change in regime policy or behavior
Recipient Country Governments	North Korea	"Triaging" access to food—ensure survival of groups key to regime	• Perhaps a million people starved • Regime controlled access to food and survived • Underground private markets emerged—contrary to government policy
	Sudan	Manipulating IDP registration—encourage return	• IDPs threatened with aid cut-off, but agencies—not government—blamed • Agencies reversed cut-off policy
Rebel Movements or Non-state Actors	Ethiopia	Diverting funds—buy arms	• Not clear—evidence so limited that the accusation was formally withdrawn
	Biafra	Landing or currency-exchange fees—finance conflict	• Biafra was ultimately defeated • 180,000 people starved • Aid manipulation likely prolonged the war—and hence the suffering and loss of life

Actors	Country	Action—Goal	Outcome
Humanitarian Agencies	Darfur	"Food for access" or "protection"— prevent attacks	• Food diverted (undermined impartiality and neutrality) • Contributed to general deterioration of security
Recipient Communities	Southern Sudan	Food taxation— support army	• Food diverted to army • Humanitarian impact not clear
	Somalia	Food aid redistribution— ensure inclusion	• Not clear: likely reduced impact of food aid • Likely mitigated local conflict

Chapter 11

Protection and Instrumentalization

The Contemporary Solferino?

Norah Niland

The bloody aftermath of the Battle of Solferino inspired Henri Dunant to push for neutral, well-organized, and readily available life-saving help. Dunant's focus was on the rescue and care of wounded soldiers. His efforts led to the First Geneva Convention in 1864 and the subsequent development of international law for the protection of victims of armed conflict. A century and a quarter later, humanitarian personnel began to rethink the measures needed to improve protection for crisis-affected populations. This included steps to strengthen their own interventions to enhance the safety, dignity, and well-being of civilians endangered or harmed by inadequately restricted warfare. The context was the demise of the Cold War and, with it, the end of bi-polarity and the sponsorship of proxy wars. A dramatic spike in the numbers of wars, mostly internal and characterized, frequently, by the targeting of ethnic or particular groups and related large-scale displacement, was a major determinant of revised humanitarian policy in the early 1990s.

The end of the Cold War also opened the way for a dramatic increase in the scope and leverage of humanitarian aid as donor governments, in particular, sought to contain refugee flows and chaotic situations. The presence of relief agencies in war zones expanded significantly. There was significant investment in policy, operational, and advocacy initiatives to address protection concerns. Such efforts were widely seen as critical for effective humanitarian action and have, unquestionably, been vital in saving lives in many diverse settings. Nonetheless, efforts to enhance protection have frequently been inadequate or of marginal value, including in recent high-profile crises. The evidence of the past two decades indicates that a

219

number of hard-won advances in strengthening protection are paralleled by patterns of instrumentalization that exacerbate rather than alleviate the threats faced by at-risk communities.

This chapter is about the egregious protection failures that occur when the humanitarian imperative is not prioritized; it focuses on settings where the dignity and safety of those in need of life-saving help were jeopardized as a result of the instrumentalization of relief strategies and programs. It looks at different patterns of instrumentalization including, for example, when the need for protection was ignored, sidelined, or made more acute by the actions of different stakeholders inside and outside the humanitarian arena. Experience shows that the protection of at-risk groups was undermined when relief or other actors prioritized political or other objectives inimical to the best interests of those in need of robust humanitarian endeavor. History also tells us that the absence of leadership and of an agreed-upon humanitarian protection strategy has on various occasions failed to ameliorate, or gave rise to, situations that exacerbated threats to the life and dignity of endangered individuals. The scope of this chapter does not allow for a comprehensive review of all protection-oriented initiatives since the end of the Cold War. The focus is on measures undertaken in the context of humanitarian action. It does not, for example, deal with steps taken by the UN Security Council or the Responsibility to Protect (R2P) initiative.[1]

As the twenty-first century and new power equations unfold, the continued credibility and value of institutionalized compassion is greatly dependent on the manner in which threats that imperil the safety and dignity of endangered communities are addressed. In line with the focus of the "Golden Fleece," this chapter examines a number of experiences that point to the need to review some default assumptions including in particular those that deprioritize the protection needs of vulnerable individuals in crisis settings.

Armed Conflict and Protection: A Long History

War has been a constant throughout history, but so have efforts to avoid it, to limit its use, and to mitigate its consequences for affected communities. History is replete with instances of barbarity, on and off the battlefield. Simultaneously, societies everywhere have seen warfare as a tool that needs to be used with caution and care.

From earliest times, norms in diverse cultural, social, and political settings dictated that warfare should be limited and conducted within specific boundaries. Certain categories of people were exempt from deliberate harm, and particular types of behavior were prohibited. In ancient China, for example, great importance was accorded to the protection of civilians;

strictures on war were codified and stipulated that warriors should "not kill the common people."[2]

In more recent times the inhumanity of the Battle of Solferino (June 1859) so perturbed Swiss businessman Henri Dunant that he organized surrounding communities to help those left half-dead on the battlefield. His subsequent efforts to ensure that war had legally prescribed limits led to the first Geneva Convention (1864) and the creation of the International Committee of the Red Cross (ICRC) in 1863 and the Red Cross Movement (1919).

Initiatives to limit suffering have generally gained momentum in the aftermath of atrocities involving appalling levels of death and suffering. This was the case after World War II when the full horror of the Holocaust became known. The inhumanity of gas chambers and mass extermination, the reality of concentration camps, the wholesale bombing of cities, and the obliteration of Hiroshima and Nagasaki gave rise to a fast-paced schedule of law making and codification. This included the Universal Declaration of Human Rights (1948), the 1949 Geneva Conventions, and the 1951 Refugee Convention.

The sentiment of "never again," and the endeavor to give it meaning, are exemplified in Article 3 common to the four 1949 Geneva Conventions. These conventions are dedicated to ameliorating the condition of the injured, those who are sick, prisoners, and civilians in wartime. Common Article 3 has the merit of extending the principles of the Geneva Conventions to internal or non-international armed conflicts. Thus, whatever the parameters of the conflict, war makers have a responsibility to comply with fundamental humanitarian norms; pleading "sovereignty" in the face of war crimes will do little to minimize international censure, at least in the court of public opinion.

The Fourth Geneva Convention spells out clearly that civilians have a protected status that should be upheld in *all* circumstances. Article 27 is precise in stipulating that civilians "shall at all times be humanely treated, and shall be protected especially against all acts of violence or threat thereof."[3] Respect for the life and dignity of individuals not directly engaged in hostilities captures the essence of the Geneva Conventions adopted after World War II. When the universal value of respect for human life was codified and coupled with principles of neutrality and nondiscrimination—all must be assisted without distinction—the humanitarian imperative gained legitimacy and leverage.

Thanks to the 1949 Conventions, the imperative to prioritize humanitarian action above all other considerations is now widely acknowledged as indispensable to the task of protecting life and mitigating suffering in the midst of violent strife. This is reflected in research commissioned by the ICRC on the occasion of the sixtieth anniversary of the 1949 Conventions. It found that 75 percent of those interviewed in a cross-section of countries favored compliance with rules limiting the extent, and reducing the impact of armed conflict.[4] Overall, "97% of those interviewed say that there should be a clear distinction between combatants and civilians when carrying out attacks."[5]

Throughout the Cold War, and with the exception of the ICRC and the United Nations High Commissioner for Refugees (UNHCR) that have clearly specified and universally acknowledged protection responsibilities, humanitarian organizations were primarily concerned with the provision of relief focused on material needs. For the most part, relief agencies operated on the periphery of war zones and were preoccupied with refugee flows that were often the result of Cold War agendas that encouraged people to flee their country of origin. Until the passage of the US Refugee Act (1980), US policy on refugees was meant to contribute to "the overarching objective of damaging and ultimately defeating communist countries."[6] However, this type of political manipulation was not, in general, an issue of great concern in humanitarian circles. It was only in the late 1970s and 1980s, as Cold War rivalries and proxy wars became more pronounced and provoked seemingly unending and protracted refugee situations, that the issue of politicization and misuse of humanitarian aid began to rise to the surface. Reference to "refugee warriors" emerged in the 1980s in relation to settlements supported by UNHCR and others. These "refugee warrior communities served as important instruments both in the interventionist policies of external powers and in regional power struggles."[7]

The tumbling of the Berlin Wall at the end of 1989 heralded a spike in the incidence of major emergencies; the number of large-scale emergencies jumped from five between 1985 and 1989, to twenty in 1990, and twenty-six in 1994.[8] As the threat of war between states receded, states at war with themselves gave rise to a host of new concerns that were, in part, driven and shaped by the "CNN factor." The real-time, and sometimes saturation, media coverage of scenes of suffering moved crises to the top of policy agendas.[9] The reverse also happened: some crises, such as the Sudan in the early 1990s, were effectively ignored when Somalia was commandeering the headlines.[10]

Direct exposure to the immediate, indirect, and accumulated costs of war influenced humanitarian thinking and agendas. Reduced refugee flows, given their loss of *realpolitik* significance, gave rise to a focus on uprooted people who were involuntarily displaced within their own country.[11] The emergence of internally displaced persons (IDPs) as a population of concern coincided with a reduction in asylum opportunities and difficulties in mobilizing the necessary level of financial resources to maintain decent care and maintenance programs in protracted refugee camp settings. The majority of the IDP populations whose plight made headlines in the 1990s were the victims of wars that also took a heavy toll on those who lacked the resources or opportunity to flee. ISPs (internally stuck people) tended to receive much less attention than their compatriots who were displaced and stood a better chance of receiving help. The wide-scale preoccupation with IDPs to the exclusion of others who were equally in need of help was due in part to donor allocation of resources; there was a high demand on humanitarian assets generated by people in camps and the protection problems that often arose in such settlements. There was also a tendency of some relief agencies to opt for high-profile camp settings. This pattern persists in situations where relief agencies have contributed to involuntary population movements by effectively ignoring the plight of the non-uprooted. The situation in Liberia shortly after the signing (August 2003) of the Accra Peace Accords is a case in point. Aid agencies focused almost exclusively on IDPs, even though it was apparent that many others were equally in need; as a result, many desperate families moved into camps that were rife with protection problems, including rape.[12]

The on-screen reality of war and suffering in the Balkans (1991–95), Somalia (1992–93), and the numbing images of genocide in Rwanda (1994) were defining experiences in the immediate post–Cold War years. Humanitarians were obliged to rethink what was needed when civilians were directly targeted and were not merely the unfortunate victims of cross-fire incidents and encounters between conflicting armed groups. The issue of protection—what should and could be done to safeguard the lives and dignity of civilians who were targeted or subjected to violence, abuse, and discrimination—was central to the policy discourse in humanitarian circles as the crises of the 1990s unfolded.

Defining Protection

Protection is a term that is context and event specific; it has different connotations depending on the circumstances in which it is employed. The ICRC organized a series of workshops in the late 1990s that resulted in the definition of protection, in a humanitarian context, as *"all activities, aimed at obtaining full respect for the rights of the individual, in accordance with international humanitarian, human rights, and refugee law."*[13] Widely seen as conceptually sound, this definition lacks precision and allows for great variation in its interpretation and application. Its translation into policies and practices in line with humanitarian principles, and that actually make life safe or safer for at-risk individuals, has proven problematical. There is a great deal of confusion in relief circles as to what is appropriate and realistic in terms of what humanitarians should or can do when faced with discrimination, abuse, or violence that jeopardize the lives of those who constitute the humanitarian caseload in dangerous settings. In practice, humanitarian actors have a very limited capacity to counter such behavior directly even as they, rightly, pursue measures aimed at preempting or mitigating threats that put lives at risk.

Protective humanitarian action, based on this author's field experience, requires a sound analytical framework that clearly identifies crisis-related patterns of harm, including discrimination, that put lives at risk. Protective measures should inform, and be part of, the overall humanitarian response at the strategic and operational levels. Effective interventions are, for example, likely to include action that helps enhance the safety of civilians confronted with targeted or generalized threats, helps combat discrimination or impediments blocking or reducing access to essential services that have immediate ramifications for survival and well-being, and seeks to secure respect for the dignity of those adversely affected by crises.

There are many issues and obstacles that restrict or undermine protection initiatives, including those mobilized by endangered communities or in tandem with relief actors. Protective action tends to be particularly contentious and difficult to achieve in settings where official or de facto authorities are responsible for violence against civilians. Protection initiatives also suffer when there is a dearth of support for the humanitarian imperative and the obligation to prioritize life-saving activities over other considerations.

Frequently, humanitarian actors are part of the problem. The default position of many relief agencies and programs is to privilege the provision of assistance, as this is easier to negotiate and organize than efforts needed, for example, to counter abusive policies and practices. Such an approach can, on occasion, be attributed to "politics" or the lure of cash and profile. However, it is equally true that protection issues are a major preoccupation in relief circles; this concern is one of the defining features of post–Cold War approaches to situations of humanitarian concern. But there is a long and sorry record of decision making by humanitarian actors who ignored or marginalized the critical need for protective measures when effective humanitarian action was the objective.

Examples of instrumentalization that had significant ramifications for protection include relief operations that failed to acknowledge *all* of the factors that jeopardized the lives of crisis-affected communities. As a result, life-endangering threats and the means to counter or mitigate these were ignored. In some settings abusive authorities felt emboldened when their harmful practices were not queried.

Instrumentalization by government and de facto authorities range from coopting or using relief interventions for non-humanitarian purposes, to blocking or inhibiting the presence of humanitarian personnel and, by extension, access to life-saving assistance. Examples also include the alignment of relief agencies with particular strategic or military objectives or the failure of the aid community to adjust policies when political or security dynamics change. The rest of this chapter focuses on selected emblematic cases that illustrate the critical role that protection issues play in crisis situations and the ramifications for those in need when instrumentalization reigns supreme.

Thai-Cambodian Border Politics and Protection

Aid agencies on the Thai-Cambodia border operated effectively as partners to a political agenda that undermined the safety of survivors of genocide in one of the most egregious examples of instrumentalization that had massive protection ramifications.[14]

The routing of Pol Pot and the Khmer Rouge (KR) regime, responsible for the deaths between 1975 and 1979 of more than a million Cambodians out of a population of 7.3 million, was not welcomed in Beijing, in Southeast Asian countries, or in Western capitals.[15] Hanoi's intervention (December 1978), in response to KR military incursions into Vietnam, was seen as a threat to the region, particularly Thailand. It greatly irked China, the major backer of the KR government of Democratic Kampuchea. Washington linked arms with Beijing with the shared aim of isolating Vietnam. Moscow supported Hanoi and its installation of the Heng Samrin regime in Phnom Penh.

The disintegration of KR control freed Cambodians to search for family members and food; millions returned to their places of origin, and others sought refuge on the Thai-Cambodian border. Early in 1979, as the world became aware of the desperate, emaciated condition of Cambodians, a major relief effort swung into action. From the outset, humanitarian action was buffeted by Cold War *realpolitik* that transformed the suffering of the Cambodian people into an instrument for the realization of strategic objectives.[16] When, in February, the Phnom Penh government warned of food shortages, donors insisted that assistance be provided, under UN auspices, along the Thai border where the KR had found refuge. Pol Pot's cohorts had herded together fighters, their families, and other civilians with the clear intent of using them to fight the Heng Samrin regime, which in turn made "cessation of aid to the border a condition of working in Cambodia."[17] It took nine months for the ICRC and UNICEF, a collaboration known as the Joint Mission, to negotiate access, monitoring, and distribution arrangements acceptable to Phnom Penh and its opponents who supported the relief operation on the Thai-Cambodian border.

Around the same time, a consortium of mostly European NGOs negotiated a deal with the Heng Samrim regime in Phnom Penh to provide much-needed assistance within Cambodia on the understanding that they would not participate in the Thai border operations. The ICRC called these arrangements a "catastrophic breach of principle."[18] In sync with the times, most aid actors maintained their own "Cold War" as those on "the Border," as it came to be known, and in Phnom Penh studiously avoided formal interaction and collaboration with each other. This effectively meant two relief operations. Both were a casualty of the parameters established on the one hand by Phnom Penh, and on the other by its opponents; Western and other capitals that supported the KR and other groups of anti–Heng Samrin fighters set the parameters for relief agencies working on the Thai-Cambodian border.

Early in 1979, China, Thailand, and the United States were busy working out modalities to resuscitate the KR, despite the fact that a short while previously Pol Pot and his murderous clique had been loudly condemned for crimes against humanity and gross violation of human rights.[19] The provision of a sanctuary, which came with military as well as relief supplies for the remnants of the Pol Pot regime in Thailand, helped the KR maintain control of a captive population with little distinction, if any, between civilians and combatants. This arrangement also helped Pol Pot's supporters maintain the fiction that the Democratic Kampuchea regime could legitimately retain Cambodia's seat at the United Nations.

In addition, Bangkok insisted that relief for uprooted Cambodians be provided in a string of settlements that straddled the border so that these camps would act as a buffer in the event of a Vietnamese incursion into Thailand. Early in 1979, Thai authorities had rejected an offer of assistance by UNHCR, arguing that the Cambodians were "illegal immigrants," thereby denying them their right to asylum.[20] This marked the opening of one of the most shameful chapters in the history of international protection. It showed the extent to which the humanitarian imperative to prioritize the safety of civilians, including refugees, was disregarded by donor and other UN member states. It highlighted the limited resolve of UNHCR that did little to challenge a pattern of *refoulement* involving thousands of Cambodians. This included the forced return of some 45,000 Cambodians who were pushed back by Thai authorities over the steep, mined cliffs of Preah Vihear in mid-1979. ICRC protested, but the UNHCR, the US Embassy, and other such entities remained silent. UNHCR had pursued a policy of trying to appease Thailand but to little avail. The Thai authorities complained that the Cambodian refugees were "conceived by US policies during the 1970–75 war and were delivered by Vietnam. Why should they be left on our doorstep?" The Swedish Ambassador cabled Stockholm to advise that the Thai decision "had been taken in the conviction that the international community has shown a notorious lack of interest in this question."[21]

The history of the early days of relief efforts to assist Cambodians showed that most aid agencies had little hesitation in being coopted into a strategy that allowed for the provision of material assistance but undermined physical as well as legal protection. This put the lives of thousands in danger when, for example, they were coerced or held in camps that were a target as well as a tool of war making. The fact that this strategy was geared to facilitating the reemergence of the KR and renewed fighting is a shocking indictment of the willingness of aid actors to be instrumentalized in a manner that was clearly detrimental to the safety of Cambodians inside and outside the country.[22]

Geo-political agendas played a significant role in demarcating the shape and content of the Cambodian aid operation, but so did the lack of leadership and commitment to humanitarian principles in relief circles. Humanitarian agencies demonstrated little interest in working together to challenge inherently harmful policies; they did not attempt to identify or pursue strategies geared to securing support for programs that reflected humanitarian values. There was no concerted attempt to exploit the limited opportunities available to counter the protection problems that were an in-built feature of the politicized relief apparatus. When ICRC and UNICEF indicated their desire to leave the border settlements in 1980, given their growing disquiet on a number of issues including the diversion of food to fighters, the World Food Programme, Catholic Relief Services, and World Relief showed no such qualms. In 1982, the UN Border Relief Operation (UNBRO), led by the WFP, replaced the Joint Mission. This coincided, roughly, with the formation in exile of the tripartite Coalition Government of Democratic Kampuchea (CGDK) that included the KR, Prince Sihanouk's United Front party (FUNCINPEC), and the Khmer People's National Liberation Front, an attempt by Beijing and Washington to make the KR more palatable.[23]

Intense shelling, a routine feature of Phnom Penh dry-season offensives, resulted in the destruction of many border camps under non-KR control in 1985.[24] Camps that previously straddled the Thai-Cambodian frontier were rebuilt on the Thai side of a defensive anti-tank ditch so that that the "displaced" Cambodians were now clearly resident in Thailand. They were confined to a restricted area in closed camps and had no possibility of returning to their home locations in Cambodia.[25] Cambodians who sought refuge continued to be denied their right to asylum and the possibility of resettlement to a third country. The destruction of the border settlements and the relocation of the population to camps that were built on Thai territory should have been an opportunity for aid agencies and donors to reassess their role in relation to vulnerable Cambodians inside and outside the country. The relocated settlements should have been of particular interest to UNHCR, but it opted to remain aloof, arguing that its presence would act as a magnet that would attract more Cambodians seeking asylum. In January 1980, Bangkok put an end to a short-lived "Open Door" policy that allowed UNHCR to register asylum applicants. Registration with UNHCR was seen as synonymous with resettlement, but the CGDK, its allies, and UNHCR were reluctant "to see a potential quarter million or more Cambodian applicants" queuing up for entry to Western countries.[26]

Protection problems persisted in the border camps; UNBRO and some individual aid workers did attempt to ameliorate these but with limited success.[27] UNBRO saw its primary role as ensuring a steady supply of relief goods and services; the misuse of relief assets, including to feed combatants, and the protection implications thereof were largely seen as matters beyond its area of responsibility.[28] UNHCR did eventually agree to engage with the Border population; it took responsibility for "voluntary repatriation" of all Cambodians in Thailand upon the signing of the Paris Peace Accords in October 1991.[29] This brought an end to an aid effort that was often contrasted favorably with other humanitarian programs, including by UN High Commissioner for Refugees Sadako Ogata, who claimed that Cambodians were the "best cared for refugees in the world" as she expressed concern that the level of support provided could act as a disincentive to voluntary repatriation.[30]

In sum, the instrumentalization that bedeviled the Cambodian relief operation effectively denied legal and physical protection to the vast majority who sought refuge by crossing into Thailand and helped maintain a war effort that was deadly, divisive, and destructive. Manipulation for political advantage also hindered the provision of timely and adequate relief to Cambodians unable or unwilling to flee a country devastated by years of war and genocide. In the process countless numbers of avoidable deaths occurred. Aid actors were mostly passive and knowingly complicit, even as some personnel attempted to ameliorate protection problems in the late 1980s. The United Nations did not translate US and Thai insistence that it be present on the Border into a strategy geared to maximizing compliance with core humanitarian principles. The role of UNHCR was particularly disquieting both in terms of its reluctance to take a robust stance on protection and its decision to distance itself from the Border population; it maintained this policy in 1990 as peace talks got under way and aid agencies on the Border began to advocate for a neutral camp that was not aligned with different warring factions. UNBRO eventually did, when pushed, attempt to mobilize action on a number of protection concerns. For the most part, however, UNBRO and its NGO partners were content to not question the cynical manipulation of Cambodian suffering and relief efforts that contributed to sustaining a political and military apparatus. Assistance to the Border population ensured a ready supply of food and other relief goods and services to individuals in need of help. Simultaneously, however, the relief program fostered conditions that undermined the safety of those who sought refuge and the well-being of those who had not fled. The Cambodian relief operation was not unique in terms of the problems posed by Cold War agendas. Aid agencies, however, showed a unique inability to learn from this experience, notwithstanding the demise of bi-polar politics.

Rwanda: Little Space for Humanitarian Values

Less than a year after the Cambodian refugee saga drew to a close with UN-supervised elections in July 1993, humanitarian agencies were confronted with the consequences of the Rwandan genocide and its aftermath. The Security Council and other key actors in the international community demonstrated a cruel disregard for incomprehensible levels of brutality and manipulation of relief programs to the detriment of efforts to protect civilians. This mirrored many of the problems that disfigured initiatives to help Cambodians in the 1980s.

An estimated 800,000 people, primarily Tutsis as well as some moderate Hutus opposed to the supremacist policies of the Kigali government, were slaughtered between April and mid-July 1994 when the genocidal regime was routed by the RPF (Rwandan Patriotic Front). The speed and methodical nature of the killings, coupled with widespread rape, was matched by the deliberate inaction of those in the international community that had a duty and capacity to intervene to stop the genocide. The Clinton administration downplayed the scale and significance of the killings and impeded effective action by the UN Security Council; this included a decision in April 1994 to reduce the UNAMIR (UN Assistance Mission for Rwanda) force from 2,500 to 270. In June, the Security Council approved Operation Turquoise, authorizing France to secure "safe areas" in Rwanda. This was contentious, given prior French support for the Hutu regime and fears that it undermined UNAMIR.

When the narrative switched, mid-1994, from bloodbath to victims in need, the international community suddenly found its humanitarian compass and rushed to help some two million Rwandans who had poured into neighboring countries and overwhelmed the relief system.[31] A wave of epidemics resulted in the death of some fifty thousand Rwandans; this included a mix of civilians, killers, their associates, and those fearful of RPF retribution.[32]

With echoes of Cambodia, Zaire's strongman, Mobutu, provided a safe haven to the retreating Forces Armées Rwandaises (FAR) and their political associates to resuscitate the *génocidaires,* an agenda of little meaningful concern to the international community. The use of humanitarianism as camouflage proved pivotal for the rearming of the reassembled government-in-exile that effectively controlled the exodus and the running of huge camps close to the Rwandan border in Zaire. Extremist Hutu forces benefited from the manipulation and diversion of relief supplies, inhibited repatriation, and soon commenced cross-border raids.

UNHCR was not prepared for the militarization and criminalization of camps housing hundreds of thousands of Rwandans. It was not in a position to physically counter threats that put lives at risk and thus advocated for a series of security measures.[33] The UN secretary-general sought and failed to secure the help of member states to provide troops to maintain security in the camps.[34] UNHCR, as a last resort, raised funding for a police contingent provided by Mobutu that "compounded the problem by siding with the criminals."[35]

UNHCR and a large number of relief agencies that had flocked to Zaire were confronted daily with the twin problems of masses of people—more than half of them children—in need of humanitarian action and the stark reality of *génocidaires* intent on resuscitating their program of extermination and rape. The humanitarian community lacked leadership and direction and failed to define an overall protection strategy geared to the safe return of those Rwandans who were not fearful of prosecution or persecution and did not wish to remain in the increasingly violent camps.[36] UNHCR, in common with other humanitarian organizations, had limited room to maneuver, but agencies further reduced their leverage by not coalescing around a proactive protection strategy.

MSF France and the IRC withdrew from Zaire at the end of 1994 convinced that instrumentalization was detrimental to the safety of Rwandans on both sides of the border. This high-profile withdrawal did not prompt the wider aid community to rethink its options, which were generally defined as "assisting or abstaining." Humanitarian actors did not take a position on the need to distinguish between those who required help and those who should have been excluded from refugee status, given the atrocities they had committed, their manipulation of relief, and the violence they sustained in the camps and in Rwanda.

UNHCR initially favored voluntary repatriation but then abandoned this approach given its concerns that RPF forces were involved in the targeted killing of Hutus.[37] In April 1995, discussion on repatriation ceased when, in line with Kigali policy to close displaced person camps in Rwanda holding approximately 1.5 million IDPs, some four thousand Hutus were killed by the armed forces of the new Kagame regime during the closure of a camp at Kibeho. Persistent human rights violations in Rwanda were, rightly, of major concern to UNHCR and others. However, support for *génocidaire*-dominated camps on the borders of Rwanda could not be considered an ethical or viable humanitarian option. When the UN Security Council demonstrated a clear lack of commitment to international law, the relief community could have been more vocal and forthright in mobilizing public support for measures conducive to durable humanitarian outcomes. The relative silence of humanitarian actors, and UNHCR's preferred "go it alone" approach, compounded the problems resulting from a combination of instrumentalization and inaction in the face of resurgent *génocidaires*.[38]

In the absence of political support to address effectively an untenable situation, protection issues increased, repatriation was put on hold, and regional tensions mounted.[39] The situation changed swiftly and significantly in November 1996 when anti-Mobuto forces, led by Laurent Kabila and supported by Rwanda and Uganda, swept through the Kivus, scattering refugees and Hutu forces, who fled westward. As power changed hands in Zaire, renamed the Democratic Republic of the Congo (DRC) in May 1997, UNHCR and the wider aid community tried to regain some humanitarian traction; much effort was expended in locating and repatriating camp residents who had moved westward and helping those who were pushed back to Rwanda at the end of 1996.

Instrumentalization of the need for and lack of protection fueled the politics of violence, conflict, and suffering that continued to be an issue in the Great Lakes region at the time of writing. The use of rape as a weapon of war has persisted; on January 1, 2011, more than fifty women were gang-raped in an incident allegedly involving DRC army personnel.[40] An enduring lesson, underscored by the conflict and political turmoil that has cost the lives of tens of thousands in the eastern DRC alone, is the vital importance of facing up to the protection dimension of crises at the outset and being proactive in mobilizing attention to humanitarian considerations when lives are on the line. It is no less important that humanitarians intervene in a manner that does not exacerbate or contribute to the politics of violence, exploitation, and discrimination. A commitment to reflect on, and learn from, experience could also help avoid or minimize instrumentalization and the reduction of protection failures in the future.[41]

Afghanistan: Safe Haven for War Making

The long war in Afghanistan, now in its fourth decade, has taken an enormous toll on the Afghan people. According to a survey by the ICRC, almost all Afghans—96 percent—have been affected either directly or indirectly by warfare; almost half (45 percent) indicated that a family member had been killed, 43 percent said they had been tortured, and a little over one-third (35 percent) had been wounded.[42] During the 1980s, more than five million Afghans sought refuge in Iran and Pakistan. A common feature of different periods of warfare was the limited investment in measures needed to address the protection requirements of war-affected communities.

A nonchalant disregard for humanitarian principles by most relief agencies, some of whom were established in solidarity with the anti-Soviet cause, greatly undermined the credibility, and by extension the effectiveness, of a relief system widely seen to be part of the Cold War Western agenda. Few questions were raised when many of the Western-backed "freedom fighters" morphed into warlords as they fought one another in a brutal bid for power after the departure of the Soviets in 1989 and the fall of the Najibullah regime in1992.[43] Humanitarian actors were effectively bystanders as former *jihadists* pillaged and raped, killed tens of thousands of civilians in targeted and indiscriminate attacks, and reduced much of Kabul to rubble. The mayhem contributed to the Taliban rise to power and their capture of the capital in September 1996.

The period of Taliban rule from the end of 1996 to the end of 2001 obliged relief entities to rethink their role and modus operandi as Afghans struggled to cope with a much-changed political and security environment. Whereas mujahideen violence against women was a factor in the emergence of the Taliban, who sought to curb rape and other such atrocities, the issue of deep-seated discrimination against females in Afghan society only gained prominence when Mullah Omar's fighters reached Kabul.[44] Relief actors shifted gear as concerns about human rights and the protection of civilians rose to the top of policy agendas in agency headquarters and donor capitals.

Aid agencies coalesced to address protection problems in Afghanistan, including initiatives to resist the denial of asylum on Afghanistan's borders. However, the absence of donor support, coupled with UNHCR's attempts to forge a compromise with Pakistan, contributed to many Afghans being denied entry to neighboring countries or coerced to return to Afghanistan.[45]

The lack of support for international protection became more pronounced immediately after 9/11, when the relatively porous border with Pakistan was "sealed." This apparently occurred at the request of Washington and in line with the policy U-turn of Pakistani strongman General Musharraf in order to inhibit the escape of al Qaeda and Taliban militants. UNHCR also did a policy U-turn and was vocal in its pleas to allow Afghans to cross into Pakistan, but many who tried to flee the B-52 bombings that commenced in October 2001 were unable to do so.[46]

Afghanistan, in the wake of 9/11, was a country brimming with expectation and hope. Very quickly, however, it became apparent that the safety of Afghans and their aspirations for a dignified life were not the focus of those who, literally and figuratively, were calling the shots and shaping the country's future. As the aid community ballooned and the narrative of nation-building obscured the centrality of the GWOT agenda, relief actors opted, once again, for politics over principles. These choices had severe consequences for Afghans in need of protection as the state-building project faltered, the insurgency took hold in 2005, and armed conflict intensified in 2006.

The implications of new political agendas became apparent relatively early in 2002 when the UN declined to take a robust stance on a well-documented pattern of targeted attacks on minority groups in the north of the country and stringent limitations on the role of women in public life in western Afghanistan.[47] Also in 2002, the protection functions of the original humanitarian office were curtailed and transferred to the political wing of the mission, thereby undermining their ability to function impartially.[48] The centrality of the United Nations Assistance Mission in Afghanistan (UNAMA) to the state-building project, and its pro-government posture as the insurgency strengthened, greatly constrained the UN's ability to address conflict-related threats to civilians.

UNAMA was slow to acknowledge that the country was not in "post conflict" mode and was antagonistic during the early years of the insurgency to any interaction with the armed opposition. When the United Nations organized a high-profile, and much needed, workshop in 2007 to identify protective measures for war-affected communities, it invited senior ISAF and Afghan authorities, who represented one set of belligerents only.[49] This one-sided approach, however, was of growing concern to an increasing number of relief actors, particularly in the NGO community. Early in 2008, a small coalition of NGOs, with some UN humanitarian support, began to lobby for the establishment of an independent OCHA presence distinct from UNAMA and its broader state-building agenda, which was focused on the partisan task of strengthening the legitimacy of the Karzai government.

The growing awareness of the need for a humanitarian infrastructure independent from political and military agendas greatly facilitated the formulation of a humanitarian strategy aimed at reducing the impact of the war on civilians. Operating within the parameters and overall strategy of the Humanitarian Protection Cluster, UNAMA's Human Rights team and its partners, including the Afghanistan Independent Human Rights commission, systematically investigated and analyzed patterns of harm in a manner that allowed for evidence-based advocacy and public reporting that was credible and accessible to a large swathe of public opinion. The rapid collection of data in war-affected communities was crucial; hours after one particularly deadly Coalition airstrike in Shindand, western Afganistan, in August 2008, grainy but powerful mobile-phone footage of the bodies of women and children taken by a local teenager proved critical in pulling together an objective analysis of what had happened.[50] ISAF had stated that those killed were insurgents. Confronted with the evidence, ISAF was forced to acknowledge that there had indeed been civilian casualties. ISAF apologies and expressions of concern for this and other similar incidents were, at the time, unprecedented and were a significant factor in shaping subsequent Coalition decision making on how to prosecute the war.

The fact that UN and other efforts to enhance the protection of war-affected communities were insulated from partisan agendas was unquestionably key to the credibility of public reports and behind-the-scene advocacy with the conflicting parties.[51] This was of particular importance in an environment where humanitarian donors were, with the exception of Switzerland, belligerents in Afghanistan. The focus of the protection strategy on identifying and mitigating patterns of harm rather than a "name and shame" approach was no less important as it facilitated constructive dialogue with different stakeholders, ranging from warring parties to village elders, and the emergence of a broad consensus that the protected status of civilians should be respected. The protection strategy was proactive and benefited from strong and informal partnerships with affected communities and other important stakeholders beyond the humanitarian arena.

It could be argued that efforts to enhance the protection of war-affected Afghan civilians constituted a positive form of instrumentalization because it obliged both the ISAF leadership and the Taliban high command to come to grips with the consequences of their operations on civilians. Evidence-based advocacy had a direct and positive impact on the prosecution of the war; both sets of warring parties issued guidance and directives that underscored the need to avoid harming civilians. Thus, although the intensification of the hostilities continued to result in avoidable civilian deaths, at the time of writing these had not kept pace with the increased incidence of warfare.

No Solferino for Sri Lankans

A thumbnail sketch of the conflict in Sri Lanka, and its bloody ending on the beaches of Mullaitivu in the last so-called No-Fire Zone that had been declared by the Colombo government, necessarily omits a lot of nuance and detail.[52] The basic ingredients of a quarter-century of armed conflict and its consequences, including the death of eighty thousand people, are nonetheless telling.[53] The war had its roots in inequities, driven in part by a national language policy that favored the use of Sinhala over Tamil. The war was also fueled by the exploitation, for political gain, of perceptions of marginalization that exacerbated tensions among different groups. Resentments and grievances came to a head in 1983 when a series of attacks by the Liberation Tigers of Tamil Eelam (LTTE) on the army and police in the north of the country led to anti-Tamil riots in Colombo; the riots marked the beginning of a bitter war and a fruitless endeavor for Tamil self-rule. Both sets of warring parties exhibited great contempt for the well-being of civilians, who were tortured, killed, imprisoned, and denied basic freedoms of expression and due process. Humanitarian agencies had very limited space in which to operate.

The conflict and related atrocities shifted into a new phase in 2005, when Mahinda Rajapakse came to power in Colombo, vowing to end the violence by military rather than political means. Rajapakse was adept at using anti-Western rhetoric to stoke Sinhalese chauvinism while resisting repeated calls to investigate numerous reports pointing to war crimes attributed to government and LTTE forces.[54] In addition, Rajapakse successfully repackaged the conflict and his determination to wipe out the Tamil Tigers as an endeavor that was part of the GWOT. This relabeling was seen to delegitimize Tamil grievances and justify the use of overwhelming and indiscriminate force. The Rajapakse war effort benefited from the tacit approval of the United States, United Kingdom, Russia, India, Pakistan, and others eager to see an end to the LTTE. Colombo also benefited from its strategic alliances and the support it received from new donors, in particular China, which provided more than US$1 billion in loans in 2008 alone.[55]

The balance of power between the warring parties shifted toward the latter part of 2006, and the end of the war came into view as the government regained territory in LTTE strongholds. During the final months of sustained warfare, from January to May 2009, thousands of civilians were slaughtered when they were trapped and pounded by artillery fire in an ever-smaller sliver of land; the government pursued its objectives of destroying the LTTE, who, in turn, did their utmost to block the escape of Tamils trying to flee deadly bombardments.[56] Survivors of the war, who had crossed into government-held territory, including thousands of children and the elderly, were confined in closed camps where access to humanitarian assistance was restricted.[57]

Sri Lankan government authorities and the LTTE were foremost responsible for the consequences of their cruel and callous treatment of civilians as they pursued their respective war aims. The member states of the United Nations, in particular those on the Security Council, were nonchalant in their de facto complicity with the Rajapakse regime and its instrumentalization of messaging on the safety of civilians, notwithstanding a great deal of public hand-wringing by the United States, United Kingdom, and others during the end days of the war.[58] The UN Security Council meets routinely on protection of civilians as a "thematic" concern but opted for breakfast and UN basement consultations as the slaughter in Mullaitivu unfolded. Nations as diverse as China, Russia, Japan, Vietnam, Libya, and Turkey concurred that the indiscriminate killing of civilians was an internal matter that did not necessitate meaningful UN Security Council action. Rajapakse's grotesque use of the sovereignty card to avoid independent investigation of the wholesale slaughter of civilians was made possible, in part, by the role of China on the Security Council. Rajapakse also benefited from the double standards of non-aligned and other UN member states that were energetic—and rightly so—in their support of an official UN enquiry into the role of Israeli forces in Gaza (January 2009), when an estimated fifteen hundred Palestinians died, but blocked similar investigation of events in Sri Lanka.

Humanitarians also bear a heavy burden of responsibility for the thousands killed, maimed, and interned, given their general lack of preparedness and investment in efforts that would have increased their leverage when dealing with the well-known machinations of the Rajapakse regime and its LTTE opponents. Fifteen years and numerous studies after the genocide in Rwanda, humanitarians were no better able to challenge the indifference of the Security Council or to mobilize the political will needed to secure respect for the protected status of civilians.

Relief actors were outmaneuvered by the repressive measures, intimidation, and gross distortions that were the hallmarks of the Colombo government. The brutality of both sides was never in doubt, but proactive measures to combat blatant untruths and the organization of an overall protection strategy never occurred. Tourism increased in 2009 notwithstanding a global pandemic alert and open warfare on civilians as the island continued to bask in its sunny reputation. Relief personnel were "preoccupied with tarpaulins" and unending negotiations on access when unrestrained violence and contempt for the safety of civilians were the critical life-threatening issues.[59] The lack of strong and effective UN leadership, including the refusal of senior officials to speak out forcefully when they had valid information on the lethal nature of the tactics employed by government and LTTE forces, and the deadly consequences for those trapped on the coast, raise questions about the utility of the investment made in numerous initiatives in recent years to secure or enhance the protection of civilians facing imminent life-threatening dangers.

When UN Human Rights Commissioner Navanethem Pillay did go public in March 2009 with concerns about the nature and scale of the harm being inflicted on civilians, it was effectively too little too late in mobilizing support for people who should have been protected rather than trapped and shelled incessantly in a clearly defined killing zone. The unrestrained brutality and carefully crafted narrative that attempted to disguise and disregard the consequences of policies that were contemptuous of the protected status of civilians, coupled with the lackluster efforts of most relief actors to shield humanitarian action from the machinations of a regime that considered universal norms as irrelevant irritants, have set precedents that will likely complicate attempts to avoid instrumentalizion in the future.

Conclusions

A great amount of energy and political capital was invested in the late 1940s in the rapid codification of norms enshrining the protected status of civilians to act as a bulwark against a repetition of the inhumanity of World War II. Very quickly, however, the understanding that war- and crisis-affected individuals should not be subjected, deliberately or inadvertently, to violence, harm, abuse, or unwarranted deprivation and suffering that put their lives in danger was reduced to the provision of material assistance. With the exception of a handful of agencies, the Cold War era was largely a period of indifference to the critical importance of addressing the consequences of policies and practices that jeopardized the safety and dignity of those in need of humanitarian action.

The manipulation of the right to asylum and the granting of refugee status was mostly a non-issue for the majority of humanitarian actors. In light of Cold War era politics, the humanitarian community allowed itself to be coopted into agendas and processes that were antithetical to the essence of compassion and the imperative that humanitarian considerations be prioritized when lives are at risk. As a result, humanitarian agencies played a significant role in political processes that used or legitimized violent or unethical practices that endangered the very individuals who, in principle, were the intended beneficiaries of the massive relief programs organized on their behalf.

The experience of Cambodians and relief agencies in the 1980s was largely ignored when, a short while later, the humanitarian community was confronted with the Rwandan genocide and its aftermath. Once again, protection issues were sidelined as assistance became the central focus of attention. This happened in settlements where a climate of fear, intimidation, and violence often proved deadly for camp residents, who were under the effective control of *génocidaires* inhibiting voluntary repatriation. As in other settings, UNHCR proved unable to mobilize the support that was needed to give meaningful effect to the notion of international protection. The majority of relief actors chose to make pragmatic compromises that disregarded the need of uprooted Rwandan civilians to be protected from threats that endangered their survival. Being pragmatic, as well as principled, is always a necessity in volatile crisis settings. This does not mean that bona fide humanitarians can be oblivious to, or worse, accomplices, however unwilling, to policies and strategies that are inherently unsafe and antagonistic to effective humanitarian action.

The focus of this chapter is on the protection consequences of instrumentalization. As such, it is not a review of initiatives that avoided manipulation, helped saved lives, or provided a modicum of dignity for those in need of humanitarian action. A comprehensive review of humanitarian endeavor in recent decades would, unquestionably, show that even in the worst of situations, such as Somalia or Sri Lanka, different initiatives helped enhance the protection of particular groups or helped reduce abusive and discriminatory practices. It is also worth underlining that, frequently, it is at-risk individuals, their families, and their neighbors who play the biggest role in countering threats that put lives in danger.

Nonetheless, it must be of concern that recent humanitarian history shows that, notwithstanding significant investment by humanitarians in policy, advocacy, and operational tools to augment their contribution to help save lives at imminent risk, there are numerous instances where the critical necessity of protective action was ignored or suffered from the self-inflicted instrumentalization of relief agencies. Indeed, while it is common, and politically correct, to highlight the importance of protection and gender concerns, all too often aid agency analysis, needs assessment, and programming is preoccupied with material assistance and devoid of meaningful protection measures. History also shows that, in addition to downplaying or ignoring the protection dimension of threats or processes that put lives at risk, humanitarians have prioritized the well-being of one group, such as the internally displaced, over other crisis-affected people who were unable to flee or were not the subject of a media blitz. Humanitarians have a responsibility, in the first instance, not to be the architects of instrumentalization, while simultaneously resisting manipulative policies and practices.

Given that life-threatening protection deficits are routinely sidelined or ignored at the strategic as well as the operational level, the relief community needs to rethink what constitutes a situation of humanitarian concern and how it defines effective humanitarian action. It would also appear opportune to evaluate the effectiveness of measures and related resource allocations that have been rolled out in recent years to combat policies and practices that are harmful to at-risk populations.

The disconnect between a decade of Security Council thematic discussions and statements on the protection of civilians, and determined inaction when, for example, thousands of Sri Lankans were being bombarded on a shrinking stretch of beach in 2009, deserves thorough scrutiny. The full impact of UN Security Council Resolution 1973 (March 2011)—in principle, adopted to protect Libyan civilians confronted with the wrath of Colonel Qadhafi when rebel forces challenged his regime—has yet to be ascertained. The significance of this resolution will, in all probability, only become clear when a situation with echoes of Sri Lanka or Libya triggers questions about the type of action needed to secure the safety of lives imperiled by armed violence or targeted attacks on civilians.[60]

Unquestionably, relief agencies frequently have limited room to maneuver when confronted with situations of great humanitarian concern. But it is also apparent that the humanitarian collectivity, including those with leadership and senior management responsibilities, have limited commitment to learning and being accountable. Too often there is a studied reluctance to forcefully challenge entrenched political interests and agendas that are harmful to civilians. Those with leadership responsibilities within the humanitarian arena need to be visionary, credible—in the sense of defining viable strategies and mobilizing support in and outside formal power structures—and proactive in organizing system-wide approaches that address the full spectrum of threats that puts lives at risk.

ICRC studies show that universal humanitarian norms enjoy a high level of support and that acts of noncompliance with international law, or practices at odds with a dignified life, run counter to the values and aspirations of war-affected populations as well as the larger global community that has signed the Geneva Conventions and the Universal Declaration of Human Rights. This indicates that humanitarians have significant leverage when it comes to countering willful or incidental harm to civilians. The relief community should build on the experiences and insights of the past two decades and pursue a long-haul campaign—clearly identified as nonpartisan—at the international level to mobilize the support of citizens, as well as governments and non-state actors, for policies that prioritize the protection of civilians over other considerations.

Looking ahead, relief personnel will probably struggle to operate as effective humanitarians in a world shaped by new dynamics and changing power structures. The increasing incidence and severity of disasters and protracted crises in urban as well as rural settings where the state and its governance structures are weak, dysfunctional, contested, or dominated by a self-interested security apparatus will pose problems that hinder the organization of timely and effective humanitarian action.

Humanitarians need to discard the deeply entrenched tendency to pursue "assistance" to the exclusion of humanitarian action that is designed to tackle the full panoply of threats that puts lives at risk. The relief system needs to commit to undertaking situation analysis and needs assessments geared to the organization of protective humanitarian action.

Humanitarians need to aggressively address the changes that are redefining the Westphalian system of inter-state relations and the concept of state sovereignty. Today, it is widely acknowledged that the notion of absolute sovereignty is outdated in an interdependent world; situations where authorities are unable or unwilling to safeguard against atrocities—including genocide, the willful massacre of civilians, and crimes against humanity—are rightly a matter of international concern. However, the relief system needs to be alert to the dangers of humanitarianism being used as the proverbial fig leaf for interventions by external actors with ulterior motives. Equally, the relief community needs to strengthen partnerships with, and invest in, indigenous entities and mechanisms geared to countering agendas that seek to justify or camouflage the victimization of certain individuals and groups as an internal, domestic prerogative. Humanitarians should also be better prepared to challenge forcefully policies that rationalize harm or result in suffering that is degrading or detrimental to the protected status of civilians.

Living up to the ethos of Solferino in the age of citizen reporters, accidental activists, and electronic social networks should provide inspiration to humanitarians everywhere to step up efforts to mobilize and expand support for humanitarian values. Not to do so is to condemn crisis-affected individuals and communities to new and old forms of instrumentalization that sacrifice or sideline the need for concerted action on protection problems, with deadly and detrimental consequences for untold numbers of people facing imminent life-threatening dangers.

Part Four

CONCLUSIONS

Chapter 12

So What?

ANTONIO DONINI AND PETER WALKER

This chapter is in three parts. The first provides a meta-analysis of the material presented in the preceding chapters and focuses on key findings and common themes. The second deals with obstacles to change. The third looks at key trends and anticipates what the manipulation and politicization of humanitarian action might look like in the future.

What Do the Findings Tell Us?

Our chapters have illustrated a number of old and recurring pathologies in the manipulation and politicization of humanitarian action. We have highlighted the challenges faced by humanitarian actors in recent crises—Afghanistan, Darfur, Haiti, Somalia, Pakistan—and some older ones—Biafra, Vietnam, Cambodia, Palestine—lessons still pertinent today. Our two thematic chapters (10 and 11) underscore how food aid—the most common humanitarian commodity—has been consistently manipulated for political or military gain and has been put in danger or sacrificed on the altar of *realpolitik*. Time and again, our chapters show, humanitarian assistance and protection have been deliberately denied or under-resourced, used as a fig leaf or a pawn for partisan agendas. State and non-state actors, donors, and aid workers themselves have often privileged the provision of material assistance—the relatively easy part of humanitarian action—over efforts to uphold the dignity and protection of groups and individuals at risk. The fact that the "can do" mentality of many aid workers often does not extend to dealing with the protection and other non-material needs of the disaster survivors they strive to assist is symptomatic of system failure.

In addition to the litany of old and familiar patterns of instrumentalization, we have identified a host of new issues that have a negative impact on humanitarian action. These include the increasing convergence of political/ security concerns and crisis response, something that has been present as far back as Biafra and Indo-China (Chapters 1 and 2) and even earlier, for example, in Palestine, where humanitarian assistance was conceived to "normalize" an intractable political situation (Chapter 7). However, recent crises—Afghanistan, Somalia, Darfur—have given new impetus to the trend toward the incorporation of humanitarian action in liberal peace or world ordering frameworks. Afghanistan and Somalia (Chapters 4 and 6) have been laboratories for the testing of new technologies that affect humanitarian work and/or put aid workers at risk. These range from civilian-military hybrids, such as the Provincial Reconstruction Teams, that blur the lines between the political and the humanitarian, the use of drones and human terrain mapping, as well as "joined-up" or integrated approaches developed by the United Nations and major donors. The criminalization of certain types of activities in fraught environments where aid agencies risk violating anti-terrorist legislation—in Somalia and Palestine, but also potentially in many other crises—are of particular concern, as is the consequent increasingly risk-averse posture of many agencies that refrain from intervening in such environments. Politically motivated attacks against humanitarian workers in Afghanistan, Somalia, Darfur, Pakistan, another relatively new and troubling phenomenon, have resulted in the emergence of new forms of architecture (the fortified aid compound) and approaches (remote management and the transfer of security risks to local staff) that increase the physical and emotional distance between aid workers and the communities they purport to assist.

Humanitarian actors have had a tendency to avoid or circumvent the state. Many NGOs were born "against" the state and have applied, sometimes with arrogance, often with paternalism, this ethos to their work in crisis and conflict. In Haiti (Chapter 9)—the "republic of NGOs"—the role of NGOs in undermining national capacity has been particularly egregious. But the relationship between the humanitarian enterprise and the state is rapidly changing.

On the one hand, Western agencies are increasingly coaxed, wittingly or not, into becoming servants of the state in pursuit of liberal peace agendas, while the reward systems they are subjected to press them increasingly to act as a business if not like a government.[1] The agencies that are able to withstand such pressure—the ICRC, MSF, and a handful of other "Dunantist" organizations that take their inspiration from the Red Cross principles and are able to assert their autonomy from partisan agendas—are very much a minority.

On the other hand, geo-political shifts, national political agendas, and better information on the functioning of the enterprise are preparing the terrain for the emergence of nationalist and sovereignty-based discourses and anti-aid rhetoric in many crisis situations. The expulsion of thirteen NGOs from the Sudan (Chapter 5) and the dramatic collapse of the protection regime due to the curtailment of space and agency for humanitarian actors in the final phases of the conflict in Sri Lanka (Chapter 11) are cases in point. Such challenges to the post–Cold War humanitarian order are likely to persist and even accelerate given the loss of influence of the traditional Western bloc countries and the growth of indigenous relief capabilities in many middle-income countries in the South. Our research on Pakistan (Chapter 8) documents the challenges of operating in a "natural disaster mode" in contexts affected both by conflict and the ramifications of the global war on terror. While outside life-saving assistance will undoubtedly continue to be welcome, Sri Lanka and Pakistan are harbingers of an era in which the provision of international protection is likely to be much more difficult and perhaps controversial.

Meanwhile, the growth and institutionalization of the humanitarian enterprise does not seem to have immunized it against instrumentalization. Much effort has gone into improving the technical proficiency of the system through standards, coordination mechanisms, clusters, standing agreements, improved operating procedures, and the like. These changes make humanitarian action functionally more predictable, yet the clash between the pragmatism of *realpolitik* and the ethical values at the heart of the humanitarian message remain unresolved. Our findings show a worrying disconnect between the inertia of a humanitarian establishment intent on reproducing and expanding itself, and the daily reality of the physical and structural violence faced by those it purports to help. Much lip service is paid to the perceptions of, and accountability to, the millions living *in extremis,* but the system of large agencies and donors that sets the stage of the humanitarian theater remains stubbornly self-referential and built around systems, practices, and reward structures that often value growth, if not turf, over principle and effectiveness. Moreover, it remains inescapably Northern and Western both in reality and representation.

The picture that emerges is a troubling and sobering one. The continued intrusion of partisan politics, power, and economics into the humanitarian endeavor takes many forms and is likely to be a permanent feature of crisis and conflict in the foreseeable future. This raises fundamental questions regarding the nature of the humanitarian enterprise and the ambiguities that surround its functioning.

The Nature of Humanitarianism

The core message of our book is that there has never been a golden age of humanitarian action. Our chapters document the tension between the aspiration to a gold standard and the reality of instrumentalization. They also show the ability of humanitarian agencies to resist the encroachment of politics and greed, sometimes successfully and against great odds. The historical chapters (1 and 2) highlight a few such victories as well as a litany of defeats. Our more recent case studies document how the tension between principle and manipulation has increasingly become systemic. Much as the authors of this book would like to reject the notion, manipulation is in the DNA of humanitarian action. Politicization and manipulation go with the territory. Moreover, protestations to the contrary notwithstanding, humanitarians often have mud and sometimes blood on their hands.

Some, of course, willingly accept being used, if not abused, in support of partisan agendas or economic gain. As our chapters demonstrate, humanitarian assistance has prolonged wars (Biafra) and provided a lifeline for genocidal or abusive regimes (Cambodia, North Korea); from Afghanistan to Zimbabwe, by way of Vietnam, Central America, and Somalia, it has been used as a tool to advance Western agendas, as a band-aid to contain festering (political) sores, as a way of "doing something" other than hand-wringing or looking the other way. Our studies also show that aid actors themselves have not been immune from using their presence and power to advance their own (or their sponsors') political agendas or to jostle for position and funds in the increasingly competitive political economy of the humanitarian enterprise.

The jury is still out on whether quantitatively and qualitatively instrumentalization is markedly greater now than in times past. Are instrumentalizers more adept in using humanitarian action as a tool? Are the instrumentalized more or less able to resist instrumentalization? On the plus side, there is much more awareness in aid agencies, the general public, and increasingly among vulnerable groups about the "politics of humanity," which includes both the responsibility and the expectation that people surviving disasters have a right to assistance and protection. Normative frameworks are in place and increasingly accepted that make it easier to document, if not resist, blatant violations of the humanitarian ethos. Relatively transparent information is available, including to recipient countries and communities, as never before on the inner workings of the aid system.

On the minus side, mainstream Western humanitarian agencies are increasingly integrated and subjected to growing isomorphism. Going against the grain butts against power dynamics that push in the opposite direction.

As with other aspects of globalization, the processes of humanitarian action and the standards that guide them are decided by outsiders and imposed through network power.[2] The top-down nature of the enterprise affects not only the response but also, and perhaps more important, the conceptualization of crises. As humanitarians, we address those vulnerabilities that we recognize and fit our schemas; we speak to those who speak our language and who have copied our institutions; we impose our mental models; we tend to shape reality in our image rather than trying to see it from the ground up. Given the sociological, economic, and political pressures to conform, it is ever more difficult for humanitarian actors to navigate against the headwinds of manipulation. On balance, the sheer size of the humanitarian enterprise and its central role in international relations makes instrumentalization more difficult to resist today than in the past. Humanitarians, nowadays, have a much better sense of what is wrong but are increasingly constrained in doing what is right.

Humanitarianism is variously understood as an ideology, a movement, a profession, a political economy, an enterprise, an "establishment," that is, a kind of informal network of powerful individuals and groups with shared values. One of the peculiar things about humanitarian action is that it is experienced as a transaction without reciprocity. As many have noted,[3] it is a dominant discourse that shapes the relationship with the "other" and in extreme cases creates its own reality on the ground.[4] More fundamentally, perhaps, it is a discourse of inequality that is about bio-politics—what Didier Fassin calls "the politics of life."[5] That compassion entails an asymmetrical relationship is nothing new. The social relationship between the two parties, regardless of the intentions of those concerned, is based on an essentially unequal exchange. Compassion is conceived as a moral sentiment where reciprocity is impossible: "hapless victims" can only receive; they know instinctively that "what is expected of them is the humility of the obliged rather than the claim of the rights holder."[6] As the African proverb says: The hand that gives is always above the hand that receives. Unlike the citizen, who, in theory at least, can punish the state through elections, the "victim" has no recourse, no possibility of redress against the governance of humanitarianism.

Because it is now center stage rather than at the margins (see Chapter 1) and because of the resources and influence that it mobilizes and moves, humanitarian action has crossed the threshold of power. It has transitioned through growth and institutionalization from a powerful discourse to a discourse of power, from mobilizing myth to overpowering enterprise. At its most extreme, the bio-political power of giving (or not) is about "bare life"; it implies choosing among "lives that are exposed and lives that are saved"[7] and those who remain in a transient or, more often than not, permanent state of purgatory. What we have here is a kind of primordial form of instrumentalization that is inherent in the humanitarian relationship.

Moving from the nature of the relationship to its projection on a global plane, we face more questions and challenges. Because it is dominantly an exchange without reciprocity, there is a disconnect (and a growing one in the context of globalization) between the lofty universalist and principled goals of humanitarianism and the messy reality on the ground. "There is nothing so ethnocentric, so particularistic, as the claim of universalism."[8] The cold metal of the water pump provided by the well-meaning principled humanitarian can feel quite different to the "hapless victim" or to the militant insurgent. Rather than as an expression of compassion or solidarity, it could be seen as redolent of arrogance, alien values, or a history of colonialism and domination.

Can the fundamental nature of the humanitarian relationship be changed? The first challenge for those who recognize themselves in the values inherent in humanitarianism is to determine whether or not it is feasible, intellectually and practically, to devise a more equal and culturally grounded approach to providing assistance and protection to people *in extremis*, that is, an approach that is based on truly universal values—a sort of "universal universalism"—rather than on the currently dominant Western universalism. Such a construction would also have to challenge how we conceive the notion of impartiality, the central notion of humanitarianism, and one that at present draws much of its validity from the assumed objective, external, unbiased, and thus unconnected and unidirectional nature of the relationship between aid givers and aid receivers. The second challenge is to figure out if this would result in forms of humanitarian action less susceptible to instrumentalization.

Some will no doubt argue that the humanitarian transaction can become more equal, more culturally sensitive, more grounded. And indeed some progress has been made thanks to the adoption of standards of accountability to intended beneficiaries and increased information on, and access to, mechanisms of redress for those at the receiving end of sub-par humanitarian interventions. So far, however, there is no consensus, no clear picture of what a new humanitarian paradigm might look like. Is it a big picture ethical framework applicable across all cultures? Or perhaps a coalition of compatible universalisms? Should an open debate where "we" do not determine "their" agenda conclude that some new and more acceptable synthesis is indeed possible, this would go a long way in reestablishing the *bona fides* of a humanitarian apparatus that is currently seen as blinkered and compromised. This would imply addressing the question of whether the relationship between the "giver" and the "receiver" is inherently a disempowering one or whether it could tend toward equality.[9] It would also imply turning on its head the top-down nature of the current enterprise.

Humanitarian actors often find themselves in the uncomfortable situation of being "condemned to repeat."[10] It is neither practical nor useful for Northern humanitarians to claim a monopoly in holding up a Sisyphean boulder that may well end up crushing them. It is essential that they reach out to others. Many studies have shown that there is a core of humanitarian values that cuts across all cultures,[11] and this common substratum is certainly a reality on which to build. To be successful, however, any such attempt would have to be grounded in an approach that allows perspectives other than the dominant Western universalist discourse to emerge and be heard.

Obstacles to Change

Does it have to be this way? Is the future of humanitarianism a projection of its past agonies, triumphs, and disappointments, or is there realistic hope of change? To answer these questions we need to look at the future through three lenses. *First*, what are the systemic barriers to change that plague the humanitarian business now and for the foreseeable future? How can these barriers be overcome to combat instumentalization? *Second*, how will the environment in which humanitarianism is practiced change? And *third*, what change models are being experimented with to face this new future, and how successful do we think they will be in maximizing the humanity and minimizing the manipulation of aid?

What stops well-meaning people, which is what most employees of humanitarian agencies are, from doing the right thing? One of the enduring features of the humanitarian business is that those operating in it are the first to identify its shortcomings and point to how they would like it to be. Why, even though individually aid workers and mangers are committed to the ideal of independent and impartial action, is it so difficult to attain? We believe that one of the most persistent barriers to change is the disconnect between the mental models on which present-day humanitarianism is based, and the reality those models purport to describe and predict; use the wrong model, and you get the wrong answer. Our chapters on Afghanistan, Darfur, and Somalia show the perils of relying on models that fit with political pressures or agency aspirations rather than a solid analysis of on the ground realities. This modeling problem manifests itself in five common ways, all of which make it easier for programs to be instrumentalized.

My World/Their World

Mark Duffield has described the humanitarian world in almost medieval terms. At its heart are the operational agencies, their donors, and their public support, all part of the global metropolis of the North along with the gated communities of the South, keen to join the metropolis.[12] For "us" in the metropolis, "them" out there in the borderlands are a source of fear, risk, and instability. As far back as the mid-nineteenth century the Indian Famine Codes were devised less to alleviate the suffering of starving Indians than to ensure that labor was available to bring in the grain harvest to feed the armies of the British Empire.[13] Containing the crisis was the order of the day, and this same concern is at the heart of today's instrumentalization of aid, although today it is in the name of counterterrorism, or access to raw materials, or growing the consumer market rather than protecting the empire.

The model reinforces a Northern view of humanitarian crises as a threat to "our" order. The purported solution lies in stabilization, thus lending intellectual weight to the rationale for instrumentalizing aid. The model also sees humanitarianism as essentially interventionist; "we" intervene in "their" crisis to help them, and that fits easily with a foreign policy that uses all tools to defend national interest. Likewise, the traditional view of humanitarianism, as essentially charitable with passive supplicants, rather than with assertive claimants, sits comfortably with this world ordering model. In other words, the emphasis is on solutions proposed or imposed from afar rather than on what the problem looks like for those concerned. Most humanitarian aid agencies, because of the dominance of Northern funding, Northern culture, and Northern senior staff, are not immune to the allure of this model.

State Avoiding

This interventionist mindset leads to a second barrier to change. As our chapters have shown, humanitarian agencies are often wary of working through the state, and sometimes quite rightly so! In many countries the state and its predatory behavior are as much a driver of suffering and insecurity as any outside agent or calamitous event. But the dilemma is that, ultimately, the state is the unavoidable provider and arbiter, an institution whose role is to provide services and governance to a population. Two generations ago disaster response to famines, floods, and earthquakes was seen as a separate endeavor from providing relief in war zones (which in nearly all cases was actually provided outside the war zone itself). Notions of neutrality and state mistrust were less prevalent, and consequently working with and through state structures was more normal.

As we shall see later in this chapter, there is every reason to suppose that crises driven by climate change and extreme weather events will become more frequent and affect more countries than today. Thus responding to a crisis shifts from an exceptionalist stance to one of normalcy. If this is the case, then aid agencies need to regain that ability to think first in terms of working with and through local and national structures rather than around them. The increased emphasis given to building resilience in national systems, as part of longer-term disaster response, is a welcome move in this direction. Engaging with local and national structures as partners forces informed dialogue and the negotiation of position. This form of relationship is far less open to instrumentalization than one that fosters suspicion and mutual distrust. Of course, this is a judgment call. If the state is predatory, if the systems are so broken or so corrupt that they present a real barrier to effective and efficient aid, then aid agencies have every reason to seek alternative ways to assist. Even in predatory states, however, responding to crisis and protecting citizens is a fundamental sovereign duty, and aid agencies as well as donors, if they are to be anything other than providers of band-aids, need to find ways of working with the state to help and if necessary denounce it into meeting its responsibilities. It is also true that states are not monolithic. If there is no space to work with the government, there may be space to work with a line ministry, or a municipality, or a technical institution. Even in a weak state like Haiti (Chapter 9), where the aid system largely circumvented the state, there were technical capabilities that could have been leveraged rather than ignored.

Emergency?

When is an emergency not an emergency? Or rather, when does emergency become normality? Most humanitarian assistance today goes into operations that have been running for five years or more. Maybe as much as 45 percent goes into programs more than eight years old.[14] In Sudan, Somalia, and Afghanistan, let alone Palestine, there are populations who have been receiving humanitarian aid for over twenty years. Each successive rotation of aid workers and funders sees the emergency and continues to address it as a humanitarian crisis. There is no question that there is acute suffering and no question that, if such assistance were withdrawn, rates of malnutrition, morbidity, and mortality would rise rapidly; but pumping life-supporting but not life-changing aid into a region year after year really does create a strong ethical dilemma. In effect such humanitarian programs deal with symptoms, not causes. Addressing them is a necessary and urgent task from a humanitarian perspective. Nonetheless, people are consigned to an endless purgatory. Aid is certainly keeping them alive but offering no real hope of a better future. Normally, one would expect development agencies to work alongside their humanitarian counterparts and focus on building the future, but most development agencies look for stability before setting up shop, and stability is not the order of the day in Somalia or Afghanistan. This "drip feed" of humanitarian action providing a sort of social welfare net is in and of itself a highly manipulative act. Many authoritarian regimes use social welfare "to instill public confidence and to quell social discontent," and as "a weapon to target politically important groups."[15] Aid is, in effect, being used as a tool by the state or by external donors to quell popular political action and add legitimacy to an otherwise illegitimate government.

The question here is not whether humanitarian action should be transformative (the traditional principled view is that it should not). Humanitarians, of course, need to continue to address acute vulnerability situations. But whose responsibility is it to address never-ending chronic or protracted political crises that generate humanitarian need? The system remains ill equipped to deal with these—as in Palestine, Afghanistan, Darfur—and provides an easy cover for the failure of political and development strategies. The mental model no longer fits the reality on the ground, even if it fits the comfort zone of predictable funding.

Starting Models and Dominant Narratives

A fourth barrier is the tenacity with which starting models get locked into humanitarian programming and become the dominant narrative. When external agencies first arrive at a crisis, they instantly look for comparison with previous events—the humanitarian equivalent of generals refighting the last battle—or to categorize the crisis into a generic form they feel comfortable with. Thus Afghanistan after 9/11 was viewed as "post conflict" (Chapter 4). Darfur in the mid-2000s was seen as a local clash of dubious Arab/Islamic nomadic groups versus sympathetic African/sedentary communities (Chapter 5). These narratives of the crisis quickly lock in and shape all subsequent programming—even if the model is patently wrong, pushing the program away from being evidence driven and rendering it more susceptible to manipulation.

Afghanistan was not post conflict; Darfur was far more complex than a sideshow to the GWOT. This lock-in is partly intellectual and partly structural. It is intellectual because planning in ambiguity is deeply uncomfortable. We instinctively build models to simplify and look for comparisons. It is structural because most funding for relief in major crises comes in the form of donor government contracts. Where the crisis has a high political profile, the donor will want to be seen to be acting quickly, and this often means acting before people's needs and possible operational modalities have been explored. Funding is pledged and contracted on the basis of best guesses. And once contracted, with fixed deliverables and salaries assured, agencies are loath to alter course, partly out of concern to keep the donor on board and partly because the contracting, accounting, and logistical systems that are quickly established require considerable work to alter. It is much easier to implement the contract and hope that it is "more or less okay." The donor reward system breeds organizational inertia and lends itself to a complicit relationship that sacrifices independence for the "greater good" that can be done with the larger cash flows, and in so doing agencies render themselves far more susceptible to being instrumentalized.

What You Measure Is What You Get

Finally, there is the barrier of measurement. Agencies typically are very good at measuring and tracking the inputs to their programs (finance, personnel, and supplies), the processes these inputs feed (logistics systems, the supply of water, health care, food, and so on), but become progressively poorer at measuring and monitoring as they move downstream to program outputs and outcomes and, at the end of the line, hardly ever measure or evaluate impact. And yet it is in impact that the consequences of instumentalization become apparent. There is an implicit assumption in this model that if the diagnosis and prescription are correct, the prognosis is a foregone conclusion. The intervention is modeled as a low-risk endeavor. The reward system is such that agencies focus more on meeting the reporting requirements of donors than on truly understanding the impact on the ground. True, it is difficult and expensive to measure impact. Aid programming is just one out of many variables in a crisis-affected community and often may not be the most influential one. The impact of aid programming may not always be immediately obvious. Impact may not show until months or years after the program has ended. The impact may be entirely unexpected, so even if an agency is committed to measuring impact, it may miss the target, looking for what it expected would happen and not for what did happen.

Where are the disaster survivors in all this? Research conducted by our own authors and many others[16] has shown time and again the disconnects between "outsiders" and "insiders" in disaster response. While many aid agencies and individual aid workers are aware of programming and organizational constraints and try to remedy them, the views of the end users are neither systematically canvassed nor necessarily valued. All too often when they are canvassed it is done to confirm the validity of an agency's programming, much as a consumer company holds focus groups to develop the products it wants, far less as an attempt truly to understand the potential or desired impact of a program. This underscores a real and often damaging clash between the value systems of "locals" and "outsiders." The consequence is that the "otherness" of the humanitarian enterprise can undermine the effectiveness of assistance and protection activities. The recurring questions communities ask about the motivation, agenda, modus operandi, and cultural baggage of Western aid agencies is clearly troubling. "Why do these young people come to our country?"—people ask—"Is it because they can't find work at home?" or "They want to help, but they tell us what to do without asking us."[17]

The nuances are different, but the message from the field research is the same: humanitarian action is a top-down, externally driven, and relatively rigid process that allows little space for local participation beyond formalistic consultation. Much of what happens escapes local scrutiny and control, making it highly susceptible to outright manipulation or system protectionism. Never far from the surface are perceptions that the aid system does not deliver on expectations and is "corrupted" by the long chain of intermediaries between distant capitals and would-be beneficiaries.

These barriers become all the more important when we look to the future, to a world where, if our predictions are correct, humanitarian crises will be more prevalent and humanitarian action will increasingly be a formal, legislated part of managing international crises.

Looking Beyond the Horizon

The past decade has seen a rash of major complicated disasters: the Asian tsunami, the Haitian earthquake, the Pakistani floods, the Japanese tsunami, drought and famine in the Horn of Africa. A complex mix of extreme weather, economic collapse, and the breakdown of governance is seemingly tipping an increasing number of communities from subsistence to destitution. Is this surge a statistical anomaly, or a glimpse of things to come? Looking forward a generation, we believe that climate change, globalization, demographic shifts, and the increasing shift of risk and crisis from rural to urban environments mean that these complex, repeating, and pervasive disasters will become the norm rather than the exception. The major crises of today highlighted in this book—Sudan, Afghanistan, and Sri Lanka—represent the extreme end of this trend. As important, though, is the next tier, which may not be heading for fragile-state status but will see a significant increase in the frequency and complexity of crises in their territories. In these countries, as crises become more pervasive and their containment more central to the state agenda, the risk of the instumentalization of aid can only increase. Researchers who have examined the relationship between disaster occurrence and violence over the past fifty years find that increases in "natural" disasters significantly increase the risk of violent civil conflict both in the short and medium term, specifically in low- and middle-income countries that have intermediate to high levels of inequality, mixed political regimes, and sluggish economic growth.[18]

Climate Change

Climate change is likely to have a negative impact on food security in both Africa and Asia. In Africa, shorter growing seasons and reduced land area suitable for farming will drive net food production down. If there is no adoption of more advanced agricultural technologies, yields are estimated to fall up to 50 percent during the period 2000–2020. South African smallholders are forecast to suffer up to a 90 percent decline in income by 2100 as a result of climate change.[19]

In Asia, climate change is forecast to force yields down by 30 percent by 2050, mostly through increases in average temperature; a 1° C increase in average temperature causes a 10 percent decline in rice yield.[20] Climate change will also reduce land available for agriculture. According to the International Panel on Climate Change, climate change will trigger a threefold increase in food prices by 2080.[21]

Recent new projections of climate change–associated sea level rise suggest up to a 1.4 meter rise by 2100. On present population projections this would displace from coastal settlements some 100 million people in Asia, 14 million in Europe, and 8 million each in South America and Africa. Take a look at a world map, and the correlation between coastal locations and mega-cities becomes all too clear.[22]

Writing in a special issue of *Disasters* devoted to the impact of climate change, Van Aalst emphasizes not just the predictable increases in sea level rise or extreme events, but just as important, the lack of predictability associated with climate change. "Climate change does not just cause changes in known hazard risks, but also raises the level of uncertainty, and will generate surprises. Disaster risk reduction and more robust development planning are crucial in adapting to the increasing risks associated with climate change."[23]

What we really need to know is how society and our systems of governance will react to these increasing levels of stress and uncertainty? Fortunately, we have a great laboratory to see how climate change affects human society;

it's called history. Human history is peppered with periods of rapid climate change. If we go back to the middle Holocene seven thousand to fifty-five hundred years ago, records laid down in the sediments of the rivers flowing out of today's Sahara show that before 3700 BCE this was a fertile place. Then something changed, the rivers dried up, the savanna turned to much more marginal land, and the only places left habitable were the valleys where ground water came to the surface, forming oases. This rapid change took place over a period of about seven hundred years and drove a major change in society—away from a hunter-gatherer and pastoralist existence to a more concentrated urban society in oasis settlements. It also led to shorter and more violent lives, to a more authoritarian form of government, and to the first-ever land disputes in the Sahel.[24]

Fast forward to 400 CE and we find the breakup of the Roman Empire coinciding with another period of rapid climate change, forcing mass migrations across Europe: Goths, Visigoths, and Vandals, all on the move in search of survival.[25] Take another step forward to the beginnings of the "little ice age" in Europe, around 1570 and a twenty-year period of systematic decline in temperature. Crop yields plummeted or failed, throwing this agrarian economy into rapid decline. Analysis of parish and court records again shows a strong positive correlation between the change in climate and rise in crime and violence across the continent.[26]

And finally, recent economic research in the Sahel, still dominated by agrarian communities, shows that in a year of bad rainfall, gross domestic product (GDP) driven by agriculture tends to fall by maybe 5 percent, and that for every 5 percent fall in GDP, the probability of marked civil unrest goes up by 50 percent.[27]

The message is clear: society does not cope well with stress, particularly stress applied at a pace it cannot adapt to. When stress outpaces social adaptation, things break. Thus climate change is likely to trigger more "natural" disasters and more conflict and governance-related crises. More states are likely to see the manipulation of aid as a legitimate tool, either to stabilize someone else's rogue state or to pacify their own discontented and potentially rebellious population. All other things being equal, the pressure on agencies and states to instrumentalize aid is set to rise.

Globalization

Climate change is not the only change hitting us. The globalizing of the economy is unleashing major economic, social, and political change, and we are struggling to bring our human adaptation up to speed. In the literature on globalization and disasters, the term *globalization* is used in two ways: first, to allude to the fact that disasters are no longer local affairs; and second, in its more normal usage, to explore the relationship between a globalizing economy and the occurrence of disasters.

David Alexander, writing on the globalization of disasters, shows how what used to be localized affairs are now global, and as global systems become more connected, these local affairs also have global effects. Alexander is an optimist. He holds that

> the global problem of disasters can be solved with existing scientific and technical know-how, provided this is applied consistently and appropriately. Rather than substantial increases in knowledge of hazard phenomena the solution requires better organization, more concerted effort and substantial reallocation of resources.

He goes on to worry, though, that "the world community has not yet reached the threshold for radical change towards a much more effective approach to the disasters problem."[28] A less optimistic view would see the globalization of disasters as both a threat to global security and an opportunity for political and commercial gain. The critique of disaster capitalism championed by Naomi Klein is explicit in affirming that crises, and by extension aid agencies, are deliberately manipulated for commercial and political gain.[29]

In a study on the relationship between globalization and disasters today, Torben Juul Andersen[30] found that the economic impact of disasters was most intense in countries with a relatively undiversified economic base. Thus, diversifying the sources of economic growth is a basic sound risk management strategy. On the face of it, this seems to argue that globalization and the economic growth it brings are good for the crisis affected, rendering them less at risk, but the devil is in the detail. Anbarci, Escaleras, and Register used the Gini coefficient as a measure of economic inequities within a country and found a positive relationship between inequity and the level of fatalities in similar-sized earthquakes. They postulate that in societies with a high Gini coefficient, typically countries at the lower end of the socioeconomic spectrum in the global South, governance is weaker, and consequently building codes and planning restrictions more likely to be bypassed, leading to less safe cities.[31] Similarly, in an analysis of the disaster record over the past twenty years, Raschky showed that "countries with better institutions experience less victims and lower economic losses from natural disasters."[32] Again, the issue is not the magnitude of growth but its quality, as manifest in improved governance and an ability to curtail gross disparities in economic well-being.

Globalization is creating tremendous wealth. The rise in living standards in Southeast Asia is something many of us only dreamed of a generation ago. The political rise of China, now the world's number two economy and the biggest investor in Africa,[33] would have stunned the political pundits of the 1970s. The ability of mobile-phone technology and social-networking media to allow remote African villages to have banking facilities and become part of the global credit culture, or the use of Facebook, LinkedIn, and Google Maps to plan and execute peaceful revolutions in Georgia, Tunisia, or Egypt, seem like the plot of a sci-fi movie. The wired militant and the citizen reporter herald a new and perhaps more democratic era, but it does have its dark side. Globalization is driving the most rapid increase ever in wealth disparities, to a point where studies show that inequalities in the United States and China now outshine those of the Roman Empire, the Ottoman Empire, or nineteenth-century Britain (though to be sure there are considerable challenges in understanding ancient inequities and applying today's economic tools to their measurement).[34] Globalization is a gravy train that seemingly comes as a package—all or nothing—and that "all" embraces free-market economy, consumerism, scientific positivism, and a dismissal of religion unless it supports the greater objective of the free market. The considerable network power of globalization shapes institutions, values, and behavior to the far ends of the world and reinforces the marginalization, if not demonization, of communities or movements that reject the dominant model.

These disparities and exclusions, coupled with a sense, for those at the bottom of the economic miracle, that they are either left behind or impotent in the control of their destinies, fuels violence and discontent. In its most extreme form it pushes whole cultures to feel abandoned and discriminated against. Thus, like climate change, globalization has the potential to drive causes of political discontent and violence, and yet, unlike climate change, almost every nation believes it has a vested interest in making globalization happen and in ensuring that it is part of that happening. The temptation to use humanitarianism as a tool in pursuit of this dream will be strong.

If we were only facing a near future of rapid climate change, that would be worrying enough, but this change is taking place at the same time as globalization, although as we write in early 2012, the shortcomings of global capitalism, as it plays out in Greece and the Occupy Wall Street protests, are there for all to see. Our global society is riding two roller coasters, and we control neither of them. So, here are the key questions: What can human society do to adapt quickly enough to absorb the stresses of change, stresses we cannot predict? And what do humanitarian actors need to do to prepare for the crises to come, and how can they ensure that what they do is free, or at least freer from instrumentalization?

Change Through Standard Setting

In the past decade many attempts have been made to move humanitarian aid to a more evidence-based and professional basis through the setting of universal standards and pushing for various forms of certification. The assumption is that the humanitarian system fails to change and adapt because it is ill-disciplined, reactive rather than learning, and based on anecdote not evidence. If this is the problem, then initiatives that create generally accepted standards, like the Sphere project, or the Humanitarian Accountability Partnership will drive change. The UN humanitarian reforms of the early and mid-2000s, including the creation of the "cluster system" for assigning responsibilities in crisis response, were driven by a similar model, and current efforts to reform disaster-response law take a similar approach.[35]

In essence, this approach is about improving efficiency and effectiveness in the global humanitarian endeavor. This is a necessary change, but on its own it carries a high risk. The emphasis on the technical—training and creating a profession—unless complemented by efforts to increase the independence of the enterprise and free its agencies from the dominance of the global North by delinking competence and employability from nationality, has the potential to reinforce instrumentalization. The emphasis on technical standards also downplays the inherent governance problems consistently demonstrated across the crises covered in this book. A rigid professional approach nudges the receiver of aid into a passive role. It may help agencies in doing things right, but it makes no comment on whether they are actually doing the right thing.

Change Through Finance

A second change model that is prevalent today is change through finance. This model posits that because financing of humanitarian aid is limited, late, and often tied, it constrains agencies from doing the right thing. The solution offered is to reform the financial tools of the system. The drive to create the Consolidated Appeal Process (CAP) in the 1990s and the creation on the Central Emergency Response Fund (CERF) and similar pooled mechanisms a decade later are products of this model.[36] Pooled funds now account for 8.4 percent of annual humanitarian spending. Another part of the model is the creation of tools to track global spending. The UN's Financial Tracking System is a prime example, as is the annual *Global Humanitarian Report*.[37] But, as with change through standards, the model is essentially a technical fix—the improvement of the efficiency of the system.

An extension of this shift is to rethink the whole notion of aid as a supply chain. In the 1980s, Amartya Sen eloquently demonstrated that famines are about market failure, not food failure, and thus the implicit solution is a market fix. Today, the use of cash distributions in emergencies is on the rise. Receiving cash rather than food or other goods is empowering. You decide what to do with your cash. Supplying cash calls for new local partners, Hawalas in Somalia, mobile-phone companies in Kenya, credit-card companies in Pakistan.[38] Perhaps here is a potential for remodeling aid? Adam Smith would be proud of us!

Change Through Doing the Right Thing, Not Just Doing Things Right?

Where this takes us, we believe, is to a realization that while present efforts to reform the system are laudable and necessary, they are in no way sufficient to render the system fit for the future. We offer the following alternative.

First, we—agencies, states, and crisis-affected populations—need to change our perception of crises. In the future, crisis will be normal, not exceptional. This implies that expecting the unexpected should become part of the normal business of government. It means seeing international humanitarian assistance as a normal part of the sovereign relations among states, not as a sign of weakness or the acceptance of charity.

Second, if international agencies are to play a more central global role in crisis response, they have to be much more serious about de-coupling their agendas and funding from the foreign policies of major states. This is no simple task. It requires both a policy and in some ways an ideological commitment to the notion of independence and a wide raft of practical changes. Above all, it requires committed leadership.[39]

Ironically, aid agencies have it within their power to break the mould. At present, states wishing to put funding into humanitarian crises need the agencies. The state-led or corporate alternatives are not there yet. Solid humanitarian leadership that challenges the history of instumentalization will also need to challenge the structures that allow it to flourish. As long as funding is largely from powerful states and is of a voluntary, reactive nature, it acts as a dampener on independence. Perhaps part of the solution lies in the expansion of the pooled funds, allowing for a buffer to come between the state and the agency. Almost certainly part of the solution lies in a diversification of funding sources with the emerging powers of Brazil, India, China, and Russia contributing more and perhaps even through a system of assessed contributions, as we have for UN peacekeeping missions today. This would also help to address the issue of the self-referential nature and undemocratic governance of a system that can decide where, and where not, to intervene, which lives deserve to be saved and protected and which can at best hope for purgatory or limbo. Alongside funding is the issue of the work force, which is still dominated in the managerial ranks by the North. This has to change. More managers and leaders who are from crisis-affected states and who have lived through crises themselves will enrich the endeavor and its overall credibility.

Finally, we may need to challenge the notion that in a globalized world only global institutions can thrive. Good crisis response is highly context specific. If humanitarian aid encompassed local humanitarian groups as partners and decision makers, rather than sub-contractors, the balance of power in an enterprise that is still very much "of the North" could be redressed and the hold of instumentalization would be weakened. Better dialogue and engagement between Northern and emerging or different traditions of responding to crisis and conflict can only be beneficial, as they would lead to a better understanding of shared goals and new challenges. For example, if it is true that in the future the state will play a much greater role in the response to climate-related, urban, or technological disasters, this presents both risks and opportunities for humanitarian actors—particularly as regards the protection of those affected or displaced. Global and local players will have to work together in order to minimize the risks and maximize the opportunities for a principled and effective response. Not doing so will likely increase the manipulation and politicization of humanitarian action.

The great thing about the future is, nothing is certain, particularly in economics and politics. Aid agencies can choose to carry on business as normal, and in so doing some will prosper financially; or they can choose to play an innovative role in helping communities and societies adapt to the new world ahead. A riskier course to be sure, but then, humanitarianism's greatest successes have all come when we have taken risks and had the courage to run with them.

Conclusion

There is no monopoly on humanitarian action; there is no orthodoxy. Perhaps this is a good thing. There is room for principled, traditional, Dunantist approaches, particularly in conflict situations and fraught political environments, where, as our chapters have shown, neutrality and independence are often the best and sometimes the only way to provide life-saving help to at-risk groups. A protected niche for such activities, built around the ICRC, MSF, and other principled organizations that are committed to impartiality, independence, and neutrality, needs to be guaranteed. And for the rest, different flowers will bloom; pragmatist, local, solidarist, even militant and politicized approaches will continue to mix and match in the relief arena. Not all will qualify as "humanitarian." All will be at risk of instrumentalization to a greater or lesser extent. Perhaps all we can hope for is a greater clarity around who is doing what and why. If the goals are clearly stated, this would help to protect the Dunantist quarter from the more extreme forms of instrumentalization.

The good news is that everyone is increasingly connected; states, insurgents, civil society organizations, and even beneficiaries have access as never before to information on what humanitarian agencies purport to do, where the money is coming from, where their projects are. This can become a formidable tool for accountability, responsibility, and transparency; empty promises, sloppy programming, shady deals, but also successful programs will be easier to document. The evidence will be easier to gather and to disseminate.

Humanitarians, beware! These are small signs that the enterprise is changing. It is becoming more open and less unidimensional, perhaps even more equal. Mobile-phone technology, as used in Kenya and Haiti, is starting to give voice to disaster survivors. New agencies operating internationally from Turkey, Malaysia, and Bangladesh are also starting to challenge the dominant humanitarian paradigm. Diversification is likely to increase and amplify.

While diversification will undoubtedly shake up and energize the humanitarian marketplace, at the same time we will need to guard against opinion masquerading as evidence. Research, objective and well designed, carried out independently of the vested interests of agencies and donors, is the fuel needed to drive any informed debate about the future. The Oxford historian Tim Garton Ash recently published a book entitled *Facts Are Subversive*. A wonderful title, but also a truism. Facts change the world and last; unsubstantiated opinion may rise like a fad, but ultimately it fails to achieve.

In closing, while we can certainly applaud the improvements in the functioning of the humanitarian machine, there is no cause for resting on our laurels. Our chapters and our earlier research confirm that the humanitarian enterprise is vulnerable to manipulation by powerful political forces far more than is widely understood. Its practitioners are more extended and overmatched than most of us realize. If, as stated previously, living with disasters is the "new normal," the disconnect between the needs of affected groups and the assistance and protection actually provided will continue to grow. Failure to address and reverse present trends will result in the demise of an international assistance and protection regime based on time-tested humanitarian principles; humanitarianism as a compassionate endeavor to bring succor to people caught up in disasters may become increasingly alien and suspect to those it purports to help.

The humanitarian project is in more serious trouble than is widely understood or acknowledged. We are doubtful that the current love affair of Western/Northern states with humanitarian action will continue far into the twenty-first century. This love affair is currently based on two notions: that humanitarian action is functional to the security interests of the countries that are its traditional benefactors and therefore shape the humanitarian enterprise, and that the current political economy of humanitarian action will continue to be dominated by like-minded Northern- and Western-driven values, behaviors, and styles of management. Clearly, these assumptions no longer hold in a multi-polar world. The humanitarian enterprise, and its Northern donors, must quickly come to grips with a new and rapidly changing reality in which a multiplicity of actors—state and non-state, private and public, local and global—will define the environment of action, which will no longer be the preserve of the North.

Humanitarianism, as traditionally framed and implemented, may well come to occupy a smaller place on the international screen, relegated to crises with low political profile in which the strategic interests of the major powers are not perceived to be at play. The assistance and protection needs of the Afghanistans, Somalias, and Darfurs will continue to pose major challenges. Needs in such high-profile conflicts seem likely to be addressed increasingly, if at all, by an array of nontraditional actors, including international military forces, private contractors, and non-state actors, rather than by card-carrying humanitarian agencies.

Over the past decade and a half, the humanitarian agenda has expanded to encompass activities such as advocacy, rehabilitation and peacebuilding, and development. Some would say that it has drifted away from its traditional moorings. An evolution toward a more modest humanitarianism, delimited in scope, objectives, and actors, would not be an entirely negative development. It would reflect a realization that current global trends and forces that generate a need for humanitarian action can be neither redirected nor significantly contained by the humanitarian enterprise itself. This does not mean that humanitarians are uncommitted to a more compassionate, just, and secure world, but rather that they are realistic in recognizing that their first obligation is to be effective in saving and protecting lives that are in imminent danger.

Humanitarian action is about "injecting a measure of humanity into situations that should not exist."[40] Buffeted by strong crosswinds, the flickering light of humanitarianism continues to shine. It lights a narrow path strewn with obstacles and compromises. Not all will be overcome. Holding the line of principle, working wherever the needs are most urgent, and looking for opportunities to push back partisan agendas continue to be fundamentally necessary and worthwhile activities despite, or perhaps because of, the challenges identified in this book. As General Dallaire reminds us in his Foreword, change is possible, and we are not condemned to repeat the past if we are willing to learn. Giving up is not an option!

Notes

Foreword

1. Colin L. Powell, "Remarks to the National Foreign Policy Conference for Leaders of Nongovernmental Organizations," US Department of State, October 26, 2001, available online.

2. David Rieff, "How *NGOs* Became *Pawns* in the *War on Terrorism,*" *The New Republic* (August 3, 2010).

3. Alex De Waal and Rakiya Omar, *Humanitarianism Unbound*, Africa Rights Discussion Paper Number 5 (1994), 24–25.

4. Kurt Mills, "Neo-Humanitarianism: The Role of International Humanitarian Norms and Organizations in Contemporary Conflict," *Global Governance* 161 (2005); David Chandler, "The Road to Military Humanitarianism: How the Human Rights NGOs Shaped a New Humanitarian Agenda," *Human Rights Quarterly* 678 (2001).

1. Introduction

1. Extrapolating from Development Initiatives data for 2010 contained in *Global Humanitarian Assistance Report 2011,* available on the devinit.org website.

2. Abby Stoddard, Adele Harmer, and Katherine Haver, *Providing Aid in Insecure Environments: Trends in Policy and Operations,* HPG Reports 23 (London: ODI, September 2006), available online.

3. Gary Bass, *Freedom's Battle: The Origins of Humanitarian Intervention* (New York: Alfred A. Knopf, 2008).

4. Michael Barnett, *Empire of Humanity: A History of Humanitarianism* (Ithaca, NY: Cornell University Press, 2011), 38.

5. Ibid., 34.

6. David Rieff, "Millions May Die . . . or Not: How Disaster Hype Became a Global Business," *Foreign Policy* (September–October 2011).

7. Quoted in Barnett, *Empire of Humanity,* 104.

8. This research, "Humanitarian Agenda 2015: Principles, Power, and Perceptions," involved thirteen country case studies of local perceptions of the work of humanitarian agencies, various country updates. A synthesis report summarizes the findings: A. Donini et al., *The State of the Humanitarian Enterprise*, Feinstein International Center (2008); all outputs available at fic.tufts.edu.

9. For example, Linda Polman, *The Crisis Caravan: What's Wrong With Humanitarian Aid* (New York: Metropolitan Books, Henry Holt and Company, 2010).

2. The Emperor's Old Clothes

1. Michael Barnett and Thomas Weiss, *Humanitarianism in Question: Politics, Power, and Ethics* (Ithaca, NY: Cornell University Press, 2008), 21.

2. *Un Souvenir de Solferino* was the title of Henri Dunant's 1862 book. In addition to describing the Battle of Solferino, it called for "some international principle, with the sanction of an inviolable convention, which might constitute a basis for the relief of the wounded in the various countries of Europe." This was where the idea of the Red Cross began.

3. Kurt Mills, "Neo Humanitarianism: The Role of International Humanitarian Norms and Organization in Contemporary Conflict," *Global Governance* (April–June 2005).

4. Old Jamaican saying.

5. David Rieff, *A Bed for the Night: Humanitarianism in Crisis* (New York: Simon and Schuster, 2002), 54.

6. Michael Maren, quoted in ibid., 219.

7. Ibid., 272.

8. Steven Hansch, "Lives Lost, Lives Saved: Excess Mortality and the Impact of Health Interventions in the Somalia Emergency," Refugee Policy Group (Washington, 1994), available on the desastres.usac.edu.gt website.

9. Count Nikolai Ignatieff was the great-grandfather of Michael Ignatieff, author of many books and articles on humanitarian intervention and former leader of Canada's Liberal Party.

10. Viggo B. Olsen, *Daktar: Diplomat in Bangladesh* (Old Tappan, NJ: Spire Books, 1975), 321.

11. Lawrence Ziring, *Bangladesh: From Mujib to Ershad* (Karachi: Oxford University Press), 72.

12. On September 30, 1971, the Washington *Evening Star* wrote: "In India, the situation is rapidly becoming intolerable. It is now estimated that more than 8 million East Pakistanis, most of them Hindus, are jammed into refugee camps along the border. . . . The sheer number of these refugees, increasing at a rate of about 50,000 a week, imposes a hopeless burden in India. And with the possibility of widespread famine in East Pakistan, the refugees flood, if anything, is expected to increase in the months ahead. Inevitably the pressure on the Indian government to take some decisive action is building up."

13. Not to mention US Secretary of State Colin Powell's profound opposition to American intervention in Bosnia and his hope that a diversion in Somalia would make a Bosnian adventure less politically desirable.

14. See, for example, Samantha Power, *A Problem from Hell: America and the Age of Genocide* (New York: Basic Books, 2002), 13.

15. Gary Bass, *Freedom's Battle: The Origins of Humanitarian Intervention* (New York: Alfred A. Knopf, 2008), 322.

16. Theodore Roosevelt, quoted in Bass, *Freedom's Battle*, 329.

17. Theodore Roosevelt, quoted in Power, *A Problem from Hell*, 12.

18. Winston S. Churchill, *The Gathering Storm* (Boston: Houghton Mifflin, 1948), 166.

19. Ibid., 176.

20. The provocation for the incident was a series of lightning Biafran air raids on three Nigerian air bases. Ironically, the purchase of the tiny Biafran aircraft and the raids were organized by a Swede, Count Carl Gustav von Rosen, who had flown relief flights to Biafra. He said after his raids that "I soon realized that every priest, every doctor, every black man and white man in Biafra was praying for arms and ammunition before food" (quoted in John de St. Jorre, *The Nigerian Civil War* [London: Hodder and Stoughton, 1972], 334).

21. John J. Stremlau, *The International Politics of the Nigerian Civil War* (Princeton NJ: Princeton University Press, 1977), 244.

22. Ibid., 240.

23. Ibid., 241.

24. Beverly Carl, deputy chief of the Nigeria/Biafra Relief and Rehabilitation Program, USAID, quoted in Stremlau, *The International Politics of the Nigerian Civil War*, 242.

25. Susan Cronje puts the figure for Nigerian arms expenditure at US$40 million in her book *The War and Nigeria* (London: Sedgewick and Jackson, 1972), 392–93.

26. Mahmood Mamdani, *Saviors and Survivors: Darfur, Politics, and the War on Terror* (New York: Pantheon Books, 2009), 70.

27. Caroline Moorehead, *Dunant's Dream: War, Switzerland, and the History of the Red Cross* (London: Harper Collins, 1998), 420.

28. Ibid., 419.

29. Jean-Claude Favez, *The Red Cross and the Holocaust* (Cambridge: Cambridge University Press, 1999), 273.

30. Ibid., 282.

31. Barbara Rieffer-Flanagan, "Is Neutral Humanitarianism Dead? Red Cross Neutrality: Walking the Tightrope of Neutral Humanitarianism," *Human Rights Quarterly* 31/4 (November 2009).

32. Ibid.

33. Moorehead, *Dunant's Dream*, 141.

34. J. C. Ridpath, E. S. Ellis, J. A. Cooper, and J. H. Aiken, *The Story of South Africa* (Guelph, ON: World Publishing Co., 1902), 824:

35. Many were also deported to islands such as St. Helena and Bahamas, from which escape was impossible.

36. Moorehead, *Dunant's Dream*, 145.

37. Ibid., 148.

38. John Stuart Mill, quoted in ibid., 128.

39. Peter Taylor, quoted in ibid., 176.

40. The quotation has been much repeated. See, for example, Daniel J. Graeber, "When Steel and Guns Meets Bread and Water," *Human Rights and Human Welfare* [online journal], University of Denver.

41. Rieff, *A Bed for the Night*, 153.

42. The Code of Conduct is available on the ifrc.org website.

43. Michael Barnett, *The Empire of Humanity: A History of Humanitarianism* (Ithaca, NY: Cornell University Press, 2011), 31.

3. Humanitarian Action and Politicization

1. For another historical review, see Michael Barnett's *Empire of Humanity: A History of Humanitarianism*, which identifies three ages of humanitarianism: 1800–1945 (Imperial Humanitarianism), 1945–89 (Neo-Humanitarianism), and 1989 to the present (Liberal Humanitarianism) (Ithaca, NY: Cornell University Press, 2011).

2. For a bibliography of research as well as individual reports, visit fic.tufts.edu. Of particular relevance are two works by S. Neil MacFarlane, *Politics and Humanitarian Action*, Occasional Paper 41 (2000), and *Humanitarian Action: The Conflict Connection*, Occasional Paper 4 (2001); see also S. Neil MacFarlane and Larry Minear, *Humanitarian Action and Politics: The Case of Nagorno-Karabakh*, Occasional Paper 25 (1997).

3. "The United Nations and Decolonization," www.un.org/Depts/dpi/decolonization/history.htm.

4. See, for example, Mitchell K. Hall, *Vietnam War*, 2nd ed. (Harlow, UK: Pearson Education Ltd., 2008).

5. George C. Herring, "Special Issue: Non-Governmental Organizations and the Vietnam War," *Peace and Change* 27/2 (April 2002): 162.

6. US Ambassador Ellsworth Bunker, quoted in Perry Bush, "The Political Education of Vietnam Christian Service, 1954–1975," *Peace and Change* 27/2 (April 2002): 209–10.

7. Quoted in Bush, "The Political Education of Vietnam Christian Service, 1954–1975," 215.

8. Delia T. Pergande, "Private Voluntary Aid and Nation Building in South Vietnam: The Humanitarian Politics of CARE," *Peace and Change* 27/2 (April 2002): 166.

9. Ibid., 165.

10. Scott Flipse, "The Latest Casualty of War: Catholic Relief Services, Humanitarian-ism, and the War in Vietnam, 1967–68," *Peace and Change* 27/2 (April 2002): 247–48.

11. Ibid., 265.

12. Paul A. Rodell, "International Voluntary Services in Vietnam: War and the Birth of Activism, 1958–1967," *Peace and Change* 27/2 (April 2002): 225, 226.

13. Flipse, "The Latest Casualty of War," 266.

14. Quoted in Chester Crocker, *High Noon in Southern Africa: Making Peace in a Rough Neighborhood* (New York: W. W. Norton, 1982), 291.

15. Jeane J. Kirkpatrick, *Dictatorships and Double Standards* (New York: Simon and Schuster, 1982).

16. John C. Danforth, telephone interview, April 5, 2010.

17. COMECON was the East Bloc's response to the West's Organisation for European Economic Co-operation (OEEC).

18. Elizabeth Piet, "McPherson Recalls Years under Reagan" (June 7, 2004; modified August 28, 2009), available on the statenews.com website.

19. McPherson has a photograph near his desk of the meeting with President Reagan at which the Ethiopia decision was taken. He points out that the decision was supported by Ambassador Kirkpatrick (correspondence with the author, May 16, 2011).

20. *Washington Times*, May 10, 1985, quoted in Larry Minear, *Helping People in an Age of Conflict: Toward a New Professionalism in US Voluntary Foreign Assistance* (New York: InterAction, 1988), 36.

21. Gil Loescher and John A. Scanlan, *Calculated Kindness: Refugees and American's Half-Open Door* (New York: The Free Press, 1986), xviii.

22. Ibid., 189.

23. This and the following section were drafted by Ian Smillie.

24. John Diefenbaker, quoted in Linda Freeman, *The Ambiguous Champion: Canada and South Africa in the Trudeau and Mulroney Years* (Toronto: University of Toronto Press, 1997), 23.

25. Freeman, *The Ambiguous Champion*, 29.

26. Oliver Tambo, quoted in Tor Sellström, *Sweden and National Liberation in Southern Africa*, vol. 1 (Uppsala: Nordiska Afrikainstiutet, 1999), 508.

27. Kees Biekart, *The Politics of Civil Society Building* (Amsterdam: International Books and the Transnational Institute, 1999), 176–77.

28. "Consensus during the Cold War: Back to Alma-Ata," *World Health Organization Bulletin* 86/10 (2008): 10.

29. Helga Baitenmann, "NGOs and the Afghan War: The Politicization of Humani-tarian Aid," *Third World Quarterly* (January 1990).

30. Larry Minear, "Humanitarian Intervention in a New World Order," *Overseas Development Council Policy Focus* 1 (February 1992).

31. The relevant UN resolutions are available online.

32. Fred C. Cuny, "Humanitarian Assistance in the Post–Cold War Era," in *Humanitarianism across Borders: Sustaining Civilians in Times of War*, ed. Thomas G. Weiss and Larry Minear (Boulder, CO: Lynne Rienner, 1993), 157.

33. Andrew Natsios, *The Great North Korean Famine* (Washington DC: United States Institute of Peace Press, 2001), 150.

34. Andrew Natsios, "Feed North Korea: Don't Play Politics with Hunger," *Washington Post*, February 9, 1997; also in Natsios, *The Great North Korean Famine*, 144.

35. Michael Clough, *Free at Last? US Policy toward Africa and the End of the Cold War* (New York: Council on Foreign Relations, 1992), 118.

36. Larry Minear and Philippe Guillot, *Soldiers to the Rescue: Humanitarian Lessons from Rwanda* (Paris: OECD, 1996).

37. See, for example, Antonio Donini et al., *Humanitarian Agenda 2015: Principles, Power, and Perceptions* (Medford, MA: Feinstein International Center, 2006); see, in particular, the discussion of coherence (22–27).

38. Joel Charny, "Upholding Humanitarian Principles in an Effective Integrated Response," *Ethics and International Affairs* 18/2 (2004): 13. See also InterAction, "Humanitarian Exemption to the Integration Rule," Policy Statement (December 2001).

39. Dorothea Hilhorst and Maliana Serrano. "The Humanitarian Arena in Angola, 1975–2008," *Disasters* 34/52 (April 2010).

40. David Wood, "What's Missing in the War on Terrorism: An Overarching Strategy," *Newhouse News Service* (June 19, 2002).

41. The full title of the legislation was Uniting and Strengthening America by Providing Appropriate Tools to Intercept and Obstruct Terrorism Act of 2001.

42. Edgardo Ramos and Clifford W. Nichols III, "Legal Dimensions of International Grantmaking: The USA Patriot Reauthorization Act, Treasury Guidelines, and Executive Order 13224: An Update on Implications for Grantmakers" (Council on Foundations, 2006), available on the usig.org website.

43. "Charities End Dialogue with Treasury over Guidelines that Stifle Effective Global Grantmaking," Council on Foundations press release (November 22, 2010).

44. Donini et al., *Humanitarian Agenda 2015*, 21.

45. Mark Bradbury and Micheal Kleinman, *Winning Hearts and Minds? Examining the Relationship between Aid and Security in Kenya* (Medford, MA: Feinstein International Center, 2010), 72.

46. Douglas J. Feith, *War and Decision: Inside the Pentagon at the Dawn of the War on Terrorism* (New York: Harper, 2008), 98.

47. Name of official withheld under ground rules of interview.

48. "Guidelines for Relations between US Armed Forces and NGHOs [nongovernmental humanitarian organizations]," available on the US Institute for Peace website (usip.org). See also InterAction, "Guidelines for Relations between U.S. Armed Forces and Nongovernmental Humanitarian Organizations in Hostile or Potentially Hostile Environments," InterAction Policy Paper (January 2011).

49. Name of official withheld under interview ground rules.

50. Telephone interviews, April 19, 2010, and May 6, 2011. For a comment about Afghanistan during the Cold War, see John C. Whitehead, *A Life in Leadership: From D-Day to Ground Zero* (New York: Basic Books, 2005), 217.

51. Joel R. Charny, "Upholding Humanitarian Principles in an Effective Integrated Response," *Ethics and International Affairs* 18/2 (2004): 20.

52. For an examination of US allocations as contrasted with those of other donor governments, see DARA, *The Humanitarian Response Index 2010: The Problems of Politicization* (Madrid: DARA, 2010).

53. Ross Douthat, "Whose Foreign Policy Is It?" *New York Times* (May 9, 2011).

54. On the role of the media, see Larry Minear, Colin Scott, and Thomas G. Weiss, *The News Media, Civil War, and Humanitarian Action* (Boulder, CO: Lynne Rienner, 1996).

55. Jo Becker, "With US Leave, Companies Skirt Iran Sanctions," *New York Times* (December 24, 2010).

4. Afghanistan

1. Michael Ignatieff, "Nation-Building Lite," *New York Times* (July 28, 2002).

2. Or perhaps even a "cannibalistic" state. See K. Meredith, S. Villarreal, and M. Wilkinson, "Afghanistan: The De-evolution of Insurgency," *Small Wars Journal* (October 2010).

3. Very little scholarly analysis of the role of NGOs in Afghanistan has been written during the Cold War period or since. An exception is Helga Baitenmann, "NGOs and the Afghan War: The Politicization of Humanitarian Aid," *Third World Quarterly* (January 1990). Between 1990 and 2002, only a handful of studies deal with the issue: Antonio Donini, *The Policies of Mercy: UN Coordination in Afghanistan, Mozambique, and Rwanda*, Occasional Paper 22 (Providence, RI: Thomas J. Watson Institute for International Studies, 1996); Gilles Dorronsoro, "Les enjeux de l'aide en Afghanistan," *Cultures and Conflicts* 11 (Autumn 1993); Pierre Centlivres and Micheline Centlivres-Demont, "État, islam et tribus face aux organisations internationals: Le cas de l'Afghanistan, 1978–1998," *Annales. Histoire, Sciences Sociales* 54/4 (1999): 945–65. Fiona Terry's *Condemned to Repeat: The Paradox of Humanitarian Action* (Ithaca, NY: Cornell University Press, 2002) contains a chapter on manipulations around the Afghan refugees issue and its implications for humanitarianism; it contains a brief analysis of the cross-border "solidarity" days.

4. Centlivres and Centlivres-Demont, "État, islam et tribus face aux organisations internationals," 951.

5. Donini, *The Policies of Mercy*, 35n27.

6. According to one observer, there were seventy-five foreign NGOs with offices in Peshawar at the end of the 1980s (Marvin Weinbaum, *Pakistan and Afghanistan: Resistance and Reconstruction* [Boulder, CO: Westview Press, 1994], 59).

7. Even MSF, today one of the paragons of principled humanitarianism, had no qualms about taking sides (Terry, *Condemned to Repeat*, 73).

8. Dorronsoro, "Les enjeux de l'aide en Afghanistan," 7.

9. Personal recollection.

10. Interviews with former MSF staff.

11. Weinbaum, *Pakistan and Afghanistan*, 70.

12. Donini, *The Policies of Mercy*, 35.

13. See Antonio Donini, "Principles, Politics, and Pragmatism in the International Response to the Afghan Crisis," in Nation-Building Unraveled? Aid, Peace, and Justice in Afghanistan, ed. Antonio Donini, Norah Niland, and Karin Wermester (Bloomfield, CT: Kumarian Press, 2004), 120–24.

14. On negotiations with the Taliban, see A. Donini, "Negotiating with the Taliban," in *Humanitarian Diplomacy: Practitioners and Their Craft,* ed. Larry Minear and H. Smith (Tokyo: United Nations University Press, 2007).

15. For a detailed analysis of the Strategic Framework, see Donini, "Principles, Politics, and Pragmatism in the International Response to the Afghan Crisis," 126–30, and the bibliographical references provided therein. See also, Mark Duffield, Patricia Gossman, and Nicholas Leader, "Review of the Strategic Framework for Afghanistan" (Islamabad: Afghanistan Research and Evaluation Unit, 2001).

16. In early 2002, an Afghan analyst remarked: "The Taliban are like broken glass. You don't see it, but when you walk on it, it hurts" (personal communication).

17. A fact facilitated by the appointment of Lakhdar Brahimi, who had given his name to the "Brahimi Report"—the UN's rulebook for integrated missions—as SRSG. See "Report of the Panel on United Nations Peace Operations," UN Report A/55/305–S/2000/809 (August 21, 2000).

18. See Norah Niland, "Justice Postponed: The Marginalization of Human Rights in Afghanistan," in Donini, Niland, and Wermester, *Nation-Building Unraveled?* 61–83.

19. Fiona Terry, "The ICRC in Afghanistan: Reasserting the Neutrality of Humanitarian Action," *International Review of the Red Cross* 93/881 (March 2011): 176.

20. Riccardo Mungia, a water engineer, was killed by Taliban in March 2003 (ibid., 175).

21. "Afghanistan: A Call for Security," 17 June 2003 statement signed by more than 50 humanitarian, human rights and civil society organizations; available online.

22. Michael Ignatieff, *Empire Lite: Nation-building in Bosnia, Kosovo, and Afghanistan* (London: Vintage, 2004).

23. The incorporation of relief and other forms of assistance into military operations is nothing new. US NGOs were willing participants in such approaches during the Vietnam War. Most US NGOs—and most of the NGOs involved in Vietnam were American—positioned themselves by default if not by design as virtual extensions of US policy in the region, working in close partnership with the US government. See Chapter 3 in this volume and George C. Herring, ed., "Special Issue: Non-Governmental Organizations and the Vietnam War," *Peace and Change* 27/2 (April 2002).

24. There was no single model for PRTs. Some were more civilianized or, like the Dutch PRT in Oruzgan, under civilian command. In theory this meant that assistance activities maintained some separation from military objectives. Others were more militarized and more integrated. On balance there has been a progressive militarization of PRTs with civilians increasingly excluded from decision making (see Sippi Azarbaijani-Moghaddam et al., *Afghan Hearts, Afghan Minds: Exploring Afghan Perceptions of Civil-Military Relations* London: British Agencies Afghanistan Group and European Network of NGOs in Afghanistan, 2008). For a critique of the British approach, see Stuart Gordon, "The United Kingdom's Stabilisation Model and Afghanistan: The Impact on Humanitarian Actors," *Disasters* 34(S3) (2010): S368–S387.

25. ISAF press release, December 23, 2007, available on the nato.int website.

26. "New DoD Policy Outlines Military Health Support in Global Stability Missions," DOD Press Release, May 24, 2010.

27. Anthony H. Cordesman, "The Uncertain Lessons of the Afghan and Iraq Wars" (Washington DC: Center for Strategic and International Studies, August 17, 2009), available on the csis.org website.

28. A. Wilder, "A 'weapons system' based on wishful thinking," *The Boston Globe* (September 16, 2009). A series of reports by the Feinstein International Center at Tufts University analyses the experience of hearts and minds programs in Afghanistan; see Paul Fishstein and Andrew Wilder, *Winning Hearts and Minds? Examining the Relationship between Aid and Security in Afghanistan,* Feinstein International Center, Tufts University, January 2012.

29. Development Alternatives Inc.—now known simply as DAI—is a for-profit company that implements many USAID projects. Because it works in ways similar to NGOs but usually with armed escorts, this blurs the line between nongovernmental and militarized assistance.

30. Personal observation.

31. It was since joined by Somalia in this dubious honor.

32. To be fair, at the time of writing, some preliminary contacts had been made with the Taliban leadership but with no visible results.

33. UN General Assembly Resolution 46/182, which established the Department of Humanitarian Affairs (DHA, now OCHA), specifically gives OCHA the responsibility of "actively facilitating, including through negotiation if needed, the access by the operational organizations to emergency areas for the rapid provision of emergency assistance by obtaining the consent of all parties concerned, through modalities such as the establishment of temporary relief corridors where needed, days and zones of tranquility and other forms" (Annex, para. 35 (d)).

34. Terry, "The ICRC in Afghanistan," 177.

35. "Afghanistan: A Return to Humanitarian Action" (Geneva: MSF, April 2010), available on the msf.org website.

36. See, for example, UN Security Council Resolution 1868 (2009), extending UNAMA, para. 4 (b); Resolution 1917 (2010) (b), extending UNAMA, para. 5 (b); and Resolution 1890 (2009), extending ISAF, para 5.

37. See, for example, "UN Afghanistan" (October 23, 2009), available on the xinhuanet. com website.

38. "I express my admiration for all the dedication of the women and men of the United Nations, voluntary humanitarian workers, NGOs and other members of the international community, including ISAF (International Security Assistance Force) for their dedication and commitment," press conference, Kabul, November 2, 2009, available on the unama. unmissions.org website.

39. Statement of the Islamic Emirate of Afghanistan, November 5, 2009, available online. The statement goes on to lament, "We have not seen any resolution by the Security Council, which speaks of grace, tolerance and altruism."

40. This was a recurring theme in interviews with Afghan analysts and NGO and UN staff in Kabul in 2010.

41. Several factors conspired to create this information vacuum: the bunkerization of aid agencies, growing risk aversion, lack of monitoring of projects in insecure areas, remote control management, and so forth. Attacks against aid workers have had a chilling effect. These factors were compounded by the reluctance, with few exceptions, to engage in contact and relationship with the armed opposition(s).

42. This trend, which does not only apply to Afghanistan, is analyzed by Mark Duffield, who describes the international gated communities in urban areas, the fortified aid compounds, and the protected means of transport that link these secure sites into an "archipelago" of international aid (Mark Duffield, "Risk-Management and the Fortified Aid Compound: Everyday Life in Post-Interventionary Society," *Journal of Intervention and Statebuilding* 4/4 [2010]).

43. Quoted in Terry, "The ICRC in Afghanistan," 188.

44. The Feinstein International Center's Humanitarian Agenda 2015 research on local perceptions of the work of aid agencies has documented "coherence" issues in thirteen countries. All the studies and the final report, *The State of the Humanitarian Enterprise,* are available at fic.tufts.edu.

5. Diminishing Returns

1. Julie Flint and Alex de Waal, *Darfur: A Short History of a Long War: African Arguments* (London: Zed Books, 2005).

2. Helen Young, Abdal Monim Osman, Yacob Aklilu, Rebecca Dale, Babiker Badri, and Abdal Jabbar Fuddle, *Darfur—Livelihoods under Siege* (Medford, MA: Feinstein International Famine Center, Tufts University, 2005). Available online.

3. UNAMID, a multidimensional peacekeeping operation, included military, civilian police, political, civil affairs, rule of law, human rights, humanitarian, reconstruction, public information, and gender components.

4. *Al Rayaam* [newspaper] (Khartoum) (July 27, 2010), in Arabic, available online.

5. The International Donors Conference for Development and Reconstruction in Darfur, co-organized by Turkey and the Organization of the Islamic Conference, Cairo, March 21, 2010.

6. According to the UN peacekeeping mission in Darfur, 440 fighters died during the month of May in clashes between rebel movements and the government.

7. Although following the February 2010 trip by Chad's President Deby to Khartoum, President al-Bashir announced that Sudan was ready for full normalization of relations.

8. *Sudan Humanitarian Update, 3rd Quarter 2010* (Khartoum: United Nations Office for the Coordination of Humanitarian Affairs, November 10, 2010).

9. The DCPSF, according to its website, seeks "to complement assistance channeled through bilateral and multilateral humanitarian funding streams such as the CHF [Common Humanitarian Fund]." Broadly, the DCPSF was established to support peacebuilding and reconciliation at the local level through support to early recovery/foundational activities.

10. DCPSF, *Overview of Current DCPSF Partners and Projects* (Khartoum: Darfur Community Peace and Stability Fund, 2010), available online.

11. Of the 434 quick-impact projects started in 2008, only 72 were completed by 2010. See "Key Facts and Figures for Sudan with a Focus on Darfur" (Khartoum: Office of the Resident and Humanitarian Coordinator, United Nations, 2010).

12. "Mapping and Capacity Assessment of Civil Society Organizations (CSOs) in Darfur: Darfur Livelihoods Programme" (Khartoum: Partners in Development Services, 2009).

13. See reports by Physicians for Human Rights, International Crisis Group, and Human Rights Watch, available online.

14. *Food Security and Nutrition Overview in North Darfur* (Khartoum: Save the Children UK, 2004); Franceso Checchi, *A Survey of Internally Displaced People in El Geneina, West Darfur* (Paris: Epicentre, Médicins Sans Frontières, 2004); Evelyn Depoortere, Francesco Checchi, France Broillet, Sibylle Gerstl, Andrea Minetti, Olivia Gayraud, Virginie Briet, Jennifer Pahl, Isabelle Defoumy, Mercedes Tatay, and Vincent Brown, "Violence and Mortality in West Darfur, Sudan (2003–4): Epidemiological Evidence from Four Surveys," *The Lancet* 364, (2004): 1315–20; WHO, *Retrospective Mortality Survey among the Internally Displaced Population, Greater Darfur, Sudan, August 2004*, European Programme for Intervention Epidemiology Training (2004).

15. Paul Harvey, *Towards Good Humanitarian Government: The Role of the Affected State in Disaster Response*, HPG Report 29 (London: Humanitarian Policy Group, Overseas Development Institute, 2009).

16. Mahmood Mamdani, "The Politics of Naming: Genocide, Civil War, Insurgency," *London Review of Books* 29/5 (2007).

17. Sara Pantuliano and Sorcha O'Callaghan, *The 'Protection Crisis': A Review of Field-Based Strategies for Humanitarian Protection in Darfur,* HPG Discussion Paper (London: Humanitarian Policy Group, Overseas Development Institute, 2006), available online.

18. *Darfur Humanitarian Profile No. 4* (Khartoum: Office of the UN Resident and Humanitarian Co-ordinator for the Sudan, 2004), available online.

19. Helen Young and Daniel Maxwell, *Targeting and Distribution: Darfur Case-Study* (Medford MA: Feinstein International Center, Tufts University, 2009), available online.

20. Ibid.

21. Commentators Julie Flint and Alex de Waal warned at the time that something like this was likely to happen: "The immediate dangers are easy to foresee. The very people the ICC seeks to defend—the survivors of the Darfur war—are the most vulnerable to whatever steps the regime takes in its fight back" ("This Prosecution Will Endanger the People We Wish to Defend in Sudan," *The Observer* [2008]).

22. For example, according to John Holmes, the UN emergency relief coordinator: "What we'd like to do is to have ideally the NGOs who were there before back, because they were the experts at these food distributions. If not, we will have to find other ways of doing it. The World Food Programme did do this, what I would call a quick and dirty food distribution using some local committees, but that's not an acceptable way of doing it for the sustainable future. So we'll have to try and find other ways of doing that" (Margaret Warner, "New Concerns Stir on Darfur's Humanitarian Situation, Margaret Warner Interviews John Holmes on PBS Newshour, 2009," available online).

23. Helen Young, Karen Jacobsen, and Abdal Monim Osman, *Livelihoods, Migration, and Conflict in West and North Darfur, 2006–2007. Part Two: Case Studies and Annexes* (Medford MA: Feinstein International Center, Tufts University, 2009), available online.

24. UN News Centre, "Joint AU-UN force in Darfur Still Lacking Crucial Equipment, Ban Says" (May 5, 2010), available online.

25. The most common indicator used to gauge the severity of a humanitarian crisis is the prevalence of global acute malnutrition, and the benchmark or threshold that corresponds to a humanitarian emergency is 15 percent. A doubling of this rate to 30 percent represents a "famine/ humanitarian catastrophe" (FAO, Integrated Food Security Phase Classification: Technical Manual: Version 1.1 (Rome: Food and Agriculture Organization of the United Nations, 2008), available online.

26. UNICEF, "Nutrition Full Report October 2009–January 2010: Darfur Nutrition Update" (Khartoum: UNICEF, 2010).

6.   When State-Building Fails

1. Declan Walsh, "US Extends Drone Strikes to Somalia," Guardian.co.uk, June 30, 2011.

2. Office of the United Nations Resident and Humanitarian Coordinator for Somalia, press release, Nairobi, July 20, 2011.

3. Michael Maren, *The Road to Hell: The Ravaging Effects of Foreign Aid and International Charity* (New York: The Free Press, 1997).

4. Ken Menkhaus, "Stabilisation and Humanitarian Access in a Collapsed State: The Somali Case," *Disasters* 34/3 (Blackwell Publishing, 2010): 323.

5. Africa Watch, *Somalia: A Government at War with its Own People* (Washington DC: The Africa Watch Committee, 1990); Amnesty International, *Somalia: A Long Term Human Rights Crisis* (London: Amnesty International, September 1988).

6. S. Hansch, S. Lillibridge, G. Egeland, C. Teller, and M. Toole, *Lives Lost, Lives Saved: Excess Mortality and the Impact of Health Interventions in the Somalia Emergency* (Washington DC: Refugee Policy Group, 1994).

7. Mark Duffield, *Global Governance and the New Wars* (London: Zed Books, 2001).

8. Walter Clarke and Jeffrey Herbst, *Learning from Somalia: The Lessons of Armed Humanitarian Intervention* (Boulder, CO: Westview Press, 1997).

9. Walter Clarke, "Failed Visions and Uncertain Mandates in Somalia," in Clarke and Herbst, *Learning from Somalia*, 9.

10. The international response to the Haitian earthquake is a recent manifestation of this (see Chapter 9).

11. Alex de Waal, *Famine Crimes: Politics and the Disaster Relief Industry in Africa* (Oxford: Jame Currey; Bloomington: Indiana University Press, 1997).

12. Ethiopia through the 1996 Sodere peace conference; Egypt through the 1997 Cairo conference; Djibouti through the 2000 Arta peace conference; and the 2002–2004 Somalia National Reconciliation Conference in Kenya, facilitated by IGAD.

13. Mark Bradbury and Vince Coultan, *Somalia Inter-Agency Flood Response Operation Phase I November-December 1997: An Evaluation* (Nairobi: UNICEF Somalia, July 1998).

14. United Nations Development Programme, *Somalia Human Development Report* (Nairobi: UNDP, 2001), 119–20.

15. This included telecommunications and money transfer companies, which are important for the remittance economy that is an essential element in the livelihoods of many Somalis.

16. In 1991, people in northern Somalia formed the secessionist Republic of Somaliland; in 1998, people in northeast Somalia formed the Puntland Federal State of Somalia; and in 1999, the Rahanweyn Resistance Army, with Ethiopian support, won control of Bay and Bakool regions.

17. The SACB was created as an outcome of the October 1993 Addis Ababa peace conference, on the eve of the departure of US forces from Somalia, when large parts of Somalia were said to be moving toward relative stability.

18. In 1996, UNDP Somalia produced a regular update entitled "From Relief to Development: Situation Report."

19. UN Department for Humanitarian Affairs, *UN Consolidated Inter-Agency Appeal: Somalia* (Geneva: December, 1996).

20. Mark Bradbury, "Normalising the Crisis in Africa," *Disasters* 22/4 (Blackwell Publishing, December 1998).

21. Bradbury and Coultan, *Somalia Inter-Agency Flood Response Operation*.

22. Harmony Project, *Al-Qa'ida's (Mis)Adventures in the Horn of Africa*, Combatting Terrorism Center, West Point (2007).

23. International Crisis Group, *Somalia: Countering Terrorism in a Failed State*. Africa Report No. 45 (Nairobi and Brussels: International Crisis Group, May 23, 2002), 2.

24. Emmanuel Goujon, "AMISOM Hires Bancroft Global Development to Train AU Peacekeepers on Finding Explosive Devices in Mogadishu," *Middle East Online* (May 29, 2009).

25. Robert Maletta and Joanna Spear, "Humanitarian Assistance: A Security Perspective," in *Security and Development in Global Politics: A Critical Comparison* (Washington DC: Georgetown University Press, August 2011).

26. OCHA, *Humanitarian Funding Analysis for Somalia* (March 2011); UN *Consolidated Appeal for Somalia* (2009). According to OECD data, ODA (official development assistance) receipts for Somalia increased from US$28 per capita in 2005 to US$84 in 2008.

27. Ken Menkhaus, "The Crisis in Somalia: Tragedy in Five Acts," *African Affairs* 106/204 (2007): 357–90.

28. The Alliance for the Restoration of Peace and Counter-Terrorism ironically included warlords who a decade earlier had plagued the US intervention.

29. Cedric Barnes and Harun Hassan, *The Rise and Fall of Mogadishu's Islamic Courts,* Africa Programme Briefing Paper (London: Chatham House, April 2007).

30. AMISOM is mandated to support the efforts of the transitional federal institutions to stabilize the country and further dialogue and reconciliation; to facilitate the provision of humanitarian assistance; and to create conducive conditions for long-term stabilization, reconstruction, and development.

31. Integrated Regional Information Networks (IRIN), "Somalia: UN Calls for Immediate Re-engagement," ReliefWeb (January 18, 2007).

32. Robert Maletta, "Somalia: An Accountability-Free Zone?" *Humanitarian Exchange* 40 (Overseas Development Institute [ODI], September 2008), 2–4.

33. IRIN, "Somalia: Displaced People Branded 'Terrorists' by Mogadishu Mayor," ReliefWeb (August 22, 2007).

34. Al-Shabaab claimed responsibility for the attack that killed 70 people.

35. UNHCR, "Somalia: Total IDPs (February 2011)" (February 18, 2011), available on the unhcr.org website.

36. UNHCR, "Somali Refugees in the Region (as of March 2011)" (March 24 2011), available on the unhcr.org website.

37. UNHCR, "UN Leaders Raise Alarm on Plight of Somali Refugees in Kenya" (April 3, 2011), available on the unhcr.org website.

38. Food Security Assessment Unit, "Special Brief—Post Gu '07 Analysis" (Nairobi, August 24, 2007); OCHA, *Somalia Humanitarian Overview* 4/3 (Nairobi, April 2011); Food Security Nutrition Analysis Unit, *Post Deyr Analysis* (Nairobi, February 15. 2011).

39. See the series of articles on the humanitarian crisis in Somalia in *Humanitarian Exchange* 40 (ODI, Humanitarian Practice Network, September 2008).

40. OCHA, *Inter-Agency Consolidated Appeal for Somalia 2011* (Geneva: OCHA, 2010)

41. Bradbury and Coultan, *Somalia Inter-Agency Flood Response Operation.*

42. Authors' interview with NGO consortium, Nairobi, Kenya, March 2010. The precise number of international and national NGOs operational in Somalia is unknown. There are 70 international and national NGOs registered with the Somalia NGO Consortium, and 210 Somali NGOs in the south and central regions receive funding through the UN system.

43. OECD, *Monitoring the Principles for Good International Engagement in Fragile States and Situations Country Report: Republic of Somalia,* draft (March 2011); OCHA, *Somalia-Humanitarian Access Updates* (May 1–31, 2010, and January 1–31, 2011).

44. United Nations Security Council, "Letter Dated 23 November 2010 from the Chairman of the Security Council Committee Pursuant to Resolutions 751 (1992) and 1907 (2009) concerning Somalia and Eritrea Addressed to the President of the Security Council" (November 24, 2010), 5.

45. S. Hansch, "Crisis Report: Somalia," in *The Humanitarian Response Index 2009* (2010), 1.

46. Jan Egeland, Adele Harmer, and Abby Stoddard, "To Stay and Deliver: Good Practice for Humanitarians in Complex Security Environments," OCHA study (2011), 12.

47. Hansch, "Crisis Report: Somalia."

48. UN News Center, "Somalia Now World's Most Dangerous Place for Aid Workers, says UN Official" (April 24, 2007).

49. Maletta, "Somalia: An Accountability-Free Zone?"

50. OCHA, *Somalia: Humanitarian Access Update* (January–December 2009).

51. Mohamed Mukhtar, *The Boom in Somalia's Roadblocks* (February 21, 2008), unpublished.

52. OCHA, *Somalia: Humanitarian Access Update* (January–December 2009).

53. Authors' interviews with INGOs, Nairobi, March 2010.

54. Human Rights Watch, *Shell-Shocked: Civilians under Siege in Mogadishu* (Washington DC: Human Rights Watch, August 2007); Amnesty International, *Routinely Targeted Attacks on Civilians in Somalia* (London: Amnesty International, May 2008).

55. The European Commission, the United Nations, and the US embassy in Kenya did make statements on the fighting in Mogadishu in 2007, but only after NGOs sent a joint statement of concern to political missions.

56. Security Council Report, Cross-Cutting Report No.2 Protection of Civilians (October 14, 2008).

57. Chris Tomlinson, "EU 'Complicit in Somali War Crimes,'" *The Independent* (April 7, 2007). The silence was noticed by many Somalis who complained that they were "second-class citizens" when it came to receiving protection under international laws.

58. Daniel Wallis, "Somalia Has Best Chance for Peace in Years— UN," Reuters/ReliefWeb (January 18, 2007).

59. Action Contre la Faim (ACF), "The Need to Strengthen the Distinction between Humanitarian Aid and Political Agendas in Somalia," letter to UN humanitarian coordinator for Somalia (Nairobi, January 21, 2007).

60. Katharine Derderian, Eric Stobbaerts, Lesha Singh, Simone Rocha, and David Melody, "UN Humanitarian Reforms: A View from the Field," *Humanitarian Practice Network* 39 (London: Humanitarian Policy Group/ODI, June 2007).

61. Department for Political Affairs, "Concept Note for a High-Level Meeting on Somalia in the Margins of the AU Summit, 30 or 31 January 2011" (Addis Ababa: Department of Political Affairs 1 Africa Division, January 5, 2011).

62. Interviews with INGOs, Nairobi, Kenya, March 2010.

63. NATO and the United States provide logistic support to AMISOM troops drawn from Uganda and Burundi.

64. Matt Bryden and Jeremy Brickhill, "Disarming Somalia: Lessons in Stabilisation from a Collapsed State," *Conflict, Security, and Development* 10/2 (London: Routledge, May 2010), 241–62.

65. Authors' interview with donor representative, Nairobi, Kenya, March 2010.

66. AMISOM, *AMISOM Deputy Head Visits Injured Soldiers*, press release, June 6, 2011.

67. OECD, *Principles for Good International Engagement in Fragile States and Situations* (April 2007).

68. Authors' interviews with INGOs in Nairobi, Kenya, March 2010.

69. Egeland, Harmer, and Stoddard, "To Stay and Deliver," 16.

70. Al-Shabaab declared responsibility for these attacks and those in Bosasso in Puntland.

71. Interview with INGO employee, Nairobi, Kenya, March 2010.

72. United Nations Security Council, letter (November 24, 2010), 5.

73. UN employee interviewed in Nairobi, Kenya, March 2010.

74. See Bradbury and Coultan, *Somalia Inter-Agency Flood Response Operation*.

75. "Rules and Regulations," *Federal Register* 74/1 (Friday, January 2, 2009). For more details, see "Issue Brief: USAID Must Consider Alternative Vetting Approaches," available on the charityandsecurity.org website.

76. The humanitarian exemption to this only extends to medicine and religious materials.

77. The authority of the secretary of the treasury is established by the USA Patriot Act of October 2001.

78. Between February 2007 and March 2008, USAID provided over US$319 million in assistance to Somalia through international and local NGOs and UN agencies.

79. OCHA, *Somalia: Humanitarian Access Update* (01 to 31 January 2010).

80. OCHA, *Somalia: Humanitarian Access Update* (February 1–28, 2010).

81. UN employee interviewed in Nairobi, Kenya, March 2010.

82. Basil Katz, "U.S. Says Not Playing Politics with Aid to Somalia," Reuters/AlertNet (February 19, 2010).

83. UN Security Council, Resolution 1844 (2008), para. 8 (c).

84. United Nations Security Council, *Report of the Monitoring Group on Somalia Pursuant to Security Council Resolution 1853 (2008)* (March 10, 2010). WFP had contracted out the delivery of food aid to Somali businesses since the mid-1990s as a way of transferring the security burden to local actors. While intended to minimize attacks on food convoys, critics suggested that it enabled the contractors to create militias.

85. United Nations Security Council, *Security Council Extends Mandate of Group Monitoring Weapons Bans in Somalia, Eritrea, Unanimously Adopting Resolution 1916 (2009)* (March 19, 2010).

86. UN Security Council, *Security Council Committee on Somalia and Eritrea Issues List of Individuals Identified Pursuant to Paragraph 8 of Resolution 1844 (2008)* (April 12, 2010).

87. United Nations Security Council Resolution 1916 (2010) Adopted by the Security Council at its 6289th meeting, on 19 March 2010 (UN 19 March 2010)

88. Authors' interviews with international NGOs, Nairobi, Kenya, March 2010.

89. United Nations Security Council, *Letter dated 12 July 2010 from the Chairman of the Security Council Committee established pursuant to resolutions 751 (1992) and 1907 (2009) concerning Somalia and Eritrea addressed to the President of the Security Council* (July 13, 2010), 8.

90. OCHA, *Humanitarian Funding Analysis for Somalia* (March 2011).

91. OCHA, *Humanitarian Funding Analysis for Somalia* (September 2010).

92. United Nations Security Council, *Letter* (July 13, 2010); United Nations Security Council, *Letter Dated 23 November 2010 from the Chairman of the Security Council Committee pursuant to resolutions 751 (1992) and 1907 (2009) concerning Somalia and Eritrea addressed to the President of the Security Council* (November 24, 2010).

93. "UN Rejects Claims Aid Diverted to Somali Rebels," Reuters/AlertNet (February 17, 2010); interview with INGO employee, Nairobi, Kenya, March 2010.

94. UN OCHA, *Somalia Humanitarian Overview* 4/3 (Nairobi, April 2011); Food Security Nutrition Analysis Unit, *Post Deyr Analysis* (Nairobi, February 15, 2011); FSNAU *(Food Security and Nutrition Analysis Unit), Quarterly Brief* (Nairobi, June 20, 2011).

95. United Nations Security Council, *Report of the Monitoring Group* (March 10, 2010).

96. Letter from the RC/HC of Somalia to His Excellency Claude Heller, Chairman, Security Council Committee Established Pursuant to Resolution 751 (1992) and 1907, Concerning Eritrea and Somalia (March 23, 2010).

97. Authors' interview with INGO employee, Nairobi, Kenya, March 2010.

98. Ibid.

99. United Nations Security Council, *Letter* (November 24, 2010).

100. United Nations Security Council, "Resolution 1972 (2011), Adopted by the Security Council at its 6496th meeting, on 17 March 2011" extended the "carve out" to sixteen months, and the reporting period was doubled to eight months.

7. Palestine

1. In December 1987, the first Palestinian uprising (*intifada*) against Israeli occupation began. The uprising was a nonviolent civil disobedience and resistance movement in which Palestinians protested Israel's continued occupation and rule over Palestinians. The uprising began in the Jabaliya refugee camp and quickly spread throughout the Gaza Strip, West Bank, and East Jerusalem, lasting six years. Israeli forces killed more than a thousand Palestinians during this period and enacted measures such as "breaking the bones" of demonstrators in order to quash protest. The uprising ended when the Oslo Accords were signed, launching the negotiations process. In contrast, the second Palestinian *intifada* was largely disorganized and did not involve civil disobedience measures. It was ad hoc in nature, but also marked by violence claiming over fifty-five hundred Palestinian lives and one thousand Israeli lives.

2. A comparison of total donor contributions to UNRWA and to the PA, 1994 to 1999, from *Aid, Diplomacy, and Facts on the Ground: The Case of Palestine*, demonstrates the drop in international donor funding to UNRWA in favor of the PA. For example, in 1995, the ratio of international contributions to UNRWA to those of the PA was 54.5 percent; by 1999, the ratio was a mere 39.3 percent.

3. Examining the funding of UNRWA from the mid-1980s to 1999, it can be seen that the average annual increase in funding was an estimated US$12.3 million. In 1993, with the signing of the Oslo Agreements, this changed with the agency's income increasing, on average, by a mere US$1.7 million annually (*Report of the Commissioner-General of the United Nations Relief and Works Agency for Palestine Refugees in the Near East, 1994–1995 to 1999–2000*).

8.   Politics, Rhetoric, and Practice of Humanitarian Action in Pakistan

1. In July 2011, a *Guardian* investigation uncovered that the CIA of had organized a fake charity vaccination program in the town where it believed Osama Bin Laden was hiding in an attempt to obtain his DNA (Declan Walsh, "Aid Agency Withdrew Pakistan Staff after CIA Fake Vaccination Scheme" (September 28, 2011), available on the guardian.co.uk website.

2. Matt Waldman, *The Sun in the Sky: The Relationship between Pakistan's ISI and Afghan Insurgents*, Discussion Paper 18, Carr Center for Human Rights Policy, Kennedy School of Government, Harvard University (June 2010).

3. There are several armed militant groups operating in and from Pakistan that could fall into one of the following headings: (1) sectarian groups, (2) Afghan Taliban, including the Mullah Mohammad Omar movement based in Quetta or the Haqqani Network based in North Waziristan, (3) al Qaeda and its affiliates, or (4) Pakistan Taliban, like the Tehrik-e-Talibaan Pakistan (TTP), which openly targets government officials, armed forces, and civil law enforcement agencies (as well as any foreign actor who supports them).

4. Muhammad Amir Rana, "Pakistan: Under Attack from Within," The Afpak Channel, February 10, 2011, available on the afpak.foreignpolicy.com website.

5. Formerly called North-West Frontier Province (NWFP).

6. Christopher Rogers, *Civilian Harm and Conflict in Northwest Pakistan* (Washington DC: Campaign for Innocent Victims in Conflict, 2010).

7. "US Senators Link Pakistan Aid to Haqqani Crackdown," BBC (September 22, 2011).

8. First Kashmir war (1948), second Kashmir war (1965), Kargil war (1999).

9. "Who Has the Bomb," *Time* (June 3, 1985).

10. Bruce Riedel, *The Future of Afghanistan and Pakistan—podcast* (Washington, DC: Brookings Institution, 2011), available on the brookings.edu website.

11. WHO data from 2006, available online.

12. For a comparison with other countries, see "Total expenditure as % of GDP (most recent) by country," nationmaster.com website.

13. According to the Pakistani Earthquake Reconstruction and Rehabilitation Authority, erra.pk/eq2005.asp.

14. International Crisis Group, *Pakistan: The Worsening IDP Crisis*, Asia Briefing (Islamabad/Brussels: ICG, September 16, 2010).

15. Neta C. Crawford, *War Related Death and Injury in Pakistan, 2004–2011* (Boston: Boston University, September 2011), available on the costsofwar.org website.

16. Fiona Terry, *Condemned to Repeat? The Paradox of Humanitarian Action* (Ithaca, NY: Cornell University Press, 2002), 78.

17. Ibid., 66.

18. Ibid., 71.

19. The Edhi Foundation appears to be somewhat atypical in its expertise on emergency assistance. Founded in 1951, it provides medical aid, family planning, and emergency assistance through over three hundred centers across the country, in big cities, small towns, and remote rural areas.

20. Andrew Wilder, *Humanitarian Agenda 2015—Perceptions of the Pakistan Earthquake Response*, Feinstein International Center (February 2008), available online.

21. Tahir Andrabi and Jishnu Das, *In Aid We Trust: Hearts and Minds and the Pakistan Earthquake of 2005*, Policy Research Working Paper (Washington, DC: The World Bank, October 2010), available online; Wilder, *Perceptions of the Pakistan Earthquake*; Inter-Agency Standing Committee, *Real Time Evaluation of the Application of the IASC Cluster Approach in the South Asia Earthquake* (Islamabad: IASC, February 2006).

22. It included US, British, NATO, and Australian military forces working together under Pakistani leadership.

23. Lieutenant General Ahmed Nadeem and Andrew McLeod, "Non-interfering Coordination: The Key to Pakistan's Successful Relief Effort," *Liaison Online* 4/1 (2008), available on the coe-dmha.org website.

24. Ibid.

25. Ibid.

26. Inter-Agency Standing Committee, *Real Time Evaluation of the Application of the IASC Cluster Approach in the South Asia Earthquake*.

27. http://www.pdma.gov.pk/About_PDMA.php.

28. Andrabi and Das, *In Aid We Trust*.

29. UNDG, "Delivering as One: Making the UN System More Coherent, Effective, and Efficient," available on the undg.org website.

30. Author's interview with the head of the ICRC delegation in Pakistan, August 24, 2010.

31. See "Malakand Comprehensive Stabilisation and Socio-economic Development Strategy" (August 2009), available on the pdma.gov.pk website.

32. Humanitarian Policy Group, *A Clash of Principles? Humanitarian Action and the Search for Stability in Pakistan*, HPG Policy Brief, Humanitarian Policy Group (London: Overseas Development Institute, September 2009).

33. John Cosgrave, Riccardo Polastro, and Farwa Zafar, "Report: Inter-Agency Real-Time Evaluation of the Humanitarian Response to Pakistan's 2009–2010 Displacement Crisis," DARA (July 2010), 49, available on the daraint.org website.

34. Amnesty International, *"As If Hell Fell on Me," The Human Rights Crisis in Northwest Pakistan* (London: Amnesty International, 2010), 65.

35. "Special Support Group for IDPs Formed: DG ISPR," *Associated Press of Pakistan* (September 5, 1912), available on the app.com.pk website.

36. Michael Young, "The Uses of Adversity: Humanitarian Principles and Reform in the Pakistan Displacement Crisis," *Humanitarian Exchange* (March 2010).

37. Michael Georgy, "Aid Must Follow Pakistan Military Gains," *Reuters* (April 27, 2010), available on the uk.reuters.com website.

38. On October 5, 2009, the WFP office in Islamabad was attacked by a suicide bomber, killing five people. On February 18, 2010, four aid workers working for Mercy Corps were kidnapped 125 miles north of Quetta. One was killed and the three others were released on July 15, 2010. On March 10, 2010, seven people working for World Vision were killed in their office in Mansehra district.

39. Mark Duffield, *Risk Management and the Fortified Aid Compound—Everyday life in Post-Interventionary Society* (European Interagency Security Forum, 2010), available on the www.eisf.eu website.

40. Ibid.

41. Humanitarian Policy Group, *A Clash of Principles?* 3.

42. Nicki Bennett, *Missing Pieces? Assessing the Impact of Humanitarian Reform in Pakistan*, Briefing Paper (Oxford: Oxfam International, October 1, 2009), 13, available on the oxfam.org.uk website.

43. Ibid., 12.

44. Action Points of the Policy and Strategy Meeting held on June 23, 2010, at the Civil Secretariat, Peshawar.

45. At the time of writing (early 2012), the military had still not signed them.

46. It is worth noting that other NGOs had developed acceptance strategies that relied on a principled approach and negotiation; see, for example, Ingrid Macdonald (Norwegian Refugee Council), "Securing Access through Acceptance in Afghanistan and Pakistan," *Humanitarian Exchange Magazine* 49 (January 2011), available online.

47. Even when MSF opened a base in Sukkur, Sindh, to respond to the flood-affected people, it dedicated a day of briefing for any newly recruited staff on MSF mission statement, practices, and principles.

48. This strategy later was also progressively adopted by MSF.

49. David Batty and Saeed Shah, "Impact of Pakistan Floods as Bad as 1947 Partition, Says Prime Minister," *Guardian* (August 14, 2010). Available on the *guardian.co.uk* website.

50. As a comparison, more than two million people were affected by the earthquake that hit Haiti on January 12, 2010.

51. *Zindabad* means "long live" in Urdu. See Zeeshan Haider, "Pakistan Military Enhances Image with Flood Relief Effort," *Reuters* (August 17, 2010), available online.

52. "Pakistan Army's Flood Relief Efforts," *Inter Services Public Relations Pakistan* (August 27, 2010), available online.

53. Jorge Benitez, "NATO Responds to Pakistani Request for Relief " (August 9, 2010), available on the www.acus.org website.

54. Andrew Wilder, "Aid and Stability in Pakistan: Lessons from the 2005 Earthquake Response," *Disasters* 34, supplement (October 2010), S406–26.

55. Jamaat-ud-Dawa is a prominent example of an Islamist organization thought to be a front for Lashkar-e-Taiba.

56. Zeeshan Haider, "Pakistan to Clamp Down on Islamist Militant Charities," *Reuters AlertNet* (August 20, 2010), available on the alertnet.org website.

57. Ahmed Rashid, "Pakistan Floods: An Emergency for the West," *The Telegraph* (August 12, 2010) , available on the telegraph.co.uk website.

58. "Pakistan: Take the Politics out of Humanitarian Aid" (December 21, 2010), available on the actalliance.org website.

59. Richard C. Holbrooke, speaking on the Charlie Rose Show, quoted in Salmon Masood, Neil MacFarquhar, and Thom Shanker, "U.S. Offers Aid to Rescue Pakistanis and Reclaim Image," *New York Times* (August 14, 2010), available online.

60. Mosharraf Zaidi, "Why Doesn't the World Care about Pakistanis?" *Foreign Policy* (August 19, 2010), available online.

61. Sarah Collinson, Samir Elhawary, and Robert Muggah, "States of Fragility: Stabilisation and Its Implications for Humanitarian Action," HPG Working Paper, *Disasters* 34 (October 2010), S293.

62. The calculation is derived from the table titled "Total Humanitarian Funding Per Donor in 2010," available on the fts.unocha.org website.

63. Jonathan Whittal (MSF), "'We Don't Trust That': Politicised Assistance in North-West Pakistan," *Humanitarian Exchange Magazine* 49 (February 2011), available online.

64. OCHA, "Guidelines on the Use of Military and Civil Defense Assets in Disaster Relief—'Oslo Guidelines'" (November 2006), available online.

65. Both Pakistani and other governments lent assets.

66. World Food Programme, "Pakistan: 6 Months On, Food Aid Helps to Power Flood Recovery" (January 25, 2011), available on the wfp.org website.

67. Nicki Bennett (OCHA), "Civil–Military Principles in the Pakistan Flood Response," *Humanitarian Exchange Magazine* 49 (February 2011), available on the odihpn.org website.

9. Haiti's Bitter Harvest

1. *Chronicle of Philanthropy*, "How Charities Are Helping Haiti: How Much They Raised and Spent" (Washington DC: Chronicle on Philanthropy, 2010).

2. UN Office of the Special Envoy of Haiti, September 30, 2011.

3. Six-week study of eight IDP camps, June–July 2011, including eight hundred household surveys. The author was the principal investigator.

4. ACTED and International Organization for Migration (IOM), "Enuête IOM–Acted: Intentions Des Déplacés Haïti" (Port-au-Prince: Acted and IOM, 2011).

5. Alex Dupuy, "Disaster Capitalism to the Rescue: The International Community and Haiti after the Earthquake," *NACLA Report on the Americas* 43/5 (2010).

6. Yolette Etienne, "Haiti and Catastrophes: Lessons Not Learned," in *Tectonic Shifts: Haiti since the Earthquake*, ed. Mark Schuller and Pablo Morales (Sterling, VA: Kumarian Press, 2012).

7. Quotes not otherwise attributed stem from conversations with the author.

8. Mark Schuller, "Haiti's 200–Year Ménage-À-Trois: Globalization, the State, and Civil Society," *Caribbean Studies* 35/2 (2007).

9. Evans Jadotte, "Income Distribution and Poverty in the Republic of Haiti" (Quebec: Poverty Monitoring, Policy, and Analysis, 2006).

10. Michel-Rolph Trouillot, *Haiti, State against Nation: The Origins and Legacy of Duvalierism* (New York: Monthly Review Press, 1990).

11. Alex Dupuy, *Haiti in the World Economy: Class, Race and Underdevelopment since 1700*, ed. Ronald H. Chilcote, Latin American Perspectives Series (Boulder, CO: Westview Press,

1989); David Nicholls, *From Dessalines to Duvalier: Race, Colour, and National Independence in Haiti*, 2nd ed., Cambridge Latin American Studies No. 34 (New York: Cambridge University Press, 1996).

12. The US military invaded Haiti twenty-six times from 1849 to 1915, when it began a nineteen-year occupation.

13. James Ferguson, *Papa Doc, Baby Doc: Haiti and the Duvaliers* (Oxford: Basil Blackwell, 1987), 70.

14. Mats Lundahl, "History as an Obstacle to Change: The Case of Haiti," *Journal of Interamerican Studies and World Affairs* 31/1–2 (1989); Robert Rotberg, "Preface: Haiti's Last Best Chance," in *Haiti Renewed: Political and Economic Prospects*, ed. Robert I. Rotberg (Cambridge, MA: World Peace Foundation; Washington, DC: Brookings Institution Press, 1997).

15. Mark Weisbrot, "Structural Adjustment in Haiti," *Monthly Review* 48/8 (1997): 27.

16. Michael Deibert, with an introduction by Raoul Peck, *Notes from the Last Testament: The Struggle for Haiti* (New York: Seven Stories Press, 2005); Alex Dupuy, *The Prophet and Power: Jean-Bertrand Aristide, Haiti, and the International Community* (Lanham, MD: Rowman and Littlefield, 2007); Robert Fatton, *The Roots of Haitian Despotism* (Boulder, CO: Lynne Rienner Publishers, 2007); Phillipe R. Girard, *Paradise Lost: Haiti's Tumultuous Journey from the Pearl of the Caribbean to Third World Hot Spot* (New York: Palgrave Macmillan, 2005); Robert Rotberg, "Haiti's Turmoil: Politics and Policy under Aristide and Clinton" (Cambridge, MA: World Peace Foundation, 2003).

17. Noam Chomsky, Paul Farmer, and Amy Goodman, eds., *Getting Haiti Right This Time: The US and the Coup* (Monroe, ME: Common Courage Press, 2004); Alex Dupuy, "From Jean-Bertrand Aristide to Gerard Latortue: The Unending Crisis of Democratization in Haiti," *Journal of Latin American Anthropology* 10/1 (2005); Yves Engler and Anthony Fenton, *Canada in Haiti: Waging War on the Poor Majority* (Vancouver: Red Publishing; Winnipeg: Fernwood Publishing, 2005); Peter Hallward, *Damming the Flood: Haiti, Aristide, and the Politics of Containment* (London: Verso, 2007); Randall Robinson, *An Unbroken Agony: Haiti, from Revolution to the Kidnapping of a President* (New York: Basic Civitas Books, 2007).

18. Rene Hendriksen, Lance B. Price, and James M. Shupp, "Population Genetics of *Vibrio Cholerae* from Nepal in 2010: Evidence on the Origin of the Haitian Outbreak," *mBIO* 2/4 (2011); Renaud Piarroux et al., "Understanding the Cholera Epidemic, Haiti," *Emerging Infectious Diseases* 17/7 (2011).

19. Michel-Rolph Trouillot, *Silencing the Past: Power and the Production of History* (Boston: Beacon Press, 1995).

20. James Roberts and Ray Walser, "American Leadership Necessary to Assist Haiti after Devastating Earthquake" (Washington DC: Heritage Institute, 2010).

21. UN Office of the Special Envoy for Haiti.

22. Fritz Deshommes, *Néo-Libéralisme: Crise Économique et Alternative de Développement*, 2nd ed. (Port-au-Prince: Presses de l'Imprimeur II, 1995); Alex Dupuy, *Haiti in the New World Order: The Limits of the Democratic Revolution* (Boulder CO: Westview Press, 1997); idem, "Globalization, the World Bank, and the Haitian Economy," in *Contemporary Caribbean Cultures and Societies in a Global Context*, ed. Franklin Knight and Teresita Martinez-Vergne (Chapel Hill: University of North Carolina Press, 2005).

23. Mark Schuller, "Invasion or Infusion? Understanding the Role of NGOs in Contemporary Haiti," *Journal of Haitian Studies* 13/2 (2007).

24. Ibid.

25. See, for example, Jean Anil Louis-Juste, "Haïti, L'invasion des Ong: La Thèse n'est pas aussi Radicale que son Sujet" (Port-au-Prince: Faculté des Sciences Humaines, Université d'État d'Haïti, 2007).

26. Paul Farmer, *The Uses of Haiti*, 2nd ed. (Monroe, ME: Common Courage Press, 2003): 368.

27. Mark Schuller, "Gluing Globalization: NGOs as Intermediaries in Haiti" *Political and Legal Anthropology Review* 32/1 (May 2009).

28. Dupuy, *The Prophet and Power*; Hallward, *Damming the Flood*. While the authors have had a vehement public disagreement over Aristide's role in his ouster, both detail the role of foreign agencies and the NGOs they supported in his forced removal.

29. USAID, "Fiscal Year 2004 Budget Justification-Haiti," available on the usaid.gov website.

30. Sauveur Pierre Étienne, *Haiti: L'invasion des Ong* (Port-au-Prince: Centre de Recherche Sociale et de Formation Economique pour le Développement, 1997); Alliette Mathurin, Ernst Mathurin, and Bernard Zaugg, *Implantation et Impact des Organisations Non Gouvernementales: Contexte Général et Étude de Cas* (Port-au-Prince: GRAMIR, 1989).

31. Kim Ives, "New Wikileaked Cables Reveal: How Washington and Big Oil Fought PetroCaribe in Haiti," *Haiti Liberté* and *The Nation* (June 1, 2011).

32. Hallward, *Damming the Flood*.

33. Mark Schuller, *Killing with Kindness: Haiti, International Aid, and NGOs* (New Brunswick, NJ: Rutgers University Press, 2012).

34. Mark Schuller, "Gluing Globalization."

35. Alice Morton, "Haiti: NGO Sector Study" (Washington DC: World Bank, 1997), 25.

36. Disaster Accountability Project, "One Year Follow Up Report on the Transparency of Relief Organizations Responding to 2010 Haiti Earthquake" (Washington DC: DAP, 2011).

37. Paul Farmer, *Haiti after the Earthquake* (New York: Polity Press, 2011).

38. Ansel Herz, "Wikileaked Cables Reveal—As US Militarized Quake Response, It Worried about International Criticism," *Haiti Liberté* and *The Nation* (June 15–21, 2011).

39. Joris Willems, "Deconstructing the Reconstruction: The IHRC," in *Tectonic Shifts: Haiti since the Earthquake*, ed. Mark Schuller and Pablo Morales (Sterling, VA: Kumarian Press, 2012).

40. New York University School of Law's Center for Human Rights and Global Justice, "Sexual Violence in Haiti's IDP Camps: Survey Results," in *Tectonic Shifts: Haiti since the Earthquake,* ed. Mark Schuller and Pablo Morales (Sterling, VA: Stylus/Kumarian Press, 2012), 162-64.

41. Mark Schuller, "Unstable Foundations: The Impact of NGOs on Human Rights for Port-Au-Prince's 1.5 Million Homeless" (New York: The City University of New York; Port-au-Prince: l'Université d'État d'Haïti, 2010).

42. Up to four people per camp were interviewed, and given the research context, it is likely that a camp committee member either responded or influenced the choice of respondents or responses.

43. Dr. Evan Lyon, quoted in "Partners in Health Physician on Haiti: 'Cholera Will Not Go Away until Underlying Situations That Make People Vulnerable Change,'" *Democracy Now!* (October 26, 2010).

44. Schuller, "Unstable Foundations."

45. Mark Schuller, "Mèt Ko Veye Ko: Foreign Responsibility in the Failure to Protect against Cholera and Other Man-Made Disasters" (New York: The City University of New York; Port-au-Prince: l'Université d'État d'Haïti, 2011).

46. International Action Ties, "Vanishing Camps at Gunpoint: Failing to Protect Haiti's Internally Displaced " (Port-au-Prince: International Action Ties, 2010); idem, "'We Became Garbage to Them': Inaction and Complicity in IDP Expulsions, a Call to Action to the US Government" (Port-au-Prince: International Action Ties, 2010).

47. See also Farmer, *Haiti after the Earthquake.*

10. "Those With Guns Never Go Hungry"

1. Alex de Waal, *Famine Crimes: Politics and the Disaster Relief Industry* (Oxford: James Currey, 1997); see also Michael Maren, *The Road to Hell: The Ravaging Effects of Foreign Aid and International Charity* (New York: The Free Press, 1997).

2. Mitchel Wallerstein, Food for War, Food for Peace: United States Food Aid in a Global Context (Cambridge: MIT Press, 1980).

3. This story has been fairly well explored previously. See, for example, Christopher Barrett and Daniel Maxwell, *Food Aid after Fifty Years: Recasting Its Role* (London: Routledge, 2005). This chapter focuses specifically on instrumentalization for strategic and military purposes.

4. BBC News, "Bob Geldof Demands Proof of BBC Ethiopia Aid Report" (March 7, 2010); "BBC Apologizes over Band Aid Money Reports" (November 4, 2010). Both are available on the bbc.co.uk website.

5. See Jeremy Lind and Jude Howell, *Civil Society under Strain: Counter Terrorism Policy, Civil Society, and Aid Post 9/11* (Bloomfield, CT: Kumarian Press, 2010). See also Reuben Brigety II, *Humanity as a Weapon of War: Sustainable Security and the Role of the US Military* (Washington DC: Center for American Progress, 2008).

6. Center for Global Development, "The Pentagon and Global Development. Making Sense of the DOD's Expanding Role," Working Paper 131 (Washington DC: Center for Global Development, 2009).

7. Andrew Wilder and Stuart Gordon, "Money Can't Buy America Love," *Foreign Policy* (December 1, 2009).

8. See, for example, William Frej and David Hatch "USAID: A New Approach to the Delivery of US Assistance to Afghanistan," *Prism* 1 (2010): 87–94. The USAID Strategy in Afghanistan notes that "all existing and planned non-military assistance resources to align US civilian assistance with the President's strategy" to "disrupt, dismantle and defeat al Qaeda in Pakistan and Afghanistan" (87–88).

9. *The Guardian*, "Protests as UK Security Put at Heart of Government's Aid Policy" (August 29, 2010).

10. Matthew LeRiche, "Unintended Alliance: The Co-option of Humanitarian Aid in Conflicts" *Parameters* 34 (2004), 104.

11. Ibid., 105. Emphasis added.

12. See D. Maxwell et al., "Targeting and Distribution in Complex Emergencies: Participatory Management of Humanitarian Food Assistance," *Food Policy* 36 (2011): 535–43.

13. For in-depth background on these points, see Barrett and Maxwell, *Food Aid after Fifty Years.* But note that while much of the discourse about contemporary food aid still presumes it to be an instrument of surplus disposal or "dumping," in fact the age of global surplus agricultural production ended in the mid-2000s, and surplus disposal is no longer a rationale for food aid.

14. Daniel Maxwell, "The Politicization of Humanitarian Food Assistance: Using Food Aid for Strategic, Military, and Political Purposes." In *Problems, Promises, and Paradoxes of* .

Aid: Africa's Experience, ed. Muno Ndula and Nicholas van de Walle (Capetown: University of Capetown Press, 2011). The case studies included Afghanistan, Biafra, Ethiopia, North Korea, Sri Lanka, Somalia, Sudan, Vietnam, Yemen, and Zimbabwe.

15. Robert Paarlberg, *Food Trade and Foreign Policy* (Ithaca, NY: Cornell University Press, 1985).

16. Robert Paarlberg, *Politics: What Everyone Needs to Know* (Oxford: Oxford University Press, 2010).

17. Joanna Macrae and Anthony Zwi, "Food as an Instrument of War in Contemporary African Famine—A Review of the Evidence," *Disasters* 16 (1991): 299–321.

18. Antonio Donini et al., *The State of the Humanitarian Enterprise: Humanitarian Agenda 2015: Final Report,* Feinstein International Center Report (Medford, MA: Tufts University, 2008).

19. Wilder and Gordon, "Money Can't Buy America Love."

20. In 2002, for example, the World Food Programme held workshops with staff to discuss these problems and how to prevent them in operational terms on the ground. See WFP, "Food Aid in Conflict Workshop Report." Another such workshop was held in 2009.

21. See the 1949 Geneva Conventions and additional protocols of the International Committee of the Red Cross, first published in 1974.

22. Alain Mourey, "Famine and War," International Review of the Red Cross 285 (1991): 549–57.

23. Michelle Cepede, "The Fight against Hunger," *Food Policy* 9/4 (1984): 282–90.

24. The Code of Conduct for the International Red Cross and Red Crescent Movement and NGOs in Disaster Relief (1994), para 4, available on the ifrc.org website.

25. See, "Signatories of Code of Conduct," available on the.ifrc.org website.

26. The Sphere Project, *Humanitarian Charter and Minimum Standards in Disaster Response* (Geneva: The Sphere Project, 2004), 156. The more recent third edition (2011) of the Sphere Guidelines makes more or less the same point but has less specific language.

27. European Commission, *Humanitarian Food Assistance Policy*, ECHO SEC 374 (ECHO, Brussels, 2010). See also the Good Humanitarian Donor Initiative, "Principles and Good Practice of Humanitarian Donorship" (2003; last updated April 2008).

28. Mary Anderson, *Do No Harm: How Aid Can Support Peace or War* (Boulder, CO: Lynne Rienner, 1996).

29. CARE International, *Benefits/Harms Framework* (Atlanta: CARE, 2002).

30. Euronaid, "Code of Conduct for Food Aid" (Brussels: Euronaid, 1995). See also, Club du Sahel, "Food Aid Charter" (Bissau: CILSS/Club du Sahel, 1990); and Food Crisis Prevention Network, "Charter for Food Crisis Prevention and Management" (Paris: Food Crisis Prevention Network and OECD, 2007).

31. Many more are explored in Maxwell, "The Politicization of Humanitarian Food Assistance."

32. Author's interview notes, February 2010.

33. Some food aid continued to reach Mogadishu city and the Afgooye corridor just to the city's northwest.

34. Jeffrey Gettleman, "U.N. to End Some Deals for Food to Somalia," *NY Times* (March 12, 2010); and "Somalia's President Assails U.N. Report on Corruption," *NY Times* (March 17, 2010).

35. See, for instance, the apparent disagreement between the UN humanitarian coordinator and the SRSG at the time. This kind of disagreement between the "political UN" and the "humanitarian UN" is not uncommon, particularly since so-called integrated missions have become the norm.

36. Barrett and Maxwell, *Food Aid after Fifty Years,* 45.

37. WFP database, cited in Barrett and Maxwell, *Food Aid after Fifty Years,* 46.

38. Tony Blair, for example, said basically the same thing as prime minister of the UK. *New York Times* (October 5, 2001).

39. Remarks by Secretary of State Colin Powell, Fiftieth Anniversary of Food for Peace, Washington DC, July 21, 2004.

40. Marc-Antoine Pérouse de Montclos,"Humanitarian Aid and the Biafra War: Lessons Not Learned," *African Development* 34 (2009): 71.

41. FIRUP program documentation, USAID.

42. Andrew Baron, "Mixing Fighting and Food in Afghanistan," *Stars and Stripe*s (September 15, 2009).

43. Andrew Wilder, "Losing Hearts and Minds in Afghanistan," *Viewpoints* Special Edition, "Afghanistan 1979–2009: In the Grip of Conflict" (Washington DC: The Middle East Institute, December 2009), 143–46.

44. Jim Lobe and Eli Clifton, "Obama Calls for More Development, Counter-Insurgency Aid," InterPress News Service (February 1, 2010).

45. Andrew Natsios, *The Great North Korean Famine* (Washington DC: United States Institute of Peace Press, 2001).

46. Ibid.

47. Ibid.

48. Ibid.

49. Stephen Haggard and Marcus Noland, *Famine in North Korea: Markets, Aid, and Reform* (New York: Columbia University Press, 2007).

50. Ibid.

51. Ibid.

52. Selig Harrison, "Promoting a Soft Landing in Korea," *Foreign Policy* 106 (1997): 56–75.

53. Natsios, *The Great North Korean Famine,* 221.

54. Author's interview notes, June 2005. It took some convincing to reverse these policies before any harm was done.

55. These are described in greater detail in Maxwell 2011.

56. John Okpoko, *The Biafran Nightmare: The Controversial Role of International Relief Agencies in a War of Genocide* (Enugu: Delta of Nigeria, 1986).

57. Laurie Wiseberg, "An International Perspective on the African Famines," *Canadian Journal of African Studies* 9 (1975): 293–313. See also, de Waal, *Famine Crimes.*

58. This made these aircraft a legitimate military target under IHL—though the Biafra war preceded some of the additional protocols of the Geneva Conventions. Indeed the war *was* the cause of some of the 1977 protocols being added.

59. De Waal, *Famine Crimes,* 76.

60. "BBC 'Timewatch' Interview with Frederick Cuny, BBC News (January 1995). Reproduced by PBS, available online.

61. De Waal, *Famine Crimes,* 74. And yes, there actually was a Biafran Propaganda Secretariat!

62. Pérouse de Montclos, "Humanitarian Aid and the Biafra War," 74.

63. Ibid., 69.

64. See Ian Smillie, Chapter 3, this volume.

65. H. Young and D. Maxwell, *Targeting in Complex Emergencies: Darfur Case Study,* part of a larger study commissioned by WFP, Feinstein International Center Report (Medford, MA: Tufts University, 2009).

66. Ibid.

67. Ibid.

68. Ibid.

69. Mahmood Mamdani, *Saviors and Survivors* (New York: Pantheon Books, 2008). Also see Helen Young et al., *Livelihoods, Power, and Choice: The Vulnerability of the Norther Rizaygat, Darfur, Sudan.* Feinstein International Center Report (Medford, MA: Tufts University, 2009); and Alex de Waal, "Counter-Insurgency on the Cheap," *Review of African Political Economy* 31 (2005), 716–25.

70. Daniel Maxwell and John Burns, "Targeting in Complex Emergencies: Southern Sudan Case Study" (Medford, MA: Feinstein International Center, 2008).

71. Luka Biong Deng, "*Famine in the Sudan: Causes, Preparedness and Response: A Political, Social and Economic Analysis of the 1998 Bahr el Ghazal Famine,*" Institute of Development Studies Paper (Brighton: University of Sussex, 1999).

72. Ibid., 95.

73. Mark Duffield et al., "Sudan: Unintended Consequences of Humanitarian Assistance: A Report to the European Community Humanitarian Office" (Dublin: The University of Dublin, Trinity College, 2000), 27.

74. Maxwell and Burns, "Targeting in Complex Emergencies."

75. Susanne Jaspars and Daniel Maxwell, *Targeting in Complex Emergencies: Somalia Case Study,* part of a larger study commissioned by WFP, Feinstein International Center Report (Medford, MA: Tufts University, 2008). See also, Alex De Waal, *Famine Crimes.*

76. Ibid. Partially in response to this, the ICRC set up "soup kitchens" or "wet feeding programs" to increase its ability to target food and to reduce the risk of looting. See Susanne Jaspars, *Solidarity and Soup Kitchens: A Review of Principles and Practice for Food Distribution in Conflict,* HPG Report 7 (London: Overseas Development Institute, 2000).

77. Paarlberg, *Food Trade and Foreign Policy.*

78. Wilder and Gordon, "Money Can't Buy America Love."

11. Protection and Instrumentalization

1. In 2006, UN Security Council Resolution 1674 affirmed the importance of the "Responsibility to Protect"; it spells out the role of external intervention when individual states are unable or unwilling to protect citizens from genocide, war crimes, and crimes against humanity.

2. Zhu Li-Sun, "Traditional Asian Approaches—The Chinese View," *Australian Yearbook of International Law* (1980), 143.

3. Article 27 also stipulates that women "shall be especially protected against any attack on their honour, in particular against rape, enforced prostitution, or any form of indecent assault."

4. ICRC Survey, "Our World, Views From the Field, Opinion Survey and In-depth Research in Eight Countries (Afghanistan, Colombia, Georgia, Haiti, Liberia, DRC, Lebanon, and the Philippines)," Ipsos Research (February 2010), 10.

5. ICRC Survey.

6. Kathleen Newland, "Impact of US Refugee Policies on US Foreign Policy: A Case of the Tail Wagging the Dog?" in Threatened Peoples, Threatened Borders: World Migration and US Policy, ed. Michael S. Teitelbaum and Myron Weiner (New York: W. W. Norton, 1995).

7. Gil Loescher, *The UNHCR and World Politics, A Perilous Path* (Oxford: Oxford University Press, 2001), 11.

8. John Stremlau, *People in Peril: Human Rights, Humanitarian Action, and Preventing Deadly Conflict*, Report to the Carnegie Commission on Preventing Deadly Conflict (May 1998), 1, available online.

9. Virgil Hawkins, "The Other Side of the CNN Factor: The Media and Conflict," *Journalism Studies* 3/2 (2002): 225–40.

10. Ibid., 227.

11. An analysis of the 1990s "shows that preventing, responding to, controlling or ending refugee outflows" was an important part of US policy objectives (Newland, "Impact of US Refugee Policies on US Foreign Policy.")

12. Author's notes, Monrovia, December 2003.

13. ICRC, "Strengthening Protection in War, Workshops at the ICRC, 1996–2000" (Geneva: ICRC, 2001), 19.

14. Millions of Cambodians died as a result of the war in Vietnam and B-52 carpet bombing that contributed to the Khmer Rouge (KR) rise to power. Damien de Walque, "The Socio-Demographic Legacy of the Khmer Rouge Period in Cambodia," *Population Studies* 60/2 (2006): 223–31.

15. "Country Studies, Cambodia," http://countrystudies.us/cambodia/40.htm.

16. The United States provided tacit support for China's February 1979 attack on Vietnam; it also encouraged continued support to the KR. Elizabeth Becker, *When the War Was Over* (New York, Simon and Schuster, 1986), 440.

17. Fiona Terry, *Condemned to Repeat? The Paradox of Humanitarian Action* (Ithaca, NY: Cornell University Press, 2002), 143.

18. William Shawcross, *Quality of Mercy: Cambodia, Holocaust, and Modern Conscience* (New York: Simon and Schuster, 1986), 166.

19. In 1978, President Jimmy Carter denounced the KR as "the world's worst violators of human rights" (quoted in Grant Evans and Kevlin Rowley, *Red Brotherhood at War* [London: Verso Editions, 1984], 221). Western nations at the UN Sub-Committee on Human Rights condemned KR atrocities; a few months later, however, the UN Human Rights Commission decided to shelve proposals for an investigation (UN E/CN.4/SR.1510).

20. In sharp contrast to those who had sought asylum prior to the toppling of the KR regime, new arrivals were classified as "illegal immigrants" (Shawcross, *Quality of Mercy*, 83–84).

21. Ibid., 88–92.

22. Efforts to isolate Hanoi and punish Phnom Penh included very limited support by Western donors for relief efforts in Cambodia and the imposition of sanctions that precluded development assistance, including World Health Organization (WHO) technical support.

23. Nayan Chanda, *Brother Enemy: The War after the War* (New York: Harcourt Brace Jovanovich, 1980), 391.

24. UNBRO recorded eighty-five camp evacuations between 1982 and 1984–85; sixty-five of these occurred under intense artillery fire. Office of the UN SRSG, "Cambodian Humanitarian Assistance and the UN, 1979–1991" (Bangkok: United Nations, 1992), 42.

25. At this point there were an estimated 250,000 "displaced" Cambodians on the border, a figure that increased to 350,000 by December 1991 (Courtland Robinson, "Refugee Warriors at the Thai-Cambodian Border," *Refugee Survey Quarterly* 19/1 [2000]: 29–31). This figure included some 50,000 under the control of the KR (Human Rights Watch, *Khmer Rouge Abuses along the Thai-Cambodian Border* [New York: Human Rights Watch, 1989]).

26. Robinson, "Refugee Warriors at the Thai-Cambodian Border," 30.

27. Problems included coerced relocations, such as the transfer of some fifteen thousand refugees from UNBRO-supported camps in the latter part of 1988.

28. In a 1995 interview, UNBRO's former Deputy Director Patrick van de Velde noted that it was important "to make a distinction between what UNBRO wanted to do—feed and care for civilians in camps—and what politics was using UNBRO for." In Robinson, "Refugee Warriors at the Thai-Cambodian Border," 28.

29. The voluntary aspect of repatriation soon became a moot point, given the unwritten understanding that all Cambodians in Thailand had to return before elections; a handful of reluctant returnees were advised that they did not qualify for refugee status (author's personal notes, Cambodia, 1993).

30. Ogata (1991), cited in "The Thai/Cambodia Border Camps 1975–1999," available on the websitercg.com website.

31. Various countries deployed military contingents to assist the relief operation; this included a three-thousand-strong US force.

32. Terry, *Condemned to Repeat?* 171.

33. HCR had learned little from its experience a short while earlier in Tanzania, where the *génocidaires* took control as the camps took shape.

34. HCR proposed various measures, including the disarming of FAR troops and the removal of Hutu extremists (UNHCR, *The State of the World's Refugees 2000: Fifty Years of Humanitarian Action* (Oxford: Oxford University Press, 2000), 51.

35. Sreeram Chaulia, "UNHCR's Relief, Rehabilitation, and Repatriation of Rwandan Refugees in Zaire (1994–1997)," *The Journal of Humanitarian Assistance* (2002), available online.

36. Subsequently, HCR officials acknowledged that they should have been more vocal and forceful in highlighting the significance and centrality of protection issues (ibid., 5).

37. HCR concluded on the basis of a field assessment (known as the Gersony Report) that the RPF had killed some thirty thousand people as they fought government troops. The United Nations in Kigali, and government authorities, disagreed that RPF killings were pre-planned and systematic (author's notes, Rwanda, 1994).

38. HCR's bilateral and non-nuanced approach to the new RPF regime with the findings of an investigative report that pointed to massacres allegedly at the hand of RPF forces, coupled with an in-house policy paper that advocated the replication of UNBRO to allow for HCR's withdrawal from camps in Zaire, were indicative of HCR's penchant to operate unilaterally and without the support of the wider humanitarian community (Terry, *Condemned to Repeat?* 197).

39. OHCHR, "Report on Most Serious Violations of Human Rights and International Humanitarian Law Between 1993 and 2003 in the Democratic Republic of Congo (DRC)," issued in 2010, documents serious violations that have fed continuing turmoil.

40. BBC, "DR Congo Army Commander Transferred after Rape Claims" (January 19, 2011).

41. Commenting on the camps, UNHCR official Killian Kleinschmidt noted, "There were many mistakes but I still don't know what we should have done differently as humanitarians and as human beings" (Chaulia, "UNHCR's Relief, Rehabilitation, and Repatriation of Rwandan Refugees in Zaire [1994–1997]," 1).

42. ICRC/Ipsos, *Our World: Views from the Field: Afghanistan,* Opinion survey and in-depth research (Geneva: ICRC/Ipsos, 2009), 11–12.

43. Some NGOs were unconditional supporters of the mujahideen; critics of their human rights violations "were seen as apologists for the Soviet and Afghan armies." Helga Baitenmann "NGOs and the Afghan War: The Politicization of Humanitarian Aid," *Third World Quarterly* 12/1 (1990): 78.

44. Amnesty International, "Women in Afghanistan: A Human Rights Catastrophe" (London: Amnesty International, 1995).

45. In March 2001, High Commissioner Lubbers indicated in public his interest in assisting the return of some 1.5 million refugees, thereby undercutting the position of UN staff working in Afghanistan. See Norah Niland, "Taliban-Run Afghanistan: The Politics of Closed Borders," in *Human Rights and Refugees, Internally Displaced Persons, and Migrant Workers,* ed. Anne Bayefsky (Leiden: Martinus Nijhoff, 2006).

46. Uli Schmetzer, "Pakistan Strives to Push Back Flood of Afghans," *Sun Sentinel* (Islamabad) (October 23, 2001).

47. Norah Niland, "Justice Postponed: The Marginalization of Human Rights in Afghanistan," in *Nation-Building Unraveled? Aid, Peace, and Justice in Afghanistan,* ed. Antonio Donini, Norah Niland, and Karin Wermester (Bloomfield, CT: Kumarian Press, 2004), 75.

48. Alex Costy, "The Dilemma of Humanitarianism in the Post-Taliban Transition," in Donini, Niland, and Wermester, *Nation-Building Unraveled?* 148.

49. UN Secretary General Ban Ki Moon visited Kabul on November 2, 2009, after five UN staff members were killed in an attack on their guest house. When he commented on the rising toll of civilian casualties in Afghanistan, he said that he really appreciated "all this noble sacrifice by many American soldiers" as they fought "terrorists and illegal armed groups." Analysts quickly noted that such "blunt remarks against one side in an ongoing conflict were unusual for a top UN diplomat." Jim Michaels, "UN Secretary-General Assails Taliban over Civilian Deaths," *USA Today* (July 14, 2011).

50. Personal records. In the interest of full disclosure, I was the then director of the UNAMA human rights office, which concluded that ninety-two civilians, including many women and children, had been killed (UNAMA Human Rights, "Afghanistan, Annual Report on the Protection of Civilians in Armed Conflict" [Kabul: UNAMA, January 2009], available online.)

51. Norah Niland, "Impunity and Insurgency: A Deadly Combination in Afghanistan," *International Review of the Red Cross* 92/880 (December 2010) (Cambridge University Press).

52. For a thorough analysis of the underlying causes of the conflict, its political context, and the gruesome final months of fighting as the protected status of civilians was ruthlessly ignored by both sets of warring parties, see Gordon Weiss, *The Cage: The Fight for Sri Lanka and the Last Days of the Tamil Tigers* (London: Bodley Head, 2011).

53. Lionel Beehner, "What Sri Lanka Can Teach Us about COIN," *Small Wars Journal* (August 2010), 2, available online.

54. The ICG concluded that both sides "repeatedly violated international humanitarian law" and that evidence indicates that the Sri Lankan security forces "committed war crimes" and called for an investigation into allegations of intentional shelling of civilians, hospitals, and humanitarian operations. International Crisis Group, "War Crimes in Sri Lanka" (May 2010).

55. Nimmi Gowrinathan and Zachariah Mampilly, "Aid and Access in Sri Lanka," *Humanitarian Exchange* 43 (June 2009).

56. Gotabaya Rajapakse, defense secretary and brother of the president underlined that the aim was "to destroy the LTTE at any cost. There was no ambiguity in that." Anbarasam Ethirajan (BBC News), "How Sri Lanka's Military Won" (May 22, 2009).

57. Ryan Goodman argues that IHL prohibits unlawful detention in internal conflicts, including in relation to intelligence gathering "Rationales for Detention: Security Threats and Intelligence Value," US Naval War College, International Law Studies (Blue Book) series (April 2009).

58. Colum Lynch, "Sri Lanka's Enablers Side with Colombo in Its Struggle against Ban Ki Moon," *Foreign Policy* 8 (July 8, 2010).

59. Author's personal notes, January 2011.

60. There would be less skepticism about the motivations of Britain, France, and the United States, which took the lead in the initiation and implementation of SC Resolution 1973, if they had fewer strategic interests in Libya, had been more concerned in the past about the policies and activities of Qadhafi and his henchmen, and had not pursued regime change while ostensibly preoccupied with the protection of civilians.

12. So What?

1. A. Cooley and J. Ron, "The NGO Scramble: Organizational Insecurity and the Political Economy of Transnational Action," *International Security* 27/1 (Summer 2002): 5–39.

2. Extrapolating from Development Initiatives estimates, between two-thirds and three-fourths of all recorded humanitarian assistance is provided through the UN system, ICRC, and five consortia of transnational NGOs (World Vision, CARE, Oxfam, Save the Children, and MSF).

3. See, for example, the case studies of the Humanitarian Agenda 2015 research and the final report (A. Donini et al., *The State of the Humanitarian Enterprise: Principles, Power, and Perceptions,* Feinstein International Center, Tufts University (2008), available on the fic. tufts.edu website.

4. As when UNHCR "creates" its own forms of sovereignty in refugee camps. See Amy Slaughter and Jeff Crisp, "A Surrogate State? The Role of UNHCR in Protracted Refugee Situations," Research Paper No. 168, UNHCR (January 2009), available online.

5. Didier Fassin, *La raison humanitaire: Une histoire morale du temps présent* (Paris: Seuil/ Gallimard, 2010), 12.

6. Fassin, *La raison humanitaire,* 11 (my translation).

7. Giorgio Agamben, quoted in Fassin, *La raison humanitaire,* 290.

8. Immanuel Wallerstein, *European Universalism: The Rhetoric of Power* (New York: The New Press, 2006), 40.

9. Mary Anderson, "The Giving-Receiving Relationship: Inherently Unequal?" in *The Humanitarian Response Index 2008,* DARA (Madrid, September 2008).

10. Fiona Terry, *Condemned to Repeat: The Paradox of Humanitarian Action* (Ithaca, NY: Cornell University Press, 2002).

11. Among others, the studies on perceptions conducted by the Feinstein International Center (fic.tufts.edu); and CDA Collaborative Learning Projects, "The Listening Project Issue Paper: The Importance of Listening" (Cambridge MA: CDA, 2010), available online.

12. Mark Duffield, "Governing the Borderlands: Decoding the Power of Aid," paper presented at a seminar entitled Politics and Humanitarian Aid: Debates, Dilemmas and Dissension, Commonwealth Institute, London, February 1, 2001.

13. S. Sharma, Famine, Philanthropy, *and the Colonial State* (New York: Oxford University Press 2001), chap. 3.

14. Development Initiatives, *Global Humanitarian Assistance Report 2011,* 27 (figure 21), available online.

15. Kwong-leung, Tang. "Asian Crisis, Social Welfare, and Policy Responses: Hong Kong and Korea Compared." The International Journal of Sociology and Social Policy 20/5 (2000): 49–71.

16. Alnoor Ebrahim, "Accountability in Practice: Mechanisms for NGOs," *World Development* 31/5 (2003): 819, available online; CDA, "The Listening Project Issue Paper: The Importance of Listening; the case studies and final report of the Humanitarian Agenda 2015: Principles, Power, and Perceptions research project, A. Donini et al., *The State of the Humanitarian Enterprise* (2008), available on the fic.tufts.edu website.

17. Quotations are from beneficiary interviews, *Humanitarian Agenda 2015* research.

18. P. Nel and M. Righarts, "Natural Disasters and the Risk of Violent Civil Conflict," International Studies Quarterly 52 (2008): 159–85.

19. M. L. Parry, O. Canziani, J. P Palutikof, P. J. van der Linden, and C. E. Hanson, eds., *Climate Change 2007: Impacts, Adaptation, and Vulnerability: Contribution of Working Group II to the Fourth Assessment Report of the Intergovernmental Panel on Climate Change* (Cambridge, UK: Cambridge University Press, 2007).

20. Ibid.

21. R. V. Cruz, M. Harasawa, S. Lal, Y. Wu, B. Anokhin, Y. Punsalmaa, et al., "Asia," in Parry et al., *Climate Change 2007*.

22. M. Webster, J. Ginnetti, P. Walker, D. Coppard, and R. Kent, "The Humanitarian Response Costs of Climate Change," *Journal of Environmental Hazards* 8 (2009): 149–63.

23. M. K. Van Aalst, "The Impacts of Climate Change on the Risk of Natural Disasters, Disasters 30 (2006): 5–18.

24. N. Brooks, S. Di Lernia, N. Drake, I. Chiapello, M. Legrand, C. Moulin, and J. Prospero, "The Environment-Society Nexus in the Sahara from Prehistoric Times to the Present Day," *The Journal of North African Studies* 304 (2005): 253–92.

25. U. Büntgen et al., "2500 Years of European Climate Variability and Human Susceptibility," Sciencexpress (January 13 2011), available online.

26. D. Zhang, P. Brecke, H. Lee, Y. He, J. Zhang, "Global Climate Change, War, and Population Decline in Recent Human History," *Proceedings of the National Academy of Sciences* 104 /49 (2007): 19214–19.

27. Edward Miguel, Shanker Satyanath, and Ernest Sergenti, "Economic Shocks and Civil Conflict: An Instrumental Variables Approach," *Journal of Political Economy* 112/4 (August 2004): 725–53.

28. David Alexander, "Globalization of Disasters: Trends, Problems, and Dilemmas," *Journal of International Affairs* 59/2 (Spring/Summer 2006): 1–22.

29. Naomi Klein, *The Shock Doctrine: The Rise of Disaster Capitalism* (London: Penguin/ Allen, 2006).

30. Torben Juul Andersen, "Globalization and Natural Disasters: An Integrative Risk Management Approach" In *Building Safer Cities: The Future of Disaster Risk,* Disaster Risk Management Series No. 3, ed. Alcira Kreimer, Margaret Arnold, and Anne Carlin, 57–74 (Washington DC: The World Bank, 2003).

31. N. Anbarci, M. Escaleras, and C. A. Register, "Earthquake Fatalities: The Interaction of Nature and Political Economy," *Journal of Public Economics* 89 (2005): 1907–33.

32. P. A. Raschky, "Institutions and The Losses from Natural Disasters," *Natural Hazards and Earth Science Systems* 8 (2003): 627–34.

33. Jian-Ye Wang and Abdoulaye Bio-Tchané, "Africa's Burgeoning Ties with China" *Finance and Development* 45/1 (March 2008).

34. Branko Milanovic, Peter H. Lindert, Jeffrey G. Williamson, "Measuring Ancient Inequality," NBER Working Paper No. 13550 (Cambridge, MA: National Bureau of Economic Research, 2007).

35. IFRC, *International Disaster Response Law Programme*, available online.

36. P. J. C. Walker and Kevin Pepper, "Follow the Money: A Review and Analysis of the State of Humanitarian Funding," *Forced Migration Review* 29 (December, 2007): 33–36.

37. Development Initiatives, *Global Humanitarian Report 2011*, 44.

38. For an up-to-date review of research and practice, see the Cash Learning Partnership website, at cashlearning.org.

39. Margie Buchanan-Smith and Kim Scriven, *Leadership in Action: Leading effectively in Humanitarian Operations*, an ALNAP Study (London: Overseas Development Institute, June 2011): 51, available online.

40. Philippe Gaillard of the ICRC, quoted in David Rieff, "Afterword," in *Humanitarian Negotiations Revealed: The MSF Experience*, ed. Claire Magone, Michael Neumann, and Fabrice Weisman (London: MSF/Hurst and Company, 2011), 256.

Selected Bibliography

Detailed references appear in the notes of individual chapters. Only works of more general interest are listed here. Every effort has been made to ensure that the URLs in this book are accurate and up to date. However, with the rapid changes that occur in the World Wide Web, it is inevitable that some pages or other resources will have been discontinued or moved, and some content modified or reorganized. The publisher recommends that readers who cannot find the sources or information they seek with the URLs in this book use one of the numerous search engines available on the Internet.

Africa Watch. *Somalia: A Government at War with its Own People*. Washington DC: The Africa Watch Committee, 1990.

Amnesty International. *Somalia: A Long Term Human Rights Crisis*. London: September 1988.

Anderson, Mary. *Do No Harm: How Aid Can Support Peace or War*. Boulder, CO: Lynne Rienner, 1996.

Barnes, Cedric, and Harun Hassan. *The Rise and Fall of Mogadishu's Islamic Courts*. Africa Programme Briefing Paper. (London: Chatham House, April 2007).

Baitenmann, Helga. "NGOs and the Afghan War: The Politicization of Humanitarian Aid." *Third World Quarterly.* (January 1990).

Bass, Gary. *Freedom's Battle: The Origins of Humanitarian Intervention*. New York: Alfred A. Knopf, 2008.

Barnett, Michael. *Empire of Humanity: A History of Humanitarianism*. Ithaca, NY: Cornell University Press, 2011.

Barrett, Christopher, and Daniel Maxwell. *Food Aid after Fifty Years: Recasting Its Role*. London: Routledge, 2005.

Becker, Elizabeth. *When the War Was Over*. New York: Simon and Schuster, 1986.

Bradbury, Mark. "Normalising the Crisis in Africa." *Disasters* 22/4 (December 1998).

———. *Statebuilding, Counterterrorism, and Licensing Humanitarianism in Somalia*. Briefing Paper. Somerville, MA: Feinstein International Center, Tufts University, September 2010.

Chanda, Nayon. *Brother Enemy: The War after the War*. New York: Harcourt Brace Jovanovich, 1980.

Clarke, Walter, and Jeffrey Herbst. *Learning from Somalia: The Lessons of Armed Humanitarian Intervention*. Boulder, CO: Westview Press, 1997.

Collinson, Sarah, Samir Elhawary, and Robert Muggah. "States of Fragility: Stabilisation and Its Implications for Humanitarian Action." *Disasters* 34/3 (October 2010): S275–S296.

Cosgrave, John, Riccardo Polastro, and Farwa Zafar. "Report: Inter-Agency Real-Time Evaluation of the Humanitarian Response to Pakistan's 2009–2010 Displacement Crisis." Madrid: DARA, July 2010. Available online.

Deshommes, Fritz. *Néo-Libéralisme: Crise Économique et Alternative de Développement*. 2nd ed. Port-au-Prince: Presses de l'Imprimeur II, 1995.

Donini, Antonio. *The Policies of Mercy: UN Coordination in Afghanistan, Mozambique, and Rwanda*. Occasional Paper No. 22. Providence, RI: Thomas J. Watson Institute for International Studies, 1996.

Donini, Antonio, Norah Niland, and Karin Wermester, eds. *Nation-Building Unraveled? Aid, Peace, and Justice in Afghanistan*. Bloomfield, CT: Kumarian Press, 2004.

Donini, Antonio et al. *The State of the Humanitarian Enterprise*. Somerville, MA: Feinstein International Center, Tufts University, 2008.

Duffield, Mark. *Global Governance and the New Wars*. London: Zed Books, 2001.

———. *Risk Management and the Fortified Aid Compound: Everyday life in Post-Interventionary Society*. European Interagency Security Forum, 2010.

Dupuy, Alex. "Globalization, the World Bank, and the Haitian Economy." In *Contemporary Caribbean Cultures and Societies in a Global Context*, edited by Franklin Knight and Teresita Martinez-Vergne, 43–70. Chapel Hill: University of North Carolina Press, 2005.

Evans, Grant, and Kelvin Rowley. *Red Brotherhood at War*. London: Verso Editions, 1984.

Farmer, Paul. *Haiti after the Earthquake*. New York: Polity Press, 2011.

Fassin, Didier. *La raison humanitaire: Une histoire morale du temps présent*. Paris: Seuil/Gallimard, 2010.

Fishstein, Paul, and Andrew Wilder. *Winning Hearts and Minds? Examining the Relationship between Aid and Security in Afghanistan*. Feinstein International Center, Tufts University, January 2012.

Flint, Julie, and Alex de Waal. *Darfur: A Short History of a Long War*, African Arguments. London: Zed Books, 2005.

Gunewardena, Nandini, and Mark Schuller, eds. *Capitalizing on Catastrophe: Neoliberal Strategies in Disaster Reconstruction*. Lanham, MD: Altamira Press, 2008.

Haggard, Stephen, and Marcus Noland, *Famine in North Korea: Markets, Aid, and Reform*. New York: Columbia University Press, 2007.

Herring, George C. "Special Issue: Non-Governmental Organizations and the Vietnam War." *Peace and Change* 27/2 (April 2002): 162–64.

Humanitarian Policy Group. *A Clash of Principles? Humanitarian Action and the Search for Stability in Pakistan*. HPG Policy Brief. Humanitarian Policy Group. London: Overseas Development Institute, September 2009.

Klein, Naomi. *The Shock Doctrine: The Rise of Disaster Capitalism*. London: Penguin/Allen, 2006.

Loescher, Gil. *The UNHCR and World Politics: A Perilous Path*. Oxford: Oxford University Press, 2001.

Macrae, Joanna, and Anthony Zwi. "Food as an Instrument of War in Contemporary African Famine—A Review of the Evidence." *Disasters* 16 (1991): 299–321.

Magone, Claire, Michael Neumann, and Fabrice Weisman, eds. *Humanitarian Negotiations Revealed: The MSF Experience*. London: MSF/Hurst and Company, 2011.

Mamdani, Mahmood. "The Politics of Naming: Genocide, Civil War, Insurgency." *London Review of Books* 29/5 (2007).

———. *Saviors and Survivors*. New York: Pantheon Books, 2008.

Maren, Michael. *The Road to Hell: The Ravaging Effects of Foreign Aid and International Charity*. New York: The Free Press, 1997.

Maxwell, Daniel. "The Politicization of Humanitarian Food Assistance: Using Food Aid for Strategic, Military, and Political Purposes." In *Problems, Promises, and Paradoxes of*

Aid: Africa's Experience, edited by Muno Ndula and Nicholas van de Walle. Capetown: University of Capetown Press, 2012.

Menkhaus, Ken. "The Crisis in Somalia: Tragedy in Five Acts." *African Affairs* 106/204 (2007): 357–90.

———. "Stabilisation and Humanitarian Access in a Collapsed State: The Somali Case." *Disasters* 34/3 (2010): S323–41.

Mills, Kurt. "Neo Humanitarianism: The Role of International Humanitarian Norms and Organization in Contemporary Conflict." *Global Governance* (April-June 2005).

Moorehead, Caroline. *Dunant's Dream: War, Switzerland, and the History of the Red Cross.* London: Harper Collins, 1998.

Natsios, Andrew. *The Great North Korean Famine.* Washington DC: United States Institute of Peace Press, 2001.

Niland, Norah. "Impunity and Insurgency: A Deadly Combination in Afghanistan." *International Review of the Red Cross* 92/880. Cambridge University Press, December 2010.

———. "Taliban-run Afghanistan: The Politics of Closed Borders." In *Human Rights and Refugees, Internally Displaced Persons and Migrant Workers*, edited by Anne Bayefsky. Leiden: Martinus Nijhoff, 2006.

Okpoko, John. *The Biafran Nightmare: The Controversial Role of International Relief Agencies in a War of Genocide.* Enugu, Nigeria: Delta, 1986.

Paarlberg, Robert. *Food Trade and Foreign Policy.* Ithaca, NY: Cornell University Press, 1985.

———. *Food Politics: What Everyone Needs to Know.* Oxford: Oxford University Press, 2010.

Pantuliano, Sara, and Sorcha O'Callaghan. *The "Protection Crisis": A Review of Field-Based Strategies for Humanitarian Protection in Darfur.* HPG Discussion Paper. London: Humanitarian Policy Group, ODI, 2006.

Pelling, Mark. *Adaptation to Climate Change: From Resilience to Transformation.* New York: Routledge, 2010.

Piarroux, Renaud, Robert Barrais, Benoît Faucher, Rachel Haus, Martine Piarroux, Jean Gaudart, Roc Magloire, and Didier Raoult. "Understanding the Cholera Epidemic, Haiti." *Emerging Infectious Diseases* 17/7 (2011): 1161–67.

Polman, Linda. *The Crisis Caravan: What's Wrong with Humanitarian Aid.* New York: Metropolitan Books, Henry Holt and Company, 2010.

Rieff, David. *A Bed for the Night: Humanitarianism in Crisis.* New York: Simon and Schuster, 2002.

Rieffer-Flanagan, Barbara. "Is Neutral Humanitarianism Dead? Red Cross Neutrality: Walking the Tightrope of Neutral Humanitarianism," *Human Rights Quarterly* 31/4 (November 2009).

Schuller, Mark. "Unstable Foundations: The Impact of NGOs on Human Rights for Port-Au-Prince's 1.5 Million Homeless." New York: The City University of New York; Port-au-Prince: l'Université d'État d'Haïti, 2010.

———. *Killing with Kindness: Haiti, International Aid, and NGOs.* New Brunswick, NJ: Rutgers University Press, 2012.

Schuller, Mark, and Pablo Morales, eds. *Tectonic Shifts: Haiti since the Earthquake.* Sterling, VA: Kumarian Press, 2012.

Sharma, S. *Famine, Philanthropy, and the Colonial State.* New York: Oxford University Press, 2001.

Shawcross, William. *Quality of Mercy: Cambodia, Holocaust and Modern Conscience.* New York: Simon and Schuster, 1984.

Stoddard, Abby, Adele Harmer, and Katherine Haver. *Providing Aid in Insecure Environments: Trends in Policy and Operations.* HPG Reports No. 23. London: ODI, September 2006.

Stremlau, John J. *The International Politics of the Nigerian Civil War*. Princeton NJ: Princeton University Press, 1977.

Terry, Fiona. *Condemned to Repeat: The Paradox of Humanitarian Action*. Ithaca, NY: Cornell University Press, 2002.

Trouillot, Michel-Rolph. *Haiti, State against Nation: The Origins and Legacy of Duvalierism*. New York: Monthly Review Press, 1990.

Waal, Alex de. *Famine Crimes: Politics and the Disaster Relief Industry in Africa*. Oxford: James Currey; Bloomington: Indiana University Press, 1997.

Waldman, Matt. *The Sun in the Sky: The Relationship between Pakistan's ISI and Afghan Insurgents*. Discussion Paper No. 18. Carr Center for Human Rights Policy, Kennedy School of Government, Harvard University, June 2010.

Weiss, Gordon. *The Cage: The Fight for Sri Lanka and the Last Days of the Tamil Tigers*. London: Bodley Head, 2011.

Wallerstein, Immanuel. *European Universalism: The Rhetoric of Power*. New York: The New Press, 2006.

Whittal, Jonathan. "'We Don't Trust That': Politicised Assistance in North-West Pakistan." *Humanitarian Exchange Magazine*. London: ODI, February 2011.

Young, Helen, and Daniel Maxwell. *Targeting and Distribution: Darfur Case-Study*. Medford MA: Feinstein International Center, Tufts University, 2009.

Contributors

Mark Bradbury is a social analyst who has worked in Africa as a teacher, aid practitioner, and researcher. He has worked in Somalia and Somaliland since the late 1980s and has been the director of the Rift Valley Institute Horn of Africa Course since 2008. He has studied international responses to humanitarian crises in Sudan, Somalia, Sierra Leone, and Kosovo, and has authored numerous articles and reports on conflict and development, humanitarianism and complex emergencies, the politics of aid, and fragile states. His publications include *Normalising the Crisis in Africa* (1998), *The 'Agreement on Ground Rules' in South Sudan* (2000), *Becoming Somaliland* (2008), *Whose Peace is it Anyway? Connecting Somali and International Peacemaking* (2009), and *Winning Hearts and Minds? Examining the Relationship between Aid and Security in Kenya* (2010).

Diana Buttu is the Eleanor Roosevelt Fellow of the Human Rights Program at Harvard Law School and a fellow at the Middle East Initiative at the Harvard Kennedy School of Government. She previously served as legal adviser to the Palestinian negotiating team (2000–2005) and later to President Mahmoud Abbas (2005). Buttu served as legal counsel to the Canadian Department of Justice and served as a clerk to Justice Campbell of the Federal Court of Canada. She holds a BA in economics and Middle East studies from the University of Toronto, a JD from Queen's University, an LL.M. from the University of Toronto, a JSM from Stanford Law School, and an MBA from the Kellogg Northwestern School of Management. She is a frequent commentator on Middle East affairs and has written extensively on the Israeli-Palestinian negotiations process.

Lt. Gen (Ret) the Honorable Roméo A. Dallaire, Senator, has had a distinguished career in the Canadian military. In 1994, General Dallaire commanded the United Nations Assistance Mission for Rwanda (UNAMIR). His book on his experiences in Rwanda, entitled *Shake Hands with the Devil: The Failure of Humanity in Rwanda*, garnered numerous international literary awards and was the basis of a full-length feature film in 2007. Since his retirement from the military, Senator Dallaire has focused on the issue of child soldiers, founding the Child Soldiers Initiative (www.childsoldiersinitiative.org), and has worked to bring an understanding of post-traumatic stress disorder to the general public. He has been a visiting lecturer at several Canadian and American universities and has written widely on conflict resolution, humanitarian assistance, and human rights. Senator Dallaire has received numerous honors and awards, including the Order of Canada in 2002. His most recent publication is *They Fight Like Soldiers, They Die Like Children*.

Antonio Donini is a senior researcher at the Feinstein International Center at Tufts University, where he works on issues relating to humanitarianism and the future of humanitarian action. From 2002 to 2004 he was a visiting senior fellow at the Watson Institute for International Studies at Brown University. He has worked for twenty-six years in the United Nations in research, evaluation, and humanitarian capacities. His last post was as director of the UN Office for the Coordination of Humanitarian Assistance to Afghanistan (1999–2002). Before going to Afghanistan he was chief of the Lessons Learned Unit at UN OCHA, where he managed a program of independent studies on the effectiveness of relief efforts in complex emergencies. He has published widely on evaluation, humanitarian, and UN reform issues. In 2004, he co-edited the volume *Nation-Building Unraveled? Aid, Peace, and Justice in Afghanistan.* Since then he has published several articles exploring the implications of the crises in Afghanistan and Iraq for the future of humanitarian action as well as on humanitarianism and globalization. He has coordinated the Humanitarian Agenda 2015 research project that analyzed local perceptions of humanitarian action in thirteen crisis countries, and in 2008 he authored the final HA 2015 report, *The State of the Humanitarian Enterprise.*

Robert Maletta is an independent researcher. His knowledge of humanitarian affairs and complex environments is informed by extensive field experience in the Horn of Africa and senior level management of INGOs in Somalia, Sudan, and Rwanda. Additionally, he has documented peacebuilding and conflict-management activities in Somaliland, South Africa, Uganda, and northern Kenya for purposes of raising awareness among policymakers and educating peace practitioners. He was Oxfam's senior policy adviser for Somalia and led Oxfam's advocacy on humanitarian issues at the regional and international levels.

Daniel Maxwell has been on the faculty since 2006 of the Feinstein Center at Tufts University, where he leads the research program in food security and livelihoods in complex emergencies and teaches food security and humanitarian studies. From 2008 to 2011 he was the chair of the newly formed Department of Food and Nutrition Policy in the Friedman School of Nutrition Science and Policy at Tufts. Prior to coming to Tufts, he was the deputy regional director for CARE International in Eastern and Central Africa from 1998 to 2006. In addition to his primary responsibility for the oversight of Country Offices, he was responsible for program development, emergency preparedness and response, monitoring and evaluation, and technical support for ten countries in the Great Lakes and the Greater Horn of Africa. From 1995 to 1998, he was a Rockefeller Post-Doctoral Fellow at the International Food Policy Research Institute. Prior to earning his PhD, he worked for Mennonite Central Committee for ten years in Tanzania and Uganda. His research has focused on food security and livelihoods in protracted crises, disaster-risk-reduction programming, and food security measurement. He is the co-author, with Chris Barrett, of *Food Aid after Fifty Years: Recasting Its Role* (2005), and more recently co-author, with Peter Walker, of *Shaping the Humanitarian World* (2009). He was the co-author and editor of the 2010 FAO Report *The State of Food Insecurity in the World.*

Larry Minear is a researcher and writer on humanitarian action in conflict situations. Co-founder of the Humanitarianism and War Project in 1991, he spearheaded efforts, first at Brown University and later at Tufts, to analyze the responses of the international community to the major conflicts of the post–Cold War period. He is the author of *The Humanitarian Enterprise: Dilemmas and Discoveries* (2002) and, with Ian Smillie, of *The Charity of Nations: Humanitarian Action in a Calculating World* (2004). He retired from the Feinstein International Center in 2006. His most recent book is *Through Veterans' Eyes: The Iraq and Afghanistan Experience* (2010).

Norah Niland has spent much of her professional life with the United Nations, both in the field (including assignments in Sri Lanka, Thailand, Cambodia, Liberia, and Afghanistan) and at UN headquarters on humanitarian, human rights, and development issues. Currently, she is a research fellow at the Graduate Institute in Geneva. Norah separated from the UN in January 2011, having departed Afghanistan a few months earlier upon completion of her assignment as director of human rights in UNAMA and representative of the High Commissioner for Human Rights. Before this, Norah was in charge of policy development with UN OCHA in Geneva. In 2003, Niland spent a sabbatical year with the Human Security Institute, Tufts University, as a visiting research fellow. A published author, Niland has an M.Phil (peace studies) from Trinity College, Dublin.

Marion Péchayre is a PhD candidate in development studies at the University of London's School of Oriental and African Studies. Her thesis focuses on the politics of "humanitarian triage" of INGOs in Pakistan from a social-anthropological perspective. Prior to returning to the university, she worked for an INGO in several countries, including Afghanistan, Pakistan, Bangladesh, Myanmar, and Sri Lanka.

Mark Schuller is assistant professor of African American Studies and Anthropology at York College (CUNY). Supported by the National Science Foundation and others, Schuller's research on globalization, NGOs, gender, and disasters in Haiti has been published in over a dozen book chapters and peer-reviewed articles, as well as public media, including a column in *Huffington Post*. He is the author of *Killing with Kindness: Haiti, International aid, and NGOs* (2012) and co-editor of four volumes, including *Tectonic Shifts: Impacts of Haiti's Earthquake* (2012). He is co-director/co-producer of the documentary *Poto Mitan: Haitian Women, Pillars of the Global Economy* (2009). He chairs the Society for Applied Anthropology's Human Rights and Social Justice Committee and is active in many solidarity efforts.

Ian Smillie is a founder of the Canadian NGO Inter Pares, was executive director of CUSO, and is a long-time foreign aid watcher and critic. He has worked in several conflict and post-conflict situations, including those in Nigeria, Bangladesh, Bosnia, Sri Lanka, and Sierra Leone. As a development consultant he has worked with many Canadian, American, and European organizations. He is the author of several books, including *The Charity of Nations: Humanitarian Action in a Calculating World* (2005, with Larry Minear), *Freedom from Want: The Remarkable Success Story of BRAC* (2009), and *Blood on the Stone: Greed, Corruption, and War in the Global Diamond Trade* (2010). Smillie helped develop the seventy-government Kimberley Process, a global certification system to halt the traffic in conflict diamonds. He was the first witness at Charles Taylor's war-crimes trial in The Hague.

Peter Walker was appointed director of the Feinstein International Center at Tufts University in 2002 after twenty-five years of field work in humanitarian crises around the world. In 2007, Walker was made Rosenberg Professor of Nutrition and Human Security. At the center Walker is actively involved in research examining the future global drivers of humanitarian crises, the effectiveness of international humanitarian systems, and the creation of international professional-accreditation systems. His recent book, with Feinstein Center faculty member Daniel Maxwell, *Shaping the Humanitarian World*, provides a robust history of humanitarianism linked to an inquiry into its future as a global venture. In the 1990s, while working for the International Federation of Red Cross and Red Crescent Societies, Walker was instrumental in championing the need to professionalize the disaster-response business, developing the global *Code of Conduct for Disaster Relief Workers* and steering the development of the international *Sphere Standards,* a major NGO and UN collaborative effort to develop universal competence standards in humanitarian assistance. In 1993, Walker founded the annual *World Disasters Report,* which has now become a standard reference text in the humanitarian business.

Helen Young is a research director at the Feinstein International Center at Tufts University. For more than twenty-five years Helen has combined practical field experience working with agencies, with action research, publishing and producing best practice guidelines, training packages, minimum standards, and sectoral policies. She first worked in Sudan in 1985, and spent two years based in North Darfur working with Oxfam GB. Since 2004, she has led the Tufts Darfur Livelihoods Programme, generating original research in partnership with a wide range of national and international partners. She has been the co-editor of *Disasters* since 1998, and author of more than fifty peer-reviewed articles, books, book chapters, published reports, and conference papers.

Index